A HISTORY
OF THE CHURCH

"THOU ART PETER"
A third century fresco; the Ipogeo del Viale Manzoni, Rome

A HISTORY OF THE CHURCH

CHAPTER I

THE WORLD IN WHICH THE CHURCH WAS FOUNDED

I. THE ROMAN IMPERIAL UNITY

IT is not possible to understand the early history of the Church without some knowledge of the political and cultural world into which the Church came, of the Roman Empire, that is to say, as it was in the century which followed the Battle of Actium (31 B.C.), of Hellenism, of the older pre-Hellenistic civilisation still alive below the surface, and of the rich diversity of the Empire's religions. The Empire in which the first Christian propagandists worked was a vast state whose forty provinces took in roughly all Europe west of the Rhine and south of the Danube, with the island of Britain, Asia Minor, Syria, Palestine, Arabia and Egypt and the north coast of Africa thence to the Atlantic. Rome, its central capital city, had begun its history as a city-state. Then, as the head of a league of similar local states, as the chief state of an Italian federation, it had acquired, in little more than a century and a half, in a variety of ways, province by province, the greatest of antique Empires. Spain, Sicily, Sardinia and Corsica were the spoil of the wars with Carthage. The best part of Asia Minor came through the will of the last of its native kings. Gaul was the product of Julius Cæsar's military genius. Syria, Palestine and the rest of Asia Minor of that of his rival, Pompey. Egypt was the conquest of Augustus himself. Much of the East came with little native resistance: Gaul, on the other hand, cost nine years of Cæsar's campaigns; Italy was only reconciled to Roman hegemony after the bloody Social War (90–88 B.C.), while in Spain two centuries elapsed between the first occupation and the final definitive victories.

The provinces differed as much in the character of their pre-Roman civilisation as they differed in the circumstances which had subdued them to the Roman power; and hence they differed no less greatly in the degree to which the Roman power "romanised" them. In Greece and Asia, Rome subdued politically peoples who were, culturally, her superiors. In Syria, and especially in Egypt, there was a civilisation older still than that of Greece,

1

"hellenised" now for several centuries; in Gaul a native Celtic civilisation, of yet another type; in Spain a population of fierce local clans where each separate valley was a new, separate people. Greece and Asia were politically organised, famous for their cities, centuries before Roman history began; while in the West it was Rome who introduced the "city," and, in many western provinces, cities were rare even centuries after the Roman occupation.

From the days when she was merely the head of a league of Italian city-states, Rome had shown unique capacity for combining diversity in union, a political flexibility always ready to find new relationships on which to build alliances. Hence in the Empire, where no part was less firmly bound to Rome than another, and every part as firmly as possible, each part was yet bound by special links forged by the special circumstances of its conquest. All were equally subject; but in the manner of the subjection and in its implications there was diversity. To the immense population of this vast state the empire gave two hundred years of internal peace —an achievement that has had few parallels in history. It developed the Hellenistic civilisation it found in possession, and brought that civilisation—the best material civilisation the world had ever known—to countries which otherwise, in East and West alike, would never have known it. It was through the Roman town—the *civitas*, the city, that is, and the surrounding countryside attached to it—that this work of civilisation was accomplished. For the city was no mere agglomeration of buildings, its population nothing more than the association of a few thousand or a hundred thousand individuals. The Roman towns were, as far as the thing was possible within the structure of the Empire, city-states, conscious of their existence as such, each with its own personality, centres of strong local patriotism and self-confidence.[1] In varying degrees the towns were all of them self-governing, independent of the central government's bureaucracy except for certain taxes and the provision of recruits for the army. From this point of view the Empire was a vast federation of self-governing cities. The constitution of this local state varied according to its charter. There was provision always for magistrates who acted as judges, settled the local taxes and collected them, saw to the upkeep of roads and the post. The magistrates were elected, as was also the city's senate; and the elections were realities. There was, finally, in the city, the popular assembly; year by year representatives of all the cities of a province met at the provincial capital for the solemn rites with which the Emperor and the Genius of Rome were worshipped.

[1] *Cf.* Reid, *The Municipalities of the Roman Empire.*

A HISTORY
OF THE CHURCH

By PHILIP HUGHES

VOLUME ONE

THE CHURCH AND
THE WORLD IN WHICH THE
CHURCH WAS FOUNDED

NEW YORK
SHEED & WARD

NIHIL OBSTAT: REGINALDUS PHILLIPS, S.T.L.
CENSOR DEPUTATUS
IMPRIMATUR: E. MORROGH BERNARD
VIC. GEN.
WESTMONASTERII, DIE 15A FEBRUARII, 1947

PRINTED IN THE U.S.A.

To

MY FATHER AND MOTHER

PREFACE TO THE SECOND EDITION

THE unexpected chance that this first volume of *A History of the Church* needs to be re-set before it can be reprinted has given me the very welcome opportunity of revising the text, of correcting errors of fact, and of adding considerably to the bibliographical notes. The only notable addition to the text is the short section on Mani and his religious system as the study of the Chester-Beattie papyri has now made this known.

The long history is divided on lines that are, I venture to think, truer to fact than the more usual divisions. This volume deals with *The Church and the World in which the Church was Founded*— that world which was politically Roman and culturally Hellenic; and it takes the story as far as the breakdown of that culture in the West and its transformation, in the East, into the new Byzantinism. The second volume is called *The Church and the World the Church Created*. It deals with the fortunes of the Church in that medieval world built up on the debris of the Romano-Hellenic culture in the West; and it ends at the time when that new culture is beginning to turn against its chief architect—the close of the thirteenth century. Finally there remains the story of *The Church and the Revolt against it of the Church-created World*, and this, in the third volume, now published, is told as far as the appearance of Luther.

PHILIP HUGHES

CONTENTS

LIST OF ILLUSTRATIONS

This Provincial Assembly also came in time to have a political importance. It became, for example, the organ through which complaints were made to the emperor. For the centre of the empire, its ruler, was the city of Rome, still in theory a republic of which the emperor was but the chief magistrate. When after a century of terrible civil wars—Marius, Sulla, Pompey, Julius Cæsar, Antony—the victory of Actium (31 B.C.) left Cæsar's nephew, Octavian, sole master of the Roman world, he was able to build on the ruins of the old republic, where an aristocratic senate had been omnipotent, a new state. The form of the old he carefully preserved, but the reality was the rule of a military chief, an autocrat obeyed by virtue of personal oath of allegiance. The basis of his power was his victorious army, and thence derived one of the empire's great problems: how to keep this army of professional long-service volunteers, who yet were citizens, from interfering in political life for its own profit. Here the personality of the reigning emperor mattered enormously, and while Augustus' first successor Tiberius (14–37) succeeded as Augustus himself had done, five emperors, within sixty years of the death of Augustus, had died violently at the hands of the troops and civil war had revived again (68–69). There followed a century of capable rulers—Vespasian to Marcus Aurelius (69–180), and then in 192 the army, increasingly out of hand, brought about another century of civil wars and finally a re-organisation of the Imperium, under Diocletian and Constantine, that made it a new thing. It is this Empire of the Antonines, either functioning (98–180), or in dissolution (180–284), that is the political background of primitive Christianity.

But the emperor was much more than the chief magistrate of the republic, omnipotent because he commanded an army that was bound to him by personal ties. He was the direct ruler of many of the provinces—Egypt, one of the wealthiest, was practically a vast imperial estate. There had thus grown up inevitably a great corps of the emperor's personal servants, paid to watch over his personal and imperial interests throughout the provinces—to gather monies due to him, to administer his properties, to safeguard his interests in the multitude of cities against distant local rapacity or indifference, to execute his decrees and to see that others observed his laws. Here was a whole superstructure of offices and officials, concerned principally with Finance and Law, and of this, as well as of the army, the emperor was the absolute chief. The chief authors of this system were Claudius (41–54), Vespasian (69–78), and Hadrian (117–138). Inevitably, with the passing years, the importance of this imperial bureaucracy grew. Duties of supervising local government were

laid upon it, and in the end the local elective governments came
to be of secondary importance beside the paid, Rome-appointed
official. In somewhat similar fashion the Law too developed, the
emperor being omni-competent and his decisions becoming a
source of law, judicial and administrative. When to this is added
the development of the religious cultus of the emperor it will be
easily understood how by the fourth century the Roman Emperor
had become an absolute monarch of the pre-classical, oriental type.

The Roman Empire was not merely one politically, it was one
also in culture; and this second unity outlasted the first, survived
indeed to be a main foundation of all subsequent culture, to
influence the Church in no small degree, sometimes aiding, sometimes hindering the development of her institutions, her expansion
and her very doctrines. Politically the Empire was Roman;
culturally it was, not Greek, but Hellenistic.

This Hellenistic Culture was the product of the political conquest
of the East by the Macedonian king, Alexander the Great
(336–323 B.C.).

The Macedonians, though the language they spoke was undoubtedly a Greek dialect, and though they were probably Greeks
by blood, were none the less reckoned barbarians by the Greeks
of the classic culture. The Macedonian conquest of the East
was therefore, from its beginning, a victory for a "Grecianism"
that had never been purely classical, for a culture almost entirely
Greek but a culture already mixed, and ready therefore to adapt
itself to other cultures. The opportunity came with Alexander's
conquest of the Persian Empire.

Persia had menaced the Greek civilisation—that is, roughly,
all that we know as "the East," had seemed bound inevitably
to replace *in the West* all that we know as "the West"—for a
century and a half already when Alexander became king, 336 B.C.
The lack of unity among the Greek city-states, the wars between
them—the long Peloponnesian War 431–403 B.C.—were an
eternal invitation to Persian aggression. To defend the West
against this, unity was essential; and to unite Greece in a league
directed by himself was the aim of Philip of Macedon (360–336).
By 337 he had accomplished it. The following year, however, he
was assassinated, and it was Philip's son, Alexander, who led
the alliance to victory. The story of his conquests reads like a
fairy tale, Asia Minor, Syria, Egypt, Assyria, Babylonia and
Persia itself, and even beyond the Indus—in thirteen years he was
master of the world from the Himalayas to the Adriatic. Then,
unexpectedly, he died, thirty-three years of age.

That his Empire should descend intact to his baby son was not
to be expected. It became, naturally, the much-disputed spoil

of his leading generals, and thus Macedonian dynasties were established in Asia Minor, Syria and Egypt—the only parts of the conquest that concern this story. These original dynasties vanished, the kingdoms were divided still further. From Syria were formed Armenia, Cappadocia, Pontus and Bithynia within a hundred and fifty years. The Celts came in (278 B.C.) and established themselves in Galatia, while the impotent Seleucid kings looked on from Antioch; and in self-defence against the invaders the natives established the Kingdom of Pergamum. Finally into Persia itself came the Parthians, "the Turks of Antiquity," destined to harass and wear down the Roman Empire for centuries. Thus, with Greek or Macedonian dynasties ruling, the hellenising of the East was only a matter of time. By the time of the Roman Conquest it was largely accomplished, and thenceforward Rome is the agent of Hellenism's expansion in the West.

Alexander had dreamed of a real union of all the races he conquered, their fusion into one new people. He had planned the administration of his Empire on this principle and had himself married a Persian. This fusion of Europe and Asia on a basis of Greek culture, Hellenism did not achieve; nor did it ever make Greeks of the Orientals. Nevertheless it transformed the East for centuries, and for this transformation the chief credit once more is Alexander's. He promised to be as great a ruler as he had been a general in the field. His conquests he welcomed as enlarging the scope and opportunity for the development of the Greek mind, the spread of Greek ideas and ideals of life, of the Greek scientific achievement. Aristotle had been his tutor and the cultural sequel to his conquest was natural. He was the world's great city founder, and the seventy which claim him as their founder were all of them Greek in form and spirit, so many active centres whence diffused Greek thought and life. Alexander's successors were, in this respect, his enthusiastic imitators. A vast scheme of colonisation went with the foundations, and soon the East was filled with Greek traders, Greek artisans, Greeks to organise and exploit native talent, native industry, and especially land. The superiority of Greek methods and policies whether in diplomacy, in politics, or in the exploitation of natural resources, brought a new age of prosperity and peace to the East—to the profit indeed principally of the Greeks. The East—Asia Minor, Syria, Egypt—became one vast market, Greek controlled.

At the head of this new hellenised world were the Greek rulers, secure because conquerors, and more stable still because they inherited, for their native subjects, the divinity acknowledged in the native kings they had dispossessed. Between these Greek rulers and their native subjects there grew up a new, extensive and wealthy middle class of commercials, industrials and middle men of all kinds. This class again was almost entirely Greek. The centres of its wealth were the hellenised towns; and the natives, dispossessed, were bound to the soil, a despised and impoverished class. Between the town and the country, drained for its advantage, there was inevitably a chronic hostility, and an allied hostility between natives and foreigners. The new social and political strain gave to the old native religions a new importance—they were the one means left for the corporate expression of "national" feeling. Of all these countries Egypt affords the best example of this oppression, for in Egypt the government owned and controlled everything—agriculture, industry, trade. The country was one vast royal estate, its people the ruler's slaves or serfs.

Hellenism, then, was but a veneer, its cities a superstructure. There was never any real fusion between Greeks and natives, although the higher classes of the natives were almost always Greek in thought, speech and habits of life. Nevertheless, although the older life still ran on, below the surface and beyond the attention of this Greek-educated world, the hellenistic veneer was universal and the unity it gave, through the centuries before the political unity was achieved and for long after that political unity was lost, was very real. Such is the value of Greek thought even when it exists, as in Hellenism, in combination with non-Greek elements. All through this cultural Empire all who were educated—and indeed the whole population of the towns—were Greek in speech; they read the same classical poets, saw the same classical plays, listened to the same classical oratory, studied the same classical thinkers. Their schools, their gymnasia, their temples, their theatres, their very cities were of the one type. They shared the one common, cultural ideal, what the Romans were to call *humanitas*, the gift proper to this culture, for lack of which the rest of the world was "barbarian," and with this they shared the complementary notion of the "civilised world." This culture had the same attraction for those outside it as, in later centuries, the material order and prosperity of the Roman Empire had for the Germanic tribes beyond the frontier. The powerful ideas latent in it travelled far beyond the limits of the material expansion of the race—and, much later, they were to assist in that re-birth of the East which characterised the late Empire and early Middle Ages, Sassanian Persia for example, and the Arabia of Mohammed.

In religion Hellenism helped to spread the new idea of a connection between religion and morality—the result partly of contact with eastern religions—and the idea also of a relation between present conduct and the life after death. It assisted the development and spread of Greek mystery religions from Italy to Egypt and the Caucasus. It favoured the gradual introduction of Eastern cults into the Greek world. In Art and Letters the Hellenistic Age adds the Comedy of Manners, the Mime, a satirical, topical "revue", and the first of the Idylls, those idealisations of country life by the products of town civilisation in which every sophisticated culture delights. We can note, too, a new intelligent, scientific interest in the non-Greek peoples, no longer dismissed, undiscussed, as "barbarians;" and the appearance in history of another characteristic product of sophistication, the myth of the "noble savage." Hellenism produced, also, romances and fairy tales, influenced here by the East. One feature all these forms of literary activity share—they are the product of careful attention to literary form. The history of the "writer by profession" has begun, of the study of language, of letters, of the History of Letters, of the first public libraries. The use of books spreads; to possess books becomes the mark of a gentleman and the book trade develops. Historians especially flourish, are in demand even, and each monarchy, each city has its official historiographer. Translations are popular and translators busy. One subject that occupies them is the Sacred Books of the Eastern Religions. The Bible is now for the first time translated into Greek—the Septuagint.

Of the hellenistic achievement in Architecture, Sculpture, Painting, its systematic and scientific town-planning—which gives to the West its first well-ordered towns—we can only make a mention. It is an age also of scientific discovery, and of amazing inventions through the application of the natural sciences—especially is there progress in Anatomy, in Physiology, in Astronomy, Mathematics and Mechanics. It is an age of learning, and an age where learning becomes the concern of the State. Schools, libraries, learned societies even—at Alexandria the Museum—are maintained at the State's expense. All this is, in the main, the product of Greek culture working in an immensely wider field, and in that field influencing, slowly and never completely, but influencing none the less, the ancient East. In one respect only does the East in return seriously influence the Greek culture, in the point where that culture was so poor in thought as to be childish—its religion. Here Hellenism truly is debtor to the East.

II. THE PAGAN RELIGIONS OF THE ROMANO-HELLENISTIC CULTURE

"The teachings of Christianity are to-day so familiar, they have dominated our philosophy so powerfully and for so long a time, that it is only with difficulty that we can realise their superhuman character. To regain that notion we must for a moment tear ourselves from this Christian world where we live, and mix once more with the Jewish and pagan crowd to whom the apostles first preached the gospel. There, without at first paying heed to the new teaching that is about to make itself heard, we must listen to the chatter of the crowd as it surges about us, and through the popular legends and the speculation of the élite, strive to reach the religious beliefs as the disciples of Jesus encountered them. Then when the voice of these new teachers does reach our ears we shall recapture something of that note of newness with which their message seized on those who first heard it."[1]

We may distinguish roughly three main religious influences in that world into which Catholicism came. There were first of all the religions associated with the culture of classic antiquity, of Greece that is, and Rome. There were the religions which originated in the pre-Roman culture of the Empire, Celtic religions in the West and—much more important in the history of the Church—the ancient religions of the East. Of these last, one, by its nature a religion apart, demands special treatment. It is the third of these main religious currents—the religion of the Jewish people.

The Jews were but a fraction of the Empire's huge population, and outside that fraction flourished the amorphous thing we conveniently label Paganism. On the surface Paganism presented, throughout the Empire, the more or less uniform aspect of the Romano-Hellenic cults which had become the fashionable thing with the expansion and centralisation of the imperial system. But just as the older culture and older social tradition survived beneath the new political structure, so there survived too the older religious beliefs and practices. The religion of any given city then, of any given family, even of the individual, would present a curiously rich diversity in which could be distinguished, strata by strata, the remains of more than one religious development and conquest.

The Greek contribution to this world of religions was twofold. There were the earlier beliefs, animistic and anthropomorphic which grew and developed through centuries of whose history we know little or nothing, and which are best known to us through the epic poetry. There were the numerous beliefs and systems that grew up in reaction against this primitive naturalistic religion.

The earlier religion saw a superhuman power at work in the play of natural forces and their products. Trees, streams, sky and air, the earth itself were reverenced as the effects of the superhuman, finally identified with the superhuman, and as such

[1] Lebreton, *Origines du Dogme de la Trinité.*

personified and worshipped. Some of these naturalistic gods were conceived as having human form; and gradually, from out this vast number of the gods so conceived, a few, absorbing the functions of the less important, came to be considered as ruling, in a more or less ordered hierarchy, this supernatural construction. With them were associated lesser gods—the deified achievements of humanity—the heroes. With each god, demi-god and hero went the appropriate myth, and to each was paid his due worship. This cult was a public, community affair, a matter of ritual acts. Sacrifices placated the divinity, oracles discovered its will, and at times magic arts constrained it. Ritual acts were the affair of the priests—their sole function. Fixed dogmatic teaching there was none; nor did these religions provide any sanctions for the morality of conduct. "Doctrine mattered little. The ritual practices were the real affair of religion. It was ritual that was of obligation, an obligation generally of extreme urgency."

There was a vague belief in a future life that was the same for all mankind, a few lucky descendants of the Olympian gods excepted; for this future life was hardly conceived as a thing to be coveted. The words Homer puts into the mouth of Achilles are but an expression of a despair as widespread as the mythologies themselves: "Better to be the most wretched slave on earth than among the dead to be the King of all." In the heaven where dwelt the divinities of this unmoral, anthropomorphic religion, life was the life of earth; and with human virtues, human vices—and among them the most human of all—found there their celestial counterpart. Violence, covetousness, treachery, injustice and an anarchy of sex morality played their part in the life of the divine patron as habitually, as unashamedly and as unremorsefully as in the lives of the worst of his earthly clients.

With any development of intellectual life the growth of reaction against such a religion could only be a matter of time. The mythology, thanks to the gifted race's imagination and to its literary genius, became at once the source and inspiration of all that was most characteristic in the national life, and, accepted in its main lines wherever the race spread, the basis of whatever unity it possessed. But the effect of imaginative and artistic development was to humanise the gods until they became indistinguishable from creatures, and presently, for the intellectuals, little more than the playthings of the race's brilliant fantasy. When to the early poets there succeeded the first philosophers, and the later critical dramatic poetry, the inevitable antagonism between Greek religion and the Greek intelligence began to show rapidly. Zeus, Hera, Artemis, Apollo and Aphrodite; Furies, Nymphs, Pan and the Satyrs could not forever dominate any human intelligence;

and the Greek intelligence was soon to show itself in a strength and acuteness never since surpassed.

The first product of the reaction was the spread, side by side with the ancient public religions, of new secret cults, open only to the initiated, in which the dissatisfaction with the older cults' puerilities and the newly-aroused intellectual speculation found something of satisfaction. These were the Mystery Religions and the Orphic cults.

The Mysteries were magnificently organised dramatic spectacles, dramas in which were represented the most primitive of the myths, through which—and not through any dogmatic teaching or special esoteric revelation—the candidate was initiated into a new assurance of his present acceptability to the god and of his future eternal happiness in a world to come. He prepared himself for the event by ritual purification in the sea or in the appointed river, by fasts and special abstinences. He was sworn to secrecy; he offered the appointed sacrifices; he was fed with the mysterious sacred food; and then, in the night that followed, spectator of the sacred mysterious drama, he became one with the blessed body of the elect.

The Orphic cults all developed about the same time: roughly, it is in the sixth century before Christ that their first historical traces can be found. Orphic religion is at once a mystery and a philosophy. Man is a being in whom there works a dual principle. From the Titans, from whose ashes he partly derives, he inherits a principle of evil. From the god Dionysos, slain and devoured by the Titans—the crime for which they merited destruction— he inherits a principle that is good. Whence the necessity for man to free himself from the evil element of his nature, so that what is divine in him may triumph. This emancipation is the object of the Orphic rites. They include repeated purifications; sacrifices where no blood is shed; the dramatic representation of the myth of the slaying of Dionysos, in which the candidates devour the raw flesh of the bull in whose form he is presented as being slain; and, finally, the revelation to the newly-initiated of the infallible, sacred, saving formula which will secure him safe passage through the nether world. The natural anxiety for a happy future life finds an assurance; and with these theories of man as a fallen god and of the saving rites of purification, the idea of morality for the first time enters Greek religion. These teachings, and the ceremonial effect of the mysteries' setting, made of the new movement a formidable rival to the futile formalism which preceded it.

A more direct blow to its life was the criticism of the new moral philosophy. "Never did people of so advanced a culture have so childish a religion," says M. Cumont; and the culture was about to destroy that religion for ever, as a force in the lives of that élite whose leisure for thought makes it the arbiter of a people's destiny. In the wake of this new religious movement, then, there followed a moralist criticism of the old cults which mocked at the domestic absurdities of Olympus and heaped on the Olympians the reproach of all the misery of the world they were conceived as ruling. Belief in such gods is futile, a waste of life, the greatest of follies. Such is the inevitable conclusion, and if in Sophocles and Æschylus the genius of poetry remained conservatively loyal, in the plays of Euripides the new criticism found an exponent as powerful and profound as his appeal was popular. The moral problems of personal responsibility for which Orphic religion offered a solution passed into the philosophical discussion of the day, and became for a long time one of its most popular topics. Through the personality of Socrates, and the art of Plato, moral philosophy bred a new notion of righteous living and a noble idealism of life which, owing nothing to the older religion's inspiration, could not, from its very superiority to that religion's ideals, be anything else than a force making for its destruction. The new philosophy offered to men a better way; and if it led to an imitation in life of the divine, it did so without the aid of the old beliefs, using the rites, where they were used, simply as symbols of civic duty.

Speculative Philosophy completed the work of destruction. Where the moral theorists laid bare the inferiority and uselessness of the ancient cults, the rationalists who accompanied and followed them broke up, with the acid critique of their direct attack, whatever hold they might have on reason. This movement reached its perfection in the work of Aristotle (384–322) whose genius built up a vast encyclopaedia of knowledge in which religion and morality found their place, based this time on critical reasoning from observed facts.

Greek Thought and the official Greek religion henceforth went their separate ways. At its best the Thought was immensely superior to the Cults, and even though in the centuries that followed the golden age Philosophy declined and decayed, the cults never recovered their one-time uncontested supremacy. The conquests of Alexander the Great, which opened new spheres of influence to Greek culture, spread its medley of religions and philosophies throughout the East. Oriental religions in turn affected the religion of the conquerors, and with the political revolutions brought about the last stage of religious transformation. The old official religion had been too intimately associated with the local city-state not to lose some if its importance when the city-state fell. Alexander, on his death, was ranked among the gods—an example only too quickly followed in the case of his multitude of successors in all the countries into which his vast Empire was partitioned. The myths ceased to have any meaning other than mythical; and slowly Greek religion took its place as one element among many in the great movement which, throughout the Empire, was slowly fusing all beliefs and cults into one amorphous unmeaning thing.

As with the Greeks of Homeric times, so it was with the Romans; their earliest religion was animist in its basis. Natural forces, air, fire, water, the sky, the lightning and the storm—these manifestations of superhuman power, won a reverence from that association, and were envisaged as the manifestations of the divine personalities who dwelt in them. More peculiarly Roman, and more in keeping with the Roman character, was the notion of the divinity as the guardian of life, the patron of all its actions. From this notion sprang a whole host of minor deities; for every act of life had its appropriate deity, under whose invocation and with whose aid, the life was lived, the action performed. So in infancy it was Educa that taught the child to eat, and Potina to drink. Cuba watched over his cradle, and while Ossipago strengthened his bones and Carna his flesh, Statanus secured that he stood upright and Abeona that he walked. Fabulinus, Farinus and Locutius initiated him in the art of speech, Terduca cared for him as he went to school and Domiduca as he returned . . . and others of the vast army assisted at every act of every stage of adolescence and maturity.

A second particularity of this early Roman religion was its domestic character. The Roman family was itself a sacred thing. Each member had his guardian deity; the Lar Familiaris guarded the field in which the house was built, and in the house itself the shrine of the Penates, with its daily ritual of oblations, was the very centre of family life. The strength of the domestic religion was shown perhaps most of all in the cult of the dead—a cult designed to placate the shades of the departed, to supply their wants in the life to which they had gone, and, in the last development, to establish a communion and intercourse between them and the worshippers.

But the gods of the Romans—even, originally, the major gods Jupiter, Juno and the rest—were powers rather than persons. The practical, unimaginative character of the people coloured its religion. There was no speculation as to the nature of the gods, no imaginative mythology, no artistic representation, no temples even. Religion, like the world of fact, was something to be used, not a theme for meditation. The Roman, in whom the notion of contract was instinctive, dealt with his gods accordingly.

The appointed ritual produced the ordained effect; and all his service of the gods was wholly legalist, wholly formalist, the careful execution of man's share of the bilateral agreement. Mysticism, love of the gods, devotion—in the usual sense of the word—could have no place in such a religion; and Cicero was never truer to tradition than when he defined sanctity as the science of ritual.

With this legalist spirit, there went the kindred notion of authority. Not that there was any priestly caste. The priest is no more than a master of ceremonies, seeing to the exact observance of the rite. In the domestic cults it was the head of the house who officiated, and in the public cults it was the magistrates or the colleges of priests assimilated to them. But Roman religion was a political thing. The city was the family developed, and was itself a sacred thing, a holy place. Hence not only was the supervision of domestic cults a duty of its magistrates, but as the city developed, as it conquered its weaker neighbours, the victory had a religious character and it was in the imposition and acceptance of the Roman religion that the new political gains were consolidated. Thus by a development very different from that which followed the Greek conquest of the East under Alexander, the Roman gods entered as victors into the pantheon of whatever people the Romans overcame. It was a trait in their religious mentality in which the later cult of the State, or of the emperor, was to find a strong foundation. Civic Authority and Religion went ever together, but with the State in unquestioned primacy. The priesthood had no influence in political life. Rather it was the politician who usurped the priesthood.

As the Roman city grew in importance, other forces began slowly to influence its religious development, of which by far the most important were from Greece. From the sixth century B.C. the tide flowed ever more strongly, and Greek Anthropomorphism with its mythology entered into rivalry with the impersonal native Roman austerity. Greek rites too were introduced despite repeated prohibitions, and presently, in the usual way, the new foreign deities were adapted to and identified with the ancient gods of the fatherland. With the Greek religions came, too, the Greek scepticism; and in Rome, as in Greece, the mythology reacted unfavourably on the religion that bred it, once philosophical criticism was free to deal with the mythology.

III. THE RELIGION OF THE JEWS

Against all the hundred religions of antiquity the religion of the Jews stands out a thing unique. Alone of them all it has survived. Zeus and Minerva, Osiris, Astarte, gods of the East and of the West are long since merely names; but to this day the Jews survive and the God Whom they worshipped in the far off centuries when these other cults too had their millions of devotees is still their God, worshipped now not only by Jews but by hundreds of millions of every race and nation.

By its subsequent history, then, the religion of ancient Jewry is a thing apart. It is no less clearly distinguished from the rest by the doctrine which is its core, and by the historic character of its origin. Judaism was the revelation made by God to a particular people; the revelation of a doctrine concerning Himself, of a moral teaching, and of the fact of their own special relation to Him with the promise to them of a special rôle in all subsequent ages. The history of the Jewish people is the development of the tradition of this revelation. By that revelation, which from the beginning is consistently presented as the free act of the Divine goodwill, the race is constituted a sanctuary wherein lie safeguarded the true belief in the only God, the true principles of moral conduct and the tradition of God's promise. Within this sanctuary of the chosen race the divinely revealed religion lives, and develops as from an internal principle; its implications brought out, its detail defined, in later revelations through nearly two thousand years.

There is only one God, who is master of the world and the source of law, just, moral. He represents in Himself an ideal of moral perfection and insists on its reflection in the lives of all He associates with Himself. He is not, then, indifferent to the moral quality of men's actions, but from the beginning demands of them truth and obedience to His law. This "ethical monotheism" survived and developed in a world whose spirit and tendencies were so hostile to it that the mere survival is "a phenomenon unique of its kind. . . . It is a feat greater than the men who bring it about, and, contrasting as it does with the *milieu* wherein it is produced, puts the ordinary logic of history to flight." For this monotheism is, with the Jews, the popular belief. It is not a higher teaching in which only the élite of these people are initiated.

It was to Abraham—the chief of a group of Hebrews living in Chaldea—that, in a world rocking in political convulsion, the revelation was made. He obeyed the call, accepted the charge, believed the promise; and left, with his people, the moral decadence that lay around. To God he and they were now specially covenanted, and thereby separated from the rest of mankind. With this separation the history of Jewry begins. The development falls naturally into two uneven periods divided by the political destruction of the Jewish nation under the Babylonian kings

(586 B.C.), and in the first and greater half of the development we may reckon roughly three principal stages. These are the primitive revelation to Abraham; the second revelation and re-organisation under Moses; and the work of preservation through the Prophets.

Moses, the leader personally called by God to whom first God makes known His nature in His name—Iahweh (He Who Is) is the restorer of Abraham's tradition which, in the centuries of his descendants' slavery to Egypt, had almost perished. Moses it is who leads the people from Egypt and in the forty years of their wanderings makes a nation of this loose association of Abraham's children. Throughout, and consistently, he acts as the agent of Iahweh in obedience to frequent and explicit divine directions. But his influence in history is greater still as the divinely directed legislator. Here the traditional revelation is expressed once more, but with a new protective precision; and, with a wealth of detail, its moral principles are applied to the Hebrew's everyday life. Iahweh is God, and Iahweh alone is God. Israel is Iahweh's people, His property; and if there is an alliance between Him and them, once more it is His good will and choice that is its foundation. He is the God of holiness of life, the enemy of violence and injustice. The sexual aberrations so closely and so universally interwoven with the contemporary idea of religious practice, are particularly obnoxious; and He exacts from all a purity of soul of which the carefully ordained bodily purity is but the sign. Throughout all the multitude of detailed observances there runs this idea of personal holiness as the end of life. The spirit of filial fear is to be the spirit of their observance and from the beginning the duty of charity and love of one's fellows is enforced. The law, its ideals and its motives, is for all; whence its power as the instrument of this people's moral and religious education. Its theocratic character, and the repeated insistence, whether in matters of ritual or of legal prescription as generally understood, on the supreme importance of the inner law of mind and conscience, safeguard it from the deadening effect that is the sure end of all mere codes of right behaviour. In this insistence Jewish law is unique, as it is unique in its aim of personal sanctification.

The cult remains, in principle, the same as that revealed to Abraham: prayer and sacrifice. Human sacrifices are from the beginning forbidden, and there is an emphatic prohibition of any attempt to represent in images Iahweh who is a spirit. The sacrifices are offered in one place only, before the Ark of the Alliance—a chest of cedar wood that holds the sensible memorials of the divine dealings with Moses. There is an elaborate official ritual and a priestly caste, hereditary in one of the twelve tribes.

Moses is the man of his people's period of transition—ruling and teaching for the forty years that lie between their leaving Egypt and their arrival in "the Promised Land," the Canaan to which Iahweh, centuries before, had directed Abraham. Their arrival and the death of Moses came together; and with their entry into this new country came a violent religious reaction. The temptation to abandon their austere religion, once escaped from the desert that was its natural setting, was strong. The Jews lived now in an easier, more generous land where everything called to the senses; and the native religions which, on every side, canonised moral corruption, afforded them an example which they imitated only too readily. Hence with their new political and social relations periods of apostacy, more or less open, from the worship of Iahweh; an ever-present danger of corruption of that worship and its teaching; and, in the new little kingdom, a more or less general moral decay.

So it was to be for some centuries: a never ending struggle between the traditional "ethical monotheism" and the inviting appeals of sense; but never does the tradition, doctrinal or moral, wholly disappear and unlike, for example, the Philistines, the Hebrews retain their individuality: they are never absorbed by the civilisations around them. This survival was due to the labours of the Prophets, spiritual free-lances whom from time to time Iahweh raised up to preserve the tradition and to develop it. At every critical moment of the kingdom's history they appeared, Iahweh's messengers, speaking in His name, attesting the authenticity of their message by miracles and prophecies. Careless of the dignity or office of the guilty, they denounced unsparingly the moral corruption and the defections from Mosaic orthodoxy, recalling unceasingly the special vocation of the Jews and their special duties towards Iahweh who had called them. In times of political defeats they taught from contemporary events the lesson of Iahweh as God outraged by man's sin and punishing for man's correction. Salvation, reconciliation with God, Who was the nation's life, was possible through penance—for along with the notion of divine justice the Prophets developed, too, the correlative idea of the divine pity for man and the idea of Iahweh's special fatherly care for the Jews. More than ever is the holiness of God insisted on, of Iahweh, Who is the God not only of Israel but of all mankind, Master of the tyrants whom He suffered to oppress them as truly as He is Master of the defeated and broken nation. Wickedness will be punished, no matter what the race of the wrongdoer; and Israel is encouraged to submit with resignation to the divine justice, with an affectionate, filial piety that discerns the love behind a father's wrath. As the inevitable catastrophe draws on, the denunciation of wickedness in high places grows ever more severe, and the sternest critics of religious abuses are here no philosophers from outside but Iahweh's own accredited ambassadors. And with the increasing vehemence of the reproach, the spirituality of the message grows ever deeper. More and more do the Prophets develop the notion that it is the piety and fidelity of the individual that is the one security for the present, the one hope for the future. Finally Nabuchodonosor captures the Holy City; the Temple that is the one centre of religious life is destroyed, and the last remnant of the people carried off into captivity; and in the midst of the lamentations and the cruelty of the oppressors, there comes from the broken heart of Israel the Prayer of Jeremias, the most sublime of testimonies to the ideal of the individual life with God, the highest moral achievement of all the earlier Old Testament writings.

The Prophets had yet another rôle. They kept ever before the mind of the Jew, and never more than in these hours of defeat, the promises made of old to Abraham that from his race there should one day come the glory of the world; and in their successive reminders the promises became ever more precise. For the faithlessness of His people had not alienated Iahweh for ever. Present disaster is but the means to their betterment and closer union with Him. Far from being unmindful of His ancient promises of a Saviour, He chooses the present time of catastrophe to renew them yet more splendidly, and thereby to heighten and spiritualise His chosen people's hope.

IV. TENDENCIES IN THE RELIGIOUS WORLD OF THE FIRST CENTURY A.D.

It remains, before we come to the story of the new religion, to note some of the tendencies at work, when it appeared, in the old religions whose leading features we have surveyed. The new religion came into existence on the morrow of a political revolution whose effect was world-wide, the transformation into a personal autocracy of the oligarchy which, through the power of Rome, controlled civilisation. That revolution was itself the last of a succession which, through nearly three centuries, had slowly changed the main conditions of social life, and in changing these had influenced the religious ideas and practices of a whole world. In those three hundred years there had been at work a continuous steady pressure working towards the political unity of civilisation, and destroying, as it progressed, the multitudinous barriers to freedom of thought and intercourse which the rivalry of a hundred states and cultures had thrown up in sheer self-defence. It had worked most powerfully for a more generous philosophical conception of man's relation to his fellows, and had even given the beginnings of a setting of fact to such philosophical theories as that of the universal brotherhood of men. This gentle and more generous spirit passed from the philosophers to the very citadel of particularism and privilege—the law, and the revolution was reflected in the first western legislation that can truly be called social.

And, it needs no stating, this new force, bred of a new political and social unity, influenced no less strikingly the traditional notions of religion. For the intellectuals of Paganism there was that new thing the moral philosophy of the Stoics; and while some turned in desperation from the critic-riddled mythologies to the despair of scepticism, the neo-Pythagorean philosophies with their teaching of a divine providence and their liturgy of healing and purification attracted others. In this pagan élite we have the spectacle of a doctrinal enthusiasm reflected in, and influenced by, every form of intellectual activity, seeking restlessly but untiringly a system which will satisfy both intellect and heart. One of the most striking examples perhaps of this coincident doubt and desire, of the prevalent alternation of credulity and scepticism is Cicero. Cicero, conservative and respectful to tradition—no embittered liberal in revolt like Lucretius—who, in one mood, invoking his genius to move the people to gratitude for Jove's safeguarding of Rome can speak as a theologian, appears in quite another guise in his philosophical writings and his private correspondence. Do the gods exist ? The question, self-found, he proceeds to discuss it. "No doubt it is hard to say 'no', if the matter is discussed in a public reunion. Amongst ourselves . . . nothing easier than to say 'no.' I am myself one of the pontiffs. I really believe we ought to preserve with jealous devotion all the ceremonial of the public cult. For all that, I should like to be able to prove to myself that the gods do exist, not the mere likelihood of their existence but to prove it as a certainty. I have so many difficulties troubling me in this matter that sometimes I come to think that really there are no gods." The like interest, the same anxious desire, finds an echo in all that was best in the literature of the time. Vergil, Plutarch, and Seneca most of all, reflect it in a kind of continuous ground rhythm that once in a while rising to the surface swells their genius to its full.

What of the crowd, the vast mass of Pagans ? Here, too, the new spirit of brotherhood showed itself in the innumerable associations—*collegia*—for mutual assistance.

We note, too, the decline of certain cults. But the traditional paganism survives, still a force if only in the weight of its inertia.

Especially does it survive in the local cults, the worship of the special protecting gods of the town, of the professions and trades and of the family, and in the cult of the dead. Local patriotism is here their inspiration, and their ritual observances become a matter of civic duty—a reflection in religious matters of the rich and varied municipal life that was for so long the Empire's main strength; and the obligation of worship presses universally on every citizen. Even the élite who find their spiritual salvation in far different ways bow in practice to the prevailing spirit; and Seneca can end a devastating criticism of the cult of the gods of the Capitol with the practical recommendation that every wise man will worship them, not that this pleases the gods, but because it is commanded by the law.

And this traditional paganism remained for the mass of its clients substantially the same, anthropomorphic, a hero-worship, a magical cult, undoctrinal, unmoral, idolatrous. Philosophers might, by allegorising, seek to refine and purify it; they might give the myths a higher meaning through symbolic interpretations. But philosophers are rare. The average man has his bread to earn and lacking the time, if not the aptitude, for speculation, gives himself generally to the practice of life as he finds his fellows practising it. Hence polytheism survives the criticism of the thinkers, and the myths their ridicule; and idolatry remains so widespread, so universal a fact of life, that the pagan élite can mock at it as unsparingly as the later Christian Fathers. And with the universal idolatry there still flourished the old super-stition and the old obscenity which the idolatry preached, only too often, from a hundred divine examples. "I am well aware," the words are those of a pagan, Denis of Halicarnassus, "that many philosophers explain allegorically the greater part of these filthy fables. But this philosophy is the possession of a very few only. The mass of mankind, the ordinary folk, accept the stories in their worst sense. Either they despise gods whose lives are so depraved, or, since the gods themselves are shown not to abstain from them, they come to the pitch that they do not recoil from the very vilest of vicious deeds." It is not unfair to say that the survival of this old classic paganism was due "in great part to the feebleness of its control over moral conduct, character and the passions, to the sanction it gave to every surrender to the beast that sleeps, alas, at the heart of each one of us."

Paganism's idea of God had in it no element of grandeur, of holiness, of sanctity; and in its practice, adoration and love could find no place. It was in fact little but a mentality, an attitude of mind which went with a certain routine of ritual. Though it accompanied every action of life, it did so only as an

empty gesture, barren of influence, powerless to affect life itself
or thought. Nevertheless the founder of the new political regime,
Augustus, saw in it a means of control, a source of power, which,
patronised, fostered, protected by the state, might become,
because of its universal diffusion through the vast empire of so
many races and tongues, a permanent reserve of support. Hence
his vigorous and continued attempts to restore and reform it;
his rich endowment of its temples; and his own public assiduity,
and that of his successors, in the observance of its rites. There is
attributed to one of his counsellors, Maecenas, a speech which
sums up the new state policy in religious matters "Honour the
gods according to the customs of your forefathers, see to it that
others honour them too. As for those who would introduce
among you any strange novelties of religion, hate them and let
them feel your hatred. . . ." Such novelties there were indeed
to be, for underneath the universal state-protected Hellenistic
Paganism the old cults of Egypt and the East were once more
slowly stirring. With their ideas of spiritual purification, of
redemption from sin, and of personal immortality, expressed in
a ritual incomparably seductive, these cults were later to do much
to transform, yet once more, the religion of the populace; but for
yet another century they were to move only very slowly, their
influence as yet hardly felt outside the underworld of the great
cities of the East. Of greater immediate importance, in the first
century A.D., was the new cult of the State itself, now in course
of slow transformation to a worship of the reigning Emperor,
and rapidly becoming the most popular cult of all.

Emperor worship was not a Roman invention. It appears,
long before Rome was a power, in ancient Egypt, and it was
sufficiently widespread throughout the East for Alexander to use
it as a means of consolidating his conquests. The generals, who
on his death divided up his Empire among themselves, took the
practice as part of the legacy and it was already an established
tradition when, in turn, these kingdoms fell before the Roman
power. Roman philosophy, associating immortality with the
great heroes of humanity—an immortality they shared with the
gods—may have prepared the way in the west. For the hero
lives for ever with the gods, soon he comes to be likened to them,
to be considered after death as one of them. But once more it is
in the east that the beginnings are to be found, in the cult there
rendered to the different generals and proconsuls. Thus at the
beginning of the second century Flaminius, the conqueror of the
Macedonians, is associated in 196 at Chalcis with the cult of
Herakles and Apollo. A century later the custom is general and
Cicero can cite a cult of Verres as a count in his famous indictment,

and make it a boast that he himself refused the proffered divine honours during his proconsulship of Cilicia. The Civil War helped greatly in the development of the practice, and the assassination of Julius Cæsar was the occasion of the first official divinisation, the law of 44 B.C. which decreed to the dead hero the title of "Divine." In the Civil Wars which filled the next few years the rival leaders generously appropriated to themselves like honours—all but Octavian. With characteristic caution he waited until with his final victory the honours came to him more surely than if they had been self-conferred. The title of Augustus conferred by the Senate in 27 B.C. had in it already something of the divine, and soon there began at Rome a private cult of the Genius of Augustus. In the provinces progress was more rapid, and altars were erected even during his lifetime to Augustus himself, though at Rome itself it was not customary, for yet another century or more, so to deify the reigning sovereign.

With the emperor there was associated in the ritual the goddess Rome; and presently the two became confounded and, worshipping the emperor, the citizen worshipped his country. It was not merely in a spirit of servility and flattery that this new imperial cult originated and developed. Round it there clustered from the beginning a host of nobler associations. There was thankfulness for the peace and prosperity that succeeded a century of bloody civil war, appreciation of Augustus as the deliverer from an age of anarchy; there was something of the sentiment of pride of race, almost of patriotism; and in this cult all the popular veneration for the majesty of the State's power found a natural and congenial expression, until in the end it became the very touchstone of loyalty and good citizenship. It was of all cults the most popular; and, excelling all others in the pomp that surrounded its celebrations and in the prestige of its priesthood, more than any other it came to stand as the established religion of the State.

It is not, however, in the development of any one particular religion that the most characteristic feature of the religious life of this age is to be sought. More significant, and of ultimately greater importance, is the tendency of all these cults to amalgamate. The new political unity; Rome's new rôle as the capital of that new unity, the city where the vast Empire's innumerable religions were to meet and to live together, and through which as through a great clearing house of culture the hundred fashions of thought and life were to pass, and to return, refashioned, to the distant provinces; the quasi-official propaganda of the Roman religions; all fostered this new levelling tendency. Rome had conquered Carthage and Greece, Asia Minor, Syria and Egypt, and in turn those ancient civilisations, like some captive mistress, were to enslave their conqueror. The subject peoples brought with them into the Empire their gods as they brought their other cultural habits, and the strangers soon appeared in every city side by side with the native deities, sometimes in rivalry, some-times roughly identified by a similarity of myth or an identity of divine function. Sometimes the different religions co-existed in a strange companionship that was unconscious of basic incom-patibility, or again, combining, they gave rise to newer cults.

This tendency to assimilate and level the cults of the world, which was at work throughout the countries ringed around the Mediterranean Sea, began unmistakably to show itself after the conquests of Alexander. It developed with ever increasing vigour for the next four or five centuries. The nature of the pagan cults assisted the development. They lacked organisation, lacked a body of religious doctrine and consequently there was in them no place for anything corresponding to an Act of Faith. The clients of the different gods were not therefore "members" of the cults as a Christian is a "member" of his Church. Remembering also that Paganism's one obligation was observance of ritual, it is easy to understand the speedy development of this syncretist tendency. Nothing could have been more congenial to the nature of Paganism. But it would be erroneous to suppose that Syn-cretism made for greater simplicity, for a real unity that would take the place of the old confusing multiplicity of gods and cults. The final result of the movement was confusion greater than ever. It introduced new complexities, and, by its juxtaposition of gods, multiplying ever more and more the number of dwellers on Olympus, it made rather for polytheism more and more hopelessly. For the one Jupiter whom the ancient Roman knew, there were now, to the delight of the sceptic, half a dozen—as often as not rivals—to conciliate whom simultaneously called for considerable tact on the part of the pious. So for example Xenophon records how, on his return from Asia, he sacrificed in turn to Zeus Eleutherios and to Zeus Basileus. All in vain. Matters were rather worse than before. He learnt from one learned in such affairs that the jealousy of Zeus Meilichios was the obstacle, and hastening to propitiate the last, he finally received an answer to his prayers. Thanks to the syncretist development "Ideas become more indistinct; but no single idea of divinity clearly emerges. This theocrasia . . . did nothing for monotheism but a great deal for scepticism and the darkest superstitions."

In the six hundred years that lay between Nabuchodonosor's final destruction of their ancient kingdom and the coming of

Christianity, the Jews had suffered under a series of political revolutions. Their Babylonian conquerors had fallen to the Persians, and the Persians to Alexander. Alexander's Greek successors had, by their attempted suppression of Judaism, roused a revolt that resulted in an independent Jewish state and finally this had fallen to the Romans. Each of the political systems under which the Jews had lived had left its mark on national characteristics, but none had effected a change equal to that which resulted from the years of exile that followed the conquest of Nabuchodonosor. The exiles were indeed allowed to return by the Persian who conquered Nabuchodonosor's hapless descendant, but the Jewry of post-exilic times was a new thing, and the restored national life was no mere resumption of the old.

Henceforth there were indeed to be two Jewries, for not all the exiles returned, and from the Babylonian captivity the historian has ever before him this dual development of the race and its religion. The colonies of those who chose permanently to exile themselves from Palestine were for the most part, originally, in the valley of the Euphrates the land of the captivity; but later, and especially in the years that followed the conquests and death of Alexander, it was the countries of the hellenic. culture, more particularly Egypt, that attracted them and Alexandria itself became a second Jerusalem. With the Roman conquest of the East, and the consequent political unity of the whole Mediterranean world, the Jews spread into the Latin West. All the Mediterranean countries now knew them, as they themselves could boast. There was a colony of 10,000 (men alone) at Rome in the reign of Tiberius (A.D. 14–37) and about the same time they are reckoned at one in seven of the population of Egypt. Harnack estimates that they formed 7 per cent. of the total population of the Empire in the reign of Augustus.

The Jewry of Palestine and that of the Dispersion are equally important in a study of Christian origins, for the Palestinian Jewry was the birthplace and cradle of the new religion, and the Jewry of the Dispersion was its first means of propaganda, the bridge by which it entered the world of Paganism outside Palestine. The two Jewries were greatly affected by every phase of contemporary religious development; they were affected in widely different ways. For the exiles who returned to Palestine, there had followed a full restoration of the forms of the pre-exilic religious life. Jerusalem was once again the Holy City, the Temple was rebuilt, and the prescribed routine of daily sacrifice and ritual prayers was resumed as though no calamity of war had ever interrupted it. The main effect upon this Jewry of the contact with the religions of their conquerors, had been to strengthen and confirm its own traditional faith. Especially were these Jews strengthened in their hold on the doctrine that Iahweh is God and is alone God. The old fight of the Prophets against idolatry is never again to need renewing. In none of the Prophets who follow the captivity is there any reference to it as a national sin. Iahweh is more clearly seen as the Creator and Preserver of all mankind, and if known in an especial manner to the Jews, knowable to the rest by His work of creation and His providence. More than ever is emphasis laid on the fact that He is the God of Holiness, of Justice in the moral sense, requiring in this an imitation of Himself in those He has created. The political catastrophe has served to emphasize that something more is required for future salvation than the mere fact of birth into the race of His choice.

Man is body and soul, is immortal, and around his relations with Iahweh his Creator, through the Law set for his observance, there now begins a whole world of new speculation and thought. Man's universal inclination to evil, his weakness in the presence of temptation to wrong-doing, are a legacy from the failure of the first of mankind, Adam. But the weakness is not fatal. An observance of the Law is possible and will ensure salvation. Observance of the Law is possible, but it is increasingly difficult; for one of the chief results of the exile has been a cult of the Law for its own sake, a cult that has gradually overlaid its first simple austerity with a mass of deduced precepts such that only the scholar trained in the Law can safely find his way through the mazes, and the Law begins to cover the minutest detail of all the myriad acts of life. To teach the law, to interpret it, there has gradually grown up the "corps" of the Scribes. They are an extra-levitical religious force, standing to the priesthood much as the new law cult stands to the Temple liturgy of sacrifice; and the foundation of their prestige is their service in the dark days of the captivity, when, deprived of that liturgy, Jewish piety was saved by study and meditation on the Divine Law.

This cult of the Law was now perhaps the chief force in the religious life of the Palestine Jewry, and in its most enthusiastic devotees developing ever more surely into a barren and exaggerated formalism. It was not, however, the only force in that life; and the Jew, torn between the consciousness of his own weakness and the austere fact of the well-nigh unobservable Law, about which the Scribes in their many schools disputed, turned for consolation and encouragement to the mercy of the Law's author. Since the captivity there had gradually developed the notion of an individual responsibility in spiritual matters, and along with this a sense of Iahweh's providence as a quality by reason of which men, not merely in the mass, as a chosen nation, but even as individuals, were important and matter for the Divine Concern. Side by side with the cult of the Law there was a cult of the Psalms; and in the interior life thus fed and stimulated, the pious Jew escaped at once the deadening formalism of a merely external law observance, and the consequences of a fatal identification of the Divine Lawgiver with His unauthorised human commentators.

The rôle of the prophet diminished; and with the death of Malachi there began a long period of four centuries in which the Jew, while the different pagan empires disputed his kingdom among themselves, lived spiritually on the riches of his past, giving himself to the twin cults of the Law and the life of interior holiness and to meditation on the manner and the time of the next showing forth of Iahweh's mercy—the looked for coming of the Messias. Here speculation was rich and varied indeed, much of it stimulated and coloured by pagan motives of eschatology, and related almost always to the anticipated end of Iahweh's earthly creation. Sometimes the coming of the promised Saviour is expected as coincident with the end of the world, as the judgment of Iahweh through him on His defeated enemies. Another school looked for the Saviour's reign as an earthly preliminary to the promised eternity of bliss. After his victory over Iahweh's enemies, he will, as ruler of the world, transform it through justice and peace, judging mankind and allotting to each his punishment or reward. The wicked shall be punished for ever in flames, the good be received into paradise, a high place where they shall see Iahweh and rejoice with Him for ever. The Messias himself was conceived as a great prince to be sent by God to establish His kingdom on earth, as a warrior and judge, as the king who will reign eternally. Generally, too, he is conceived as already existing, awaiting the day of his coming; but he is never conceived as himself divine, nor did the general conception ever associate with his coming and the execution of his mission the idea of vicarious suffering and expiation.

For this Palestinian Judaism the conquests of Alexander were the beginning of much new development. The hellenistic culture which thereafter spread over all the semitic East could not leave it untouched. From Alexander himself, and from the Ptolemies to whom Palestine fell as a province on Alexander's death, their religious institutions had nothing but protection. But the victory of the dynasty of the Seleucid rulers of Antioch (198) brought about, with the change of ruler, the novelty of an aggressive movement on the part of the state to hellenise not merely the secular culture of the Jews but their religion also. The Jews were to syncretise Judaism at the order of the hellenic Paganism that

was now their master. A national insurrection was the consequence; and after a series of bloody wars the Jews, under the
heroic Judas Maccabeus, not only secured their threatened religious
independence, but shook themselves free of the rule of the foreigner.
The new political independence lasted for a century until, in
63 B.C., Jersualem fell to Pompey's armies and Rome. It was a
century of religious revival. The hellenistic influences of the
pre-Maccabean generations did indeed survive, especially among
the families of what may be called the ecclesiastical nobility, and
those from whose ranks the leaders in public life were recruited.
This was the party of the Sadducees, who reduced observance of
the Law to the minimum of what was actually written, and
rationalised, as far as they could, the ancient beliefs. Sadducees
formed a tiny colony of Hellenism in the very heart of Jewry,
controlling political life through their wealth and through their
command of the high priesthood which money had brought
them.

This attitude of compromise with the foreign culture was,
however, the attitude of the few; and the mass of the nation
followed rather the influence of those jealous doctors of the Law,
the Scribes. Striving to keep themselves clear of the pagan
culture's corrupting influence, they "separated" themselves from
its every manifestation—whence the later name by which they
were called, and called themselves, Pharisees, the Separated.
Their spiritual lineage was from the heroes who had formed the
armies of Maccabeus, and the traditional religious patriotism of
the sect won it a deep and constant influence with the mass of
the Jews.

The Judaism of the Dispersion is best studied as it appeared in
Alexandria its most influential centre, the second city of the
Empire, the Metropolis of the East, the capital of the Dispersion,
and for the Jew the second Jerusalem. It is hard to exaggerate
the importance of the fact of the Dispersion in the early history
of the Catholic Church. From Antioch to Italy and through
Gaul to Spain the chain of Jewish colonies spread, and it was
around these islands of belief in the pagan sea that the first
Christian groups were formed. Through the loosely federated
colonies of the Dispersion the new religion was to find a material
facility of propaganda such as no other religion could hope to
possess. In the colonies of the Dispersion the Jews lived their
own life. They did not intermarry with the surrounding Gentiles,
and, careful of their traditional cult of morality, they habitually
avoided the amusements that were the core of the pagan social
life—the theatres, the circus, the baths. They were exempt from
the charge of public office as they were debarred from military

service; and as members of a privileged religion their synagogues received protection and they themselves were judged according to their own law.

It was nevertheless, impossible for them to live entirely uninfluenced by their surroundings. They became Greek speaking, for example, and forgot their Hebrew to such an extent that it was necessary for their own use to have their sacred writings translated into Greek—whence the Septuagint. With the new language they entered into contact with all the rich variety of the world's most gifted civilisation. Greece, its literature, its philosophy, its spirit of speculation on fundamental things, now lay open to the scholars and thinkers of the Dispersion. Were they to close their minds to the new influence, to shut it out as a thing necessarily accursed, in the fashion of many of their compatriots in Palestine?—or was there not a means of conciliating what was good in it with their own traditions, and so of enlarging the sphere of their influence without surrendering what was vital to their faith? The thinkers of Alexandrian Judaism chose the latter alternative, and using Greek Philosophy to universalise the Law, strove to create an entente where the corrected philosophy and the Law, philosophically explained, should be seen as two aspects of the same unity. The Jewish faith remained the same thing, with its eternal foundations of monotheism and the personál immortality of the individual soul. The best of Greek philosophy accorded here with Jewish belief; and while the Jew accepted the philosophical allegorising of the Greek myths and fables that made of them merely a vehicle for the teaching of abstract truths, he was prepared, in the same accommodating spirit, to explain allegorically, the contents of his own sacred books. It is the idea hidden behind the fact that is the all-important thing; the fact related is secondary. Greek Philosophy thus becomes a religion, accepting the principle of the supernatural; Judaism, without ceasing to be a religion, will be a philosophy, "searching beneath the word revealed, the reasonable teaching it covers."

Religious ceremonial and liturgy lost much of their importance in this presentation of Judaism, except in so far as they were symbols of truth; the old notion of the true religion as meant exclusively for the chosen race disappears, and most important of all, the concept of the promised Saviour changes fundamentally. For these philosophically minded Jews it is no longer a warrior, judge or king, who is to restore the kingdom and wreak vengeance on the enemies of Iahweh, but a triumphant, all-conquering true doctrine. Allied to this change is another in the teaching about the end of the world. Here, though the idea of a personal judgment is preserved, the teaching lacks the picturesque extravagance characteristic of the Palestinian apocalypses. Punishment or reward follows immediately on death and judgment, and the lot then assigned is irremediable, eternal.

The greatest thinker among these Jews of the Dispersion was undoubtedly Philo (25 B.C.–A.D. 41) and it is in his writings that we can best see the aims and achievement of the movement and measure how far the one fell short of the other. Here, more fully than elsewhere, can we study the process by which, interpreting allegorically the sacred books of the Jews, these thinkers strove to find in the Law of Moses the principles and the completion of the philosophical and religious systems of Greece, much as Heraclitus,[1] strove to read Stoicism into Homer. It is an astonishing combination of Judaism with the leading ideas of Platonic and Stoic philosophy, learned but vague, lacking unity, and disconcertingly contradictory even in essentials. The body is essentially evil and by its contact with the soul inevitably soils the higher principle and leads it to sin. Man cannot therefore escape sin. To live well is the end of life and morality the most important part of philosophy. Of himself man cannot live a virtuous life. His goodness is the gift of God. Man knows God—and ordinarily can only know Him—by His works, and in His attributes; but by ascetic practices and assiduous study he can arrive at the direct knowledge of God which is ecstasy. In this, the momentarily intuitive vision of God upon earth, man, lifted above the good of merely intellectual knowledge, reaches to the very essence of God and comprehends in Him the unspeakable unity of all.

Of redemption from sin, of satisfaction for sin, there is not a word; and the ecstasy held out as the end of life, is, from the intellectual nature of the process which leads to it, a privilege which necessarily can only fall to scholars and thinkers. On the other hand, although the traditional monotheism remains intact, the use of the allegorical method of interpreting the sacred writings—a practice borrowed from Stoicism—was bound to weaken the value of the writings as records of historical fact; and in the very success of the effort to justify the Jewish faith by Greek philosophy there lay the danger of compromising the unique character of that faith as the revealed religion of Iahweh the one true God.

The new religion preached by Jesus Christ came then into a world where religious questions were already eagerly discussed.

---

[1] Not, of course, the Ionian philosopher of the sixth century B.C., but the writer who, six or seven hundred years later, wrote, under the name Heraclitus, the *Homeric Allegories*.

To satisfy the universal feeling of religious desire in its myriad aspirations and hopes, a host of rival cults and philosophies, preached by enthusiastic devotees, already competed. They did not die at the sudden coming of the new thing. Far from dying they survived; some of them to flourish even more than hitherto, some of them to vex, some to assist it: all of them in one way or another to condition its development. In the particularism of Palestinian Jewry it met its first great foe; and when, thanks to this struggle, its own separate character was established, the Pharisaic spirit survived in the first Christians themselves, to menace from within the free development of the new truth. Alexandrian Judaism was more friendly, but in its very friendliness was danger, for it did not always recognise the exclusiveness which was of the new faith's essence; and the spirit in which, sometimes unfortunately, it strove to reconcile the prophets and the philosophers, survived in the first great school of Christian teachers, to assist, and sometimes seriously to thwart, the philosophical exposition of that faith too. In Paganism the new religion was to find a frank and open enemy, violent and aggressive in its political aspects, inevitably so in the developing novelty of Emperor-worship, and the most slowly worsted enemy of all in the traditional rural cults—cults to the lateness of whose overthrow there stands for witness the curious fact that one of our modern terms for heathen is the Roman word for rustic—*paganus*.

CHAPTER II

THE FOUNDATION OF THE CHURCH

I. THE FOUNDER

THE new religion whose early history is the subject of this book, has for its origin the attested fact of the birth, at Bethlehem, an unimportant town of the Roman province of Judæa, of Jesus Christ. His mother Mary and her husband Joseph, were of Galilee and it was the business of the imperial census, in the Roman year 749, which brought them travelling at this most unsuitable of times so far from their poor home. The goal of their journey was barely reached when, in an outhouse of one of the over-crowded inns of the little hill town, Mary gave birth to her Son. The life that there began is the foundation of the Church.

The Child's destiny had been foretold to His mother by the angel of Iahweh who announced to her the coming miraculous conception through the direct operation of the Most High. To Joseph, too, was given like explanatory vision and prophecy. The Child was to save His people from their sins, whence the name Joseph was charged to impose on Him—Jesus.

The documentary sources of our knowledge of that life are the writings of the immediate disciples of Jesus, set down within a generation of the end of His earthly life, the collection which we call compendiously the New Testament. Around the genuine-ness of these writings, the truthfulness of those who composed them, their value as records, a vast amount of controversy has raged. The study of the questions raised by that controversy belongs properly to a more specialised science than General Church History which must here make its own the findings of Scripture scholarship. The position assumed here is that the New Testament writings are what they propose themselves to be—authentic records of trustworthy contemporary witnesses. What kind of thing is the religion those writings describe? The first difficulty before the enquirer is that the writings do not profess to describe any religion at all, but are supplementary to the basic knowledge which they presuppose. The collection is made up of a variety of things. There are short accounts of the life and death of Jesus Christ; there is an account of the spread of His teaching in the first generation after His earthly life ended; there is a book of mysterious prophecy; and a number of letters written by His principal lieutenants explaining particular difficulties or correcting special errors in belief or practice. The New Testament can thus in no sense be regarded as a systematic exposition of the religion taught by Jesus Christ. It provides, none the less, a wealth of information about this new religion and its Founder sufficient for the historian's purpose, sufficient, that is to say, to make clear the new thing's nature.

As a religion it is alone of its kind. It is a revelation; it is a rule of conduct; it is a doctrine; it is an organisation; and in each of these aspects it is something new. This new revelation is the fulfilment of Iahweh's repeated pledge to Israel. Jesus is the long promised Saviour Who shall rout Iahweh's ancient enemy and restore Mankind to its original amity with the Creator. Jesus is the Messias. Finally He through Whom this revelation is made, the Teacher, the Founder, is yet something infinitely beyond. He is the object of His disciple's faith, no mere prophet of Iahweh, even the greatest, but Iahweh's Son, God Himself incarnate.[1]

The religion of Jesus Christ is no revolutionary thing, new in all its parts, built up on the ruins of some older thing destroyed to make way for it. It is, by its Founder's express declaration, the perfect fulfilment of the ideas and ideals already foreshadowed in Judaism; and the body of the New Testament religion is built round an idea already so familiar as to be a commonplace of Jewish piety, the Kingdom or Reign of Iahweh. "Jesus came into Galilee proclaiming the good news of the Kingdom of God" is the New Testament's first description of the divine Teacher's activity. But this Preacher of the Kingdom of God has no attachments to any of the contemporary teachers who, interpreting the messianic prophecies in material terms, eagerly dispute the details of the future King's earthly triumph. Such a kingdom has no place in the teaching of Christ. The kingdom as now announced is not the political triumph of Iahweh's chosen people over their Gentile oppressors; it is not even a restoration of the kingdom of David. It is the reign of Iahweh in men's hearts. The citizens of this kingdom are those in whose heart Iahweh reigns, and such citizenship is not a privilege of race, nor the reward of merit. It is offered to all! Repentance, faith, simple childlike humility are the disposing conditions. For the subjects of this new reign of God, the old ideals of holiness and moral goodness revealed by Iahweh to the Jews remain in all their force. The Law is not

---

[1] So great are the risks of distorting this subject by abridgment that it would certainly have been easier to have left this section unwritten. But the other risk remained that unless the essentials of the Gospel of Jesus Christ are set forth at the beginning of the history of His Church that history could hardly be intelligible.

abolished but, lived in the new spirit—the spirit of the kingdom—
is transformed in this its final fulfilment. More important than
obedience to the letter of the law is the spirit in which the law
is kept, and the new spirit is the spirit of loving dedication of self
to Iahweh, the love of all mankind in imitation of Iahweh's
universal love and for Iahweh's sake. Iahweh, the King, is
revealed as the loving Father of those He rules. It is as "Our
Father" that—in the one prayer Jesus taught His followers—the
disciple is bidden to address Him. As a father He cannot but
give good things to the children who ask. He cares for the birds,
the very flowers of the field and His children's every hair. Even
His children's ingratitude and rebellion cannot destroy Iahweh's
love; and Jesus tells the parable of the Prodigal Son to bring
home the supreme truth of this love that only the sinner's own
obstinacy can withdraw him from this eternal love's effect. Man's
love—of God, of his fellows—must strive to imitate Iahweh's
love. It must be complete, selfless, universal, not the product of
chance association, of similarity of race, or of the hope of gain.
Everything for God, for God's sake from Whom all love has
come. The "reign" is necessarily an intimate, interior thing in
man's very heart and will, its very existence calling for the continual conscious union of the disciple's soul with Iahweh. On
this interior submission all else depends. Obedience to Iahweh's
commands, then, is no mere legalist obedience, but, because of
the motive which shapes it, of the spirit which gives rise to it, a
means of ever closer union. Iahweh's love, which is the foundation
of the Kingdom, is, too, its final object and, consummated in
eternity, the soul's ultimate reward. It is impossible to exaggerate
the part of Love in this revelation of Jesus Christ.

The reign will be established slowly, gradually. Like the leaven
in meal, like the seed buried out of sight, it will grow silently in
a man's heart, in the world. Its victory is the outcome not of
violence, nor of external force, but of Love's slow persuasion.
No sudden burst of enthusiasm, then, will suffice for its establishment. A steady, persevering will alone provides the necessary
foundation. For the Kingdom will make high demands upon
its subjects. It is a treasure hidden, a pearl of surpassing value,
to possess which when he hears of it a man will sell all he has.
In a matter where anything short of absolute selflessness menaces
the whole good work, the disciple must be tested, disciplined,
must try himself by surrender, until self be no more. All is
asked of him to whom all will be given. Where is this giving up
of self to end ? For each disciple where Iahweh wills it. The extreme sacrifices—of property, of family life, of life itself—though
commended as the perfect thing, are not prescribed as equally

necessary to all. There is a way of Precept as well as this higher way of Counsel. But for all, to whichever way Iahweh calls them, there is the same spirit in which they must serve—the spirit of renouncement, self-forgetfulness, service of others, love, humility and all for Iahweh's sake, in conscious imitation of Him. The ideal is summed up in a phrase of startling realism "If any one will come after me let him deny himself, take up his cross daily, and follow me."[1] And for all there is, too, the duty of continuous prayer—for prayer, once more, is no mere external rite but a hidden interior act of union with God, its model the "Our Father." If His demands are far-reaching Iahweh's patience with those who stumble as they strive is revealed as infinite; and for the repentant, no matter what the degree of their offending, His mercy has no limits. So, too, must the disciple forgive those who injure him, forgive them endlessly, love even his enemies, bless them that hate him, pray for his persecutors and those who despoil his good name. So shall he show himself the child of his Father in Heaven.

The disciple's willing acceptance of the reign, his faithfulness to its spirit, are rewarded even in this life· by the peace for which man's innermost being yearns, and which is only possible to the man on whose affections self has ceased effectively to make demands, and by an ever-closer union with God. In the world to come there is the consummation of the union with God begun in His Kingdom on earth. Goodness and happiness then go together, and goodness is the renunciation of self and the service of others for Iahweh's sake, in a union with Him inspired by love for Him. This last qualification is all important. The spirit informing the new ideal of conduct raises it above the mere humanitarianism which, sooner or later, calls for human compensation, and can never reach perfect disinterestedness, be perfectly safe in practice for the souls who dedicate themselves to it.

In the nineteen hundred years that have gone by since Jesus preached His gospel, the phrases in which He set it have become the commonplaces of mankind. All men use them, all pay them the homage of lip-service at least. It is, on this account, difficult to understand, unless we meditate historically, how great a novelty such teaching was when it was first given. What are, if too often unpractised, the acknowledged commonplaces of modern moral idealism none the less, were then truths startling in their novelty, and, because alive, disconcerting. Nor can we ever hope to see their effect as it was produced unless we continually bear in mind Who He was that taught—a man truly,

[1] " Our accustomed ears can hardly guess what that word ' cross ' meant to His startled followers " (C.C. Martindale, S.J.).

but a Man who was God, a man through Whose real Humanity—human body, human soul, human mind, human will, human charm—a Divine Person acted. Only when read with this all important fact in mind—that Jesus Christ is God incarnate—does the story of that earthly life take on the fullness of its meaning, and the reasonableness of the steep ascetic recommendation become clear. It is a share in what He Himself enjoys that He offers to those who will follow Him. Some higher motive than the merely human must inform their allegiance. Only by rallying to His high demands can the disciple become that to which God's high ambitions destines him.

Jesus then teaches, through the new revelation of the Kingdom, a doctrine of social brotherhood which, because it is based on the transcendent truth of Iahweh's essential Love (never before so perfectly revealed), reaches the very heights of idealism. And this divinely ideal spirit is proposed as the normal habit for all mankind. There is no man in whose soul it cannot be realised, no man whose heart it cannot touch, whose life it cannot transform. The philosophers, at their best, spoke only to a tiny minority of trained minds, chosen spirits. Jesus speaks to all. For it is not by mere individual effort that citizenship is first achieved, nor does the Kingdom develop from even the best of human intentions, from the strongest of human wills. As it is more than a human morality, so the Divine shares in every state of its growth. "Without me you can do nothing" are the divine Master's own words to those who accept Him. Their good-will, their faith, are to be informed by a higher, divine life, and transformed thereby, made capable of the supernatural activities which alone can serve and maintain the new life. This new life—which alone makes possible the translation into act of the new rule of conduct—is the divine life by which Jesus lives Himself, and in which, by their new association with Jesus, the disciples mysteriously share. Jesus is the vine, they are its branches. With Him, as the greatest of all His followers is to say a few years later, they form one body, He the head, they the limbs.

The new revelation is not then—for all the universality of its appeal, promise, and plan—intended to achieve its end through individual conversation merely. The individual converted, in allegiance to the new Kingdom, reaches the destined perfection through his new status and in consequence of the association that goes with it, rather than by any virtue of his own individual act of adhesion. It is as the branch of the Vine Who is Christ, as the limb of that body whose head is Christ, that the citizen of the Kingdom is a subject for the new privileges. And that mysterious association with Christ, and hence with all those other limbs his fellow-subjects, receives visible corporate expression in the *ecclesia*—an actual society. For the Kingdom which is a seed and leaven, is also a field where the weeds grow as surely as the wheat. It is a net of fish, again, both bad and good; a palace (and Jesus names one of His followers as the keeper of its keys); a building (and the same follower Jesus names as its rock-like foundation). It is a flock which wolves can attack; a flock whose shepherd is Jesus, and which again He can commit to the care of that disciple who is key-bearer and foundation rock. Into this actual, visible, corporation the disciple enters by a visible corporal initiation—Baptism. In the Kingdom there is authority, and those to whom its Founder gives that authority are to be obeyed as He Himself is obeyed. Their authority is to teach, to teach indeed all nations, to bind and loose in His name, to forgive sins even and to retain, to admit by Baptism those who believe: and what by His commission they authoritatively decide, that, He promises them, will He finally confirm. The Kingdom will be buffeted. Hell itself will strive against it—but vainly; for He will Himself be with it to the end. The nucleus of that society in which the Kingdom is thus visibly expressed are the twelve disciples whom the record is careful to name—the Apostles; and it is one of these, Simon, who is the shepherd appointed to feed the flock, the key-bearer of the palace, the rock-like foundation and therefore renamed by the Founder Himself, and so to be known ever after, not Simon but Peter.

The Church (*ecclesia*) is however much more than the association in which the disciples are grouped under an ordered authority. It is in the Church, and through the Church, by means of that authority, that the teaching is to be preserved safe from error, the life to find true guidance. The Church is, too, the means by which the disciple is related to God. Jesus Christ and the Church together constitute the mystical Christ of which, while Jesus Christ is the head the rest of the disciples are limbs, members. This is not mere metaphor but spiritual reality. All the members live by the life of the whole, and that life is the Divine Life of the Head. Into that living body the disciple is incorporated by the ritual act of Baptism. Thereby and thereafter he shares in the Divine life, entering into a privileged relation with God, into a new relation with the other members of the body. It is through the unity of this mystical body that God has chosen to work out the salvation of mankind. This is the central point, the innermost mystery of the new religion. This is the essence of "the good news about the Kingdom of God," the fulfilment of God's promises to the Jews, the means by which man may share here on earth in the life that is divine. This unity of the mystical body is shown forth, realised and intensified through a second ritual act, the disciple's sharing in the banquet-mystery called the Eucharist, where he is given a Food which, in appearance bread and wine, is in reality Christ Himself. It is to disciples who are members of this mystical body, linked thus with the Divine in a union whence comes to them a real newness of life, a share in the divine life; to disciples illuminated in mind thereby and strengthened in will, that the high demands of conduct are made, that there is proposed the ideal of a life of love of God and of man for God's sake. The disciple, through Baptism member of the Church, member of the mystical body of Christ, is supernaturalised; and through the mystical body Christ lives on for ever in this world.

Even this is not the end of the summary of what that *ecclesia* is in which Jesus Christ set His revelation, and which He preached in His "good tidings." Jesus was the long-promised Messias. All humanity, Jew and Gentile alike, had through the sin of Adam been ever since estranged from Iahweh, "under the rule of sin." The Reconciler was Jesus Christ, and the redemption of humanity from its enslavement was wrought by His sacrificial death. Through that death came for man the possibility of forgiveness, of restoration. It is, in the Gospel religion, the source of the whole scheme's life. Man's rôle is not, however, passive. He must take the proffered thing, the new status possible through that death. He takes it by believing—it is not a reward for merit—and by being baptised. The death is for all. The offer is made to all, to Jew and non-Jew alike. Man must believe once he knows it is God Who speaks. And he must become of the Church by Baptism. Baptism, associating the disciple with Christ dying sacrificially on his behalf, associates him with Christ's consequent triumph over sin. It is, once more, as a member of the mystical body that he shares in the triumph as in the death, and thence lives on in Christ, like a branch grafted on to a tree, by the one same vital principle of the Divine life. Baptism then, the rite of initiation, is most strictly bound to the sacrificial death. Equally strictly bound to it is the other great ritual of the Eucharist, which is not only a showing forth of the mystical body's unity, but a renewal of the sacrificial death itself.

The *ecclesia* then is not a mere aggregation of individual believers, but a spiritual moral person, which continues in concrete, visible fashion the life and work of its Founder— teaching, guiding, sacrificing; which is the means through which men take hold of the gifts of the new fellowship with Iahweh. A new vital principle, a new ideal of living, divinely revealed truth eternally secured, in a living organism ruled by safeguarded teachers with authority and power to dispense supernatural aids—the Catholic Church. Its history we can study as the history of the development of Christ's teaching—the History of Dogma; or as the history of the way in which the new life has shown itself through two thousand years—the History of Christian Spirituality; or as the history of the organism as an organism. But while no study of Church History is complete which leaves out any one of these, it is truer still to say that no Church History can ever really be complete, for the essential Church History is the history of the reign of God in the millions of faithful human hearts throughout two thousand years—and this is known only to God.

The sublime religious idealism of the revelation of Jesus Christ is the teaching for which the world has all these centuries been waiting. His own life is itself the best exemplification of the way in which His teaching must, of its nature operate. For His life was hidden, remote; unobserved, for all its marvels, beyond its tiny local setting: and the propaganda, which lacked all appeal save what appeal the ideals and truth made of themselves to hearts well disposed, had so little immediate success that by the time of His death scarcely more than a hundred believing souls had given themselves to the cause.

His daily life, for all but the last three years, was apparently the ordinary well-filled day of a workman—a carpenter like Joseph His foster-father—in a small country town, with so little to distinguish it publicly from the life of those around that, on His first appearances as Teacher, those who knew Him best could scornfully point to His ordinary antecedents in final and devastating criticism of His new rôle. He was to these simply "the carpenter's son," and to His immediate relatives the subject, obviously, of an unfortunate fit of madness ! Signs and marvels had accompanied His birth. If, on the one hand, it had come about in circumstances of destitution which foreshadowed the ideal of self-renouncement for God's sake which He was ever to preach, it had yet been heralded by visions of angels; and, led by a mysterious divine star, wise men had come from the East to adore the Newly-born. At the ritual ceremony of His mother's purification the Child had been recognised in prophecy as Israel's saviour; and Divine intervention, again, had saved Him from Herod's jealousy-inspired massacre of all the children of His age. Upon that vision Joseph had fled with Him and with His mother into Egypt and there for ten years, until Herod's death (A.D. 6), they lived. The story of the next twenty years is that of the quiet ordinary life in the house of Joseph and Mary in the town of Nazareth, half way between the Carmel range and the Lake of Genesareth, a quiet of which one incident alone is known to us—

the visit to Jerusalem when the Boy was twelve, His disappearance, and His being found instructing the Doctors of the Law in the temple portico.

Twenty miles or so to the north-east of Nazareth is the little heart-shaped stretch of water called sometimes the Sea of Galilee, sometimes the Lake of Genesareth, twelve miles long in its greatest length, seven miles broad. The half-a-dozen little towns that cluster round it were the scene of the greater part of the new Teacher's activities, and it was from their population of fisherfolk that most of His first followers came.

From the beginning that simple teaching provoked opposition and misunderstanding. For the politically-minded zealots who looked for the Messias—as so much contemporary discussion presented him—as Iahweh's warrior-captain, this new teaching was a disappointment. The Pharisees too were alienated by the denunciation of the development which had made the letter of Iahweh's Law the all-important thing in orthodox Palestinian Judaism. Nowhere was He understood immediately and fully. Even the chosen band who, coming to Him in the first days, were the objects of His special instruction, and who remained to the end, whom He chose to be the nucleus of the new institution, were to the last a little impatient of the idealism, a little disappointed at the lack of earthly glamour, at the failure to conform to the hopes of orthodox religious patriotism.

None the less, wherever He went crowds awaited His coming, listened to the teaching, followed the Teacher from one town to another and even into the wilderness when He made thither for retirement. The teaching, the new voice that spoke "as one having authority," the personality, the miracles of healing wrought everywhere in all men's sight, miracles so evident, so numerous, so characteristic that He could Himself quote them as a testimony —"Relate to John the things you have seen, the blind see, the lame walk, the lepers are cleansed, the dead rise again"—as evident as that "the poor have the gospel preached to them," all these things bred immense enthusiasm but little, very little, of that solid conviction and change of heart based on belief which alone would serve His purpose.

The passing enthusiasm for novelty, for a thaumaturgus, He refused—the leaven must work according to its nature—refused it even when it would have saved Him from His hostile critics, from His enemies. For by now enemies He assuredly had; and in the later stages of His career as missionary they assist, "lie in wait," set traps to trick Him, now into the expression of some unorthodox opinion in the day's religious casuistry, now into treason against the all-powerful Emperor. The end is only a matter of time. Humanly speaking, sooner or later, should He not prevent it by His divine power, these jealous and wily adversaries will have Him enmeshed. From now on He redoubles the time, and the patience, He expends on the chosen faithful few. He explains to them gradually Who He is, His mission and destiny of suffering and death, their own future rôle in the *ecclesia*, the nature of their high vocation and the reception which will be theirs too, once they meet the world He is come to save, the world which knows Him not, wills not to know, and pursues Him to death itself. To the end, though they remain faithful, believing, obedient, the disciples hear all this with reluctance. Human nature in them is not able to reconcile this destiny of vicarious suffering with that other tradition of Iahweh, Lord of Hosts, strikingly triumphant over the wicked whether in Israel's past or in the wild apocalyptic reveries that have, for them, so often drowned the sadness of the insistent present. So with the earthbound material heart of His nation against Him, and the work of formation not yet accomplished in even His faithful few, Jesus comes to the appointed chosen death. Once more, as in the birth, the circumstances make it the supreme act of self-renouncement, once more supernatural signs accompany every phase of His life.

"The Gospel is announced; the Church is founded; the sacrifice of the cross is to confirm the one and the other." Slowly Jesus makes His way south, journeying for the last time to Jerusalem, the religious capital, where for generations now the struggle between the rationalist, Sadducee, aristocracy from whom are chosen the High Priests, and the legalist piety of the patriotic and popular Pharisee is the one absorbing evidence of religious interest. Both Sadducee and Pharisee are, for their own characteristic reasons, opposed to His mission, willing to plot His fall. This He knows, yet "steadfastly set His face to go to Jerusalem." And He foretold that in the Holy City they would lay hands on Him, mock Him, scourge Him and put Him to death: and that He would rise again the third day. On the first day of the week before the feast of the Pasch, through the streets of the Holy City filled with thousands of pious pilgrims drawn thither by the feast, in a kind of triumph—surrounded by His disciples and acclaimed by the crowd as the Holy One of God—He entered on the time of His passion. One last time the imperfect enthusiasm, which would use Him and His teaching rather than yield and be itself converted to His uses, blazed in an appearance of adhesion.

Four days later, on the eve of the Pasch, He prepared to celebrate the feast for the last time with the twelve disciples of His especial choice. At the ceremonial meal He instituted the new rite of the

Eucharist, already foreshadowed and promised in His preaching, and in a long discourse made to the Apostles the revelation of His own most intimate self. From the meal they passed to the olive grove of Gethsemane—the traitor among the Apostles, seduced by the Master's enemies, had already arranged with his enemies for His betrayal and arrest. In the garden they found Him and took Him.

He was led before the High Priests and, proclaiming His Divinity, condemned for blasphemy. But although, in his mockery of a trial, they reviled and insulted Him, more they dared not do—the Roman Authority not consulted. Whence an appeal to the Procurator of Judæa, Pontius Pilate, and a further trial. Pilate was embarrassed. His Prisoner was innocent, but the influential Jewish leaders insisted. The procurator shifted uneasily—Jesus was of Galilee, so he tried to load with the decision the shoulders of Herod, its nominal ruler. That failing, he tried a last resource —the custom of releasing annually on the feast some criminal condemned to death. But the mob and the priesthood asked in preference a highway robber lying under sentence. Finally, with taunts that affected the procurator's loyalty—"If thou release this man thou art not Cæsar's friend"—they prevailed, and Pilate, disclaiming responsibility, made over the Prophet to the priests.

"And they took Jesus and led Him forth. And bearing His own cross He went forth to that place which is called Calvary, where they crucified Him, and with Him two others one on each side, and Jesus in the midst. . . . And Jesus having cried out with a loud voice, gave up the ghost. . . . And the centurion who stood over against Him said 'Indeed this man was the Son of God.'

"Now there was in the place where He was crucified a garden; and in the garden a new sepulchre, wherein no man yet had been laid. There they laid Jesus because the sepulchre was nigh at hand. And on the first day of the week, very early in the morning, they came to the sepulchre, bringing the spices which they had prepared. And they found the stone rolled back from the sepulchre. And going in, they found not the body of the Lord Jesus. And it came to pass, as they were astonished in their mind at this, behold, two men stood by them in shining apparel. And as they were afraid, and bowed down their countenance towards the ground, they said to them: 'Why seek you the living with the dead? He is not here but risen. Remember how He spoke unto you, when He was yet in Galilee, saying: The Son of Man must be delivered into the hands of sinful men, and be crucified, and the third day rise again.' And they remembered His words.

And going back to the sepulchre, they told all these things to the eleven, and to all the rest. . . . And these words seemed to them idle tales; and they did not believe them. . . . At length He appeared to the eleven as they were at table; and He upbraided them with their incredulity and hardness of heart, because they did not believe them who had seen Him after He was risen again. . . . To whom also He shewed Himself alive after His passion, by many proofs, for forty days appearing to them, and speaking of the kingdom of God. And eating together with them, He commanded them, that they should not depart from Jerusalem, but should wait for the promise of the Father, which you have heard (saith He) by My mouth. For John indeed baptized with water, but you shall be baptized with the Holy Ghost, not many days hence. They therefore who were come together, asked Him, saying: Lord, wilt Thou at this time restore again the kingdom to Israel? But he said to them: It is not for you to know the times or moments, which the Father hath put in His own power: But you shall receive the power of the Holy Ghost upon you, and you shall be witnesses unto Me in Jerusalem, and in all Judæa, and Samaria, and even to the uttermost part of the earth. And when He had said these things, while they looked on, He was raised up: and a cloud received Him out of their sight. And while they were beholding Him going up to Heaven, behold two men stood by them in white garments. Who also said: Ye men of Galilee, why stand you looking up to heaven? This Jesus Who is taken up from you into heaven, shall so come, as you have seen Him going into heaven."

II. THE FIRST GENERATION

After the Ascension the twelve apostles returned to Jerusalem and, in fear of the Master's powerful enemies, locked themselves away, while in obedience to His last commands they awaited the imminent coming of the Holy Spirit. "Within a few days" He had said; and ten days only after His Ascension the mysterious event took place. The Holy Spirit came in the noise of a mighty wind, appearing over each as a tongue of visible fire. And they began to speak in different tongues according as the Spirit gave them to speak. The seclusion was at an end; and strengthened by the undeniable miracle they went forth to announce themselves to the world.

It was the Jewish feast of Pentecost and the Holy City was filled with pilgrims from every province of the East, from Persia and from Rome itself. The rumour of the heavenly sign spread, the crowds began to collect, and ás these pilgrims of a score of tongues understood, each in his own language, what the disciples of Jesus said, bewilderment seized on them, and anti-Christian calumny offered its first curiously futile explanation. . . . "These men are full of new wine." The calumny was the Church's first opportunity, and Peter, using it, preached its first explanatory missionary sermon, gathering in thereby the first converts—"about 2,000 souls." Repentance for past sin, belief in Jesus Christ as God and Saviour, baptism—these are the conditions of membership. For the rest the new group led the life of traditional Jewish piety: prayer, fasting, almsdeeds, attendance at the Temple, adding to this their own private reunion for the new ritual of "the breaking of the bread," and a practice of voluntary poverty. Day by day their number grew, and the miraculous signs which had supported the Master's teaching followed the work of the Apostles. Of Peter especially it is recorded that the sick were brought in their beds to the streets through which he would pass, that his shadow, at any rate, falling on them, they might be healed.

The opposition grew too. It was only a matter of weeks since the religious chiefs of Jewry had successfully pursued the Founder to His death, and here already His teaching was showing itself more successful than in His life. One of Peter's more striking miracles with its accompaniment of missionary sermon and conversions (this time 5,000) gave them their chance. Peter and John were arrested, cross-examined and forbidden further to preach or teach "in the name of Jesus." More at the moment the chief priests dared not do for fear of the people. A second attempt at repression promised to be more successful. All the Apostles were arrested and imprisoned. But an angel of the Lord came by night and released them, bidding them go immediately to the Temple to continue their work. They were re-arrested, re-examined. Once more Peter reasoned with the Council affirming again the divine character of the Master's mission, until the priests "cut to the heart began to cast about how best to slay them." It was one of their own number, Gamaliel, who dissuaded them. The movement, if it were no more than man-inspired, would perish of itself. The Council fell in with his views, had the Apostles flogged, and, with renewed prohibitions, set them free once more.

The peace which followed was short. Around the activities of a new preacher and wonder worker, Stephen, the old hatred flamed yet once again. Stephen drew on himself the hostility of the Greek-speaking Jews of Jerusalem. They challenged him to debate the new belief, and, falling victims where they had promised themselves victory, they roused the mob with the word that Stephen was a blasphemer. He was dragged before the Council and charged. No plea could avail to save one who believed that Jesus was the Messias and God, and who made the proof of this from Jewish history the burden of his defence. Stephen was condemned and, outside the walls of the city, stoned to death. This first martyrdom was the signal for a general persecution which scattered the believers through all Judea and Samaria. The Apostles alone remained at Jerusalem.

Flight however, brought little relief. The persecution was a well-organised affair and its chief agent in Jerusalem—a young zealot of the Pharisees, Saul by name—raided the houses of believers and filled the prisons with his victims. Then, turning his attention to the fugitives, he asked and received from the High Priest a commission to follow and round them up. Damascus was his first objective and thither with an escort he forthwith proceeded, "breathing out threats and slaughter against the disciples of the Lord." He was nearing the city when, blinded by a sudden light from Heaven, he fell from his horse. A voice spoke "Saul, Saul why dost thou persecute me ?" Who said "Who art thou Lord ?" And He "I am Jesus Whom thou persecutest." Saul's surrender was immediate and whole-hearted. "Lord what wilt thou that I do ?" The chief of the persecutors had become himself a disciple, the most momentous of all conversions had been made. To the Church in that hour was given the personality which more than any other has shaped its thought, its organisation, its spirit; the greatest of converts, the greatest of disciples, greatest of missionaries, thinker, ascetic, mystic, the follower in whom more than in any other is mirrored the Master.

Saul—soon to be known exclusively by his second name Paul —was a subject already marvellously adapted for his new rôle. By birth he was of the Dispersion, from Greek-speaking Tarsus in Cilicia. But his education had been in Palestine, at Jerusalem, in the school of one of the great men of the day, the rabbi Gamaliel. At Gamaliel's feet Paul had grown up, learned in biblical lore, to be a "Pharisee of the Pharisees." He knew his co-religionists as he knew himself, and, familiar with every phase of the Jewish thought of the day, moved easily in its many idioms. To the end, wherever he is dealing with Jews, whether inside the Church or outside it, he remains in his methods very much the rabbi. But his intellectual formation was not exclusively rabbinical, and though he is by no means a Hellenic type, to Hellenism he was no stranger. To this rich variety of formative influences the further fact should be added that birth in Tarsus made him a Roman citizen, gave him wherever he went within the vast empire a public status still privileged and of importance.

For a time after his conversion he gave himself to the task of explaining his conversion in the different synagogues of Damascus, and then buried himself for some years in the solitude of the Arabian desert. From this period of prayer and study he returned to Damascus with the object, once more, of converting the Jews to his new belief that "Jesus is truly the Messias." The Jews could not refute him, and to silence him they plotted his death, the governor of the city assisting them. Before the combination Paul was helpless. His time, however, was not yet; and he made a dramatic escape, lowered in a basket from the walls while soldiers watched the gates. From Damascus he went now to Jerusalem, to make himself known to Peter and the rest. He was received coldly enough until Barnabas, like himself a convert from the Diaspora, stood bond for his conversion. At Jerusalem he began again his task of explaining his new belief to the Greek-speaking Jews and once again there were plots to make away with him. A vision consoled and directed him. Jesus appeared as he prayed in the Temple, and bade him leave Jerusalem and his present fruitless task "For to the nations that are afar off will I send thee."

That vision is the first hint of what Paul is to be, the Apostle of the non-Jewish world. But not for a few years yet was the promise to be fulfilled. Paul left Jerusalem for a second period of retirement, this time in his native Cilicia. It was at the invitation of Barnabas that he returned thence to his mission of instruction and debate. This sponsor of St. Paul had, for some time now, been in charge of the believers who lived at Antioch, the third greatest city of the empire. It was a mixed congregation, fugitives from Jerusalem, converts from Judaism and, in any number, converts also from Paganism, who had come to the Church directly, without ever passing through any stage of association with the Jews. Here there was no Temple, and the Church was emancipated from any traditional connection with the synagogues. A new type of believer was developing and the town found for them a soubriquet—"at Antioch the disciples were first called *Christians*." Barnabas, sent from Jerusalem to govern this new community, saw it developing beyond his powers. He needed help, and going to Tarsus, besought Paul to come to him at Antioch. For a year they worked together "making known the Lord Jesus even to the Greeks," until (about A.D. 44) a divine monition bade the governors of the Church at Antioch set them aside for a new special work. St. Paul's ten years' novitiate was over. The promise of the vision in the Temple was to be realised. He was to go to the nations afar off. Henceforward his life is the famous series of missionary journeys: Cyprus, Cilicia, the provinces of Asia, Galatia, Macedonia, Achaia; passing and repassing through all these, establishing and organising churches, forming disciples to rule them, St. Paul, in the remaining twenty years of his life, lays the foundation on which is built the greatest part of the Church's later extension.

The procedure of St. Paul and his associates was simple. Arrived in a town, they made themselves known to its Jewish community, assisted at the synagogue service, and, when the opportunity came, explained their teaching that Jesus Christ was the looked-for Messias, the Church He had founded the fulfilment of the ancient prophecies, the Gospel the term of the Law. The final proof of this was the Resurrection, and of that historic fact they, the newcomers, were the accredited witnesses. Almost everywhere this exposition provoked violent dissensions, and if a few were converted to it, in the vast majority it bred a bitter hostility to the Christians and their institution. The mission, with its nucleus of converts, then turned to the pagans. Sometimes by disputation in the public places of the city, and again by private discussions, very slowly but persistently, the new religion was brought "to the Greeks also." So in the course of the twenty years 44–62, in all the chief cities along the coasts of the Ægean Sea and in many towns of the interior too, tiny communities of believers were organised. Ephesus, Corinth, Philippi, Thessalonica, each had its "church," and in these churches the great majority of the brethren were converts from the pagan cults. Whence very soon an important difference of opinion between the two classes of Christians, the Jewish and the Gentile, and a crisis.

The point at issue was the importance and the necessity, in the new Church of Christ, of the old Jewish Law. That the Church was open to the Gentiles no less than to the Jews had very early been made clear in a vision to St. Peter, and it was to preside over a Church made up mainly of Gentiles that the Apostles had dispatched Barnabas to Antioch. But were such Gentiles, converted now to the Church, to live as Jews ? The Jewish element in the Church continued to practise all the observances of the Mosaic piety. Must the Gentile convert do as much ? Did he come to Christ through Judaism or directly ? The question was a practical one. It involved such things as circumcision, an elaborate code of dietary regulations, a whole way of life. But it did not end there. The controversy was, at bottom, a controversy as to the relation of the Church to the old religion of the Jews. In that religion, observance of the Law had been the very means of salvation. The discussion between the two types of Christian was a discussion as to whether the Law had lost its saving power, whether a Christian could be saved through the Church alone—the Law being now abrogated, whether the Church was self-sufficient or, though a better kind of Judaism, still no more than a Jewish sect and, as such, tied to the Law.

The controversy was fierce "some coming down from Judea taught the brethren that except you be circumcised after the manner of Moses, you cannot be saved." St. Paul, as the man chiefly responsible for the new Gentile accession, and responsible, too, for the policy which emancipated these converts from the burden of the Law, was attacked bitterly. To still the controversy he and Barnabas came to Jerusalem (A.D. 51) and in a consultation of the Apostles—the so-called Council of Jerusalem—it was laid down that except for the prohibition of certain foods, the Gentile converts were free of the Law. It was a victory for St. Paul, and the circular letter announcing the decision went out of its way to give him praise for the work he had done.

But the opposition was by no means at an end. It survived to harass his work for years yet to come. At Corinth and in Galatia especially, did it trouble the peace of his converts. These Judaisers—the "false brethren" of St. Paul's *Epistles*, converts from the Pharisees and at heart Pharisees still—could not indeed go behind the decision of 51, but by insisting that the observance of the old Law added to sanctity, and was therefore the mark of the more perfect Christian, they fomented new divisions. The new controversy produced from St. Paul the most vigorous of all his letters—the *Epistle to the Galatians*—and a general manifesto on the whole question which, that it might have a greater prestige, he addressed "to all those who are at Rome the beloved of God, the chosen ones."

The Mosaic Law, he explained, as a thing useful for salvation is ended: the Sabbath, Circumcision, the whole elaborate code. There is now a new way of reconciliation with God, belief in Christ, union with Christ. The just man now lives not by the Law but by the new thing Faith. From Faith, and not from the Law, does salvation come. The whole theme is elaborately worked out, the relations between the Law and Faith, the rôle of Faith in the divine plan of salvation. To be in the Church is to be free from the burden of the Law.

Despite St. Paul's logic, and notwithstanding the Council of Jerusalem, the influence of the Judaising faction persisted, and so long as the church of Jerusalem flourished it did not lack a certain prestige. That influence was sufficiently powerful, for example, to intimidate St. Peter when, at Antioch, among the Gentile Christians, he was living with Christian freedom. He went back on his conduct, and the incident was the occasion of a passage-at-arms with St. Paul who, faced with the desertion, "withstood him to the face." Not until the end of his life, in fact, was St. Paul free from these zealots. They followed him wherever he went, sowing dissension, and, to the best of their power, undermining his authority.

Another division which troubled this first generation of Christians must be noted. It arose from the desire of private individuals to supplement and explain the official doctrine, particularly in all that related to Jesus Christ. These various private systems were alike in this that, in order to throw new light on the teaching of the apostles, they made use of Jewish beliefs, of ideas borrowed from current philosophy, and of practices and rites of the different pagan cults. Also, along with their ingenious new presentation of the teaching, they prescribed a new way of life. The Jewish Law was exalted, circumcision practised, and it was from among the Jewish Christians that the movement arose. Among the non-Jewish elements of the system was a denial of the resurrection of the body and—an aberration that will dog the Church's teaching for another twelve hundred years—the prohibition of marriage as a thing that is evil. St. Paul's *Epistle to the Colossians*, his Pastoral Epistles, the Second Epistle of St. Peter, the Epistles of St. John and St. Jude, the Apocalypse are filled with references to the new errors and to the moral disorders they produced wherever they made an entrance.

The writings which make up the New Testament were none of them written to be a primary and sufficient source of information as to what the new religion was. They were all of them evidently addressed to readers already instructed, to recall what they have learnt, to supplement it, to clear up disputes which have arisen since the first instruction. Yet, though none of them profess to describe fully either the teaching or the organisation, we can extract from them valuable information on these two points. Though the facts may be few they are certain, and among these certain facts is the character of the early propaganda and of the primitive organisation.

The new doctrine is not offered to the world as a reasoned philosophy. Its teachers do not seek to convince by any argumentation from principles, by any system of proof and deduction. It is presented as an indivisible body of truth to be received whole from the teacher, as he himself received it: and to be so received, not on any personal judgment of the reasonableness of its detail, but on the authority of the teacher. Nothing is more characteristic of St. Paul's methods, no note is so frequently sounded as this. It is to be, all through the centuries, the one answer of the Church to innovators, its one practical test of truth. This primitive apostolic Christianity is a lesson to be learnt, articles of faith to be believed, moral precepts to be obeyed, a mystery accepted on the divine authority which functions through the Apostle who is teaching.[1]

The character of the primitive organisation is no less clear; and from the Epistles of St. Paul especially, and from the Acts, we can make out the main lines of that organisation as a thing already considered traditional within twenty years of the death of Our Lord. They give us the picture of a number of Christian communities with the received and traditional catechesis just described, an internal liturgical life, a complete ascetic formation and a regular system of government, communities in which the ruler, the teacher, and the liturgical officer are one and the same.

The foundation of the whole organisation is the authority of the Apostles. The Apostle is the official witness to Christ's resurrection; and he is an Apostle by the fact of Christ's commission given to him personally. Not gifts of preaching, of organisation, not any unusual spiritual experience, not personal merit, but the fact of his having been sent by Christ in this special manner is the basis of the Apostle's authority. It is this group, "the Twelve" is Our Lord's own term for them, which, in the days which follow the Ascension, is found exercising a general authority. They are the centre of all the subsequent development, the missionary activities for example, the institution of the order of deacons, the replacing of Judas; and it is to the Apostles that St. Paul submits his claim to be acknowledged as a thirteenth Apostle, "one born out of due time" indeed but none the less of the true lineage.

In the Apostolate, then, the Church is from the very beginning endowed with authority as its principle of unity, and that endowment is recognised as the personal work of Jesus Christ. Before that authority, because it is an *Apostle* who speaks, everything else must yield. Those who exercise that authority decide but do not discuss (*cf. e.g. I Cor.* xi, 16). Here we have much in germ—the notion of the Faith as a deposit, a traditional whole handed on as it has been received, the notion of authority as the teacher, and the notion of these as things willed and instituted by Christ Himself. Side by side with this fact of the Apostle's authority we note the believers' realisation that together they form a whole, that they are very truly a new people. In the Old Testament that

---

[1] *Cf. I Cor.* viii, 4–6, vi, 9–11, xv, 1–2, 3 ; especially, for the recognised contrast between the Church and the human methods *I Cor.* i, 22–24, also *II Cor.* v, 17–20. *I Thess.* ii, 4, 9, 13. *Rom.* vi, 17.

unity had been the very evident one of race. In the Church the chosen ones are racially, "nationally," of a score of varieties, yet they are, nevertheless, immediately conscious of a unity which transcends these differences, a new spiritual unity no less real however than the old. Race no longer counts. The basis of the new unity is Faith in Christ and incorporation with Him (*Gal.* ii, 20–21).

The later Epistles of St. Paul add more details to our knowledge, in the regulations they contain for the appointment to other offices not hitherto mentioned, but whose institution these later Epistles certainly presuppose. Thus the Epistle to the Philippians is addressed (*Phil.* i, 1) to the *episcopoi* and the deacons of that church. This new term is also used (*Acts* xx, 28) of men just described (*ib.* 17) as *presbyteroi*. Throughout these later Epistles there is continual use of these two new terms, sometimes to describe the same persons (as in *Acts* xx, 28), sometimes the one term qualifying the other (*cf. I Tim.* v, 17). But always the term is used in the plural. In the Vulgate translation of the Greek of St. Paul, *episcopoi* becomes *episcopi* always, and thence in our English New Testament *bishops*. The Greek *presbyteroi* however the Vulgate sometimes renders *presbyteri* (which in our English becomes *priest*) sometimes *maiores natu* (*Acts* xx, 17) or *seniores* (*Acts* v, 6) and this in English becomes *elders*. *Bishop* and *priest* are, of course, and have been for centuries now, technical terms each with a definite unmistakable meaning. What then were the *episcopoi* and the *presbyteroi* of the New Testament? In what relation did they stand to the itinerant hierarchy of Apostles and missionaries? And since there were several in each church, how did the system give place to the system of a single bishop which has admittedly been universal since the beginning of the second century? The matter is anything but clear, and it has given rise to much controversy among Catholic and non-Catholic scholars alike. Besides the data of the New Testament writings we have, on this point, a certain amount of evidence from another contemporary document *The Teaching of the XII Apostles.*[1]

The *presbyteros* was one of the senior members of the community and perhaps, sometimes, nothing more. But sometimes the term undoubtedly describes an official, e.g. St. Paul's instruction to Titus to *create presbyteroi* for every city. The *presbyteroi* again sometimes bore the burden of presiding over

---

[1] This ancient treatise commonly known by its Greek name *The Didache* was probably written in the last quarter of the first century, where, and for whom, and by whom we do not know. It treats of Christian Asceticism, gives directions for the liturgical offices of Baptism and the Holy Eucharist, and deals with the qualifications necessary for the different Church officers. *Cf.* H. J. Chapman, O S. B., in *Catholic Encyclopedia* Art. *Didache.*

the community (*I Tim.* v, 17), or again they labour in the word and doctrine. To such *presbyteroi* is due a double honour (*ib.*). Again the body of *presbyteroi*, considered as a corporate thing (*presbyterion*) is a channel of grace (*I Tim.* iv, 14).

These new officers, during the lifetime of the Apostles, are all spoken of as named by the Apostles, either directly (*Acts* xiv, 22) or through the Apostles' immediate subordinates. In St. Paul's instructions to Timothy and Titus there is no hint that to designate *episcopoi* or *presbyteroi* is the business of anyone but the Apostle's delegate. The whole initiative is with Authority. The possession of some special gift of the Holy Ghost—the charismata which were so common a feature of the new religion's first days—tongues, miracles, prophecy or the like, does not of itself give the possessor any authority in the community. Authority only comes by designation of authority already recognised. It is never a charisma. Whatever the relations of these *episcopoi* and *presbyteroi* to each other, whatever the extent of their powers during the lifetime of St. Paul (and it is in connection with St. Paul that the question arises) the Apostle, there is no doubt about it, ruled personally his immense conquest, by visits, by letters, through delegates such as Timothy and Titus.

The next stage in the development begins when death removes the Apostles. Their office, status, power was unique. No one ever put in a claim to be an Apostle of the second generation. Because of the fact which constituted them Apostles they were necessarily irreplaceable. To their authority succeeded the new hierarchy of *episcopoi* and *presbyteroi*, and as it took their place this new hierarchy itself underwent a change. The college of *episcopoi* or *presbyteroi* who, under the Apostles, had ruled the local Church gave place to an arrangement where in each local Church there was but one *episcopos* whom a number of subordinates, now termed *presbyteroi*, assisted. By the time of St. Ignatius of Antioch (i.e. the end of the first century, within from thirty to forty years of the death of St. Paul) the new system—the so-called "monarchical episcopate"—is so universal that he takes it for granted as the basis of his exhortations.

The change took place with so little disturbance that it has left no trace at all in history. It passed with so general an agreement that one can only infer that it had behind it what alone could sanction so great a change, what alone could secure it so smooth a passage, the consciousness of all concerned that this was part of the Founder's plan wrought out in detail by the Apostles He had commissioned.

To return finally to the question of the functions of the *episcopoi* and *presbyteroi*, and the relations of the two classes to each other, one view (very ably argued by Mgr. Batiffol and the Bollandist Fr. De Smedt), is that the *presbyteros* was a man to whom was given a title of honour for special service, a distinction which of itself carried with it no power or authority. From among the *presbyteroi* the *episcopoi*—whose duty it was, under the Apostle, to rule, to teach—were naturally elected. Whence the fact that not all *presbyteroi* are also *episcopoi*. Later the *presbyteroi* who are not also *episcopoi* disappear. The name, however, survives and is henceforward used for the subordinate officials of the new system, successors in part of the old *episcopoi*, but successors with very restricted powers and with no authority independent of the bishop—as we may now call him.

One last important detail the New Testament writings give us. It concerns the inauguration of these different officers. Nomination to the office, even by the Apostle, does not of itself suffice. Before the candidate can act, something more is required. There is mention always of fasting, of prayer, and of the imposition of hands, and always this imposition is the act of those already possessed of authority. As a later, more technical language will describe it, the power of order, like the power of jurisdiction, like the faith itself, is transmitted from one generation to the next through the action of those who already possess it. Nowhere is it spoken of as coming from below as the result of popular determination, nor as deriving from the prestige of superior holiness, ability, or the possession of charismata. Though the word is not yet mentioned, the all-important fact is clear that, for the first generation of Christians, no powers were valid, no teaching guaranteed, no authority was lawful save such as came through the Apostles.

The evidence of two more sources remains to be examined before the study of the Church in its first years is complete—the letter of St. Clement of Rome to the Church of Corinth, and the letters of St. Ignatius of Antioch. This is a convenient place to say something of the origins of the Roman Church.

Who were the first members of that Church, how the new religion first came to the Empire's capital, we have absolutely no information. The first fixed date is nineteen or twenty years after the passion of Our Lord—A.D. 49 when, among the Jews expelled from Rome by the Emperor Claudius (41–54), were the two Jewish Christians Aquila and his wife Priscilla.

This sudden reversal of the imperial favour was due to riots among the Jews themselves; and the riots, says Suetonius, were provoked by a certain Chrestus—which may be literally true or may be the inaccurate fashion in which a none too well informed writer, a generation or more after the event, reports a conflict between Jews who were Christians and Jews who were not. Nine or ten years later the Roman Church is "Known for its faith to all the world", and so St. Paul addresses to it the greatest of his epistles, a public manifesto of his position on the question of the Jewish Law's status in the new religion. When in 61, St. Paul himself at last reaches Rome, as Caesar's prisoner, he finds many brethren there to aid him; and from the lodging where, under guard, he spends the two years until his appeal is heard, he directs through the Church, an active propaganda which results in many conversions. On the eve of Nero's persecution St. Paul is released (63) and undertakes his last pioneer voyage, to Spain it would seem certain, and then once again he returns to the scenes of his earliest labours. Finally he returns to Rome and, still under Nero, he is put to death.

Nowhere, it is true, does St. Paul mention St. Peter as being in Rome during his own sojourn there; nor does the account of St. Paul's arrival in the *Acts*. But a tradition, universal in the Church a century and a half later, and in whose support documentary evidence can be cited that is contemporary with St. Peter, (his own Epistle for example, Clement of Rome, and St. Ignatius of Antioch) the utter absence of any rival to the Roman claim to possess that Apostle's tomb, and the important fact that to St. Peter's one-time headship of the Roman Church its bishops, henceforward, invariably—and successfully—appeal to justify their own assumption of superior authority; this varied and undoubted evidence, indirect though it may be, leaves the modern scholar in no doubt that St. Peter came to Rome, governed the Roman Church as its first bishop once the Christians there were organised, and, crowning his episcopate by martyrdom, left to that Church as its most treasured possession his body and tomb. As to the details—when St. Peter first came to Rome, for how long he ruled the Roman Church, and, supposing the twenty-five years' episcopate (a tradition which goes back at any rate to Eusebius of Caesarea, born *c*. 270), at what dates to fix its beginning and end—we know nothing with certainty.[1] St. Peter was succeeded by Linus, and Linus by Anacletus. Of these two—the second and third bishops of Rome—we know absolutely nothing. With the fourth bishop, Clement, the case is far other, and under his direction the Roman Church is revealed in the special role which has characterised it ever since.

Clement was the head of the Church at Rome, the third successor, by the general reckoning, of St. Peter. His famous letter, written probably about the year 96, was directed to the restoration of peace at Corinth where a section of the faithful were in revolt

[1] For a longer discussion of this matter *cf. infra* pp. 59–66.

against the rulers of that church. Its importance for the historian lies in the information he can gather from it as to the constitution of this early Christianity, as to the nature of its ruling authority and as to the character of its teaching. The letter makes no mention of the charismata, so familiar a feature in the time of St. Paul, nor of any itinerant missionary authorities. The temporary structures have already disappeared, and the Church is in the first days of the new permanent régime. Unity is essential and the source and means of unity is Authority. Whence obedience to authority is the first duty of all believers. This is the leading idea of the letter. The believers are "a people" (*ethnos*) divinely set apart. They are an army in which "not all are officers . . . each has his rank, carrying out the orders of the leader." They are a "body", "the body of Christ," a flock. Authority is the source of unity, and unity is achieved by submission to the "tutelage" (*paideia*) of authority. "Let us submit to the tutelage . . . obey the elders and allow them to tutor you . . . learn to be submissive. It is better to be nothing in the flock of Christ, to be even hungry, than to appear to be great and lack all hope in Christ."

The subject matter of this education or tutelage is the traditional faith and the commandments of the Lord, "the words of the divine tutelage," things already fixed in writing. This fixed and traditional doctrine is the norm by which the believer must be guided, "Let us cease to make vain searches, let us come to the glorious and venerable fixed rule (*canona*) that has been handed down to us." This notion of determination by a fixed rule, a canon, is found in association with other things than doctrine. In the liturgical reunions, St. Clement reminds the Corinthians, offerings are to be made "not as anyone chooses and without order but as the Master ordained, at fixed and definite times. Where and by whom He Himself has arranged by His sovereign will." Wherefore "each of us, brethren, should keep to his own rank, and not transgress the fixed rule (*canona*) of his rank."

St. Clement's explanation of the historical origin of the authority he is supporting is simple. It came to its present holders from the Apostles, who received it from Christ, Who received it from God. The Apostles preached the Gospel, and the first-fruits of their preaching they made bishops and deacons. As these died, others took their place inheriting the Apostolic commission and authority. These successors of the bishops nominated by the Apostles are elected by the Church over which they are to preside, but, an important point, it is from other bishops—not from their election—that the elect receive their powers. The powers are received by transmission from one who already possesses them himself. The essence of the Hierarchy is its descent from the Apostles. These things are not the express teaching of the letter. St. Clement does not argue for them, nor make any attempt to prove them. They are facts apparently as well known to his readers as to himself, recalled as the basis for his plea for peace and concord at Corinth. The letter ends on a practical note. A delegation goes with it to explain more fully the mind of the Roman Church.

Such is the first appearance in history of the Roman Church in action—intervening in the domestic affairs of another and distant Church. Was Clement of Rome asked to intervene ? Then his letter is the sequel to the first appeal to Rome. Was his letter the fruit of his own spontaneous act ? Nothing remains to tell us. But the Roman Church is already acting as though conscious of its superior power; and this, during the lifetime of an Apostle, for St. John was still alive at Ephesus and Ephesus was much nearer to Corinth than was Rome !

This First Letter of St. Clement of Rome witnesses, then, to a general belief in the divine right of the hierarchy, in the divine origin of its power, and to the Roman Church's consciousness of its peculiar superiority. It takes these things as the facts of the situation, and it acts on the supposition that they are facts universally recognised, which do not call for proof.

Can it be said that Clement of Rome is unique, an eccentric ? That the views of his letter are the product of any local Roman "legalist" spirit ? Side by side with his letter, the letters of his contemporary Ignatius of Antioch should be read.

St. Ignatius, born about the year 60, in all probability a disciple of St. John, was the third Bishop of Antioch. He was one of the victims of the anti-Christian laws under Trajan (98–117), and it was during his journey from the East to Rome, for his martyrdom, that he wrote these seven letters. They are letters of gratitude to the different Christian communities who had come to his assistance, letters of encouragement, advice, and edification. Once more, it is to be noted, their usefulness here is their *obiter dicta*—incidental references to institutions, offices, beliefs which, the writer evidently assumed, were as familiar to his correspondents as they were to himself. The letters are addressed to the churches at Ephesus, Magnesia, Tralles, Philadelphia, Smyrna, Rome and to the martyr's disciple, St. Polycarp. The general organisation of the Church as this oriental contemporary of Clement of Rome knows it, the form of its teaching, are much as we find them in the letter of Clement and in the New Testament. St. Ignatius does but confirm, once more, evidence already examined. Like Clement he knows no "itinerant" teaching hierarchy. Like

Clement he attaches the utmost importance to internal peace and unity, and his insistence on this as the first necessity is the more striking because it is not provoked, as was St. Clement's plea, by any immediate breach. In each of the churches there is a ruling body, its officers now clearly distinguished, one bishop with several priests and deacons. This one visible bishop is in each church the representative of the invisible bishop, God. Hence obedience to the visible bishop as to God, and obedience to the college of priests as to the Apostles. Again we find the Church likened to a disciplined army; and in another very striking phrase the priests are exhorted to attune themselves to the bishop as the different strings of a harp, so that the whole church will sing as a choir with one voice. Erroneous doctrine cuts off from the Church whoever believes it. The true doctrine is the doctrine handed down. To reject this traditional doctrine, or to receive it otherwise than it has been received, to prefer any other to it, is criminal. Whoever, for example, speaks of Christ otherwise than the Church speaks, should be looked on as dead. The test of a doctrine's truth is its acceptance by the visible Church, and the sole guarantee of faith is to be one in belief with the bishop. Already dissidents are to be found who appeal to Scripture for their justification. St. Ignatius has met them: "If I can't find it in the Gospel" they protest "I won't believe." He does not produce any counter argument in reply. He brushes aside their reasoning, and against their dissidence simply sets the accepted faith. Agreement with that is the measure of the truth of their opinions.

Unity is of the highest importance, is willed by God. Unity in each local church, unity by unity of belief between all the churches of the world. The test of this unity is the belief of the local bishop, obedience to the bishop is its guarantee. There where the bishop is should all believers be gathered too, as where Jesus Christ is there is the universal Church—(*katholiké ecclesia*). St. Ignatius, looking beyond the local churches to the one great Church which in their unity they compose, has found for that unity the name which henceforth it will for ever retain—the Catholic Church.

It is not without significance that, in both these primitive fragments, there is reference to the Roman Church. Clement was himself the third of its bishops, and to it St. Ignatius addressed one of his letters. In his address he adds epithet to epithet, in eastern fashion, to show his sense of its distinction. Not as Clement wrote to Corinth does Ignatius write his exhortation; "I do not give you orders as Peter and Paul were wont to do; they were apostles." He congratulates the Roman Church because "it has taught the others," and because "in the country of the Romans it presides," a curious phrase which is meaningless unless it refers to a presidency of the church over other churches.

St. Ignatius was thrown to the beasts in a Roman circus somewhere about the year 107. In the three quarters of a century which are all that separate his martyrdom from Our Lord's Ascension, the ecclesia is visibly and evidently the Catholic Church. It is spreading throughout the Roman world. It is increasingly a gentile thing; it is a federation of communities united in belief, united in their mode of government, united in their acceptance of the belief as a thing regulated by authority, united, too, in their worship. It has received its historic name— the Catholic Church—and the rule of the Church at Rome is already foreshadowed in writing and in action, the continuation in time of the chieftainship conferred by Christ on Peter. Uniformity of belief has already been challenged, and in these challengers the Church has met the first heretics, has recognised them as such by their refusal to accept her received tradition, by their defiance of the authority of the bishop who, because he is ruler, is also teacher.

NOTE A

Although the first Christians were all of them Jews, with every year that passed the influence of the Jewish Christians diminished, once the Greeks, too, came into the Church. The failure of the efforts of one section to enforce within the new religion the observance of the Mosaic Law as such, was a very notable set-back. The Gentile converts easily outnumbered the Jewish and by the time of the death of St. Paul the Jewish Christians were already a minority. In 62 they lost the Apostle who seems to have been their especial leader—James, the Bishop of Jerusalem; and eight years later the armies of Vespasian and Titus, destroying the Holy City and the last vestiges of independent Jewish political organisation, ended inevitably the prestige of the church in which Christianity had first been organised. There would now be no repetition of the danger, which the Church had so recently escaped, that it would present itself to the world as simply another Jewish sect. The Roman soldiery had, in very grim fashion, crowned the work of St. Paul.

But for all that Jerusalem was no more, razed to the very ground as Our Lord had prophesied, with only the camp of the Tenth Legion to mark where it had stood, its Christian population continued to lead a collective life. Some vision had warned the bishop—Simeon—of the coming troubles, and the faithful had left the city in time, and settled at Pella, in the pagan country across the Jordan. Here for yet another century and more they survived, isolated from the rest of the Church and increasingly a prey to heretical developments. The belief in the essential divinity of Our Lord changed into what was afterwards called Adoptianism. He was the child of Joseph and Mary and later, because of his scrupulous fidelity to the Law, permitted to become the Christ. That destiny is open to all his followers. Whence, among these heretical Judeo-Christians—the Ebionites—a devotion to the Law unsurpassed by the Pharisees themselves. Of the sacred books which later formed the New Testament they possessed the Gospel of St. Matthew. St. Paul they held in abhorrence as an apostate and a perverter of the truth. The second generation of the Ebionites, through contact with the Jewish sect of the Essenes, added yet other beliefs and practices. They had their own theory of a double creation of good and bad, perpetuated

57

through the centuries in parallel lines of good and of lying prophets, descendants of Adam and of Eve respectively. More accurately, these are re-incarnations of the one prophet, and this one prophet it is who has appeared in Jesus Christ. He is not God. Circumcision is retained along with Baptism, a vegetarian diet is prescribed, a daily bath, and, as a means of avoiding sexual sin, marriage at the very beginning of puberty. In their Eucharist water takes the place of wine. A still later development is that of the Elkasaites of whose distinctive tenets, however, nothing is known with certainty.

Ebionites and Elkasaites were of course heretics. Side by side with them, however, but in ever dwindling numbers, the Christian Church survived for yet two centuries at least. St. Jerome writes of these survivors to St. Augustine, and finds them sufficiently orthodox in faith. Though they do not reject St. Paul, they cling steadfastly to all the customs of the Jews. In an earlier generation they had produced at least one writer Hegesippus, who, (c. 150), set himself to travel throughout the world comparing his own faith with that professed by all the bishops he encountered, and endeavouring to construct a pedigree of orthodox teachers, linking the bishops of his day with the Apostles. All the bishops he met agreed in doctrine and the doctrine was that which he himself had been taught. Also he noted the names of the bishops of the Roman Church down to Anicetus. It is evident from the few references to these Jewish Christian Churches of the East, and from the occasional confusion in what references we do possess, that they had ceased to be more than a matter of archæology to the learned men who wrote about them. By the fifth century they are nothing more than this, and thence on they are entirely lost to view.

NOTE B

(The following long note is translated, with the author's permission, from the *Histoire de l'Église*, Tome I *L'Antiquité Chrétienne* (pp. 61–67) of Fr. A. M. Jacquin, O.P., Paris, Éditions de la Révue des Jeunes, 1928. To the learned author of this best of manuals I gladly express my sincerest thanks.)

"The fact of St. Peter's martyrdom at Rome has been called in doubt, through the prejudices of Protestants first of all and then of the critics. In both cases the mistake has led to an appreciable gain in historical knowledge and to that extent has been of real service. That these doubts were mistaken is to-day unquestionable for all scholars save those who turn from the light. The critical apparatus with which Baur strove against the ancient tradition is to-day, and rightly, regarded as negligible." (A. Harnack, *Geschichte der altchristlichen Literatur*, Chronologie, t. ii, i, p. 244.)

For all Harnack's judgment, there are not lacking Protestant and rationalist historians who spend their energy defending these theses which have long ceased to be tenable. Erbes, for example, and above all, Ch. Guignebert (*La primauté de Pierre et la venue de Pierre à Rome*, Paris, 1909). This last scholar's work earned him from the pen of M. P. Monceaux a lesson in critical scholarship which hardly increased his reputation as a scholar. (*L'apostolat de Saint Pierre à Rome à propos d'un livre récent* in the *Révue d'historie et de littérature religieuses*, New Series I (1910), pp. 216–40: cf. also A. Flamion, *Saint Pierre à Rome : Examen de la thèse et de la méthode de M. Guignebert* in the *Révue d'histoire ecclésiastique*, XIV (1913), pp. 249–71, 473–88.) On the other hand a Protestant, H. Lietzmann, has just published in defence of the tradition a work of the very highest interest (*Petrus und Paulus in Rom*, 2 ed., Berlin, 1927). His choice goes to the evidence from the Liturgy and from Archæology, and he reaches the conclusion that, towards the year 200, the conviction at Rome was universal that the city possessed the tombs of SS. Peter and Paul. Other proofs, drawn from the letters of Clement and Ignatius, from the First Epistle of St. Peter, make it impossible for us to allow the theory of a legend formed in the interval between the death of the Apostles and the year 200: and this all

59

the more since no other church, whether in the East or in the West, has ever laid claim to the honour of possessing these illustrious remains.

There would then be little occasion to re-open the discussion of a question now so clearly decided, except for the fact's importance in the history of the Primitive Church and for its apologetic value as an argument for the privileges of the episcopal see of Rome. This double importance is a good reason for presenting here the arguments on which the traditional belief is based.

Moreover, the proof is by this time a commonplace, and among many others Mgr. Duchesne (*Les Origines chrétiennes*, 2 ed., pp. 82–117, Paris, s.d.: *Hist. Ancienne de l'Église*, I, pp. 61–63, Paris, 1911) has set it out with a scientific detachment which is beyond all criticism. He makes a distinction between the principal fact, about which no one can any longer have any serious doubt, and the accessory circumstances about which we have not the same historical guarantee. "It is possible," he says, "to prove that St. Peter came to Rome, and that he suffered martyrdom there: we have no evidence sufficient to fix the date of his coming nor the length of his stay." (*Les Origines chrétiennes*, p. 82.)

I. As to the first point, we can note, by the end of the second century a tradition that is precise and universal: the majority of the churches provide evidence, and that evidence is to the same effect.

1. *Alexandria*. Clement, writing about the Gospel of St. Mark, says "Peter preached the word of God publicly at Rome, and under the inspiration of the Holy Spirit made the Gospel known. Those who assisted at his sermons, and they were numerous, exhorted Mark, who for a long time had been Peter's companion, and whose memory held many of his sayings, to put these things in writing." (EUSEBIUS, *H.E.*, vi, 14.)

Origen, in his commentary on Genesis (1 iii) speaks of the activity of the Apostles. Of Peter he says "Peter appears to have preached in Pontus, in Galatia, in Bithynia, in Cappadocia, and in Asia to the Jews of the Diaspora. Finally he, too, came to Rome, and there he was crucified, head downwards, having asked to suffer in this fashion." (EUSEBIUS, *H.E.* iii, I.)

2. *Africa*. Tertullian more than once asserts that St. Peter came to Rome and there suffered martyrdom. Speaking of the church of that city he says "O Happy Church! The Apostles lavished upon it their teaching and their blood. Peter there suffered a death like to that of the Lord." (*De Praescriptione*, 36.) In the *De Baptismo*, 4, he recalls that Peter "baptized in the Tiber" that is at Rome. In another place (*Adv. Marcion*, iv, 5)

it is to the authority of the Romans that he appeals against Marcion since "to them Peter and Paul left the gospel, confirmed by their blood." A little later still, *Scorpiace* 15, he asserts that "Nero was the first to persecute the nascent faith at Rome with punishments. Then it was," he adds, "that Peter was girt by another, when he was fixed to the cross."

3. *Gaul and Asia.* St. Irenæus, Bishop of Lyons, was of Smyrnian origin, and acquainted therefore with the traditions of these two countries, to say nothing of the tradition of Rome where he had lived for some time. Now St. Irenæus has no doubts whatever that St. Peter came to Rome. According to him the gospel of St. Matthew was written "while Peter and Paul were preaching the gospel at Rome and founding the church there." (*Adv. Haereses*, iii, I.) And, a little later, wishing to base his argument on the witness of the Churches, he contents himself with giving the proof of the apostolic succession of the Church of Rome "founded and organised by the two glorious apostles Peter and Paul." (*ibid.* iii, 3.)

4. *Greece.* Eusebius (*H.E.*, ii, 25) writes as follows "Denis Bishop of the Corinthians, in a letter addressed to the Romans, thus fixes the point that Peter and Paul both suffered martyrdom at the same time. You have also, by such an admonishment, united Rome and Corinth the two trees which we owe to Peter and to Paul. For just as both the one and the other planted at Corinth and taught us, so after teaching together in Italy, at the same time they suffered martyrdom."

5. *Rome.* Leaving aside the archæological and liturgical evidence regarding St. Peter's chair at Rome, his tomb and the place where he is supposed to have lived in the empire's capital,[1] and, too, the lists of the bishops of the Roman Church, we can cite the testimony of the Roman priest Caius, who wrote during the pontificate of Zephyrinus (199–217). "In a treatise written against Proclus, the chief of the Cataphrygians," says Eusebius (*H.E.*, ii, 25) "and speaking of the places where the sacred remains of the Apostles were laid he says, 'I can show you the trophies of the Apostles. Go to the Vatican, or along the Ostian Way, there you will find the trophies of the founders of this church.'" The meaning of the expression τρόπαια has been much controverted, and it is suggested that it designates not the tombs of the Apostles but simple commemorative monuments. Even so it remains true that Rome, at the end of the second century, was still mindful of the memory "of the founders of this church." But there is nothing to disprove that the term in question means "tomb"; we find it used with this meaning, and Eusebius, who had before

[1] A. Profumo, *La memoria di S. Pietro nella regione Salari-Nomentana*, Rome, 1916.

him the complete text of Caius, so uses it. It is, in point of fact, the only possible meaning in this context. Caius is answering the boast of Proclus that Asia retains the bodies of the four prophetess-daughters of Philip and of their father, too, and must in turn be claiming that Rome, more gloriously still, possesses, not merely a memorial, but the very tombs of the Apostles.[1]

This examination shows then that the principal churches of the Christian world between 170 and 210 were unanimous in affirming that St. Peter went to Rome and there suffered martyrdom. Now an agreement so unanimous, among witnesses whom we may believe to be independent of one another, can only be explained by the objective reality of the fact to which they testify. That agreement is all the more impressive from the circumstance that it has not to meet any rival contrary tradition. When the Bishops of Rome claim to be the successors of St. Peter, and pride themselves on this distinction, no one throws doubt on their claim. The Eastern churches themselves bear testimony in the same sense. (*Cf.* F. Martin, *Saint Pierre, sa venue et son martyre à Rome*, in the *Révue des questions historiques*, t. xiii (1873), pp. 5–107.)

[1] The excavations undertaken, since 1915, in the basilica of St. Sebastian, which, once upon a time, from the fourth century, was a " basilica of the apostles " have brought to light, six feet below the ground, towards the centre of the building, the remains of a still more ancient building dating from the middle of the third century. It is " a small, irregular hall closed on three sides, open on the fourth in a kind of portico. The mural decorations, the inscriptions on the walls, the remains of a bench and of a fountain have led to its recognition as a room built for meetings and for banquets. Whence its now famous name ' La Triclia.' "

On what remains of the walls, no more than three feet in height, more than two hundred *graffiti* have been discovered of the names of the apostles Peter and Paul. The accompanying invocations, the occasional mention of a meal (*refrigerium*) all point to the place having been a centre of devotion, that mentioned in old liturgical and hagiographical documents as placed on the Via Appia at the place called *Ad Catacumbas*, that is to say on the site of the present basilica of St. Sebastian. What memory of the Apostles was it that was honoured here ? Before the excavations opinion was divided. " One theory held that it was the tradition of the house where the Apostles (or St. Peter only) once lived. Another the memory of a place where their bodies once rested. Those who held this second theory were in turn divided. One school accepted as true the old legend of Easterns coming to Rome to steal the relics of the Apostles and halted by the pursuit at this very place on the Appian Way. Others, who rejected this legend, held to a translation of the remains made by the Romans themselves. Whence again a further division—some holding that the bodies were buried first on the Via Ostia where are their tombs, others that the relics were taken from these tombs and hidden for a time at the Catacombs to save them from profanation during the persecution of Valerian in 258 " (G. de Jerphanion, *Les dernières découvertes dans la Rome souterraine*, in *Études*, April 5, 1922, p. 61).

The discoveries actually made do not solve the problem. They have revealed the existence of a *cultus*, without being able to suggest the motive which gave rise to it. At the most, chronological coincidences would seem to incline one to accept the hypothesis of a translation in 258. On the other hand serious difficulties can be urged against this. (*Cf.* J. P. Kirsch, *Das neuentdeckte Denkmal der Apostel Petrus und Paulus an der appischen Strasse in Rom*, in *Römische Quartalschrift für Kirchengeschichte*, xxx, (1916–1922), pp. 5–28.)

The end of the second century was too near in time to the events themselves for any legend to have formed and to have spread itself so widely. Besides, pushing the investigation back through the intervening years we find hints that fit in with the data of the tradition as early as the first century, as early as St. Peter himself.

If, for example, St. Justin and Hermas are silent about the coming of St. Peter to Rome and his martyrdom there, and there was no reason why they should speak of it, St. Ignatius of Antioch, on the other hand, in his *Letter to the Romans*, written about 110, certainly alludes to it. In touching language he beseeches those to whom he writes "to spare him any untimely benevolence" that might rob him of martyrdom, and he adds "I do not give you orders as Peter and Paul. They were Apostles and I am but a prisoner condemned to death" (*Rom.* 4). Commenting on this text, Mgr Duchesne (*Les Origines Chrétiennes*, p. 89) says very truly, "These words are not the literal equivalent of the proposition 'St. Peter came to Rome,' but, supposing that he did go there St. Ignatius would not have spoken otherwise: supposing he did not go to Rome the phrase lacks meaning."

The tradition then existed, even in Syria, from the time of Trajan. It shows itself at Rome, in the time of Domitian, in the letter of Pope Clement. Speaking of the evil effects of jealousy he shows how it caused the death of the apostles and of many other martyrs. "Cast your eyes," he says, "upon the most worthy apostle—Peter, who, victim of unjust jealousy, underwent not one or two but a whole host of sufferings, and who, having thus accomplished his martyrdom, departed for the place of glory that is his due. It was through jealousy, too, that Paul showed how [to win] the prize of patience. . . . After teaching justice to the whole world, journeying to the very limits of the West, he accomplished his martyrdom before those in authority, and left this world, illustrious model of patience, to go to the holy place. With these men of holy life were joined a great crowd of chosen souls, who, the effect of jealousy, endured many outrages and tortures, and who left among us a magnificent example. It was as the victims of jealousy that these women, the Danaïds and the Dirces, after suffering terrible and monstrous outrage, reached the goal in this race of the faith, and weak in body as they were, received their noble reward" (*Cor.* 5–6). All these victims form with the Apostles, Peter and Paul, one group. These women, came to join themselves (συνηθροίσθη) with the Apostles, and it is at Rome (ἐν ἡμῖν) that all suffered and left a magnificent example.

Finally St. Peter himself, in the letter he wrote to the churches of Asia, seems certainly to suggest that he is living in Rome at the time he is writing. To these Christians he sends the greetings of "the Church of Babylon" (*I Pet.* v. 13) that is to say of Rome, according to most exegetes. "Peter," says Renan (*L'Antéchrist*, p. 122, Paris, 1893), "to designate Rome chose the name of the capital of Asiatic wickedness, a name whose symbolical meaning all would recognise."

Thanks to this continuity in the tradition, which goes back as far as the fact itself, it is possible *to demonstrate* that St. Peter went to Rome and there suffered martyrdom. "Every other hypothesis," says M. Lietzmann, "heaps difficulty upon difficulty, and can produce in its support not a single testimony from sources" (*Petrus und Paulus in Rom*, p. 238).

II. If we desire to establish with precision the date at which St. Peter came to Rome and the length of his stay we are not any longer in a position to prove anything *demonstratively*. There are sources which all of them speak of a period of twenty-five years in connection with St. Peter's Roman apostolate, but they disagree as to the date when this period begins and also as to the events with which it is connected.

Eusebius, in his *Ecclesiastical History* (ii, 14), makes St. Peter come to Rome at the beginning of the reign of Claudius (41–54), and places his death during the persecution of Nero. His presence in the imperial city is alleged to have ruined the prestige of Simon Magus. In the second edition of his *Chronicle*, of which St. Jerome's translation is testimony (A. Schene, *Die Weltchronik des Eusebius in ihrer Bearbeitung durch Hieronymus*, Berlin, 1900), he gives as the date of arrival the second year of Claudius (42), and as the date of martyrdom the fourteenth of Nero (67).

The Liberian Catalogue, so called because in its present form it dates from the pontificate of Liberius (353–366), mentions St. Peter at the head of the list of Bishops of Rome. "Peter, twenty-five years, one month, eight days; during the reign of Tiberius Cæsar, Caius, Tiberius Claudius, and Nero; from the consulate of Minucius (Vinicius) and Longinus to that of Nerine (Nero) and Nero (Vetus)." St. Peter then is said to have come to Rome during the reign of Tiberius, Vinicius and Longinus being consuls (30): he is said to have lived there during the reign of Caligula, Claudius and Nero until death came to him during the consulate of Nero and Vetus (55).

Finally Lactantius (*De Morte Persecutorum*, 2) says of the Apostles, "They spread themselves throughout the world to preach the gospel, and for twenty-five years, to the end of the reign of Nero, were busied about the foundation of the Church through all the provinces and cities. Nero had already come into power when St. Peter came to Rome. . . . Nero was the first to persecute the servants of God. Peter he crucified and Paul he put to death."

These three texts agree in speaking of a period of 25 years. But while Eusebius and the Liberian Catalogue speak of the period as the duration of St. Peter's Roman episcopate, Lactantius' reference is to the preaching of all the Apostles, during the time between the Ascension and Nero's succession, and preceding St. Peter's coming to Rome. Again, the first two sources differ in the dates from which they make the period begin—Eusebius places the period between 42–67, the Liberian Catalogue between 30 and 55.

All the documents date from the fourth century but two of them, Eusebius and the Catalogue, derive from earlier documents, lists of bishops already existent in the third century and perhaps even in the second. (*Cf.* A. Flamion, *Les anciennes listes épiscopales des quatre grands siéges*, in *Révue d'histoire ecclésiastique*, i (1900), pp. 645–678; ii (1901), pp. 209–238.) It follows from this that it was probably from this time that the idea of twenty-five years was linked with St. Peter's Roman apostolate.

It is not, for all that, easy to understand the twenty-five years as a period of uninterrupted residence at Rome. According to the *Acts of the Apostles* St. Peter was at Jerusalem in 49 on the occasion of the conference which dealt with the question of Gentile converts to the faith. Shortly afterwards he was at Antioch where the incident related by St. Paul occurred. St. Paul's own silence in his *Epistle to the Romans*, written in 58, that of the author of the *Acts* in his account of St. Paul's captivity (61–62), the silence of the Apostle of the Gentiles in all the letters he wrote from Rome, seem to point to the fact that in these years St. Peter was not living at Rome. "All this is, no doubt, not absolutely irreconcilable with an effective residence of twenty-five years that would have to allow for necessary absences. But it is very extraordinary that these absences fall precisely at all the times concerning which we have information about Roman Christianity" (L. Duchesne, *Les Origines Chrétiennes*, p. 84, note).

According to Eusebius (*H.E.*, ii, 14), St. Peter, who routed Simon Magus for a first time in Palestine, met the imposter a second time at Rome "at the beginning of the reign of Claudius." Simon's success which had been such that he had come to be considered "as a god, honoured with a statue," disappeared and was extinguished with himself. As early as the third century the author of the *Philosophoumena* (xi, 20) had recalled this fact without, however, making any mention of the statue. The value of this testimony, and of other testimonies still more recent, is hard to assess. Eusebius, for all that relates to Simon, bases his account on St. Justin, citing his first *Apology* (26), where the magician is spoken of as follows: "He was taken for a god; as a god he had his statue; it is erected on an island in the Tiber, between the two bridges, with his inscription in Latin: *Simoni Deo Sancto*." Now it is very probable that Justin, whose historical accuracy often leaves much to be desired, has here confused Simon and the Etruscan divinity Semo Sancus. In the sixteenth century, as a matter of fact, on this very island of the Tiber, there was discovered the base of a statue with the words upon it *Semoni Sanco Deo Fidio Sacrum*. Later still, on the Quirinal, where there was a temple to this divinity, two similar inscriptions were discovered. On the other hand the literary tradition of the meeting, of which one finds traces as early as the third century, may derive from the *Acts of Peter*, which dates from this time. But this work, romantic in character, Gnostic in origin, Docetist in tendency, is too slight an authority to have any credit at all. It is to this work, too, that we owe the story of *Quo Vadis*—St. Peter leaving Rome to escape martyrdom meets Our Lord Who invites him, tactfully, to return to the city.

All things considered, if it is not possible to deny absolutely the meeting of St. Peter and Simon it is impossible at present to prove it scientifically. As far as regards St. Peter's death, on the other hand, we possess some data of the very best authenticity coming from Tertullian and Origen. The first says clearly (*Scorpiace*, 15) that he died in the time of Nero, the second (EUSEBIUS, *H.E.*, iii, I) placing the martyrdom of St. Paul at this time seems to associate with it that of St. Peter. The two writers add that he was crucified (TERTULLIAN, *De Praescriptione*, 36, *Scorpiace*, 15; ORIGEN *loc. cit.*) and Origen says, too, that he was crucified head downwards, not an unusual circumstance as the custom of the day went and one which is to be found in other cases too (cf. P. Allard, *Histoire des persécutions pendant les deux premiers siècles*, p. 79).

CHAPTER III

THE FIRST CONTACTS WITH THE PAGAN RELIGIOUS WORLD

I. THE RELIGIOUS WORLD OF THE SECOND CENTURY

THE history of the first contacts of the new religion with the religious thought of the Romano-hellenic world is only imperfectly known to us. The *Acts of the Apostles* relates, of course, the story of the conversion of the Roman officer Cornelius in the first years after Our Lord's Ascension, and describes St. Paul's varied success with the pagans of the Roman East. The *Acts* is, in a large part, the story of the origins of Gentile Christianity. Nevertheless it is not until the next century that we begin to have evidence in detail about the way the new religion affected the religious gentiles who occupied themselves with its teaching and promises; or the like evidence about the way the Church reacted to its contact with the world outside it.

That world outside was not, in the second century, by any means unconcerned with religious theories and practice. Religion was all important to it, and though the religious restoration of the first of the Roman emperors had not developed, as he had hoped, into a rebirth of the old classical Paganism, religion a hundred years after his death was flourishing and promised to flourish yet more. Development since Augustus had not, indeed, taken the direction he would have willed. It had left the Paganism of the classic pantheon to its inevitable end. It showed itself rather in the appearance of new cults, particularly in the cult of personified abstractions. Such were the new religions which worshipped Honour, Piety, Peace and—the most popular cult of all—Fortune. These new fast-spreading cults were free of the mythological foulness which had disfigured the older religion they displaced; but the gods they honoured remained, for the popular imagination, little more than abstractions before which the only attitude possible was the resignation of fatalism. Fortune might be worshipped as the supreme goddess, but Fortune was inexorable unchangeable destiny, Fate—and before Fate what use to pray or beseech?

A like fatalistic attitude to life was bred by another series of new cults now in full emigration from the East, the cult of the Sun, of the Moon and of the Stars. According to the positions of the

67

stars at the moment of birth, so must every man's life be; and the adepts of these cults set themselves to work out astrological codes by which each man's future and fate might be told. The emperors enacted the severest laws against these mischievous superstitions, but without any great success. The promise of this religious astrology was too much for human anxiety to resist, and the very emperors in whose name the laws were published were themselves the first to break them.

But the most important feature of the century's religious history was undoubtedly the progress of the ancient cults of the old pre-hellenic culture of the East. Below the veneer of Hellenism which had covered it now for generations, the East still remained the East. Egypt, Asia and Syria still retained their ancient identities, their ancient sensual and bloodthirsty gods. Slowly, now, that older East was coming to life again; and, in a kind of revenge for the Hellenistic centuries, its old religions seeped through the surface, steadily, increasingly, until by the middle of the third century they had done much everywhere to transform the religion of the city populations. These cults were popular now for the same reasons that the mystery religions had been popular in ancient Greece. They offered to their clients guarantees of special protection—very notably they offered protection against the powers of evil, against Fate itself. They gained a hold on the imagination by the splendour of their rites, their secret initiations, the spectacle of their sanctifying sacred dramas. In the assemblies which were the scene of these rites a mad enthusiasm spread through the crowd. Men stabbed themselves and each other, feeling nothing; in sheer religious exultation mutilated themselves publicly and shamelessly, passed through fire, leapt unbridgeable gulfs, gave themselves to actions of unbelievable impudicity. But more potent than the attraction of these often misunderstood aberrations was the novelty of the god's familiarity with his client. The gods of the classic Olympus had been aloof. Familiarity with them was perilous. Their company no man could hope to survive. But Isis, Mithra, the Syrian Goddess, offered familiarity, friendship: offered this, even, as the very means of their protection, as the medium. through which they wished to be worshipped.

As these cults slowly established themselves in the West, they underwent more than one important modification. The Syrian goddess, patron of reproduction, was seen by the Greeks as another Aphrodite, by the Romans as a Venus. With the identification a more open sensuality often crept into the old Paganism of the West, a new brutal bloodthirstiness. From Rome the new cults crossed the Alps, and revived by their presence the superstitions and the horrors of the old pre-Roman religion of the Celts. Always there is the fantasy of the legend, never exactly the same in any two places; always the rough and ready identification of the new and the old; the attraction of sensual novelty in the ritual, the promise of the god's intimacy, of his special protection and of a happy eternity. The man who has given himself to the god or goddess and is accepted has no more to fear. Though Fate dog his life Isis will effectually protect him. These religions introduced, too, a new kind of priesthood. Their priests were a caste apart, men whose lives were wholly given to the service of the god, and who were set apart for that service in a definite ritual, often indeed of a brutal and obscene character. They had their prophets, they had their magicians, sorcerers, soothsayers; and their establishment presented the nascent religion of Christ with yet another obstacle to overcome in its mission of winning the populace to the good tidings of the Kingdom of God. Under the working of these new influences the popular inert dislike of the Christian turns to passionate, active hatred—a hatred which skilful calumny intensifies. And as, with the third century, the Eastern cults gain a hold among the aristocracy, and can claim the emperor himself as a devotee, the possibilities of the anti-Christian influence know no limit. It is, for instance, the magician, Macrian, who converts the emperor, Valerian (253–259), from his sympathy for the Christians and makes of him one of the bloodiest of persecutors.

The mystery religions, as they developed in the century between Nero and Marcus Aurelius, were to influence the pace of the Church's development in another way. Two features they all shared—the initiation reserved to the select few and the special revelation of the god to the initiated. It was only after a laborious novitiate, and a series of tests and partial initiations, that the candidate was in the end admitted to the heart of the mystery. In every mystery religion, then, the disciples, at any given moment, were arranged in a hierarchy of knowledge, and of perfection, according to the degree of their initiation. And as knowledge of the divine secret and intimacy with the god developed together, the perfectly initiated into knowledge was alone perfectly holy, stainless and saved. This idea of a hierarchy of virtue based on degrees of knowledge was to play its part in the Church, too, once the Church came into contact with Gnosticism.

The perfection to which the initiate few thus attained was of course wholly unconcerned with moral goodness. In the dramas of the mysteries, even of the more restrained Hellenic mysteries, the subjects of the splendid spectacle were all too often the sexual relations of the god and goddess with one another and with mankind.

Moral teaching they held none; nor anything of instruction about the gods except the interminable, meaningless genealogies. And if the early Christian writers used all their eloquence to denounce the mysteries for the traps they were, the Pagans were equally outspoken. Plutarch, for example, ends his description of the myth of Isis and Osiris with the comment that to those who really believe that the gods give themselves to such a way of life there is no more to be said but what Æschylus advises, "Spit it out and rinse your mouth." Nothing in this latest development of Paganism brought it nearer to the chance of giving the world what the Gospel promised to give. It was no rival gospel that the Church had to fear in the mystery religions, or in these new cults from the East. The danger was more simple—that the mixture of charlatanry and sensuality would find so ready a response in the weakest parts of human nature that there would not even remain a beginning of natural virtue to which the super-natural could make an appeal. "The mysteries never raised man to a belief more worthy of the divinity. Rather it was man who by his interpretation of the mysteries gave them a meaning more worthy of the gods."

Such as they were, however, these religions flourished. The army, the imperial functionaries, the officials of the civil service spread them from one end of the empire to the other. The century that begins with Marcus Aurelius and ends with Aurelian (161–275) is their golden age. The old Paganism of classical times, as a force influencing men's lives, is dead. As a ritual, as a part of the day's public life, a religious consecration of the State and its institutions, it still continues. But it has long since ceased to shape men's activities. In its place are the oriental religions just described and, for the élite who think, the religious philosophies. In the Paganism of the second century these two things alone are alive.

The religious philosophy of the day made, of itself, no appeal whatever to the senses, nor to the imagination. It attempted a reasonable explanation of religion and of the mythologies, and, more than that, it presented itself as a reasoned teaching in religious matters, offering a reasoned system of morality. The philosophers were the guides and spiritual directors of that minority who wished to live an ordered, reasonable, and, as we should say, religious life. In their teaching such souls found illumination and encouragement, and it was from the philosophers of this generation that the Church recruited those converts who were to be pioneers in the work of expounding her doctrine rationally to the intellect of the non-Christian world. The philosophy fashionable in the second century is, then, not only an important element in the non-Christian life of that time, but it has its effect within the Church itself thanks to the conversion to Christianity of so many of its devotees. Two schools of this second-century philosophic thought call principally for notice—the Stoics and the Platonists.

For the Stoic all things had their origin in one single living principle, and this principle is material. From this first material principle—the purest and most subtle matter conceivable, a kind of fiery air—all other existing things have come, and will continue to come, by a process of continual degrading, a process inevitable and necessitated. In all these derived existing things, no matter how low the degree of their existence, there remains always some spark of that principle whence they first derive—whether the things be, as we should say, animate or inanimate. "This fire" the definition classic among the Stoics explained "is skilled and travels a fixed road since the world's beginning. Locked up within it are all the seminal *logoi* in accordance with which all things necessarily come into being." From this fire all things come, to it all things return; and the evolutionary process is fixed, inevitable from the nature of the fire. Returning to the original fire, they issue forth yet again—always in the same way, bound to the same evolution in the future which has shaped their history in the past; things, animals, men, the gods themselves, except Zeus whom the Stoics identify with the imperishable fire. All is governed by this unescapable law of necessity. Even the least of human actions necessarily follows from causes outside man's control, is fixed by the nature of things, is shaped by the one soul of the universe. "Man," said the Stoics, "is a dog tied to a car. He has no choice but to run in its wake."

This necessity, constraining human action, is and is not a slavery, for the soul of all things whence the necessity comes is man's soul too, and the necessity which constrains him is not the violence of another to which perforce he must submit, but the necessity of his own nature's deepest need. "Secure in his autonomy, why should the Stoic sigh for liberty?" The theory worked out in practice in very different ways. First of all it set man on an equality with the gods, for it is the one same divine soul that gives life to all. Whence a valuation of human personality among the Stoics higher than any other of the ancient philosophies ever accorded it. Whence, too, those beginnings of a care for personality in legislation, and the humanitarianism of which Cicero is a leading example. Whence also, on the other hand, a pride and self-exaltation that could end in mania.

Again, although the theory of the divine origin of all things could, and did, in Seneca for example, develop into a belief in something like Providence, the other half of the theory—the necessary evolution, the unescapable force, the inevitable, individual destruction and re-absorption,—is the very negation of Providence. This god who is in us all, who is ourselves, as he is everything, is yet unknown and unknowable, and research as to his nature can only end in ever greater obscurity. Prayer, supplication can find no place in the system—for all things that happen must happen as they happen. No effort can change them, no flight escape them. If one type of character was helped and encouraged by the system's Pantheism, braced or consoled by the belief in fellowship with the rest of creation, assuredly there were others crushed in despair by its fatalism.

The two great names among the Stoics of the second century are Epictetus and the emperor Marcus Aurelius. Epictetus is no fashionable philosopher with the entertainment of a leisured audience as his highest aim. He is a man with a mission, and his hearers were earnest and devoted seekers after a higher life. He set before them an ideal of austere detachment from the chances of life. Sickness, old age, misfortune, death itself should have no power over the Stoic; no power to disturb the calm, happy freedom of this man whom reason controlled. Such ills, when they threatened his peace, should be looked in the face, understood for what they were, and, their whole power for ill thus reasonably examined, they would cease to trouble. Was not man his own only master? containing within himself the only real good? and did he not live as part of a great universe of existence? What matter if his rôle in that great plan was meaner than another's.

To the whole it was equally necessary, and in this consideration of his contribution to the need and welfare of the whole the reasonable man would find compensation and consolation for the chances of life. Should this Pantheism fail to console, a further solution still remained. "There is one who provides me with food and with raiment . . . when he no longer gives he signifies to me that it is time to depart, he opens the door and calls. Whither does he call me? Towards a term which cannot affright thee, for it is thence thou didst originally proceed, towards friends and kinsfolk and the elements of things. What in thee is fire, to fire will return; what in thee is earth, to earth; what air, to air; what is water, to water yet again. There is no Hades, no Acheron, no Cocytus, no Periphlegethon, but everywhere is filled with gods and with daemons." But suicide is only for the weakling, blessed even as Epictetus blesses it. The ideal is acceptance of life in an indifference to its chance, an acceptance buttressed by the belief that man, too, is divine. God is in us, we are part of God and we should be loyal to what in us is divine for so we are most truly loyal to ourselves. "As the soldier swears he will prefer

Cæsar before all others, the Stoic swears so to prefer himself." Prayer and theories of divine assistance can have no place in the system, and the basis of the exalted sentiments that still move whoever studies these ancient writings is self-exaltation. Epictetus presents us with a meditation on death in which the dying man reviews his life and thanks his god for all it has been. It is no act of thanksgiving for mercies and favours, still less is it a confession; and if its underlying self-satisfaction recalls anything in the Gospel it is the famous prayer of the Pharisee.

Stoicism was never popular. Its theories, no doubt, broke too soon at the contact with reality. And it had too much scorn for the unenlightened herd to make their conversion a possibility. It remained the privilege of an élite, and even there its success was not such as to encourage its prophets. "Show me a Stoic if you know one," said Epictetus. "You will show me thousands who speak like Stoics. Show me at least some *one* who shows promise of realising this ideal. Let my old age gaze on what so far it has never been my lot to know. Show me one at least. You cannot."

Such an one we see perhaps in Marcus Aurelius. Under Domitian Epictetus had been banished from Rome as a philosopher. Now philosophy itself was on the throne. In his *Meditations* Marcus Aurelius admits us to the innermost workings of his mind. We see the Stoic theory shaping his response to the demands of life. We see the progress of self-knowledge, self-discipline, the continual examination and analysis of action and motive pursued faithfully day by day in search of truth ever more profound. All the traditional Stoic theory is here, not set out in theory for a class, but in its practical application to life. Man's share in the universal life, the common *logos*, is to Marcus Aurelius a familiar, a personal daemon. He reveres it, serves it, obeys it and for its sake will keep his life spotless. He shares, of course, the fatalist resignation to life which is the aim of the school, though the thought of the extinction which is death moves him to angry resentment. On the other hand he believes in prayer, prayer not to the gods of the classic pantheon, but to Fortune, the Sun, the Stars, Asclepios. Inevitably he is the victim of superstition, dreams and omens playing their part in his life. And the whole life is built on a foundation that is ever in movement, on hypotheses and alternatives and the uncertainty of doubt, of sentiment and guesswork. It is the end of happiness, the end of life, and from it derives that "infinite boredom" which Renan noted as characteristic of the famous work. "Infinite boredom", in life as in the *Meditations*, and "an analysis of life which leaves life little better than death."

The second great school of religious philosophy was that of the

Platonists, and this, unlike the school of Epictetus was not only popular, but as the century went on, grew to be one of the greatest forces in its religious life. For the Platonists there is a dual principle at the origin of things—spirit and matter. God is not only not identical with the world, as the Stoics proclaimed, but so transcends the world as to be beyond all power of our knowing him. In ecstasy alone can man reach to the divine. This dualism, and the doctrine of the divine transcendence, go back to Plato himself. It was his immediate successor Xenocrates who developed the system's dualism, and Plutarch derived from it the other notion of the divine inaccessibility to human reason. In the succeeding centuries these two ideas came to dominate the whole teaching of the school, and thereby inevitably lowered the system's intellectual appeal and bequeathed to it the continual menace of scepticism.

Since God was inaccessible, and since all things owed to God their origin and their continuance in being, the Platonist postulated as the medium of the divine action one or more beings intermediate between God and man, beings who shared indeed in the divine nature but who were yet subordinate to God their first origin. These are the daemons, powers, spirits, the *logos*. For the Stoics the logos was the immanent necessary law of things. For the new Platonists, it was the divine agent, and the pattern by which all things were; it was the divine element by which the other necessary element of the universal duality was corrected—all things being subject to the double law, *i.e.* of influences deriving from a thing's nature, and of influences deriving from the divine. This duality obtained in things inanimate, in man's soul too. Logos and nature, one for the Stoic, are for the Platonist rival contending forces.

Platonism had borrowed a term from the Stoics to express itself. It had borrowed elsewhere, and notably from the East. From its conception of spirit and matter as forces inevitably in conflict, a whole train of consequences were to follow. That conception was to enter the Church, to cause endless trouble in the heresies it provoked, and to be the cause, too, of more than one set-back in the development of thinkers otherwise orthodox.

These ideas of the dual principle in all reality, of a hierarchy of perfection, and of the radical opposition of matter and spirit, the Platonists popularised as Stoicism never was popularised. Around this philosophical core other doctrines gathered taken from the teachings ascribed to Pythagoras, and with them there passed to the Platonists something of that spirit which turned philosophy into a cult, with devotees, holy men, religious practices, rites and—by no means its least important feature—itinerant missionaries who gave their lives to the work of propaganda. There gathered, too, around the core of philosophy and idealism, something of the superstition and the magical practices which always attached to the self-styled disciples of Pythagoras. If such features detracted from the dignity of the philosophy they were, on the other hand, its very life as a force in public affairs. It was not long before Platonism, as a cult, absorbed the neo-Pythagoreans and quite ousted the Stoics. Later it was to inspire the bitterest and most skilful of all the attempts to destroy Christianity. Meanwhile, in that second century which at the moment occupies us, its leading figure, after Plutarch (50–125) was the lecturer, Maximus of Tyre.

The subjects of the lectures which gained him fame are the questions which the public of his day debated. Is revenge noble ? Is activity a higher life than contemplation ? Should we pray to the gods ? What is Plato's notion of God ? How can we reconcile human liberty and sorcery ? His theological teaching is a mixture of superstitious credulity and scepticism. Between God and man there is an intermediate hierarchy of daemons, demi-gods, who though they are passable are yet immortal. They are the companions of mankind, guiding and inspiring its life. "Some of them," he said, "cure sickness, or they tender advice in difficulties. They make known things otherwise hidden, they inspire the masterpieces of art. Some dwell in towns, others in the country, others in the sea. . . . They are sometimes the guests of human bodies, as in the case of Socrates, of Plato, of Pythagoras. . . . Some of them are scourges, others humane. . . . There is as great a diversity in the dispositions of the daemons as in those of men themselves." All the gods of the ancient mythology are seen now to be daemons, and Zeus identified with the supreme divine monarch. Prayer—the habit of petitioning the gods— Maximus condemns as useless. If God is Providence these things will come unsought. If God is Chance prayer cannot move it. As for the desire to possess greater virtue, no god can do more here than man can do for himself, for the source of virtue is within man himself. This last point recalls Epictetus and the Stoics, and is one of the many evidences of the eclectic character of the new Platonism of the time. Its adepts borrowed as willingly from contemporaries as from the past, borrowed ideas and terminology no less readily than ritual.

The one supreme God transcends sense. The soul is raised to communication with him by contemplation and love, and the condition of this ascent is an increasing detachment from all else. The perfection of this intellectual vision of God is indeed impossible in this life. Yet, by meditation and a life of detachment, great heights may be attained even here on earth. Not all men it is true can so raise themselves. For those who are unable there remains in consolation the contemplation of the hierarchy of semi-divine intermediaries.

"How then will you escape, how come to see God? In a word, you will see him when he calls you to come. Nor will he long delay to call. Only await his invitation. Old age is at hand which will lead you; Death, whose approach affrights the coward to tears but whom the lover of God looks for with joy, receives with courage. But, if you wish, even in this present, to know his nature how shall I explain it? God is no doubt beautiful, of all beauteous things the fairest. But it is not the beauty of a body. He is what gives the body its beauty. It is not the beauty of a field, but again that whence comes the field's beauty. Beauty of streams, beauty of sea and sky, it is from the gods who dwell in the sky that all this beauty flows, running over from a spring pure and eternal. And in the measure of their sharing this eternal stream, all things are beautiful, ordered, saved. In the measure they turn from it there remains for them only shame, death, corruption. If this satisfies, you have seen God. If not, how can you be made to understand? Do not picture to yourself size, nor colour, nor form, nor indeed any material quality, but, like a lover stripping of its varied clothing the beautiful body thus hidden from his gaze, strip away with your thought all these material imaginings. There will remain, and you shall gaze upon it, what you desire to see. But if you are too weak thus to arrive at the vision of the Father—the Demiurge, it will suffice that you actually see their works and adore their offspring in all their rich diversity. . . . Imagine a great empire, a powerful kingdom where every creature depends, and willingly, on the good will of one soul, the soul of the King, venerable, excelling in virtue . . . imagine then this King himself, immovable as law itself, communicating to those who serve, the salvation which is his. See all those who share in his power, the innumerable gods, visible some and others yet unseen. Some there are who, like guards of honour, at his side share his table and his food. Others serve them, and others there are of yet lower degree. See you not this chain, this hierarchy descending from God down to the very earth?"[1]

The charm of the vision so described, its poetry, the communication of religious emotion between master and student

[1] Maximus of Tyre, *On the God of Plato*, 11, 12, quoted LEBRETON *Origines du Dogme de la Trinité* II, pp. 75, 76.

explain much of the system's appeal. It brought about, in the end, and made generally acceptable, an idea of the infinite that grew ever vaguer, ever more indistinct; an instinctive suspicion, indeed, of distinctness and definition and reason in religious speculation; the idea of an opposition between "mysticism" and "dogma" necessary and fundamental; an exaltation of "mysticism" at the expense of "dogma," and a surrender of reason for emotion. Closely allied to this school of Platonists were those other practical philosophers who pass under the name of neo-Pythagoreans. Little as we know of them, we know that for them also matter was a principle of death, that the perfect reality was transcendent and unknowable. Between God and man, once again, there is this world of intermediaries, and one chief mediator, daemons and the Logos. The Logos again is at once God's idea or pattern according to which all things are, and the divine instrument. But it was the neo-Pythagorean school which did most, apparently, to build upon these philosophical theories a working religion. And it did so by borrowing from the East magical rites and incantations, rites of expiation and purification, mutilations and sacrifices.

All through the second century, and increasingly as the second century passed into the third, the missionaries of these new religions moved through the empire, lecturing, explaining and translating their theories into act. They consoled souls broken with sorrow and pain, they prepared for death the unfortunate whom the tyranny of the emperors condemned to suicide. "By word and example they showed to all the way of salvation."

Religions from the East offering salvation, astral religions, new cults of Fortune and the Fates, the pantheism and magic of the philosophers, mysteries dazzling by their splendour, initiations attracting by their exclusiveness, with all this rich and active diversity we have not, even yet, come to the end of the catalogue of the second century's religious activities. More important than any one of them individually is a movement which runs through them all, drawing something from each, offering something in return—a deeper insight, a truer vision, Knowledge in fact where, so far, no more has been possible than to see as in a glass darkly. This movement that claims to reveal to the religious themselves Knowledge, is the much discussed Gnosticism, and the history of the Church in the second century is very largely the history of its relation to Gnosticism.

Gnosticism is pre-Christian in its origins. It set itself to re-interpret Paganism and to re-interpret Judaism, and in the course of the interpretation it altered them radically. It offered Knowledge, the vision of God, actual communication with the divine here on earth. Like the philosophies, it made ecstasy the means of the most perfect knowledge and the ultimate aim of religious life. Like the mystery religions, it promised salvation. To all the thousands who sought security, in one or other of the myriad cults, it suggested a better understanding of those cults, the revelation of a deeper meaning in what they already believed or practised. It varied enormously, inevitably, from one exponent to another, varied according to whether it set itself to work on Paganism or Judaism or the religion of the Church; and it added new hybrid gnostic-inspired cults to those hundreds it found in possession. There were Gnostic-Pagan cults, and Gnostic-Jewish cults and ultimately Gnostic-Christian cults. But in all these amalgams we can trace some common features, can discover at work forces allied in character. There is for example, the claim that the Gnostic teaching is of divine origin, handed down through a secret chain of initiated disciples. There is a marked insistence on the dual origin of existence, and a hatred and scorn for the material world as a thing necessarily evil. God is of course transcendent, and so removed from the material world that creation is necessarily the work of intermediary powers. There is a preoccupation with theories about the creation, the end of creation, and the divine genealogies that borders on mania. There are rites, symbols, a mystical arithmetic, and exotic cults. Finally Knowledge is always presented as the privilege of the few. It is to an élite only that the real meaning of religion is offered.

It was simply a matter of time before the religion of the Church attracted the attention of Gnostics, and before Christians themselves began to turn to Gnosticism to explain the mysteries in their beliefs. With that, and the beginnings, inside the Church, of attempts to explain its belief "gnostically," the Church enters upon the first great crisis of its history.

A rich and confused amalgam of rites and beliefs and magical practices, theories to explain the origin of evil, human destiny, the relations between matter and spirit, between God and his creation, between God and Jesus Christ—the Gnostic movement within the Church was to win from the tradition some of the Church's first theologians and scholars, Tatian for example and Bardesanes. It also provoked a strong traditional reaction, and one of the great masterpieces of Catholic writing, the *Adversus Haereses* of St. Irenæus. In studying the history of this second century we are watching the first attempts of Christians to explain rationally their beliefs and mysteries and, in the story of the Gnostic crisis, can observe the natural, spontaneous reaction of the Church to its first great danger. The manner of that reaction throws an interesting light on the nature of the Church's organisation, and on second century theories about the Church's constitution and its powers.

II. THE FIRST APOLOGISTS

What was there in the religion of the Catholic Church to interest the Pagans of this century so desperately interested in religion ? Had it any "message" for the enquirer who sought security of mind and peace of soul, and sought in vain from mystery cults and magic? from first one, and then another, of the day's moral philosophies ? Celsus, the most informed perhaps of all its early opponents, was to sneer at Christianity as a religion that began with fishermen and publicans. Had it then nothing to offer to the educated, to the intellectuals ? Was it no more than an association of mutual benevolence, a friendly society with its ritual and passwords, a kindly sentimental morality ? The answer to these questions was the writings of Christianity's first publicists, the so-called Apologists.

The name Apologist is conventionally restricted to a small group of some fifteen writers. Half of them—Quadratus, Miltiades Melito for example—are little more than names to us, for their works, all but a few fragments, have perished. In other cases whole treatises remain from which we can discover the common aim which inspired this great literary effort, study its methods, and form some estimate of its importance in the development of Catholic theological thought and of the technical language in which it has come to be expressed. This second more important group includes the Greeks Aristides, Athenagoras, Hermias and St. Theophilus of Antioch, the Syrian Tatian, the Latins Minucius Felix and Tertullian, and St. Justin Martyr. In date their work ranges from the *Apology to* [*the Emperor*] *Antoninus Pius* of Aristides (between 138–161) and Hermias' *A Laugh at the Heathen Philospohers* of perhaps seventy years later. Tertullian, the greatest writer of them all, was something more than an apologist and will be discussed elsewhere. A more representative figure is St. Justin Martyr, and the school, with its merits and its weaknesses, is perhaps best described in him.

A double object inspires the writings of the Apologists. They hope to clear their religion of the calumnious charges which the Pagan world takes as proved against it, and so to persuade the emperors to a policy of toleration. They hope, also, to make clear to the associates and friends of their own pre-Christian life the beauty and truth of their new belief. They are converts from Paganism, converts from the Philosophical sects, who have not ceased to philosophise with their baptism but, realising now that their new faith is the goal of all thought, they burn with the desire to communicate this good news to those by whose side they sat in the lecture rooms of Rome and Athens, or those to whom they themselves once taught the consolations of Stoicism and the divine Plato. With St. Paul (*Philipp.* iv, 8) they made their own whatever is true, whatever is just, the virtuous and praiseworthy, wherever they found it. They carefully sought out whatever of truth or goodness there was in Pagan thought and inspiration and, made the most of it, that it might serve as a bridge for the heathens to pass from the philosophies to Christ. Christianity was the unknown good, and to it unconsciously all men of good-will tended. The Apologists hoped then to dispose the pagan mind for Christianity. They did not set out to instruct the Pagan in the full detail of Christian belief—and the Apologists' limited objective must be continually borne in mind when their writings are used as evidence of early Christian belief. From the nature of the Apologists' case, they prefer to elaborate those points where Christian teaching confirms Philosophy, to discuss natural virtues and those truths about God which are discoverable by the natural reason. All the stock topics of the day find treatment in their writings—the unity of God, the unicity of God, the soul's immortality, the future life as a sanction of morality. These are the substance of their apologetic appeal.

St. Justin was born in Palestine round about the year 100. He was not only a philosopher by education and taste, but by profession too, earning his living by teaching philosophy. In his search for truth he passed from one school to another and was Stoic, Aristotelian, Neo-Pythagorean, Neo-Platonist by turn. Finally, when thirty-eight years of age, he was converted to Christianity at Ephesus, and passing to Rome opened there a school where he taught Christianity as a philosophy. At Rome he flourished for nearly thirty years, until the malice of a rival, worsted in debate, set the persecuting laws in motion against him and, under the philosopher-emperor Marcus Aurelius, thrown to the beasts, he died a martyr in 165. His surviving works are his two *Apologies* and the *Dialogue with Trypho the Jew.* St. Justin's reasoned presentation of Christianity has for its starting point the principle that Christianity is itself a philosophy. More striking than its differences from other philosophies are the many points it has in common with them. Those differences, too, are not so much real oppositions as shades of meaning. The Faith does no more than teach with greater security what Plato and the Stoics teach. Faith teaches with divine authority, and Faith can prove with reason what it teaches. The origin of this likeness between Philosophy and Christianity is, for St. Justin, twofold. First of all, the philosophers originally learned these truths from the Old Testament—an idea popular, before St. Justin, with the philosophising Jews of Alexandria. Then—by a theory of St. Justin's own invention, destined to make a name for itself—the philosophers had profited from the activity of the Divine Logos. The Logos, whose incarnation in Jesus Christ was the beginning of Christianity, had, from the beginning, made Himself known to the Pagans as well as to the Jews. To the Jews He had spoken by the prophets and the writers of the sacred books, to the Pagans through the philosophers. This revelation through the philosophers was indeed less complete than that made to the Jews. None the less it was sufficient to make possible the philosophers' discovery of the truths of natural religion. This seed of the Logos (*Logos Spermatikos*) planted in every man's mind from the beginning, was the true source of philosophical truth. Between Philosophy then and Christianity there could not be any real and final opposition. All who have lived according to that light are Christians, Socrates and Heraclitus as truly as Abraham. Christianity is the fulfilment of Philosophy, Jesus Christ of Socrates ! The revelation through the *Logos Spermatikos* was incomplete, and from its incompleteness errors were bound to follow. Hence the mistakes of even the best of philosophers. But now, the Logos has appeared incarnate, the fullness of revelation is come by which the errors of the past may be corrected. The philosopher who is logical embraces Christianity.

The argument against the sufficiency of the philosophies of the day, thus roughly summarised, is but one side of the Apologist's work. He criticises the pagan religions, their insufficiency, their puerility, their immorality. He defends the Christians from the vile calumnies which, to the man in the street, justified the persecutions. He addresses himself also to the Jews, responsible, in the eyes of St. Justin, for many of the calumnies whose refutation occupies his time. The accord of their own prophetic writings with subsequent history and the present event, proves the Church to be the divine fulfilment of the religion of Abraham and Moses. The true Israel of to-day is the Church of Christ.

It is not easy to say how much this first learned appeal for a hearing achieved. The calumnies continued, as did the persecution. Nor have we any data by which to judge of the fruit of the Apologies among the Pagan élite. They remain, however, a valuable evidence of the first contact of Christianity with the thought of the contemporary Pagan world; and, in addition, they are of absorbing interest as the first attempts of members of the Church to clothe its traditional beliefs in philosophical language. With the Apologists Catholic Theology is born—the development of the content of Revelation by human reasoning under the guidance of that authorative teaching which, from the beginning, has been one of the new religion's most striking features. With these first beginnings of speculation on the data of Revelation there begins no less surely the trouble bred in the Church by the thinker who claims for his thought, for his own carefully worked-out explanation of the revealed tradition, a superiority over the tradition itself. Here, too, is the real origin of those discussions which fill the fourth and fifth centuries, and which can never be really understood if these primitive theologians are neglected. Inevitably the Apologist's trained mind was drawn to the exploration of the meaning of the great mysteries of the Christian tradition. The urge of his own piety, the passion to explain all, to know all that is knowable, made it impossible for him not to attempt the task of describing these mysteries philosophically.

So it was with the mystery we know as that of the Trinity. God was one. Jesus Christ was God because the Logos incarnate. And yet Jesus Christ was not God the Father. Again there was the absorbing question of the relation of the Father and the Logos before the incarnation, and the question of the eternal generation of the Logos. These difficulties did not challenge in vain. The Apologists boldly showed the way to eighteen centuries of Christian thinkers. Like pioneers of every type they had to devise instruments and machinery as they went along. The road was unplotted, the obstacles unknown and, when known, for long not fully understood; the rough tools were sometimes a hindrance as well as a help. They use, for example, the concepts and language of the philosophical schools to which they at one time adhered, and thence ensues a host of new difficulties for the student of their teaching. The modern scholar picks his way easily through the difficulties of such high speculation, equipped with a tested technical language which they lacked. Of that language they were the founders. In their stumblings and gropings it was born. Inevitably there is, at times, in their speculation an uneasiness, a confusion and an obscurity which leave room for contrary interpretations of their meaning. Little wonder, then, that the efforts of these first private theologians bred a certain uneasiness on the part of the Authority whose mission it was to preserve at all costs the traditional faith, and for whom, by comparison with that high duty, the need to explain philosophically that faith's coherence was of secondary importance.

St. Justin, faithful to the tradition, explains that there is only one God and that in God there are to be distinguished the Father, the Logos or Son, and the Holy Ghost. The Father is God as the source of divinity and is therefore the Creator who formed all things from nothing. Nevertheless, following St. John (i. 3), creation was, by the Father's will, through the Logos, and so too, through the Logos, has God chosen to reveal himself to man (*St. John* i. 18) and to redeem him. Creation, revelation and redemption are the work of the one only God. The Logos is truly God; not a creature, not an angel. "God of God Begotten" says Theophilus of Antioch. The Logos exists before all creation, is not himself made nor created, but begotten and therefore truly Son of God. The Logos then is really distinct from the Father. For all the distinction's reality, it does not imply any division of the indivisible divinity, any separation of Logos from the Father. The next two questions to suggest themselves were that of the moment of the generation of the Logos, and, deriving from this, the question of the difference in the relation of Father to Logos before and after the creation. The current philosophical theories of the day once more came to the thinker's aid. These notions the Apologists adapted to explain the Christian mystery of the Trinity.

Logos in Greek means the word as spoken, and it also means the conceived idea of which the spoken word is the manifestation. The Stoics had thence developed a theory of the Logos as immanent and as manifested. St. Justin put it to a Christian use.

The Logos existing from all eternity, did not exist from all eternity in a real distinction from the Father. As a term really distinct He exists only from the moment of the generation, and that moment was the moment of God's willingness to create. Until that moment the Divine Logos is *Logos Endiathetos*—the Logos Immanent in God. At that moment, in a manner of speaking, the Logos issues forth. Thenceforward He is *Logos Prophorikos*—the Logos Manifested—and really distinct. This is the theory which has been called (none too correctly) the theory of the temporal generation of the Logos. The Logos, moreover, since He is *in function* the minister of the Divine Will is "subordinate" to the Father—a subordination however not *of nature,* for the Logos is equally God with the Father and God is one. This is subordinationism, but only in so far as it is an attempt to describe the rôle of the Logos in the Divine ordering of things. It neither necessitates, nor implies, any theory of the inferiority of the Logos to the Father in nature.

Through the Logos manifested had come the Creation, and the partial revelation to the philosophers and to the Jews. Through the Logos incarnate in Jesus Christ had come the fullness of revelation and the Church. It is from the Church that the disciple learns of His work and its fruits, how He died on our behalf to

ransom us from the death which sin had merited. His death is
the principal cause of our redemption, and, as Jesus Christ the
Incarnate Logos restored what Adam the first of mankind had
ruined, so Mary, consenting to be the mother of Him Who is
mankind's salvation, repaired the ills that followed from Eve's
disobedience.

St. Justin is primarily a polemist. He has set himself to the
restricted task of the defence and explanation of special points,
and this to a restricted audience of Pagans. None the less he
describes the Christian life, makes clear the ritual, as well as the
doctrine, of Baptism; and he has left the most precious description
of the liturgy of the Holy Eucharist, in primitive times, which
we possess.

III. THE GNOSTICS AND THE CHURCH

St. Justin is an example of the philosopher turned Christian
who uses his philosophy to gain a hearing for the Church's
teaching. The aim of the Gnostics was far different. Where St.
Justin only strove to translate that teaching into a language
understood of the non-Christian thinking world, the Gnostics
urged that the Church's teaching should itself be remodelled.
There was a higher knowledge than that of the traditional catechesis, and only in accordance with this higher knowledge could
the revelation of God to man really be understood.

Gnosticism in its relation to Christianity is a subject of be-
wildering complexity. The simplest way to explain the very real
danger it became is, perhaps, to describe the systems of two of
the leading Christian Gnostics of the time—Basilides and Valentine.
Better so than in any other way—in a work where space is limited
—can we see how a school of thought within the Church, inspired
by an all powerful religious tendency of the time, and using its
methods, hoped to find a deeper meaning in Christianity than
that offered by the gospels and tradition, and to transform the
religion of the Church into a mystery cult of dreams and initiations.
Apart from the matter of these Gnostic-Christian speculations,
the long crisis is important in another way. For Gnosticism is
also, historically, an attempt on the part of the Christian "intellectuals"—some of them thinkers of unusual power—to usurp
a right of speculating, of systematising and dogmatising in the
strictest sense of the word after the manner of the pagan schools
of philosophy.

To the ordinary man the detailing of the beliefs and theories
of these heretics is a wearying business. Speculations seemingly
as divorced from right reason as the schemes of the professors
in Laputa, nightmarish mechanically-contrived fantasies, a

wilderness of sounding phrases and necromantic names, a chaos where sounds abound and sense is all to seek—in studying these systematic aberrations we have to remind ourselves at every turn that their bizarre extravagance covers a discussion, and an offered solution, of the most fundamental of all problems. The nature and origin of evil, of man, of God, the purpose of life and its attainment through living—these are the problems, theoretical and practical, which the Gnostic interpretation of Christianity claimed to answer. Nor was Gnosticism a mere academic discussion. It offered itself as a religious system. It had its ritual and its observances, its regulations and its officials. It was a formidable competitor to traditional Christianity, and to Gnosticism the Church lost some of its best minds and most energetic spirits. Nor did the influence of the movement end with the second century. That century witnessed a life and death struggle between the Church and the Gnostics which ended in the Gnostics' expulsion from the Church, but the defeated theories survived outside the Church to provide, for centuries yet to come, an undercurrent of influences which never ceased to irritate and disturb the development of Catholic thought.

Of Basilides himself we know little except that he flourished at Alexandria in the reign of Hadrian (117–138). The beginning and first principle of all things, according to his theology, is the unbegotten Father. Thence, by a series of successive emanations, derive the eight intermediary and complementary divinities—Nous, Logos, Phronesis, Sophia and Dynamis, and from this last couple the Powers, Archons and Angels. This personification of abstractions was all in the contemporary fashion, as was also the arrangement of intermediary divine agencies between the first principle and the created universe. The ogdoad of intermediary divinities is also a familiar notion in the religions of ancient Egypt.

The Powers, Archons and Angels made the first heaven. Other Angels, issue of these first Angels, made the second, the third and the rest of the heavens to the number of 365. The origin of the world is conceived as from two opposing principles Light and Darkness, between which there is an irreducible opposition. This dualism finds its counterpart in the opposition between the Supreme God and the first of all the Archons. This Archon, the leader of the wicked Angels, is the God whom the Jews adore. The apparition of the Holy Spirit at the baptism of Our Lord bred in him a terrible fear which was for him the beginning of Wisdom. The system offers a theory about Our Lord, about the redemption, the creation of the world and the nature of the divine life. It is a miscellany in which reminiscences of biblical theology and of

Egyptian and Persian religion find their place. In addition
Basilides lays claim to a special knowledge deriving from the
secret teaching of the Apostle St. Mathias.

In the next generation Valentine built up a system still more
complete upon much the same foundation. Where and when
Valentine was born, what influences shaped his early formation
is not known. He came to Rome in the second quarter of the
century and was sufficiently prominent in the Roman Church
at the death of the pope St. Hyginus (c. 140) to hope himself to
secure election as its bishop. He was disappointed and, according
to Tertullian, this disappointment was the occasion of his breach
with Catholicism. Tertullian's account of this crisis in the life
of Valentine has been called in question. Be it true or false,
there is no doubt whatever as to the success of the grandiose
system of which Valentine was the founder. All contemporary
writers agree that his sect was the most numerous and the most
powerful of all. In time it divided and while one school of
Valentinians spread through Egypt and Syria, the other filled
Italy and southern Gaul. It is this western Valentinianism which
is best known to us, for in Gaul it met the man who was to be its
greatest adversary and in whose writings the memory of it is best
preserved, the Bishop of Lyons St. Irenæus.

In the Valentinians the Christian aspect of the movement is
clearer than with the followers of Basilides. It is more apparently
their object to find a solution for the paradoxes of the Christian
mysteries in the fashions of contemporary ideas. Valentine sup-
poses a dual principle at the origin of things. He has the old
hatred of matter as a thing necessarily evil, and thence, in his
theology, the theory of the Supreme God in necessary opposition
to the divinity through whom He creates, and a theory of the
Incarnation that makes the humanity of Christ Our Lord a matter
of appearance only.

At the summit of all being is God, the Father, and His companion Sigé (Silence). God is One, unique, known only to
Himself, remote, inaccessible; and between God and the world is
a whole universe of "demi-gods." From the Father and Sigé
proceed Intellect and Truth, and from these Word and Life, and
from these again Man and the Church; these are the eight superior
eons. This process of generation among the eons continues until
the Pleroma is complete—the perfect society of divine beings,
thirty in all. So far all is abstraction, idea. Physical reality origin-
ates through a breach of the harmony of the ideal pleroma,
"a kind of original sin". . . . The lowest of the thirty eons,
Wisdom, conceives a desire to know the Father—an inordinate
desire, necessarily, since the Father is knowable only to His own

first born, Intellect. This inordinate desire of Wisdom is a new being, imperfect necessarily and therefore cast out from the Pleroma. Its name is Hachamoth. To prevent any recurrence of such disorder Intellect and Truth produce a sixteenth pair of eons, Christ and the Holy Ghost to teach the rest the limits of their nature. Then in an act of Thanksgiving all the thirty-two eons unite their powers and produce the thirty-third eon, Jesus the Saviour. The thirty-third eon and the eon Christ are now dispatched by the Pleroma to Hachamoth—the imperfect desire of Wisdom. From the eon Christ it receives a beginning of form and the elements of conscience—whence a sense of its own inferiority. The thirty-third eon separates the passions from it. The separated passions are inanimate matter (*hylike*); Hachamoth, freed from them, is animate matter (*psychike*). Hachamoth's vision of the Saviour results in a third substance, the spiritual (*pneumatike*). So originate the elements of the world that is to be. Hachamoth, from the psychike, produces the Creator, Demiurge, and he gives form to the rest of creation.

Demiurge is ignorant of his own origin, believes himself supreme. He is the maker of man, material and animated, the god of the Jews and the Old Testament, a bad god and to be resisted. (Whence the common Gnostic teaching of a fundamental opposition between the Old Testament and the New.) Men are of three types, according to the element predominating in them. There are material men (*hylikoi*), who cannot be saved; spiritual men (*pneumatikoi*) who have no need of salvation (the Gnostics); and animate men (*psychikoi*) who need salvation and can attain to it. For these last there is the plan of Redemption. The redeemer is spiritual, he is animate, he has the appearance of the material and, a fourth element in him, he is the eon Jesus. This eon descended into him at his baptism and remained until the trial before Pilate when it returned to the Pleroma, taking with it the spiritual element. The actor in the Passion was no more than the animate element with its appearance of matter. The Passion is not the source of redemption. Salvation, the redemption of the spiritual in man from the influence of the psychic, is due to the knowledge brought by the thirty-third eon—knowledge of the secret traditions and mysteries, knowledge of the Gospel, which can only be truly known through this esoteric knowledge. The possession of this knowledge is the key to life, and knowledge is the highest of virtues. Matter is the source of evil in man, and since the Gnostic is spiritual, his actions cannot but be good. Spirit and flesh are independent, and the spirit is not responsible for the flesh.

The system of eons proceeding the one from the other by pairs is not Valentine's own invention, and the idea of a pleroma of thirty eons is to be found in Plutarch. Peculiar to Valentine is the introduction of the two new eons Logos and Life and this, together with the presence in the lower series of the Only-begotten and the Paraclete, is no doubt explainable as a borrowing from the Gospel of St. John. But these Christian expressions are no more than trappings to decorate a pagan masquerade, mere names which have lost all their Christian meaning when they have not been distorted to a new meaning altogether.[1]

It was not through such elaborations of learned fantasy as these that the new religion was to live. This was again to show itself as primarily the tradition of an unaltered block of truth revealed once and for all. The test, for the Church, of the Gnostic theology's truth was its accord with the tradition; and the judge of that accord was to be, not the encyclopædic erudition of the Valentines and Basilides, nor even the trained minds of convert philosophers. Victory was to lie with the tradition and its sole authorised exponent the hierarchy of bishops. The adversary *par excellence* of Gnosticism in the Church, is, fittingly enough, no Apologist but a bishop, St. Irenæus of Lyons.

IV. ST. IRENÆUS OF LYONS

St. Irenæus is one of those sympathetic figures in whom all the tendencies of a time seem to meet. He was born, apparently, between the years 135–140 in Asia Minor, and in his youth was a disciple of the famous Bishop of Smyrna St. Polycarp who was, in turn, the disciple of St. John. From Smyrna Irenæus passed to Rome and, possibly at this time, came under the influence of St. Justin, reminiscences of whose work are found in all his writings. But it is not until the year 177 that Irenæus appears in history and he is then in Rome, the envoy of the Church at Lyons, recounting for the Roman Church the detail of the famous persecution. In that persecution he has himself suffered and he is by this time a priest of the Church at Lyons. By the time he returned from Rome, the persecution had given yet more martyrs to the Lyonnese Church, among them its aged bishop, Pothinus. Irenæus was elected to succeed him, and ruled for the next twenty or thirty years. How his life ended we do not know, but, traditionally, it is as a martyr that he figures in the calendar.

St. Irenæus—and the fact is immediately evident from his writings—is not an apologist. To win a sympathetic hearing from the Pagan élite whom philosophies attract is by no means

---

[1] So with Love. In the system of Valentine it is the principle of all the emanations. It is not Love in the Christian sense, however, but the simple desire of the physical pleasure associated with sex.

his object. He is a man of affairs, the busy missionary bishop of a frontier diocese, and if he writes it is to defend his people from the ever menacing heresies. He is concerned to rout the Gnostics to shatter their claims to be followers of Christ, to state yet once again the simple truths delivered to the Apostles in which alone salvation lies. And for all his admiration for St. Justin, and his use of that scholar's work, he has little patience with the attempts of philosophers to explain rationally the how and the why of the mysteries. *Quasi ipsi obstetricaverint*—"as though they themselves had been the midwives"—he says scornfully of the theorists busy with discussion on the generation of the Logos. His work marks an epoch in the development of Catholic Theology and there are not wanting scholars to see in him, in this respect, the peer of St. Augustine, the greatest force indeed between St. Augustine and St. Paul.

Yet St. Irenæus is no innovator. He has no revolutionary theories to present, no new explanations—explanations indeed he does not profess to give. But he so re-states the old traditional truths in relation to the particular danger of his day, that his restatement has a new, universal value and, beyond what he designed, it has stood ever since as a refutation by anticipation not of Gnosticism alone but of all and every heresy. Simply summarising the legacy of all who had preceded him, setting forth once again the traditional belief and practice of the Church as he knew it, he ends by sketching a theological theory of the Church and its teaching office which all subsequent discussions have merely developed. He is a most valuable witness to the second century Church's own theory of her own nature. He professes merely to state facts, to describe the reality before him, and the event is proof of his sincerity and his truth. The Church did not become Gnostic, although many Catholics were Gnostics. It threw off the doctrine, as a thing it could not assimilate. Gnosticism, and the religion of the Church as Christ would have it, are incompatible because the religion of Christ is essentially a religion of authority. The issue is the simple one of tradition against speculation. Two theories claiming to determine truth within the Church are in conflict—the Gnostics base all on the depth of their learning, Irenæus on the teaching authority in the Church. The Gnostics, witnessing to the institution they seek to subvert, gibe at "the teaching fitted for simpletons." Irenæus accepts the gibe. Upon it he builds his work. Not by the machinery of councils, nor the aid of the State, but by the simple functioning of the authority which was its essence, the Church of the second century shook itself free of its modernising children. Upon no other hypothesis than a general belief in the traditional nature of Christian teaching, and a general acceptance of the claim of the rulers to decide what was the tradition, can the passage of the Church, scathless, through this crisis be explained. If, on the other hand, the Church was as St. Irenæus describes it, the matter is self-evident.

Two books of his writing survive. The first which we have in a Latin translation, possibly contemporary with the author, and in a vast number of Greek fragments, is the work usually known as the *Adversus Hæreses—Against Heresies*. Its Greek title better describes it as *A refutation and criticism of Knowledge falsely so-called*. The second and much shorter work—*The Demonstration of the Apostolic Preaching*—is a kind of handbook for one who is already a believer, explaining the faith, with arguments and citations from Holy Scripture. It was lost for centuries and rediscovered, in an Armenian translation, as recently as 1904.

It is to the *Adversus Hæreses* that St. Irenæus owes his place in history. The doctrine of the book is the traditional doctrine. God is only fully knowable by revelation. God is one and there is only one God, God of the Old Testament and of the New alike. This one true God is the Creator of all. In God there are the three, Father, Son (St. Irenæus characteristically prefers the term Son to Logos with its associations of alien philosophies and Gnostic misuse) and Holy Ghost. The Son existed before His incarnation, for the Son is God equally with the Father. As to the mode or, moment of His generation St. Irenæus, as against the Gnostics and in marked contrast with the Apologists, has no theory to propose. These are mysteries known to God alone, and the Gnostic's elaborate explanations are mere fantasies. Nor does he offer any explanation of the origin of evil, beyond the free will of man and the fact of the first man's fall and its consequences. That falling away from God at the beginning of things has affected all subsequent humanity. From its disastrous consequences we are redeemed by the saving death of Jesus Christ—the Logos Himself, now incarnate. He is Saviour and Redeemer, as well as Revealer of God to man. He is truly God and truly man; and St. Irenæus is again content to record the traditional belief without any attempt to show how the two realities meet in Him. From the redeeming action of the incarnate Logos there comes to man the possibility of reconciliation with God, to be achieved by faith in Christ, obedience to His precepts, and rebirth in Him by Baptism. The mystery of the Holy Eucharist in which are really received the Body and Blood of Christ, and which is also a sacrifice, consummates on earth the work of reconciliation.

In all this St. Irenæus is not merely repeating the tradition.

He is repeating it to refute thinkers whose special error it is that they claim to arrive at the fullness of Christianity by "Knowledge." Whence the special attention he gives to the fundamental question of the sources and means by which we can come to know God and His will in our regard. Here is the very heart of what is characteristic in his work. Man, because of his finite nature, can never attain to full knowledge of God. It is no matter for surprise, then, that such mysteries as the generation of the Logos, the origin of the material escape us. Perfect knowledge is more than we can expect. Yet there is open to us a sure knowledge of heavenly things and mysteries, even a sure knowledge of the Logos—the knowledge God Himself has chosen to reveal. This knowledge is, in part, contained in the divine Scriptures. It is objected that these are often obscure, and the difficulty arises of correct interpretation, of a choice between rival interpretations. What then is the ultimate guide? Not Scripture but "the fixed, unchangeable rule of truth" which each receives in Baptism. This canon of belief is the same throughout the Church; so that the Church whether in the Germanies or in Gaul, in Spain, among the Celts, in the East, in Egypt, in Libya has but one heart and one soul, speaks with one mouth and one voice. The most eloquent of bishops cannot teach otherwise, the weakest can do nothing to lessen the tradition. So it is with the Church universal, wherever it is established. The source of this canon's value is its apostolic origin, the historically demonstrable fact that it was committed to the Church by the Apostles and has, by the Church, been ever since preserved. All those who care to know the truth can examine the apostolic tradition, shown forth clearly in every church throughout the world, guaranteed by the line of bishops which began with those whom the Apostles appointed and which continues to their successors in our own time. To trace the succession of bishops in all the churches of the world would take more space than his book can afford, he proceeds. A simpler way is to examine the succession in that see of Rome, the greatest and most venerable of all, founded by the glorious apostles Peter and Paul. By setting out the tradition it holds from the Apostles, and the faith it has taught through a succession of bishops reaching thence to our times, we bring to confusion those who, for whatever reason, gather elsewhere than they ought. And this for the simple reason that every church throughout the world is bound to bring itself into line with the Roman Church because of that Church's surer guarantees,[1] for in that

---

[1] *Propter potentiorem principalitatem. Adv. Her. III*, 3, 2. For the translation of this much-discussed phrase *cf.* Batiffol, *L'Eglise Naissante* pp. 251–2, Dawson, *Making of Europe*, p. 33 n.

Church what the Apostles handed down has ever been preserved by those who govern. In final analysis it is not human learning, not even the study of the admittedly Sacred Writings, which is the source of man's knowledge of the truths revealed. It is the teaching of the Roman Church.

Such is the famous testimony of St. Irenæus written, not as an argument to prove the papal claims against objectors, but, as a reminder of known and accepted truths, to make it easier for his contemporaries to distinguish between truth and heresy. For a Church so constituted, and so clearly conscious of its constitution, there was little to fear in Gnosticism. The seduction of the heresy, its apparent success in giving rational explanations where the Church proposed mysteries to be believed, its ritual, its exclusivism, its suggestion that the Gnostic was one of an élite—all these might lead many astray. But, upon the institution they deserted for the "knowledge falsely so-called", the theories could make no impression. The tradition was too rooted that the religion of the Church is itself a thing handed down, to be believed on Authority, to be taught by Authority; a religion in which the last word in controversy rests not with learning, but once again, with Authority.

It is the glory of St. Irenæus that his genius stated the anti-Gnostic case in this universal way. His ideas are never new. They are to be found where he too found them—in St. Polycarp of Smyrna (155) and Papias and Hegesippus and the whole line back to the Apostles themselves. But his use of these riches stamped on theology once and for all that traditional character which it still bears. He is not the inventor of the principles which he states, and thanks to the Church's acceptance of which the Gnostic influences fail—the authority of the Rule of Faith and of the Apostolic Succession, the infallibility of the Church and the united episcopate,[1] the special doctrinal authority of the Roman See. But he is the first to set them out for what they are,

---

[1] " We must obey the elders in the Church, who hold the succession from the Apostles . . . who with the episcopal succession have received the sure gift of truth. As for the rest, who are divorced from the principal succession and gather where they will, they are to be held in suspicion, as heretics and evil thinkers, faction makers, swelled-headed, self-pleasing. . . ." (*Adv. Hæreses*, iv, 26, 2.) "It is through the Church that it has been arranged for us to receive what Christ communicates, i.e., the Holy Spirit, the confirmation of our faith and the ladder to mount to God. ' For in the Church,' He says, ' God hath placed Apostles, prophets, teachers (I *Cor*. xii, 28) and all that other working of the Spirit in which none of those share who, instead of hastening to the Church, rob themselves of life by following evil opinions and a wicked way of life. For with the Church is the Spirit of God to be found, and with the Spirit of God there the Church and all grace : the Spirit indeed being truth. Those therefore who share not that Spirit are not nourished in life at the breasts of their mother, nor do they receive of that most pure stream which flows from the body of Christ " (*Adv. Her.*, iii, 24, 1).

the several parts of an amazing whole, and thereby he is the first founder of that treatise *De Ecclesia* fundamental in Catholic Theology.

V. MARCION—MONTANISM

The tableau of the life of the Church in this century of its first contacts with Pagan life and thought is not yet complete. Two more deviations from the Tradition call for record. They are the heresies called, after their founders, Marcionism and Montanism, heresies of quite another spirit than Gnosticism—organised for specific purposes all their own.

Gnosticism tended to make the traditional faith a mere introduction to the final truth of which the Gnostic alone held the key. Marcion was a revolutionary who proposed to reform the Church and to reconstitute it on entirely different foundations— an aim in which he is perhaps Luther's first precursor. That he made his own some of the ideas common to the Gnostic sects is not surprising—they were the common coin of the day's religious life. But it is Marcion's aim which fixes his place in history, and his aim is not the Gnostic ambition to discover the hidden meaning of Christianity, but the practical business of bringing back the Church to its first mission, of restoring to men what alone could save them, the original uncorrupted gospel. This, and not any enthusiasm for a hidden and higher knowledge, motived his dissension. Marcion was born a Catholic, the son of the Bishop of Sinope. He came to Rome round about the year 135, and taught there for some twenty-five years. Valentine the Gnostic and Marcion were thus contemporary celebrities in the Roman Church. In 144 Marcion was excommunicated, but in what precise circumstances we do not know. At the basis of his system is a theory of the radical opposition between the Old and New Testaments, the Law and the Gospels. The Law, harsh and inflexible, was the work of the Creator, an imperfect God to be abandoned now for the Supreme God, God of Love and forgiveness, revealed in Jesus Christ. The Gospel, then, was meant to displace the Law; the New Testament to reverse the Old. Unfortunately the Apostles, through ignorance or prejudice or lack of courage, failed in their task of purging revealed religion from the Old Testament blemishes. Whence the Old Testament ideas which remain in the Church to harass the faithful. To this failure of the Apostles there is however one very notable exception— St. Paul. For St. Paul Marcion has the most extraordinary veneration; and Marcionism is little more, on its dogmatic side, than St. Paul's doctrine of emancipation from the Law exaggerated to caricature. In the light of what he conceived St. Paul to have taught, Marcion revised the New Testament itself. From St. Paul he cast out the "interpolations" made by the Apostle's successful opponents which had masqueraded ever since as St. Paul's own words. All the remaining books he rejected as worthless except his own, amended, version of St. Luke. A book of his own composition—the *Antitheses*—in which he set forth the opposition between the Law and the Gospel completed the Marcionite Bible. A new morality, in which the fashionable notions of the day appear, accompanied the new canon of Holy Scripture. For all believers the most rigorous asceticism was prescribed as of obligation. Fasts are multiplied, abstinence from meat is perpetual, and upon all there lies the obligation of perpetual celibacy. At the end of the world God will leave the wicked to the power of Demiurge the Creator who will, thereupon, devour them.

Marcion showed himself a capable organiser, and, with the Church as his model, he set up a rival Church with a hierarchy and sacramental ritual. The movement met with success, and by the end of the century Marcionite churches were to be found in every province of the empire. Many of the Marcionites suffered death in the persecutions rather than sacrifice to the Pagan deities, and the sect continued to flourish for long after the Catholic Church had become the official religion of the Empire. In the middle of the fifth century the problem of whole villages of Marcionites in his diocese of Cyrrhus occupied the attention of the great Theodoret, and there is mention of them even so late as the tenth century.

With Montanism we move yet further from the spirit which inspired the Gnostics. Here there is nothing of philosophising, nothing of the spirit of hellenic or oriental Paganism. It is a movement where the actors are Catholics, and the action is a revolt against one established institution bred of exaggerating the importance of another—an effort to make private revelation supreme over the official teaching hierarchy. The movement first showed itself about the year 172, in the highlands of central Asia Minor, the neighbourhood of the modern Ancyra. Montanus, a recent convert, a one-time priest, self-mutilated, of the goddess Cybele began to experience "ecstasies", in the midst of which, to the accompaniment of bizarre gesticulations and long drawn out howlings, prophecy poured forth from him and new revelations. The Holy Ghost was speaking. The end of the world was at hand. The new Jerusalem was about to come down upon the earth, where Christ would reign with his elect for a thousand years. It was to come down at Pepusa, to be precise, some two hundred miles away to the east. So to Pepusa went the believers in their thousands; and in the plain soon to be favoured by the miracle a new city of the expectant sprang up. Montanus was there, and his assistants, the chief of whom, a notable novelty of the sect, were two women, Priscilla and Maximilla. Their pious exercises, the frequent ecstasies, with their accompaniment of "mystical" phenomena, served to console the faithful while in patience they waited.

Except for their insistence that through them the Holy Ghost was speaking, the new prophets do not seem at first to have made any innovations in doctrine. In morality they followed the current of contemporary rigorism, with its food taboos and its suspicion of marriage. The main feature of the movement was its belief that the end of the world was at hand. The founders died; the end of the world delayed to come; but the sect still grew, and rapidly; while from all over the Church came protestations—not against prophets as such, nor against the asceticism, but against the novelty that men should claim the authority of the Holy Ghost for things said in ecstasies whose extravagance suggested mania rather, or possession. The most important achievement of Montanism was that in the first years of the third century it made a convert of one of the very greatest of all Christian writers —Tertullian. Finally, in different parts of the Church, bishop after bishop turned to expose and denounce the sect, which thereupon showed itself a sect—for the Montanists preferred their prophets to the bishops. It was in this, precisely, that the novelty of Montanism lay—"its desire to impose private revelations as a supplement to the deposit of faith, and to accredit them by ecstasies and convulsions that were suspect." The action of the bishops seems to have checked the movement's further progress, but in places where it was once established it lasted into the fourth century. Montanists suffered martyrdom with the Catholics, and they survived the attempts of the Catholic Emperors to suppress them. By the sixth century, however, all trace of them has vanished.

The Montanist belief in the Millennium, in the theory that, as a first reward of their fidelity, the saints would reign with Christ for a thousand years upon this earth, was not, however, peculiar to the sect. Its affinity with some of the pre-Christian Jewish theories about the character of the triumph of Messias is evident. Not less evident is its connection with a literal interpretation of the Apocalypse.[1] Within the Church it makes its first appearance in the first years of the second century, with the heretic Cerinthus and with Papias the—orthodox—disciple of St. John. For Cerinthus,

---

[1] xx. 1–6.

and for the later heretical adherents to the belief, the coming reign would be a *vie de Thélème*, where previous asceticism would be rewarded by, amongst other things, a lively carnival of the flesh. The Christians who were Millenarists naturally steered clear of such horrors. What they anticipated was the triumph on earth, in an earthly life, of Christian holiness. Among those who held to this belief were such illustrious writers as St. Justin and St. Irenæus, the latter developing it as an argument against the Gnostic denial of the resurrection of the body. These very writers, however, bear witness that Millenniarism was never the general belief of the Church in their time, and it met with vigorous opposition, at Rome from the priest Caius and in the East from Origen and, especially, from St. Denis of Alexandria. By the time of St. Augustine it had disappeared from the churches of the East, and the great authority of his exposition of the texts in the Apocalypse ended, for ever, whatever hold Millenniarism still possessed in the West. Henceforward, where it does survive it is no more than an eccentricity of heretical sects. [1]

[1] *Cf.* TIXERONT *Hist. des dogmes* vol. I, ch. iv, § 8 ; BARDY, G., art. *Millénarisme* in D.T.C.

CHAPTER IV

THE CRISES OF THE THIRD CENTURY

THE history of the Church in the second century is very largely the history of its first contacts with the Pagan religions of the time. The effect of that meeting is to bring out, ever more clearly, the new religious thing's well defined form. The reaction by which it emerges unchanged—and alone unchanged—from that syncretist century of a hundred religious enthusiasms, is spontaneous. The Church does not find it necessary to add either to its traditional faith, or to the already recognised jurisdiction of its rulers, in order to stem the development within its walls of theories alien to its nature. *Sedet æternumque sedebit*—for such crises was it built. They have been no more than the occasion for its essential nature to show itself in function. They leave the Church no different, save, perhaps, for a clearer consciousness of its own nature and powers. The stress of the century which culminates in the *Adversus Hæreses* of St. Irenæus was due, primarily, to the influence on the Church of forces bred elsewhere. It was an attempt from outside to pull the Church into line with the day's religious fashions. In the century which follows St. Irenæus the crisis is wholly different. Catholics are its authors; and the struggle is one for mastery between the episcopate and individuals who, by reason of their theological skill or of the sacrifices they have made for the faith, claim for themselves and their opinions a deciding voice —as of right—in matters of discipline that involve points of belief.

It is one of the fortunate accidents of the story of the next eighty years (190–270) that these disputes involve the Roman Church, whose history over a continuous period of years is now, for the first time, revealed. As the troubles of the second century are a means to inform us what contemporary Catholics believed about the nature of Catholicism, so those of the third century throw a flood of light for us on the position, already traditional, of the Roman Church within the great whole. They supply a commentary of fact to St. Irenæus' theory, and we are thereby enabled to see at work that superior authority which he noted as the Roman See's peculiar privilege. There is a dispute concerning the calendar, disputes on the explanations of the mysteries of faith, disputes about changes in discipline, and disputes which raise the fundamental question of the relations of the Roman Church to the rest. We meet the first of the anti-popes, and the first schisms in the Roman Church itself. At the same time, thanks to the genius of

Plotinus, a last attempt is made to infuse life into Paganism—
an attempt which is, also, bitterly anti-Christian. A last new
religious revival from the East threatens yet another delay to the
Pagan's realisation that Christianity or nothing is his choice.
At Alexandria one of the greatest geniuses of all time essays a
vast synthesis of philosophy and Christian learning, and founds
a tradition of theology which is to endure for centuries.

I. THE EASTER CONTROVERSY

The actual date of the death and resurrection of Our Lord
formed no part of the Church's traditional faith. From very early
on, the different Churches followed each their own judgment in
the matter. By the end of the second century the majority of the
churches, Rome amongst them, had come to celebrate the
Resurrection on the Sunday which followed the 14th day of the
Jewish month of Nisan. The churches of the Roman province
of Asia (*Asia Proconsularis*) celebrated the commemoration of
Our Lord's death rather than His resurrection, and they kept it
on the 14th of Nisan whether that day fell on a Sunday or not.
This difference of observance was felt as a serious inconvenience;
and, in 154, the pope of the time—Anicetus—made an effort to
win over to the Roman, and more general, practice the bishop
whose prestige might have brought in the rest of the Asiatics,
Polycarp of Smyrna. St. Polycarp, invoking the great name of
the apostle St. John as the source of the Asiatic tradition, would
not be persuaded, and endeavoured in his turn to win over
Anicetus. But Anicetus, too, had his tradition—the tradition of
his predecessors in the Roman See. There the matter rested—the
harmony of charity between the two bishops in no way disturbed.
   In 167 this difference of practice again came to the fore. The
detail of the event is not known, but the Asiatic bishops are found
in that year defending their own tradition, apparently against
an attempt to introduce the more general custom. Twenty-four
or twenty-five years later, however, the question came up once
more, and it speedily developed into a crisis of the first magnitude.
It is unfortunate that we know nothing of the immediate reasons
for the action of the pope of the time, St. Victor I (189–198)
and very little of the order of the events. What is certain is St.
Victor's letter to the Bishop of Ephesus, Polycrates, in which he
bids him call together the bishops of the province of Asia and
secure their consent to the adoption of the Roman practice in
the matter of the celebration of Easter. The pope reminds
Polycrates of the apostolic origin of his see, and, presumably, of
the authority thence deriving. Polycrates called the bishops

together—from his letter to St. Victor we gather such a reunion was without precedent, and only the fact that it was ordered from Rome could have justified him in the innovation. But the bishops of Asia preferred to keep their own tradition, and in the reply of Polycrates we have a curious testimony to the fact that the theories of church government to which St. Irenæus gives expression are not any personal invention of his own. For Polycrates bases the refusal on the grounds of apostolic tradition. His practice is that of apostles too, St. Philip buried at Hierapolis and St. John whose tomb is in his own city. He makes the list of distinguished bishops and martyrs since then, and he pleads "the fixed rule of faith" which forbids innovation in the apostolic tradition. No threats, he declares, will terrify him. Greater men than he have settled the principle on which he must act "It is better to obey God than men." (*Acts* v, 29.)

The issue is simple. Two traditions equally apostolic are in conflict. On what principle shall either prevail ? Rome acted. St. Victor, apparently about the same time that he wrote to Polycrates, had written to other bishops also in the same sense. The letters of several councils of bishops in reply to his survive. They all express their agreement with Rome. "No threats will terrify me," the Bishop of Ephesus had written to the pope, referring no doubt, to some mention in the Roman letter of penalties in case of refusal. Now, by letters to all the churches, St. Victor declared Polycrates and his associates cut off and separated from the Church. It is the first recorded occasion of such disciplinary intervention on the part of the Roman Church, and its action has already all those characteristics which mark it ever afterwards. As against the Roman tradition not even apostolic traditions prevail, not even Philip nor John, since Rome is Peter and Paul.

But the matter did not end with the excommunication of the Asiatics. In more than one church it was felt that Rome had used them harshly, and appeals for a more lenient treatment began to flow in to St. Victor. Among those who pleaded was St. Irenæus himself. He urged that the difference of practice was not of those for which brotherly charity should suffer, and he recalled the previous discussion between St. Polycarp and the pope Anicetus and its happy ending. And he wrote to others besides the Bishop of Rome, rallying opinion to his view of the case. But nowhere is it suggested that the Roman bishop had outstepped his jurisdiction, that the right he was exercising, perhaps somewhat mercilessly, was not really his right. St. Irenæus was as successful in his mediation as in his theology. The pope withdrew the excommunication, and the churches of Asia continued to celebrate Easter in the tradition of St. Philip and St. John.

II.—THE MONARCHIANS—SABELLIUS—ST. HIPPOLYTUS

Of more serious intrinsic importance than this quarrel of liturgical observance was another controversy which began in the reign of this same pope, St. Victor I, and which raged around the divinity of the Second Person of the Divine Trinity, the Logos incarnate in Jesus Christ. The discussions which now began continued at intervals for the first half of the third century. Then, after a peace of fifty years, they revived, and for a good hundred and fifty years more they were the chief feature of the Church's history.

The traditional belief was simple. God is one and there is but one God. Jesus Christ is God, being the incarnate second term of the Divine Trinity, God the Son or Logos. The Logos is nevertheless not the Father. The intelligence of believers, and their piety, continued to meditate and probe these traditional data, always with a hope of better understanding, and with the practical aim of making the tradition seem reasonable to critics from outside. Two questions in the main divided the attention of these theorists, the relation between the human and the divine in Our Lord, and the way in which the divine in Our Lord was divine. This second question had been already discussed by St. Justin. Now it was the turn of the first, and when the theorists, in their efforts to conciliate seemingly contradictory beliefs, stumbled into a denial of the tradition, a school of thinkers arose to set them right who in turn stumbled into errors on the Trinitarian question.

There came to Rome towards the end of the pontificate of Eleutherius (175–189) a wealthy citizen of Byzantium, one Theodotus, by trade a dealer in leather. He had apostatised in a recent persecution, and now sought to hide his shame in the great city. He was less successful, however, than he had hoped; and taxed with his record he retorted that after all, in denying Jesus Christ he had not denied God, for Jesus was but a man, the holiest of men admittedly, upon whom the Christ had descended in the form of a dove when he was baptized in the Jordan by John, but, for all that, no more than a man. To support the theory Theodotus produced a catena of texts from Holy Scripture. The pope, St. Victor I, in 190 excommunicated him, but Theodotus remained obdurate. He gathered round him a number of adherents, and soon was the leader of a sect taken from the most erudite circle of the Roman Church. Logicians, mathematicians, scientists, they used the comparative method and along with their Bibles studied Euclid and Galen and Aristotle. The Church tradition occupied a very small place in their critical labours, where indeed grammar and logic extracted from the Scriptures all they craved to know. How long the sect continued as a sect we do not know. But through one of its members of the second generation, Artemus (fl. 235), its teaching passed to the notorious bishop of Antioch, Paul of Samosata, the friend of that Lucian who was the teacher of Arius and the real father of Arianism.

The theories of Theodotus do not seem to have seriously troubled the peace of the Church, at any rate during his own lifetime. With the contemporary theory which bears the cumbrous name of Patripassian Monarchianism it was far otherwise. The thinkers responsible for this theory were moved by the desire to safeguard the two traditional truths of the unity of God and the real divinity of Jesus Christ, and to refute the suggested contradiction between the two. But their theory only achieved its end by identifying Father and Son, thus sacrificing a third truth of the tradition, namely that the Father and Son are really distinct.[1]

The first to bring this theory to Rome was, according to Tertullian, Praxeas in the closing years of the second century. Thence Praxeas had passed into Africa where Tertullian routed him, and, better still, converted him. Another account makes Smyrna the seat of the heresy's first beginnings and Noetus its founder. From Smyrna, after the excommunication there of Noetus, it came to Rome with one of his disciples, Epigonus, somewhere between 198 and 210. The Monarchists speedily became known, and the theory became the exclusive topic of discussion in the Roman Church. Nor was the cause of truth and peace at all assisted by the presence in Rome of a double opposition to Monarchianism. The Roman Church opposed it for the innovation it was; but, at the same time, it met with opposition of a very different character, the reasoned opposition of a philosopher, from the greatest scholar in the Roman Church, the priest Hippolytus. It was the misfortune of the Roman Church that between its officials and Hippolytus there was soon a war as bitter as that between either of them and the Monarchists. Nor did Hippolytus scruple to charge the official opposition with complicity with the heretics. On the other hand Hippolytus and his followers, in their ingenious defence of one truth, came very near to denying others. The task of the historian is not made easier by the fact that our knowledge of these transactions is due, in the very largest measure, to the writings of St. Hippolytus himself,—written before the saint's reconciliation and martyrdom,

---

[1] Since they professed to uphold at all costs the oneness of the divinity, " the monarchy " as they never tire of calling it, and since they taught, in logical conclusion from their theory, that it was the Father whom Mary conceived and who died for us, the appropriateness of their many-sounding name is evident.

when, the first of all the anti-popes, he was himself leading a schism against the lawful Bishop of Rome.

When Epigonus arrived in Rome to set up his school of Theology, mindful of the condemnation at Smyrna and perhaps knowing of the fate that had befallen Praxeas at the hands of Tertullian, he tempered his zeal with caution. It was his good fortune that the pope St. Zephyrinus (199–217) was an administrator rather than a scholar, and as Epigonus and his chief lieutenant, the more famous Sabellius, showed their belief in the reality of Our Lord's divinity in an instructed attack on the recently condemned Theodotus, they speedily gained a name for orthodoxy and the favour of the pope. But if Zephyrinus, lacking both taste for this theorising and skill in its practice, saw no more in the new party than welcome allies against the Adoptionists, this was by no means the case with Hippolytus. The writings of this great man have most of them perished, but enough remains to show that in him the Roman Church possessed a scholar of an erudition like to that of Origen. With the erudition, there went, alas, an uncomfortable impatience of ignorance in high places, and a genius for rough and bitter language that recall his other contemporary, Tertullian. In the events of the next few years both the learning and the caustic wit of St. Hippolytus were to have every opportunity. He now attacked Sabellius as he had attacked Theodotus; and when the pope refused to endorse the letter of his attacks, refused to make his own the learned theories by which Hippolytus was routing the new heresy, Hippolytus turned to attack the pope. Zephyrinus, however, stood firm. He refused to enter the dangerous ground of the rival philosophical explanations of the tradition, and contented himself with a steady re-affirmation of what had always been believed "I only know one God Who suffered and died, Jesus Christ and beyond Him no other. It is not the Father Who died but the Son."

In 217, while the three-cornered controversy was still raging, Zephyrinus died. He had ruled for nearly twenty years, but during all that time there had been a "power behind the throne", a greater man than himself, on whom, wisely enough, he relied. This was his deacon Calixtus. Calixtus had had an unusually exciting life. Years before, as a slave, he had managed his master's bank. He was unlucky enough to lose his master large sums of money, some of it in bad debts where the debtors were Jews. His efforts to recover from them led to a riot and, the Jews denouncing him as a Christian, he was sent to penal servitude in the mines of Sardinia. About the year 190 he was set free and returned to Italy. The accession of Zephyrinus found him at

Antium, a pensioner of the Roman Church. The new pope brought him back to Rome and ordained him deacon, one of that council of seven who saw to the management of the Roman Church's temporal business. Calixtus was a man of affairs, a practical administrator, and in the influence of Calixtus over his master, Hippolytus saw the reason for the pope's reluctance to condemn Sabellius and the rest in terms of his theory. Hippolytus was, then, already personally hostile to Calixtus when Zephyrinus died. When Calixtus was elected to succeed him, the learned and choleric Hippolytus seceded, accusing Calixtus of Monarchianism, and of holding that the distinction of terms in the Trinity is incompatible with the divine unity.

Hippolytus had a numerous following. They gathered round him and he set up his sect as the true Church in opposition to the "Monarchist" Calixtus. Meanwhile Calixtus had acted. He condemned Sabellius and excommunicated him as an innovator in the traditional belief, but he did not, in so doing, make his own the subtle reasoning by which Hippolytus exposed the heresy and explained the compatibility of the related truths.

That reasoning is indeed subtle, and to distinguish it from the heresy which makes the Logos a second inferior God calls for a philosophical mind and much good will. Nevertheless, although he did not adopt the ideas of Hippolytus, neither did St. Calixtus condemn them.

The schism of Hippolytus—he was never thrust out of the Church but left it himself—continued long after the death of St. Calixtus (222) and of his successor Urban I. In the persecution of Maximin, which was directed mainly against the rulers of the Church, Hippolytus, a confessor now in the mines of Sardinia, found himself the fellow-sufferer of the lawful pope Pontianus (235). There, under what circumstances no record remains, he was reconciled to the power he had so long denied, and the Church honours him among her martyred saints.

III. THE PENITENTIAL CONTROVERSY—ST. CALIXTUS I

The question of Patripassian Monarchianism, or to give it its shorter name Modalism,[1] was not the only controversy in which the pope, St. Calixtus I, was involved. In that controversy he had had for his adversary the subtle, scholarly, and irascible Hippolytus. In the next, which raged round changes in the Church's penitential discipline, his action roused all the bitterness of

---

[1] *Modalism*—because for those who refused to acknowledge the real distinction between the Father and the Son, Father and Son were simply *modes* of the Divine Being.

Tertullian as well. Few men have been called upon to face two such adversaries in a short four years.

Tertullian, at the moment when he composed his bitter attack on St. Calixtus I, was nearing the end of his long and eventful career. He was born at Carthage apparently about the year 160. His father was a centurion, and Tertullian was born and bred a Pagan. It was, however, the Law and not the Army which attracted Tertullian, and it is the Roman lawyer who speaks through all his varied writing. He was converted to Christianity, became a priest of the Church of Carthage, and from 197 he is, for a good quarter of a century, the central figure of literary activity in the Latin Church. Tertullian is always the Roman, sober, practical, contemptuous of philosophy and abstraction. He is, too, always the lawyer, with the lawyer's failing of over-refinement, of quibbling even, in his destructive criticism and in his advocacy. But never was any lawyer less hindered by the dry formalities of his knowledge. For Tertullian's learned advocacy is fired by one of the most passionate of temperaments. Thence results an apologetic of unexampled vigour and violence. Tertullian is master of all the controversial talents, "the most prolific, the most personal of all these Latins", with a gift of apt and biting phrase that sets him side by side with Tacitus himself. Of no man has it ever been truer that the style is the man; and in the works of this convert genius lie the foundations of the theological language of the Latin Church.

Christianity, for Tertullian, is not the crown of all philosophical history, it is not a light to make clear riddles hitherto obscure, but a fact to be proved and a law to be explained and obeyed. Into that explanation he put all the native rigour of his own harsh temperament, all the inflexibility of the civil law in which he was a master. From the chance that it was Tertullian who was the pioneer of the Latin theological language, it gained that tradition of clear cut definition, and the beginnings of that store of terms incapable of any but the one interpretation, which, from the beginning, saved the Western Church centuries of domestic controversy and disputation.

Tertullian's temperament proved, in practice, too much for his logic; and in Montanism his strongly individualistic nature found a home more congenial than the religion of the Church. The Montanist Tertullian spent the last half of his life in reviling the Church as bitterly as he had previously reviled, on its behalf, Pagans and heretics alike. He had been a Catholic perhaps fifteen or sixteen years when Montanism began to seduce his splendid intelligence. Ten years later, when the decree of St. Calixtus roused him to write the *De Pudicitia*, he was a fully-fledged member of the sect, and so great was his influence upon it that, in subsequent years, it was as Tertullianists that the Montanists were known in Africa.

But it was as a Catholic that he wrote the greatest of all his works the *De Praescriptione Hereticorum*—a statement of the old argument which rules heresy out of court unheard, self-condemned, because self-confessed as an innovation. It is St. Irenæus' argument from tradition, but cast this time in legal form, and gaining enormously in power from Tertullian's superb exposition. Other works poured from his versatile mind, his supple mastery of the old Latin tongue bending it to new uses. Instructions for catechumens, apologies addressed to Pagans, ascetical exhortations for the faithful, and everywhere controversy, panegyrics of virginity and of that patience in which, rather touchingly, he notes himself so sadly lacking "Miserrimus ego semper aeger caloribus impatientiae." Perhaps Tertullian's greatest service to the progress of theological science is his exposition of the mysteries in the Divine Trinity. The attempts of all his predecessors in this field, from St. Justin downwards, are easily surpassed; as Tertullian surpasses, too, all later writers until Nicea. More convincingly, and more clearly, than any of them does he argue the eternal divinity of the Logos, His origin from the substance of the Father, His unity of nature with the Father, and His real distinctness from the Father. More clearly than any writer, Greek or Latin, before St. Athanasius, he explains the necessity of belief in the divinity of the Holy Ghost. But it is his exposition of the mutual relations between the Divine Three, and its unembarrassed understanding that there is no conflict between the truths of Their unity and of the Trinity, that is Tertullian's chief glory as a theologian. All his ease of careful analysis finds scope in the distinction he draws between a division of the Divine Substance and its organisation. The resulting terms of that organisation he recognises as spiritual substances, divine in nature; and, first of all writers, he gives them the name *persons*. "Unity of Substance, Trinity of Persons" the classic formula in which the traditional faith finds reasoned expression is of Tertullian's very minting. A hundred years before the event he thus anticipates Nicea, and by his immense influence wherever the Latin tongue prevails, he saves the West from years of subtle controversy and disunion.[1]

That a power to forgive sins, and to reconcile the sinner to God, was left to the Church by its Founder was undoubtedly part of the Tradition from the very beginning. "Whose sins you shall

---

[1] Tertullian was, however, considerably less successful in his theories about the divine generation of the Logos and in his argument to prove the consubstantiality of the Logos with the Father.

forgive they are forgiven them," He had said, "Whose sins you shall retain they are retained," and "Whatsoever you shall bind upon earth shall be bound also in Heaven, whatsoever you shall loose on earth shall be loosed also in Heaven." In St. Paul's letters to the Corinthians we have at least one record of the Apostle's use of his powers. A generation later we can, however, note a tendency to require that the Church be an assembly of saints, from which all who sin after their baptism should be rigorously expelled; a tendency to demand absolute sinlessness as a normal condition of membership. Baptism could not be repeated. Therefore let the baptized be warned. Should they again fall into sin, the Church had no second baptism to raise them a second time. To this ideal the evidence of everyday offered a contradiction of fact. There were Christians who sinned and sinned gravely, and who yet did not fall from their faith in Christ. Did their sins really matter ? Gnostic theories that matter and spirit were independent the one of the other, so that sin, deriving from matter, could not affect spirit, would deny to post-baptismal sin any importance at all. The more prevalent opinion in the Church judged it with the utmost severity. Such literature, of the generations immediately following that of the Apostles, as has survived is filled with evidence of this fact. The tendency is to abolish the distinction between precept and counsel, and to impose both alike, as of obligation, on all Christians. In nothing was the new rigorism more rigorous than in what related to sex. Not only, for such extremists, is virginity preferable to marriage, but marriage itself is considered a bar to sanctity. "There is no resurrection except for such as keep their virginity" one pseudo-Pauline maxim declares. True Christianity implies perpetual virginity. Baptism is equivalent to a vow of chastity. Those who uphold these opinions are the Encratites—never a sect as such, though more than one of the greatest of them ultimately fell away from the Church, but a group whose ideas were for long a feature of public opinion to be constantly reckoned with. Their views on the Church's policy in the matter of forgiving post-baptismal sin were, naturally, extremely rigid.

The Encratite view of things was not, however, the only view to find expression in the second century. There was another school of thought which kept nearer to the spirit of the Gospel. Its chief exponent, in the literature of the time which has come down to us, is the brother of the pope, St. Pius I (140–154), a priest of the Roman Church, Hermas by name. His book—the *Shepherd*—is a popular work, practical not speculative, and its aim is to bring home to the ordinary man the truth that there is always pardon for the sinner who repents—pardon at any rate once. Nor is there any mention of sins so great that they are beyond pardon. The sinner repents and God receives him back. Between the terms of the process a series of actions intervenes. The sinner, turning once more to God, re-enters the Church by acts of penance. But, for Hermas, once and once only is there for the sinner this way of forgiveness. The Encratite current runs too strongly for even Hermas to disregard it. None the less he is a witness, in a question where sources are so scarce as hardly to exist at all, that, in the Roman Church, Encratite theories were viewed with disfavour.

The rigorist reactions from the everyday immorality of Pagan life might carry away the enthusiastic Christian to assail even the lawful use of what he saw so generally abused. Hermas is a witness that not all were carried away, though all perhaps felt the strength of the tide at its full; and that the Roman Church continued to teach that to repentance sin is forgiven.

Between the *Shepherd* of Hermas and the decree of Calixtus I which roused all Tertullian's cantankerousness, there is a period of some seventy years. How the discipline had developed in that time, in some places, can be learnt from a book of Tertullian's written to instruct candidates for Baptism, the *De Penitentia*. With regard to sins committed after Baptism he teaches the same doctrine as Hermas, but without the hesitation which appears in the *Shepherd*. There still remains one more opportunity of pardon, and it is given through an external ritual which Tertullian names —the *Exomologesis*. This is a laborious, public, penitential act, which the repentant sinner voluntarily performs in atonement for his sin. The sin is declared to the bishop, he fixes the nature and the duration of the penance to be performed, and on its completion receives back the sinner into full communion. Tertullian himself describes these penitents, clad in a special dress, living under a rigorous régime of abstinence and fast, ashes on their heads, their bodies uncared for, who kneel at the door of the church beseeching the prayers of the faithful as they pass in to the services.

The Exomologesis lasted a longer or shorter time according to the sin. Of itself it was merely an offering to God in satisfaction for the wrong done. But since the Church associated herself with the penitent who undertook the penance at the bidding of the bishop, the discipline acquired a new value. The intervention of the Church made it "efficacious" for, Tertullian explains, the Church is Christ and His mediation is infallible in its effect. Two last points of Tertullian's description are to be noticed. Pardon is granted through the Exomologesis once only. The sinner who relapses must, thereafter, negotiate his own pardon with the mercy of God. Nor is the Exomologesis available for every kind of sin. Three sins, notably, are excluded—idolatry, murder, and fornication. The Church does not teach that these sins are unforgivable. Merely she will not take it on herself to forgive those who commit them. They may be admitted to the ranks of the penitent, there to remain for the rest of their life. Their penance will avail them much in the sight of God, but the Church does not formally receive them back into her communion.

It was this reservation in the discipline of the Exomologesis that Calixtus I now decided to alter. This particular reservation has no warrant in Scripture, nor does Hermas make any mention of it. In all probability it was an ecclesiastical regulation of the late second century, a special provision provoked, it may be, by some special circumstances of contemporary Pagan morality. Whatever its origin, the restriction added to the severity of the existing discipline which, Tertullian is our witness, was already beginning to defeat its own ends. For very few indeed were they who were prepared to submit to it. Whence a practice of deferring Baptism, and a crop of secret sinners. Those who knelt in sackcloth among the penitents were not, apparently, the only ones guilty of sin. More than one of those at whose knees the penitents besought prayers might fittingly, in his turn, have prostrated himself in the dust.

The system was ceasing to fulfil its purpose, and Calixtus I prepared to modify it. He announced that, henceforward, sin in sexual matters would also be forgiven through the discipline of the Exomologesis. No longer would such sinners be permanently cut off from the Sacraments, but, their penance duly performed, they too would regain their place among the faithful. Whereupon Tertullian, and Hippolytus, attacked the pope bitterly and maliciously.

It is important to notice the grounds Calixtus cites as authority for his action. They are quite simply Our Lord's words to his predecessor Peter " Upon this rock I will build My Church, to thee will I give the keys of the kingdom of heaven, Whatsoever thou shalt bind on earth shall be bound also in heaven, Whatsoever thou shalt loose on earth shall be loosed also in heaven." Calixtus explicitly claims to be the present heir of Peter's prerogative, and on this basis he acts.

IV. THE SCHISM OF NOVATIAN

The edict of Calixtus I marks an important stage in the development of the Church's discipline of penance as we know it. Thirty years later one of his successors, St. Cornelius, developing the reform, brought within the system the sin of apostasy. The action of Calixtus had led to controversy; that of Cornelius provoked a schism.

The persecution of the Emperor Decius, which had just ceased, had been altogether novel in its systematic organisation, thanks to which hardly any Christians escaped the test, save the tiny minority who had means to fly the country. The result was an unprecedented crop of more or less nominal apostasies, and the anomalous situation arose that in many places the majority of the faithful, guilty of a sin the Church refused to pardon, were out of the Church. It had long been the custom—St. Calixtus allows for its action in his decree—that although the Church did not reconcile such apostates through the Exomologesis, she accepted them as reconciled at the intercession of their more steadfast brethren, who in bonds awaited the martyr's death. This custom, owing to the crowds of repentant apostates who now besieged the prisons where the confessors were detained, suddenly threatened to break down the reservation once and for all. If these thousands were to be re-admitted at the prayer of the confessors, how could re-admission be refused any longer to those who sought it by the harder road of the Exomologesis? A further complication arose from the fact that not all these confessors were as docile to authority as they were constant in faith. What authority had allowed as a privilege, some of the confessors now began to claim as a right, and their petitions to the bishops for the reinstatement of the apostates took on more and more the appearance of commands. *Communicet ille cum suis* is a text which St. Cyprian's indignation has preserved. Not only the penitential discipline of the time was shaken, but there were the beginnings of a threat to episcopal authority also. As the bishops in the second century had had to defend the tradition of authority against the usurpation of learning and of private revelation, so now they faced a new menace which would subordinate their authority to the prestige of individual confessors and martyrs.

It was in Africa that the new troubles began, in the Church of Carthage whose bishop at the moment (250) was St. Cyprian. He protested against the threatened subversion of traditional practice. Such sinners were not admitted to receive the Eucharist until, having performed the appointed penance through the Exomologesis, the bishop and his clergy solemnly laid hands on them. Wherefore he forbids his priests to admit apostates to Communion on the simple presentation of the recommendation of a confessor or a martyr, that is to say, without penance done, without the Exomologesis and without the imposition of hands. The act of the martyr is an act of intercession with the bishop —an influential intercession no doubt, but no more than that. This intercessory procedure St. Cyprian proceeds to regulate. There must be no more of the collective notes. The martyr must specify by name the person for whom the indulgence is sought, and the person must be someone really known to him. These petitions the bishop will examine publicly, once peace is restored, and thereupon give his decision in each individual case. An exception is made for the apostate in danger of death whom a martyr has recommended and who cannot await the bishop's decision. Him any priest or deacon may reconcile, receiving the acknowledgement of his sin and imposing hands upon him.

These regulations brought to the surface the latent arrogance of the innovators. One martyr sent to St. Cyprian a notification for the reconciliation of all apostates wherever found. Priests were not wanting to support this new revolt, and soon, in one town after another, riots broke out as the crowds of apostates, armed with their letters from the confessors, besieged the churches demanding re-admission from the local clergy. St. Cyprian reminded the rebels that it is the bishop who rules in the Church, and that episcopal rule is the Church's foundation. Also he wrote to Rome an account of his troubles, explaining his point of view and asking for the Roman Church's support.

The Roman reply was encouraging. It explained that the mode of procedure at Rome was substantially that adopted by St. Cyprian, and it endorsed his contention that the bishop alone had jurisdiction in these matters of discipline.

So far, at Rome, no trouble had arisen from any undue interference of the confessors. In its place another question was beginning to arouse discussion. This was the fundamental question, not of how the apostates should be reconciled, but of whether they should be reconciled at all. Calixtus I thirty years before had inaugurated the practice of receiving repentant adulterers through the Exomologesis. Was it now time to extend the same favour to repentant apostates too ?

The Roman Church, at the moment of St. Cyprian's letter, was without a head, for the pope, St. Fabian, had been arrested and put to death in the January of 250, and the vigilance of the authorities had, so far, prevented the election of a successor. The reply to St. Cyprian had, then, been the letter of the clergy who governed the see during the vacancy. It was actually written by the priest Novatian—at that moment the outstanding personality of Christian Rome. In many ways he recalls St. Hippolytus, though he was cast in a smaller mould than that great man. His surviving writings recall Tertullian in their doctrine and in their manner of exposition. In the history of the development of the philosophical explanation of Revelation Novatian has an important place, and his influence on later thinkers was considerable. He is said to have been harsh in disposition, and is accused of vanity. His elevation to the priesthood had not been universally popular, and the criticism continued now while he held the important position of instructor to the catechumens. In the reply to St. Cyprian Novatian had shown signs of a spirit more rigorous than that implied by the system he described, of a fear that, in absolving the apostate, the Roman Church was losing something of its prestige and strength.

This rigorist spirit was soon to have its opportunity. The persecution ended. The bishops came back to their sees. In Africa a council of bishops adopted St. Cyprian's provisional arrangement as henceforward the permanent law of the Church in the matter. At Rome, after a vacancy of fourteen months, St. Fabian was given a successor, the pope Cornelius (March 5, 251), Novatian had been a candidate, and among his helpers in what we might perhaps call his campaign, were two of St. Cyprian's clergy, excommunicated by him for their share in the revolt of the apostates, and come to Rome to intrigue against him. Novatian was apparently to be the next pope. They joined themselves to him and they shared his disappointment. For Novatian was bitterly disappointed, and with a following among the clergy, the laity and the imprisoned confessors, he now organised a Church of his own and found three bishops to consecrate him. The new sect needed a principle by which to justify its existence. It found it in the question of the treatment of the apostates. Paradoxically, the man whom the envoys of the unreconciled and rebellious apostates of Africa had supported, now declared himself the patron of rigorism. The one point on which Novatian now condemned the Church of Cornelius and of Cyprian was that it offered pardon to the repentant apostates. Novatian not only would refuse them pardon, but, developing his first severity, he denied there was any possibility of their being pardoned at all, no matter what their sorrow, no matter how severe the reparation they made.

The new pope, Cornelius, in the autumn of 251, summoned a council of bishops at Rome—sixty of them. The teaching of Novatian was condemned and, with his supporters, he was expelled from the Church. The policy of St. Cyprian, which the bishops of Africa had already endorsed, was now adopted by the Roman Council too, and thereafter by all the churches of the world.

The Novatian schism, a conflict of personal ambition to some extent, had been much more the product of a conflict between the rigorism of the Christian pharisees and the more merciful tendency of constitutional authority. Something of that rigorist spirit was to be found in every Church, and hence Novatian, beaten at Rome, and disavowed in a series of echoing condemnations throughout the Church, was yet able to organise a strong minority. The Novatian Church had its hierarchy, its sacraments, its churches, its cemeteries. Its existence was legally recognised by Constantine (326) and not until a century later did it lose its last church in Rome. In the East and in Africa it survived even longer, still divided from the Catholic Church by the one belief that to absolve from crimes such as apostasy was beyond the power of the Church, and as late as the beginning of the seventh century it was still a useful occupation for an Alexandrian theologian to write a lengthy treatise *Against the Novatians*.

V. ST. CYPRIAN AND ROME

St. Cyprian, whose co-operation with Rome in the affair of the repentant apostates has been recounted, was at that time, only recently consecrated (248), and his consecration as bishop had followed closely on his conversion. He came apparently of a family socially distinguished, and his own education was of the best. A scholarly distinction and the courtesy of the great gentleman are apparent in all his writings, and in all that we know of his eventful career as Bishop of Carthage. St. Cyprian was of that class of men who are born to rule. The habit of decision, the instinct for responsibility, the courage to lead, all this was St. Cyprian's by nature.

He had hardly been consecrated when the persecution of Decius came to wreck the peace of the Church, and with the persecution the crisis of the confessors and the repentant apostates. He had thought it his duty not to expose himself to arrest, and it was from a secret hiding place that he ruled his flock, encouraging those whom the persecution tried and, to the best of his powers, restraining the excesses of the innovators. With the peace there came the end of the long vacancy in the Roman See, the election of Cornelius, and the schism of Novatian. Towards that schism some of St. Cyprian's own disloyal clergy had worked, and it was but fitting that he should himself be prominent in the work for peace. He checked the schemes of Novatian's envoys at Carthage, and he wrote a memorable appeal to the confessors at Rome who sided with the anti-pope. But his great contribution to the restoration of unity was his treatise *On the Unity of the Church* published at this moment. The subject of this important work is better indicated by an older title it sometimes bore, *De Simplicitate Praelatorum*, i.e. on there being but one bishop in each church— for the Church with whose unity St. Cyprian is concerned, in this work, is not the Catholic Church as a whole, but the local church, and more precisely the local church of Rome.

It has been well said of St. Cyprian that "He was a practical man without any philosophy or theology." He repeats the tradition; he borrows very largely from Tertullian; he writes a highly cultivated Latin; but there is nowhere evidence that he possessed any power of seeing general principles in the learning he had, nor of deducing thence, in his day to day application of it, further general truths. The one subject which he ventures to explore is this question of the Church and its nature. He explores it simply because exploration of it is forced on him by controversies he cannot escape. And it is in the spirit of a practical controversialist, eager to find arguments and confirmation of his policy, that he explores it. The pitfalls to which such a character is exposed, in such a work, are very easy to imagine. St. Cyprian was to experience them in very full measure.

In the *De Unitate Ecclesiae* he pleads for unity in each local church, and, well in the tradition, he finds the only hope of such unity in the obedience of all to the local bishop. Our Lord founded the first Church on one individual, Peter, as a pattern for all time. In each church there should be but one bishop as there was but one Peter. Schism is the sin of sins. To leave the bishop is to leave the Church, and to leave the Church is to leave Christ. Outside the Church there are no sacraments nor any bishops. St. Cyprian's theory, and the arguments by which he supports it, serve his restricted purpose admirably. But beyond the local church there is the whole body, of which the local church is but a part. It is possible, in arguing for the authority of the local bishop, to leave less room than will be needed if the theory is ever to be completed and take in the unity of the Church Universal. It was St. Cyprian's misfortune that he based his pleas for unity on arguments only true in part. The next five years were to make this painfully, almost tragically, clear. St. Cyprian was next to find himself in disagreement with Rome.

The first trouble was with that pope, Cornelius, to assist whom the *De Unitate Ecclesiae* had been written. The priest Felicissimus whom St. Cyprian had excommunicated for his share in the disturbances of the repentant apostates, and who, gone to Rome to appeal, had then become the ally of Novatian, now put in his appeal to Cornelius. St. Cyprian's complaint is that the pope should even listen to so discredited an intriguer. An incidental phrase of his letter witnesses to the important fact that he shared the belief, so far uncontroverted, that in the Church Universal the local Church of Rome had a special place. For St. Cyprian it is *ecclesia principalis* (a phrase which recalls immediately the *potentior principalitas* of St. Irenæus) and the "source from which the unity arises."

Pope Cornelius died in 253. His successor was Stephen I, and with the new pope St. Cyprian had a series of disagreements.

In 254 the bishops of Merida and Leon in Spain were deposed, why we do not know. The affair had apparently caused a certain commotion, for their successors thought it well to seek support in a general confirmation of their rights. So it was that they appealed for recognition to Africa and, at their Autumn meeting, the African bishops confirmed the Spanish sentences and the new elections. But the deposed bishops appealed to Rome, and Rome re-established them ! Of the rights and wrongs of the affair it is not possible to judge, for the documents have long ago perished. We can, however, note the affair as a cause of discord between St. Cyprian and Rome at the very beginning of St. Stephen's pontificate, and we can also note, in connection with it, the appearance of some disturbing new theories in St. Cyprian's theology of Church government. One such theory is that it is for the people to depose bishops who are sinners. They are the judges. Another equally mischievous novelty is the idea that only men of innocent life should be made bishops, because bishops who sin lose the Holy Spirit and all power of order; their prayers are not heard; God no longer ratifies what they do; their sacrifices contaminate those for whom they, are offered.

The next stage in St. Cyprian's development is the affair of the bishop of Arles, Marcian. He was a rigorist of the Novatian type and he refused to give his people the benefit of the new milder discipline in the matter of apostasy. Thereupon he was denounced to Rome, and at Carthage too, as a bishop who had cut himself off from the unity of the Church. It was a suitable occasion for the application of St. Cyprian's theory of deposition. He did not, however, make use of it. Nor did he leave the matter to the bishops of the accused prelate's own province. Instead he wrote to Rome, a most urgent letter. The pope, he urged, should write authoritatively to the bishops of Gaul. It is his duty to maintain the established discipline, the decision of Cornelius. He must depose Marcian and appoint another in his place. And would the pope be good enough to say whom he had appointed as Marcian's successor so that the bishops would know with whom, in future, they must communicate as Bishop of Arles.

St. Cyprian, in his indignation, has forgotten his own theory of the year before. He contradicts it. He is appealing, once more, in the traditional manner to the *potentior principalitas* of the *ecclesia principalis*. A year later and, in conflict with Rome on a question of policy, he once more involves himself in novelties and contradiction.

The subject of the new dispute was the question whether, when persons already baptized by heretics or schismatics were received into the Church, they should be re-baptized. A layman of note raised the question—a very practical one no doubt in the time of religious revival which followed the Decian persecution—and St. Cyprian replied in an elaborate letter. The baptism administered by heretics cannot be of value, he teaches, because the Holy Spirit does not operate outside the one only Church. Later in the year (255) the question was raised at the African bishops' meeting, and the same decision was given in a joint letter to the bishops of Numidia. Despite the authority that inspired the letter the discussion continued. An opposition party revealed itself, quoting against St. Cyprian and his council an older practice. To settle the matter finally a joint meeting of all the bishops of Africa and Numidia was held in the Lent of 256, and the declaration of 255 re-affirmed. St. Cyprian wrote to Rome the news of the council's decision.

Now at Rome, as at Alexandria, the teaching had always been that the baptism of heretics was valid, as it had been the teaching in Africa until about thirty years before St. Cyprian's time. There is reason to believe that the Africans knew the Roman tradition, and it is possible that during the interval between the two African Councils (Autumn 255 and Spring of 256) Rome had declared its mind. St. Cyprian, in that case, would be repeating the procedure of acting independently of Rome, as in the matter of the Spanish bishops, and his letter after the Council of 256 be, not merely an announcement of African policy, but a reply to Pope Stephen's definite declaration that if the rite be duly administered the person of the minister does not affect its validity.

Be that as it may, two facts are certain. First of all, when the African envoys arrived in Rome they found themselves treated as heretics. They were refused communion, refused even hospitality, and the pope refused them a hearing. Cyprian was regarded as the false prophet of a false Christ. The second fact is St. Cyprian's letter. For all his recognition of the *ecclesia principalis*, he writes as though, in this matter, he considered all bishops were equals; as though the administration of baptism was a detail of the local church's domestic life—and if the detail differed from church to church, that was the business of the local church and of the local church alone. To God alone is the local bishop responsible. This is hardly in keeping with the theory of 254 that bishops are to be judged by the people who elected them and, if bad, deposed. St. Cyprian is once again weaving a theory to justify his policy, and weaving it from one day to the next. Another contradiction of his own theory is the declaration, in the letter to Rome, that this question of the validity of baptism is one on which Catholic bishops can differ. In 255 he had explained to Marcian that it is an article of faith !

The letter to Rome is, in its tone, an appeal to an ally. For answer the pope notifies the Bishop of Carthage of the Law and the Tradition and, without any diplomacy, simply bids him observe it. "If therefore anyone shall come to you from any heresy whatsoever, let there be no innovation contrary to what has been handed down, namely that hands be imposed upon them in [sign of] penance." The reply is in the curt legal tone of a power too conscious of its own authority and of the obedience due to it, and too accustomed to receive obedience, to feel any need of argument. To the decision the pope simply added the reference—the already traditional reference—to the first of his predecessors in the Roman See, and to the authority thence deriving to himself. In all this there is nothing new. The one element of novelty, so far, is in St. Cyprian's theories. His action on receipt of the Roman decree adds yet another. He took fire at what he called the pope's "haughtiness, self-contradictions, wandering from the point at issue, his clumsiness and lack of foresight," and at the next meeting of the African bishops (September 1, 256) a joint reply was sent to the pope. "None of us," said St. Cyprian in his opening speech and alluding to the pope, "poses as bishop of bishops . . . each bishop has the right to think for himself and as he is not accountable to any other, so is no bishop accountable to him." The Council unanimously supported St. Cyprian.

Rome proceeded to make known its decision to all the churches. It was no longer a question merely of the correction of the Bishop of Carthage. Rome was hinting at the possible excommunication of dissidents. St. Cyprian began to look round for allies. He found a most devoted one in the Bishop of Cesarea in Cappadocia, Firmilian. Firmilian replied in a letter filled with so violent an invective against the pope that the pious pens of the copyists not infrequently refuse to transcribe it. The unity and the peace of the Church, "unity of faith, unity of truth" are assured facts. They stand in no need of any protection from a supreme judge of controversies. Almost, in the midst of this philippic, Firmilian denies the possibility of differences. The pope is worse than all the heretics, for he deliberately darkens the minds of the repentant heretics who seek light from him. As for the pope's reminder that he is the successor of Peter and therefore the final judge of the tradition, that, for Firmilian, is the crowning mark of St. Stephen's folly and pride.

Rome waited, her relations with the churches of Asia Minor as strained as her relations with Africa. Then, before any action had been taken, on August 2, 257, the pope St. Stephen died. Whether the new pope, Sixtus II, was of a gentler disposition, or whether he thought it wiser not to press the matter to a decision at a moment when the persecution was reviving, the question was left alone. Sixtus and St. Cyprian were friends and the Roman Church in the next year came to the help of Firmilian, whose diocese had suffered much in the Persian invasion. The con- troversy of the three sees had speedily travelled beyond its first issue of the worth of heretical baptism. It had raised the question of the relation between the pope and the episcopate, a thorny question which was to cause trouble again and again in the ensuing centuries, and which was not to be finally solved until the Council of 1870. Little wonder that its appearance in the days of St. Cyprian provoked such a turmoil. Of more im- portance to Church History than the evidence which that turmoil affords as to the real humanity of the great saints, is its witness to the Roman See's habit of ruling; and to the fact that, upon all the questions which the ever-widening discussion involved, it is that decisive Roman interpretation of the tradition, which had occasioned the turmoil, that secures universal acceptance and is taken as the Church's belief. "For with this Church every other Church throughout the world must bring itself to agree."

St. Cyprian, it is not hard to understand why, has been the chosen patron of those in our own times whose ideal is a Catholicism without the Roman Primacy. But so to esteem him is to do him serious injustice. The theological impasse into which, at the end of his career, his untheological mentality led him must be judged in the light of his whole life, the mood which found expression when storms provoked his gallant soul be set side by side with those calmer hours when, free from the necessity to justify a policy, "he recognised in the Roman See an altogether special importance because it is the See of that Apostle upon whom Christ conferred the primacy of apostolic authority."

Eleven months after the pope whom he had opposed, St. Cyprian, too, laid down his life in testimony of his faith, September 14, 258. The *Acta* which relate his trial and martyrdom are well known as among the most moving of all that marvellous literature: his arrest and trial, and exile, his recall and re-arrest, the second trial, its sentence of death and the serene confident beauty of his death. *Galerius Maximus proconsul Cypriano episcopo dixit: Tu es Thascius Cyprianus? Cyprianus episcopus respondit: Ego sum. . . . Iusserunt te sacratissimi imperatores caerimoniari. Cyprianus episcopus dixit: Non facio. Galerius Maximus ait: Consule tibi. Cyprianus episcopus respondit: Fac quod tibi praecep- tum est: in re tam iusta nulla est consultatio.* Then the proconsul most reluctantly, *vix et aegre*, lectured him as is the custom for judges with the man they must condemn. *Et his dictis decretum ex tabella recitavit: Thascium Cyprianum gladio animadverti placet. Cyprianus episcopus dixit: Deo Gratias.* He was led to the place of execution. He set off his outer garment, bade his servants give the executioner his alms, five and twenty pieces of gold. He bound himself his eyes, and his deacons bound his hands. "*Ita beatus Cyprianus passus est* . . . the eighteenth day before the Kalends of October, under the Emperors Valerian and Gallienus but in the reign of Our Lord Jesus Christ, to Whom honour and glory for ever and ever Amen."

The Roman Church, embodying the memory of her greatest names in the very heart of her active life, has written them into the consecration prayer of the Mass, and along with the names of these ancient popes, that of the great Bishop of Carthage who, on earth, sometimes opposed them.

VI. THE SCHOOL OF ALEXANDRIA—ORIGEN

Alexandria, in the third century, was still the intellectual capital of the Roman world. Thanks to its great library and the marvellous scientific organisation of the Museum, the city never failed to draw to itself leading thinkers of every kind of learning. It had been the centre of the learned Judaeo-Hellenic speculation associated ever after with the name of Philo; from Alexandria, too, had come many of the leading Gnostics—Valentine certainly, and Cerdon who was responsible for the Gnostic element in the theology of Marcion. It was in Alexandria, too, that the effort of philosophy to replace the Hellenistic religions as interpreter of the riddle of life now reached its full perfection. The thinkers who now built from it a kind of Hellenistic theology and mysticism were three, Ammonius Saccas (*d.* 242), Plotinus (*d.* 270) and Porphyry (*d.* 304).

Their system is Neo-Platonism properly so called. Ammonius Saccas, an Alexandrian labourer, is known chiefly by the work of Plotinus, his pupil, for, if he himself wrote at all, his works have all perished. Plotinus, also an Egyptian by birth, left Alexandria for Rome after the death of his master. There he lectured and taught for the next twenty years—the élite of the world capital filling his rooms, the Emperor Gallienus among his audience—but not until the last few years of his life did he commit his ideas to writing. As Plotinus developed Ammonius Saccas, so Porphyry, his own confidential pupil, arranged and systematised the teaching of Plotinus. But Plotinus is the real founder of the new faith and its principal saint. That faith was not, of course, anything so simple as the mere revival of a cult of Plato's philosophy. The spirit of syncretism, powerful for three centuries and more everywhere, except in the domain of the Church's tradition, showed itself very apparently in Neo-Platonism. Plato's ideas found a place in it, but so, too, did those of the Stoic Zeno, of

Pythagoras, of Aristotle, and of Philo. Finally there was the influence of the Gnostic movement, with all its strange amalgam of oriental ideas and Gnostically interpreted Christian traditions. Out of these elements the genius of the Neo-Platonists, during the third century, devised their system.

These Neo-Platonists were, however, very far from desiring any reconciliation of philosophy with the religion of the Church. On the contrary the movement was markedly hostile to the Church; Porphyry, amongst his other works, writing classical antiquity's masterpiece of anti-Christian polemic—a great work in fifteen books of which, however, only a few pages have survived. Anti-Catholic might be a truer description than anti-Christian, for Porphyry shows great reverence for the memory and character of Our Lord; and his attack, on the lines of the familiar modern historical criticism of the gospels, is directed rather against what he considered the influence of St. Paul. Porphyry lived to see the last of the persecutions in full swing; and it was the Neo-Platonist movement which, in more than one important instance, lent the illiterate and uncouth Galerius, who was that persecution's real author, a logical excuse for his hate and something of a system in his pursuit of it.

Neo-Platonism, in itself a vaguely rational justification of religious sentiment, with a worked out scheme relating the fundamental problems of the nature of God, the creation of man and man's destiny, and offering to man the chance of recovery, of a gradual ascent by increase of knowledge to the actual vision of God Himself, could scarcely ever have progressed beyond the élite of a small philosophical school But, by an ingenious exegesis of the mythologies, this religious idealism was combined with the old classical Paganism, all of whose rites and practices found in the new system an allegorical interpretation to sanction them. This sagacious combination met with much success. It helped once more to its feet the religion so often condemned to die since the days of Euripides; and whatever hold these ancient beliefs maintained for the next three centuries on the allegiance of the intelligent, can be set to the credit of the system which had at last given them a philosophical setting, something even of a body of doctrine, and which was offering to their devotees a way to heaven even in this life of earth. Of the movement's influence on the Church much must be said, but in dealing with a later period of the Church's history. The harm it did the Church of the third and fourth centuries was that, as an attractive will-o'-the-wisp, it distracted from their real goal those who anxiously sought for truth, and that it armed the fiercest of the Church's persecutors. But in a later age, through the genius of St. Augustine, and

through the writer who passed, for centuries, as Denis the Areo-
pagite, more than one idea that derived through Plotinus entered
into the service of Catholic theology and Catholic mysticism.

Of the first introduction of the Church into Egypt we know
nothing. The legend of the foundation of the see of Alexandria
by St. Mark was, apparently, unknown even to Alexandrians
before the fourth century; and except for the names of the handful
of Alexandrian Gnostics, all that we know of the Egyptian
Churches before the end of the second century is a list of bishops
of Alexandria that goes back to A.D. 61. It is only in the last
twenty years of the second century that the darkness lifts, and it
lifts to reveal to us the existence at Alexandria of a flourishing
school of Christian culture under the guidance of Pantenus.

The writings of this doctor of the Alexandrian Church have
perished. That he was a convert from Stoicism, and that before
setting up at Alexandria he had shared in the evangelisation of
"the Indians," and that among his pupils were Alexander, later
bishop in Cappadocia, and Titus Flavius Clemens who succeeded
him in the direction of the school, is the sum of our information
regarding him. For these scanty data it is to that successor that
we are indebted. Titus Flavius Clemens—Clement of Alexandria
—unlike the master to whom he owed so much and whom he so
greatly venerated, is very well known to us, is in fact one of the
best known, as he is one of the most lovable personages of the
Church's early history. His work at Alexandria, and the work of
the genius who was first his pupil there and then his successor—
Origen, was to exercise an influence far beyond the local church
that bore them to the faith. It was to be a leading influence in
Western theology until the time of St. Augustine, and to give to
the theology of the Eastern Church an orientation and a spirit
which it has perhaps never lost. Also this Alexandrian theology,
like its two great teachers, was to be a sign of contradiction among
Catholics for all time—contradiction always sufficiently lively
to be a barrier to any official recognition of the sanctity of the two
pioneers of the Church's systematic theology. Neither Clement
of Alexandria nor Origen, for all their heroic life, are invoked
as saints or enrolled among the Doctors of the Church.

Clement was born in Athens, probably about 150, a Pagan.
We are ignorant of what brought him to the faith, but he has
himself listed the different influences which, after his conversion,
perfected the formation of his Christian culture. He names a
Greek of Ionia, another of Greater Greece, a Syrian, an Egyptian,
an Assyrian and a Palestinian convert from Judaism. Then he met
Pantenus, and with him found his vocation in the explanation to
educated Catholics of the religion they professed. To the lecture

rooms of the school in Alexandria came a varied and distinguished audience, of men and women alike, drawn from the leisured and educated classes of the Church. Clement, now a priest of the Alexandrian Church, set their Faith before them scientifically. Like himself, they were, the most of them, converts from Paganism. He showed them, with all his own rich knowledge of Paganism, the world they had gained in comparison with what they had given up. At every turn he cites the treasures of that ancient culture, in which they had been bred. Its poets, its philosophers, its orators—he knows them all, and in his instructions the appropriate citation from them is always to hand. Like St. Justin he is optimistic in his view of the Pagan culture and the pre-Christian philosophies. Both have in them a vast amount of good; both rightly used can greatly assist the instructed Christian; the religion revealed to the Church is, yet once again, the crown of truth naturally known.

This cultured critique of Paganism, none the less effective for its sympathy with the Pagan's craving for certitude and security, is only one part of Clement's mission. He shows himself—this man driven by his nature to teach—equally enthusiastic, equally cultured, equally painstaking in his elaborate instructions on the life the Christian should lead. Not a single occupation of the day, not one of the phases of that sophisticated civilisation escapes him. His audience is made up of that immense majority of human beings who are tied to the life of the city by a hundred obligations. They cannot, if they would, leave the world for the desert. Clement proposes to teach them how to remain in the world and yet be perfect Christians. It is a little the mission of St. Francis de Sales fourteen hundred years later, in a civilisation so very different, and where yet human nature is so very much the same, and tried in the same way. And it is in the same spirit of cultured optimism that Clement too, priest here as well as philosopher, directs his hearers.

Finally Clement is a theologian, using his trained mind to develop the data of the traditional belief. As a theologian he knows, and respects, and makes much of "the fixed rule of the tradition." He proclaims himself as heir of the ancients from whom he learnt the Faith in the days before he met Pantenus, and is careful to note that what they taught was valuable because they had received it from the Apostles, from Peter and Paul, John and James. Peter is "the chosen one, the elect, the first of the disciples for whom alone the Saviour paid the tribute money," and so attached is Clement to Peter's prestige that he will not have it that it was Peter the Apostle whom St. Paul "resisted to his face" at Antioch. That unfortunate was another Peter, one of the seventy-two disciples ! It is from the Apostles, again, that bishops derive the authority by which they rule. Of all doctrines the Church's doctrine is to be preferred, because it is traditional. It is the rôle of Philosophy to prepare the mind to receive this doctrine, and it is on the basis of this doctrine that Clement proposes to build what is, for him, the crown of the Christian's achievement, the perfect knowledge (Gnosis) to which only the perfect Christian attains.

This superstructure, or rather Clement's view of its nature, goes beyond what the Church had ever taught. It is Clement's personal (and erroneous) contribution to the theology of man's knowledge of God. But, even for Clement, it depends for whatever truth it can claim to possess on the previous acceptance of the Church's traditional teaching. The point is important, for Clement, so often claimed as a "liberal protestant," born seventeen hundred years before his time, is a Catholic as his very mistakes clearly prove. He shares the common Alexandrian fault of an over-fondness for allegorising the meaning of Sacred Scripture, and, more seriously still, in his eagerness to discover the traditional teaching in his beloved philosophers (the Trinity, for example, in Plato) he runs the risk of deforming it. Again, though his division of practising Christians into two classes, those who live by faith and those raised to knowledge, might accord with the traditional distinction between life according to precept and life according to counsel, Clement's introduction of the Platonic idea that the possession of knowledge adds, of itself, to moral perfection opens the way to all manner of error. In the same spirit of optimism he introduces into his moral teaching a canonisation of what it is hard to distinguish from the Stoic virtue of indifference (*apatheia*).

Clement guided the school at Alexandria for more than twenty years. In the persecution of 202 he made his way to Cappadocia where his friend Alexander was now bishop, and when Alexander was imprisoned administered the see for him. The last record of him is a letter from Alexander, written in 215, which speaks of him as dead. That letter is addressed to Clement's one time pupil, Origen, now himself in turn director of the theological school. To have formed Origen is perhaps Clement's chief title to fame.

Origen, born 185, was Christian from his birth, the child of parents who lived only for their faith. Unlike Clement in this, he was unlike him, too, in race; for Origen, to all appearance, was of the native Egyptian stock. He was still a student when his father was martyred (202). The sentence entailed the confiscation of the family property, and the youth began his career as a teacher to help to keep his mother and her numerous family.

When Clement fled to Cesarea, Origen took his place as director of the theological school. The heroism to which Origen was so movingly to exhort his contemporaries, was, from his childhood, the daily affair of his life. It was about this time, too, that in an heroic misunderstanding of the Gospel text, Origen submitted to the famous mutilation which was later to form the technical justification for his dismissal from the school. Like Clement, and like St. Justin before him, Origen was not content with what chances of achieving wisdom he found at home. He travelled much. Greece, Palestine, Arabia, Antioch, Nicomedia, Rome —he had seen them all and was familiar with what each had to offer the scholar. To defend the faith against its critics he must know what the critics themselves believed, and so he spent years in the schools of the leading philosophers, and notably of Ammonius Saccas. His zeal for the study of the Bible drove him to the original texts and to learn Hebrew. He became known as the most learned of all the Christians, and it was to him that the learning-loving mother of the Emperor Alexander Severus applied for instruction as to the Church's teaching.

He was ordained priest in Palestine by a bishop other than his own, and upon his return home was solemnly deposed by the Bishop of Alexandria, and deprived of his position in the school. He betook himself to the friendly bishop who had ordained him, and thenceforward Caesarea, in Palestine, was his headquarters until in 235, driven by the persecution of Maximin, he made his way to Cappadocia. In the persecution of Decius he was arrested, imprisoned and tortured. Four years later—254—he died at Tyre. He had been for forty years the wonder of the Christian world, the oracle universally consulted on points of doctrine and of practice. His knowledge, his logic, his eloquence knew no equal, and his amazing genius was set in a life of ascetic detachment and humility.

His erudition, and his industry, were indeed immense, and its output reckoned at six thousand volumes—an enormous total even when the slender possibilities of the "book" as the ancients knew it are borne in mind. More important even than the erudition and the industry was the systematic fashion of its exposition. The learning of Clement—so far as it found expression in writing —lacks all order. It resembles only too faithfully the meadow to which he himself compared it—where all things grow and, if sought, are ultimately found. St. Justin, Tertullian, St. Hippolytus had each of them, for the purpose of his own particular controversy, used secular learning to explain and defend the tradition. But beyond the defence of special points there was as yet no Catholic Theology. The only syntheses which claimed to set out a rational orderly exposition of religious truth, from the first movements of the Divine Life *ad extra* down to the last destiny of created things, were the Gnostic systems. It is Origen's chief title to fame that, first of all Christian scholars, he set himself to construct a vast synthesis in which the many sided truths of the traditional faith should be displayed in all their related harmony. Much of that work has perished. Enough remains to make very clear the reason of the admiring veneration with which his contemporaries regarded him.

In Scripture, besides a great mass of commentaries which covered every book of the Bible, he published that stupendous instrument of textual scholarship, the Hexapla. Here were set out, in six parallel columns, four Greek versions and two Hebrew versions of the Old Testament in an endeavour to ascertain the value of the Septuagint text. Then, as an apologist, he wrote the eight books *Against Celsus*, the most perfect apologetic work of the primitive Church, in answer to the mightiest attack on Christianity that Paganism ever produced. His theological reputation depends chiefly, however, on his Summa, the *Book of Principles (Perí Archôn)*. Here, for the first time, a Christian writer, with no preoccupation with controversy to influence the order of his work or his style, endeavours to explain systematically the whole body of the tradition. That the technical language of theological science was as yet too undeveloped—to say nothing of the notion of Theology as a science—to make success possible, does not detract from the glory of the pioneer. Faults, and serious faults, were in the circumstances inevitable; and the product of Origen's mighty erudition was, in the centuries that followed his death, to be more than once the occasion of controversies that aroused the whole Church. Nor are Catholic scholars at one, even to-day, in their opinion of Origen's orthodoxy on many points. But of the genius which places him near to St. Augustine himself, of the encyclopædic learning, of Origen's real holiness of life and of his constancy in the presence of persecution, there has never been any question. In his own lifetime, for all the misunderstanding between himself and the Bishop of Alexandria, there was never any condemnation of his theories. He died venerated by all the Catholicism of his time. But almost from the moment of his death discussion began, and presently from one quarter and another condemnations began to shower upon his work—though never were any made of the man himself.

The gibe of Celsus—and of contemporary Paganism generally—that the Church has no message for any but the illiterate, Origen turns against its authors. The truth of the faith is capable of scientific proof in the Greek manner, and the Christian gladly makes use of other knowledge to explain and prove his Christianity. "The disciples of the philosophers say that Geometry, Music, Grammar, Rhetoric, Astronomy are the born companions of Philosophy. We say the same thing of Philosophy itself with regard to Christianity." Nowhere in all this early Christian literature is there a keener realisation of the beauty and the value of the Pagan culture, nowhere a greater confidence in its rôle of pedagogue to bring the Pagan mind to Christ. Not that, for Origen, the religion of the Church is merely a matter of philosophy, of principle and conclusion. It is for him as for his predecessors a thing revealed, "the model made over to the Churches," and the true prophets of Christ are they who teach the word "as the Church." The test by which he would have his hearers distinguish the true exposition of Christ's teaching from the false is the ancient one—"Make use of the Church's preaching handed down by the Apostles through the order of succession, which still to this day remains in the churches. That alone is to be believed as true, which, in every way, accords with the tradition of the Church and the Apostles."

To this tradition all else, even that pursuit of a deeper knowledge which Origen, following Clement, acclaims as a Christian's noblest virtue, is subject. To the primacy of the Church's traditional teaching, even the Hellenic culture must yield. There is no place in the Church for contrary philosophies, and to attempt to introduce them is criminal. *Hoc fecit infelix Valentinus, et Basilides, hoc fecit et Marcion haereticus.* The schools where these men expound their personal interpretations are no better than brothels. *Haeretici aedificant lupanar in omni via, ut puta magister de officina Valentini, magister de coetu Basilidis, magister de tabernaculo Marcionis.* The Church has its rulers the bishops. Not all of them, he notes, are models. "At times we surpass in pride the wicked princes of the heathens. A little more of it and we, too, shall have our bodyguard like the King. Terror walks in our wake. We live apart, inaccessible to all—and especially to the poor. To those who petition us we are haughtier than any tyrant, than even the most cruel of kings. Such is the state of things in many a famous church, especially in the churches of our greatest cities." Origen knows then what a bad bishop can be. He is not thereby confused as to the place of the bishop in the Church. The bishop is sovereign over clergy and laity alike. As he has the power to offer sacrifice, so he has the power to rule and to expel unworthy members for the safety of the whole body. Finally the bishop is the teacher. Origen makes much of the possession of knowledge as itself a virtue, and the perfect Christian is the instructed Christian, the Christian who "knows", Origen's "gnostic." Logically he makes much, also, of the Church's learned men, *doctores ecclesiae*, of whom he is proud to be one. But the final word, yet once again, is not with individual learning but with authority. In doctrine, as in morals, the bishops are the judge of what is in conformity with the tradition.

The Church's teaching is, then, the starting point of Origen's exposition. He notes that while some truths are taught as certain, others are to some extent matters for discussion. The traditional teaching of the Church is completed by the study of Sacred Scripture and of Philosophy. Origen is perhaps the most scriptural of all theologians. It is to Scripture he goes for the solution of all his problems; and Scripture for him had three meanings, the literal; the moral—that is, the meaning useful for the spiritual welfare of the soul; and finally the "spiritual"—that is, the allegory which contains a doctrine about the relation of God to His universe. Origen by no means ignores or discounts the literal sense, but it is the allegory of the moral and spiritual interpretations which most attract this great Alexandrian, as it had attracted Alexandrian Judaism centuries before him.

He is not so enthusiastic as Clement, his master, in the employment of Philosophy as an auxiliary, despite his enthusiasm for Philosophy. He does not so much use philosophical data to explain Christian doctrine, to accredit it with the Pagan world, but rather, in his theological exposition, he thinks like a philosopher. The philosopher, the enthusiast for Greek learning, is revealed in the spirit of his work rather than in the presence there of any definite philosophical teaching. For all the time Origen spent in the schools of Ammonius Saccas, he cannot be claimed as a neo-Platonist. God is one, incomprehensible, impassible; and in this unity there are the three hypostases Father, Son and Holy Ghost. The second term of this Trinity, the Son or Logos, is God, yet distinct from the Father, begotten from all eternity. "There never was a time when the Son was not," he said, refuting Arius a century before that heretical Alexandrian appeared; and the Son is of the [same] substance as the Father—the Nicene teaching and even, perhaps, the Nicene formula *homoöusion*.

So far, on these fundamental points, Origen is undoubtedly orthodox; but the faulty terminology of some of his *obiter dicta* led later to the suspicion that, in the matter of the relation of the Son to the Father, he taught a subordinationist theory. Like the Apologists who preceded him, he relates the generation of the Logos to the creation, and, a very serious error, he teaches a theory of eternal creation—there never was a time, according to Origen, when there were no creatures, God's omnipotence being eternal. Here Origen's speculation leads him to the theories for which, in the centuries ahead, he was to be most savagely attacked. For the subject of this eternal creation is the world of spirits, created equal in gifts and powers and endowed with free will. From the varying degrees in which, at the moment of trial, they were faithful to the Creator there have resulted all the subsequent inequalities of the Universe, moral and physical. Of the original spirits some became angels, the hierarchy of heavenly powers; others, the sun, moon and stars; others, the souls of men; and yet others, the demons. No term has been set to this evolution, and according to their conduct it is in the power of all spirits to regain the height from which they have fallen, and, in another world which will come into being upon the consummation of this present world, to work out their new destinies. The spirits who, in greater or less degree, fell in the hour of trial are provided with bodies of one kind or another—even the angels have a body of a "subtle" kind—and in that union of body and soul they expiate their sin and work out their salvation. But not through their own efforts alone are they saved. They are assisted by the intervention of the Logos, Who to that end, finally Himself became incarnate, uniting Himself first to a human soul and thereby to a human body.

Jesus Christ, the Logos became man; He is then really man and really God. The redeeming death of Jesus Christ was universal in its effect, profiting not only men, but all reasonable beings wheresoever found. That this treasury may be his, however, man must co-operate with God Who offers it to him. God's help is essential, a *sine qua non*, but even this is powerless unless by act and will man co-operates. One form of God's help is the gift of Faith. Another is the higher gift of knowledge (*gnosis*). "It is much better to be convinced of our teaching by reason and knowledge than by simple faith," and Origen—though not so enthusiastically as Clement—divides the faithful into two classes according to this principle. The Christian who is "gnostic" has greater obligations. He should live austerely, practising continency, preserving virginity and living apart from the world.

After death there is the life to come, and, for most men, a certain purification *in quodam eruditionis loco*, through a baptism of fire. The less a man has to expiate the less will he suffer. Heaven is the full revelation of the mysteries of God and union with Christ. The old apocalyptic notion of an actual material kingdom of Christ on earth where with His saints he will reign for a thousand years Origen rejects, as he rejects the theories of the transmigration of souls. The wicked will be punished by fire—a special kind of fire for each individual, bred of his own individual wickedness. Will this punishment last eternally?

Here Origen hesitates, and except for some of the fallen angels, teaches that in the end all God's intelligent creation will be reconciled to Him. Not all will enjoy the same degree of happiness, but all will be happy in some degree.

The premises on which the vast system is based are excellent. But along with all the vast learning, and the deep thought, that produces the system, there is an amazing amount of rash conjecture and of unproved assertion. Origen is indeed "like some great river in flood, which in its very abundance, brings down together the rich fertilising mud and the sand whence comes sterility." And in this great synthesis there is one thing lacking. Nowhere does Origen, *ex professo*, discuss the nature of the Church itself. For good or for ill, however, he was to dominate all theological development until St. Augustine, and in the East until long after. Even his opponents were obliged, in their fight against his influence, to use his learning and to copy his methods. St. Athanasius, St. Basil, St. Gregory Nazianzen, the champions of Catholicism in the doctrinal controversies of the next century, are all his pupils; for if there descended from him to the theology of the Greek-speaking Church a looseness and a vagueness from which the West was preserved, that same Church more than once found in Origen the best of defences against the speculations of heresy.

VII. MITHRAISM

Before we come to the final discussions which bring this century of controversy and crisis to an end, something must be said of yet another ancient religion from the East which, by now, was racing for the primacy of popularity. This was the cult of Mithra.

Mithra, originally, in the religion of ancient Persia is the god of Light. In the religion of the Avesta he is a god of the second rank, the judge of the dead, the god who keeps men to their promises, the god of Honour then, and especially of military honour. He sees all things and the Sun is his eye. With the fourth century B.C. the cult spread to Chaldea, and Chaldean astrological theologies influenced it, working out an identity between Mithra and the Sun God. About the same time Alexander's conquest of Persia brought Mithraism into relation with the Greek mythology, and thence derived a more æsthetic interpretation of the rites and the myth. Finally the later Roman conquest of the East opened to the cult the whole of the West, and from the end of the first century (A.D.) Mithraism was a settled religion in the West and rapidly developing. Merchants and oriental slaves took it to all the ports of the western world, but the chief agent of its spread was undoubtedly the army, and with the legionaries it soon travelled to the very frontiers. As a religion it has its foundation in the great eastern theory of the dual origin of all reality. To fight the evil principle, beings are created intermediary between God and man. Mithra is one of these heroes and gradually, as the theories develop, he comes to eclipse all the other heroes, and even the transcendent divinity, as the God of Light and the protector of mankind.

The culminating point of the Mithra legend is his victorious conflict with the bull, and from the slain bull flows all life and all usefulness. Finally Mithra ascends to Heaven in a fiery chariot driven by the Sun. He will, however, return once more. There will be a second slaying of the bull, whence will come immortality for the faithful, and then a general conflagration will destroy the wicked, the demons, and the principle of evil, Ahriman himself.

The cult was organised in circles of restricted membership which divided and sub-divided as their members increased. It had an elaborate liturgy in which ablutions, an anointing with honey, fasts, and a ritual banquet of bread and water played their part. The initiation was through seven degrees, animals were sacrificed, and the candidate was received through a baptism of blood which poured from the bull slain above him. The meetings took place in caves, and crypts built to resemble caves, decorated with pictures of Mithra slaying the bull. The weekly holy day, naturally, was Sunday and, equally naturally, the Equinoxes were regarded as a sacred season, and the date of Mithra's birth, placed at the winter solstice—December 25.

That the cult was immensely popular with the army there is no doubt, nor of its influence in the third century. But that it ever threatened the future victory of Christianity is a matter infinitely less certain. It has, however, been the subject of much loose thinking, as has been also the question of the analogies between Mithraism and the religion of the Church. Fr. Martindale[1] summarises the position very fairly, setting side by side M. Salomon Reinach's neatly phrased thesis and the no less skilfully worded examination of Père Lagrange. "M. Salomon Reinach thus sums it up: 'Mithra is the mediator between God and man; he secures salvation to mankind by a sacrifice; the cult includes baptism, communion, fasts; his disciples call themselves brothers; in the Mithraist clergy there are men and women vowed to celibacy; there is a moral code which is of obligation and which is identical with that of Christianity.' We have here a series of scornful affirmations to which Père Lagrange can oppose another series of flat denials. 'The fasts and the brotherhood we

[1] *Christus*, pp. 532–4.

can admit—and they are found in every religion that ever was. Everything else is incorrect. Mithra is called 'mediator' once—in Plutarch, and he is mediator between the God of Goodness and the God of Evil. We have no knowledge of any direct relation between the sacrifice of the bull and salvation. Nor is Mithra ever sacrificed, as was Jesus. The Mithraist baptism is a simple ablution in no way different from any other; the communion is nothing more than an offering of bread and water, nor can anyone say it was even intended to represent Mithra; women, usually, had no part in the mysteries of Mithra and could not, therefore, have been there dedicated to celibacy . . . as to men, in that respect, we know nothing except for a single text of Tertullian . . . a text which has been misinterpreted. Every moral code sets out to be obligatory, more or less, and if that of Mithra was identical with the Christian code why did Julian the Apostate—himself a devotee of Mithra—recommend the Christian code as a model to Pagans?'"

VIII. THE MANICHEES

It was in this third century, critical in so many ways for Christianity, that a new religion began to be preached which, although proscribed everywhere from its very first appearance, did not cease to trouble the peace of the world for another thousand years. This was that famous Manicheeism which Christians and Mohammedans, Pagan emperors of Rome and Chinese mandarins, all in their turn repressed with all possible severity. It was a cult that very soon disappeared from sight indeed, but it persisted as the strongest religious undergrowth of all time; and it would be a bold assertion to say that we have yet heard the last of it. There are few features of the general history of the Church better known than its persistent struggle against the Manichees—the Bougres, Cathari, Albigenses of the Middle Ages—and yet it is only within the last twelve years that we have had any truly reliable information about the origins of the sect and about its founder.[1]

Mani, a Persian by birth, set himself to found a new religion which should contain all the religious wisdom hitherto known. In this conscious and ambitious syncretist, that long drawn out

---

[1] *Cf.* P. ALFARIC *Les Ecritures Manichéenes* 2 vols. Paris 1918.
   F. C. BURKITT *The Religion of the Manichees.* Cambridge 1925.
   C. SCHMIDT *Neue Originalquellen des Manichaismus aus Ægypten.* Stuttgart 1933.
   J. LEBRETON *Gnosticism, Marcionism, Manichœism* in *Studies in Comparative Religions* (edit. E. C. Messenger, London 1934) is a good popular account written by a specialist.

business comes to its final perfection. Mani is the contemporary of those imperial patrons of syncretism, Heliogabalus and Alexander Severus, and in the years during which they enthroned the Syrian influences at Rome, Mani, from the other side of Syria, made the long pilgrimage still further to the East, in his search for yet more religious wisdom, to India and to the Buddhists.

For Mani, there had been, in the career he had chosen, three great practitioners already, Our Lord, Zoroaster, and Buddha, three interpreters of a single wisdom. They had only preached: Mani would also write, and so secure for "my religion" a world empire such as no religion had so far known. The time was indeed to come when it would, for a time, win over the great intelligence of St. Augustine in Africa, and gain a real hold as far to the east as China. And the main arm of its propaganda would be the book, and its illustrations.

There is something of Montanism in the new religion, for Mani declares himself to be one body and spirit with the Paraclete, the spirit sent by Jesus Christ. At the same time it embodies a mythological doctrine about the origin of the universe which is akin to that of such Gnostics of the previous century as Basilidie's and Valentine. And Mani owes much to Marcion also.

In this new amalgam, the existence of two first principles of all things—the good and the bad—is all important, for around the unending struggle of the good god and the bad god everything else turns. This the key to the whole system, as it is the key to Mani's explanation of the universe.

The ascetic ideal was pitched high—so high, indeed, that the sect was divided into the Perfect, bound to practice what it was the unforgiveable sin to fail in even once, and the Hearers, who accepted the ideal indeed but, fearful of their ability to live up to it, put off their reception until the last hour of life. The seeming simplicity with which the theory of a dual first principle solved the torturing riddle of the existence of evil, the stiff ascetic ideals, and the spectacle of the life of the Perfect, fascinated thousands, in Mani's time and for centuries afterwards. For these devotees the moral horrors, and such repugnant practices as the ritual slow suicide, were altogether obscured. Nothing availed, in the end, but to destroy the Manichees, as so much noxious human vermin —so, everywhere, said those to whom it fell to undertake the work of destruction. Mani was not only a cool headed prophet, but an organiser of genius. The new religion was strongly built, and the prophet's first coadjutors were well chosen. Mani's violent end—he was crucified by the Persian king Bahram in 272—did not appreciably halt the progress of his sect. It gradually drew to itself the remains of the Marcionite church, and established itself in the lands between Persia and China. It was the last phase of organised Gnosticism, and the most successful of all.

IX. DENIS OF ALEXANDRIA—PAUL OF SAMOSATA

The century which follows the *Adversus Haereses* of St. Irenæus ends, as it begins, with a Trinitarian controversy and an intervention of the Roman Church. Curiously enough it is a controversy that concerns the very points which had then engaged the attention of the pope St. Victor I. It reveals to us yet another sympathetic figure of the Alexandrian school of theology—St. Denis, Bishop of Alexandria—and a Bishop of Antioch whose life bears out to the letter Origen's anticipatory warnings on the temptations which beset prelates in the empire's greatest cities—Paul of Samosata.

Denis of Alexandria was Origen's own pupil. After a period as head of the Catechetical School he was elected bishop in 247, and he ruled the Church of the great metropolis for as long as seventeen years. It was an eventful episcopate. To begin with, there was the persecution of Decius in which the bishop was arrested. From the trial which awaited him he was, to his embarrassment, rescued by some of his flock and forcibly hurried into safety. The persecution over, he had to face the problem of the reconciliation of the repentant apostates. His solution of the question was that adopted at Rome, and he took the Roman side again when, three or four years later, St. Cyprian raised the question of the validity of heretical baptism. In the persecution which crowned St. Cyprian's life with martyrdom, Denis was again arrested, tried and exiled. How he escaped death it is hard to understand. He returned to Alexandria when the persecution ended, to find the city given over to a civil war in which it was almost destroyed. To add to the troubles the plague came to devastate the surviving population.

The years of St. Denis' episcopate were then hardly the most suitable for the exercise of the talents which had given him his place in the succession to Origen. But interest in religion was inseparable from the intellectual life of the time; the elaboration of new theories and their passionate discussion, endemic. The occasion which would call forth all the bishop's talents was bound to come.

It presented itself in a revival of the Monarchist theories of Sabellius, of which the five cities of Cyrenaica were the scene. Once more, in their zealous attempts to defend the truth that there is only one God, Christian thinkers were sacrificing the other truth that Father, Son and Holy Spirit are realities really distinct. For these neo-Sabellians the Trinity was a mere matter of names; God is one and according as He is successively Creator, Redeemer, Sanctifier, He is Father, Son and Holy Ghost. The controversy reached Alexandria in an appeal to the bishop from the contending parties. There could be little doubt where so faithful a disciple of Origen would range himself, and St. Denis wrote strongly to Cyrenaica defending the reality of the Trinity. He also wrote to the pope, Sixtus II. It was, however, the misfortune of the Bishop of Alexandria that he did not content himself with a repetition of the tradition in face of the new theory, but criticised that theory in the light of his own, Origenist theology. This, for whatever anti-Origenists there were at Alexandria, was an opportunity not to be neglected. They denounced the bishop to Rome. The pope—it was no longer Sixtus II but a successor, also named Denis—had the matter formally examined. He objected to several details of the Bishop of Alexandria's refutation of the Sabellians—his use of the word "creature" to describe God the Son, for example, and his reluctance to use the word *homoöusios* (consubstantial) to describe the relation of the Son to the Father; and he objected also that his defence of the reality of the distinction between Father, Son, and Holy Ghost by a theory of three distinct *hypostases* was so expressed that it might be taken as a theory that there were three Gods.

This was communicated to St. Denis in a private letter which invited him to explain the difficulties. With that letter there went a new public condemnation of the Sabellian theories, and also, no names being mentioned, of whoever taught that the Son was a creature, or that the three of the Divine Trinity were separate *hypostases*. St. Denis gave his explanations—four books of a "*Refutation and Explanations*"—and satisfied Rome of the perfect orthodoxy of his thought. Once more, in a vital controversy involving the traditional faith, Rome has declined to philosophise. There are in presence the innovators and the Catholic who uses against them the weapon of theological theory. Rome stands by the tradition, condemns the innovation by reference to the tradition, and as dispassionately criticises—again by reference to the tradition—the theory which the Catholic has constructed to defend the tradition. The procedure is already traditional, and it throws a great of deal light on the practical working of the *potentior principalitas* of the Roman Church.

The date of this correspondence between Denis of Alexandria and Denis of Rome is somewhere about 262. About the same time the Bishop of Alexandria was drawn into a second controversy which brought him into relation with the greatest centre of Christianity in the East—Antioch. The Bishop of Antioch at the moment was Paul, a native of Samosata. The moment was one of political debacle throughout the East. The disasters of the Persian War were a recent memory, with the defeat and the shameful captivity of the Emperor himself. The flood of the Persian invasion had barely subsided, and Antioch was under the rule of one of the border States to which Rome's weakness promised a new opportunity of expansion, the Kingdom of Palmyra and its queen Zenobia. With the new ruler, Paul of Samosata was on the very best of terms, and he contrived to combine a high position in the State Treasury with his leadership of the Church of Antioch. Cultured, wordly, profligate even, this aspect of his career fills more space in the contemporary record than the more important, but less alluring, theme of his heresies. Nevertheless, it was his heresies which finally provoked the intervention of neighbouring bishops and his deposition.

The heresies offered in sum, nothing very new. They were little more than a re-edition of the theories of Theodotus and of Artemas.

Jesus Christ was not divine in the same way that the Father was divine, for the Logos dwelt in Jesus Christ simply as in a temple. Moreover, the Divine Logos was simply an attribute or faculty of God and not a divine Person. Jesus Christ could only be said to be divine in so far as the Divinity had adopted Him. The opposition to Paul's novelties showed itself immediately, and between 263 and 268 at least three councils were held at Antioch to judge its bishop's orthodoxy. To these St. Denis was invited, but old age stood in the way of his personal intervention. The long thousand miles journey was more than he dared attempt. It was another pupil of Origen upon whom fell the rôle of defender of the tradition—Firmilian, Bishop of Cesarea in Cappadocia, the ally, ten years before, of St. Cyprian.

But Paul of Samosata was too subtle an adversary for the orthodox. Time and again he eluded the prosecution, and not until 268 was the case so handled that he was forced into an open declaration of his dissent. The hero of this was one of his priests, Malchion, the head of the school at Antioch, and its scene a council in which seventy or eighty bishops took part. Paul was deposed, Domnus elected in his place and letters sent to Alexandria and to Rome, communicating the decisions. But Paul was not at the end of his resources and, strong in the support of Zenobia, he held out for four years more, refusing to surrender either church or palace. The deadlock only ended with the new Emperor Aurelian's victory over Zenobia (272). Antioch was once more a Roman city and the suit for Paul's dispossession came before the emperor. He decided that the Bishop of Antioch was the man whom the bishops of Italy and Rome acknowledged to be such. Paul was therefore ejected.

One interesting point about this last controversy of the third century is that while the champions of orthodoxy were all one-time pupils of Origen, the heresiarch, too, made use of the master's terminology to defend himself and to baffle the prosecution. His use of one term in particular drew down upon it the censure of the bishops. This was the term *homoöusios*. Rome, seeing in it the Greek equivalent of Tertullian's *consubstantialis*, by now the consecrated term in the West to describe how both Father and Son were divine, had, a few years before, overriden Denis of Alexandria's objections to its use. Denis, a Greek, with a philosopher's experience of the subtle possibilities of his native language, had then feared that *homoöusios* might be taken to mean "*identical in person*" and therefore seem Sabellian. Now, in 268, Paul of Samosata had been able to exploit in the interests of his theory yet a third interpretation of the term. The Council of Antioch had thereupon condemned it. Sixty years afterwards and more that condemnation was to bear unlooked for fruit. For when the Council of Nicea used the word *homoöusios* to defend the traditional faith against Arianism, the heretics retorted with the charge that the Catholics were the real heretics, alleging in proof the objections of Denis of Alexandria, while the old condemnation of the term, now become the touchstone of orthodoxy, was an embarrassment for many of the Catholics. There is, however, a more intimate connection still between this crisis of 263–268, of which unfortunately we know so little, and the Council of Nicea. With Paul of Samosata there disappeared from the clergy of Antioch one of his leading allies, the priest Lucian. The name should be noted for Lucian was the teacher of Arius and the real father of Arianism.

With Aurelian's decision regarding the property of the Church of Antioch there begins a period of thirty years, of whose history we know nothing. Save for the general description—a few sentences—of Catholic life at this time in the great history of Eusebius, nothing has survived beyond names and dates in the lists of the bishops of the principal sees. When in 303 the veil lifts, it is to reveal all the horrors of the persecution of Diocletian, the Empire's last assault on the religion of the Church. That assault is the prelude to the Empire's conversion. With that conversion the setting of the Church's life is so different that we can speak of the period which follows as a new age. The formative period is now at an end. It is the history of an undeniable world force which lies before us.

CHAPTER V

THE WAY OF CHRISTIAN LIFE

Le milieu paien, cet immense océan de superstitions et de rêves que le courant chrétien dut traverser sans s'y mêler.[1]

THE current was threefold. It was a revealed doctrine, it was a thing organised, and it was a special way of life. So far we have been concerned with the fortunes of the doctrine and of the means divinely devised for its propaganda and protection as the current moves slowly through the ocean. The study is incomplete if it neglects some description of how the ideal of Christian life fared during these first momentous centuries.

The foundation of that life was the spirit of renunciation, of good things for the better, of all things for the sake of God, as the gospels describe it. For some of the Christians this knows no limits. Property, marriage, life itself they will gladly renounce to give themselves more fully to the following of Christ, Who is from the beginning the one centre of their new religious life. Others give up less, but something each must give up, for in each disciple there must be that permanent willingness to renounce whatever is asked, whenever it is asked. Renunciation is not cultivated for its own sake, nor with the purpose of perfecting the disciple's own personality. It is an imitation of Christ, made in union with Christ, its purpose ever closer union with Christ. It is an activity of that new life which has come to the disciple through fellowship in the Church and the mystic incorporation with Christ—a life which never ceases to be dependent on Christ. This life begins with the rite of Baptism; and the chief means through which it is increased and the union between Christ and the disciple consummated, is the rite of the Eucharist. This new, mystical, super-natural union with God is the source of the believer's new relation to his fellows. He is to love them as himself, not with the natural love that springs from his appreciation of their natural attractiveness, but with a super-natural love deriving from his new relation to God. God loves them, and therefore the disciple, loving God, loves them for God's sake. This love of the disciple for his fellows is the very mark by which his discipleship is recognisable.

This doctrine, which characterises especially the gospel of St. John, is also the teaching of the epistles of St. Paul. The two

[1] Lebreton, *Origines du Dogme de la Trinité*.

136

principles of spiritual self-denial and of the constant union between the believer and God are, here again, the foundation on which all is built, although St. Paul's approach to the subject is not that of St. John. Though the new life is given in Baptism, something of the old survives. Whence a lifelong contest between new and old or, as St. Paul says, between Flesh and Spirit. These terms recur often in St. Paul, and following him they become, for all time, the common coin of spiritual teaching with orthodox and heretic alike. It is important to note the meaning St. Paul gives them. By "Flesh" is not meant merely the temptation to sensuality in matters of sex. The term stands rather for human nature as the fall of the first man affected it, crippled, disordered, no longer answering naturally to reasonable control, and therefore ever afterwards a source of rebellion, a thing which the unaided human will is unable to dominate. Left to itself this fallen human nature is a source of sin. Baptism, making the baptized one with Christ, breaks that ancient dominion of the first sin over human nature, but yet not so completely that it cannot make new bids to recover. Whence the life of the disciple is a continual struggle; and St. Paul has a rich store of comparisons to emphasise this truth. A second obstacle to the disciple's progress is the World—the mass of men who, for one reason or another, live in habitual disregard of the Spirit, in habitual affection for the Flesh. No disciple can possibly love the World. In St. Paul, too, we see the two classes of disciples with greater or less perfection for their aims, and, as a means to perfection, we find recommended that peculiarly Christian notion of consecrated virginity. The notion involves no disparagement of marriage or of sex. On the contrary, whoever practises continency is considered as denying himself an important good.

In the two centuries or more which separate the Apostles from the convert emperors of the fourth century, the believer never lacked eloquent guides to remind him of the fundamental principles which should control his life. Here is a theme to which every Christian writer of these centuries returns sooner or later. "There are two roads: the road to life, the road to death," begins the *Didache*, and the parable speedily becomes a commonplace of the primitive moral exhortations. "The road to life"—the love of God, obedience to His commands, flight from sin, from sexual wrongdoing, perjury, lying, theft, avarice, blasphemy, avoidance of whatever disturbs the unity of the Church, the practice of almsgiving, the care of children, obedience to authority, humility. The apostolic theme of the continual warfare is not neglected, and the never-ceasing persecution gives rise to a whole literature exhorting to patience and constancy in the hour of trial, to confidence in Christ for Whom the martyr is privileged to suffer. To comfort and strengthen the confessor and the martyr all the great writers in turn set their genius, Tertullian, Origen and St. Cyprian very notably. In all this literature the one common, dominating feature is the reference to Christ as the centre and goal of the whole idealism as this is preached and as it is lived. It is no detached theorising about an indubitable but distant God which these theologians present, St. Ignatius, St. Irenæus and the rest. A vivid faith in His presence in the very hearts of those for whom they write is the very life of their work. And, of course, nowhere is this so manifest as with the martyrs. The martyrs were the crown of every church's achievement.

After the martyrs came another class of spiritual heroes—the *continentes* and the virgins, those who bound themselves, for the love of Christ, to a life of perpetual continency. There is no ascetical practice so praised, so exalted by these early writers as this; and the number of those who gave themselves to it is the boast of the Apologists, as it was the marvel of the contemporary Pagans who knew it. The *continentes* are cited too, and continually, as a powerful force for good among the believers themselves, a living exhortation to the whole Church. Those who so devoted themselves continued, as yet, to live with their families, but very soon they came to form a kind of spiritual aristocracy in every church, along with the widows, who, in a like spirit, made a perpetual consecration of their widowhood. From a very early time so important a matter ceased to be left to the discretion of the individual. The consent of the bishop was essential before the irrevocable life-long dedication was allowed. A ritual of consecration developed, and an age limit was introduced earlier than which no one could be accepted. The care of these specially consecrated believers took up much of a bishop's time, and warnings against the pitfalls that lay before the virgin, the especially insidious temptation to pride, self-esteem, and a contemning of the ordinary folk, fill many pages of the contemporary exhortations *Ad Virgines*. It was natural, too, at first to recommend, and later to enact, that for their own greater security, and for the seemliness of the thing, such as were thus dedicated should lead a life of retirement. They should not appear at public banquets, nor at weddings, should avoid the public amusements and the baths, should dress soberly, without jewels or cosmetics, and in public always go veiled. To the ordinary fasts which bound the whole Church they added still more, and in their retirement multiplied the hours of prayer, meeting together privately for the purpose. Naturally, occupied with little but the service of God, they soon became the Church's recognised agents for the vast charitable services which were this primitive Christianity's leading activity—care of the widows, of orphans, of the sick, and the systematic relief of the poor and distressed.

The movement did not progress without serious aberrations showing themselves from time to time. There was the tendency to value these abstinences for their own sake, to declare the use of wine for example, of flesh meat, of marriage, things evil in themselves—a tendency related, very often, to the theory that matter is necessarily evil. St. Paul had to warn Timothy against such "saints," but for all authority's faithful adherence to his example the tendency never ceased to show itself. Apocryphal *Acts* of particular apostles, forged to give a sanction to these theories, did much to make them popular, and no doubt the every day experience of the excesses of contemporary Paganism helped very considerably in the same direction. It is also interesting to notice that rigorism of this kind is associated with all the early heresies, the mark of Montanists, Marcionites and Gnostics alike.

From the tendency to control and regulate the daily life and occupation of the *continentes* was to come, ultimately, the institution of Christian Monasticism.[1] "Happy the virgin who places herself under a rule," runs a fourth century saying, "she shall be as a fruitful vine in a garden. Unhappy is the virgin who will not follow a rule, she is as a ship that lacks a rudder." From St. Jerome (347–420) and St. Ambrose (340–397) we can learn many details of what such a rule was. These ladies live at home a life of seclusion, going out rarely. They wear their hair cut short, their long-sleeved dress is black and they are veiled. They have a round of private prayer at home and certain daily prayers in common in the church. They fast, taking each day one meal only, and that without meat. This meal, too, they often take in common. They serve the poor and they attend the sick. From such a state of things to the life of a convent is but a step. As early as 270 we find St. Antony of Egypt placing his sister in a house where a number of like-minded holy women lived a common life, and by 300 such institutions were fairly numerous.

This was not the only source whence monasticism developed. There were others of the *continentes* who, although they no longer lived with their families, preferred to live alone, solitaries, on the outskirts of the towns first, and then further away still in the 'desert." Of these anchorites or hermits the pioneer is St. Paul of Thebes. More famous, however, is his disciple Antony (c. 250–355). Such was this hermit's fame that, despite his opposition, disciples gathered round him and pursued him into the very

[1] For a masterly, documented study *cf.* PIERRE DE LABRIOLLE. *Les Débuts du Monachisme* in F. & M. III 299–370.

depths of the Egyptian deserts, until, in the Nitrian desert, there were, about 325, more than 5,000 solitaries, of both sexes. They lived in separate huts without any common rule, each a law unto himself, meeting at the church on the Sundays for Mass, to receive the Holy Eucharist and a spiritual instruction. They chose their own austerities, each according to his own fancy, and were their own judges as to the extent to which these should be continued. There were hermits who hardly ever ate, or slept, others who stood without movement whole weeks together, or who had themselves sealed up in tombs and remained there for years, receiving only the least of poor nourishment through crevices in the masonry. The fervour of the oriental found in this primitive monasticism all it could crave of opportunity for sacrificial self-despoilment. In the fourth century more especially, when to the persecution there followed an era of comfort, and when, in the saying of a contemporary, there were many more Christians but less Christianity, did the zeal of the more perfect lead them into the desert.

The hermit movement presently had a competitor in the monastic movement properly so-called—the foundation in the desert of institutes where the members led a common life, working, praying, practising austerities, studying the Sacred Scriptures, under the rule of a superior. In these institutions the will of the superior was the guide and the norm. The austerities, no less than the prayers, were regulated by his discretion. The pioneer of this movement was St. Pachomius, and his first foundation—a monastery for men and one for women—at Tabennisi dates from about 320.

From Egypt the movement spread to Palestine and here a disciple of St. Antony, Hilary, devised yet a third form of the life, the Laura. The Laura was a village of cells or huts, so that each monk lived alone as did the hermits, but the community was subject to a superior as in the monastery. This system became rapidly popular, and many of these monastic villages counted each its thousand of monks. Jerusalem, in the fourth century, became a great centre for monks of every kind of monastic life, the capital, in fact, of monasticism, and St. Jerome the movement's presiding genius.

Syria had its monks, Asia Minor, too, and here, towards the middle of the fourth century, this eastern monasticism produced the great saint whose rule was to fix its characteristics for the rest of time—St. Basil (329–79). St. Basil was a reformer of the practical type. He had travelled much, had seen every aspect of contemporary monasticism in one country and another, and when he came to draw up a rule it was much more a code of life than any of the so-called rules which preceded it. He it was who invented the novitiate—a systematic probation of aspirants, who were to be trained primarily to the renouncement of their own way, obedience being the monk's great virtue and the means of his spiritual progress. And the monasteries were not to be over large —thirty or forty monks only to each superior. This was in very striking contrast to the monasteries of the Pachomian type where, as with the system of the Laura, the monks were to be numbered by the thousand.

For St. Basil the community type of life is a higher form than the hermit life; and from this moment the hermit life declines in prestige. All the monks are to come together for all the prayers, and the psalms and singing are to be varied to avoid monotony and the boredom that derives from it. The superior gives his monks instruction, confession of faults to him or to another monk is encouraged, and great emphasis is laid on the necessity of systematic manual work for each monk. The will of the superior is the monk's law in all that concerns his monastic life. Hence no room is now left for personal eccentricity, whether in the matter of devotions or austerities. All exaggerations, and the trouble they breed, disappear. To guard against pride and vanity no one may go beyond the rule except by the superior's special permission. The abstinence from meat and wine is perpetual. Silence is the law for meals, at the office and during work. The monk never leaves his monastery, except for a just cause, and even then he never goes alone. The sick are to be cared for with every comfort, and hospitality is enjoined as a primary duty. For those who refuse to keep the rule, penalties are provided. But, where St. Pachomius provides floggings and a bread and water diet for serious faults, in St. Basil's rule there is nothing harsher than a kind of temporary internal excommunication.

In the East, by the end of the fourth century, within a hundred years of its first introduction, Monasticism was established as perhaps the most flourishing of all the Church's activities. In the West, it had developed more slowly. Here, too, in every church, there had been, from the first generations, the spiritual aristocracy of *continentes* and virgins, and, for example at Rome, such women had begun already to live a common life when, towards the middle of the fourth century, the knowledge began to spread of the marvellous happenings in the Egyptian deserts. One important source of this knowledge was the accidental presence, for several years, in Italy and Gaul of the bishop of Alexandria, St. Athanasius, banished from his see by the Arianising policy of the emperor. None knew better than he the detail of the new movement—of which he was indeed one of the earliest historians—and to the presence in the West during so many years of the bishop who was, by his position, the very patriarch of nascent monasticism, and by his temperament a master propagandist, much of the sudden growth of the movement in the West may be ascribed. Another source of the West's knowledge of the ascetic marvels of the eastern Churches was the experience of the thousands of pilgrims who, in the first generations of the Christian Empire, made the long journey to Palestine to venerate the sacred places whence the Faith had come.

Some of these pilgrims, attracted by the life, even stayed on, spiritual exiles for the sake of the more perfect life. Of such westerners who so made themselves easterners the most famous is St. Jerome (347–420), and around his life may be written the whole history of early Roman monasticism. His first experience of monasticism was the five years he spent as a solitary in the desert to the east of Antioch—a desert so peopled with like-minded souls, that solitude, he found, was the last thing possible. From the desert St. Jerome returned to Rome, and for the next few years he was the centre round which the monastically-minded of the old capital—women of noble families for the most part—gathered. In this circle all the stark austerity of the life of the desert found willing adepts, under the learned direction of St. Jerome. There was the inevitable conflict with the less ascetically inclined relatives, and with the still less ascetic Roman clergy, and in the end St. Jerome and his followers left the city, to establish themselves once and for all at Bethlehem (386).

Along with St. Jerome there must also be mentioned his contemporaries the Bishop of Milan, St. Ambrose (340–397) and the future Bishop of Hippo, St. Augustine (354–430). St. Ambrose did much, by his sermons *De Virginibus*, to foster the ideal among his people and to encourage the movement. St. Cyprian is here his master, but St. Ambrose breaks entirely new ground when he suggests Our Lady as the type and model of the consecrated virgin. Milan, under St. Ambrose's direction, became in its turn a centre of the monastic life, and with the progress of the movement came the inevitable opposition. The saint's *De Virginitate* is his reply to it.

In St. Paulinus of Nola, a retired imperial official of high rank who gave himself to the life, monasticism reached another stage of development and with Eusebius, Bishop of Vercelli, it began to affect the clergy too. The priests who served the church of Vercelli lived a life in common, whose spirit was the spirit of monasticism. It is with this clerical type of monasticism that the still greater name of St. Augustine is associated. Some of the best known pages of his *Confessions* record how greatly he was influenced, at the crisis of his life, by the story of the imperial officers whom the example of the hermits in Egypt had won over to monasticism. After his return to Africa the converted scholar, giving up his career and his projected marriage, turned his house at Tagaste into a monastery. There with his friends, their property sold and the proceeds given to the poor, he led a regular life of seclusion, of prayer and study. His ordination in 391 fixed him at Hippo, and at Hippo he once more established a monastery of the same type in which he himself lived. Finally when, in 396, he became Bishop of Hippo he not only continued his own monastic way of life but brought all his clergy into it also. The episcopal palace itself became a monastery—a monastery whence, as from Marmoutier and Lérins, monks went forth as bishops to rule more than one of the neighbouring sees. St. Augustine has left descriptions of the life of the community in his sermons, a treatise *De Sancta Virginitate*, another *De Opere Monachorum*, while, from the letter he wrote to restore peace to a community of holy women, later centuries developed the so-called *Rule of St. Augustine.*

The opposition to monasticism continued. Its strength lay very largely in what remained of Paganism in the old Roman aristocracy, and more than once the city mob rioted in its anti-monastic zeal. There were also the heretics—Helvidius, for example, who preached against continency, derided the idea of mortification, and even denied the virginity of Mary. Another such was Jovinian, an ex-monk who, man of the world now and practised debauchee, turned—first of an unhappy line—to revile and attack all he once had reverenced. There was, he declared, only one heaven, only one reward for all; and since those validly baptized cannot but be saved, mortifications are but a useless show. He drew replies from St. Ambrose and—a characteristically waspish one—from St. Jerome. He was excommunicated by the pope, Siricius (384–398), but his teaching grew, and many apostasies are recorded.

It was, however, in Gaul, and not in Italy, that the first western monks really flourished, where the pioneer was the Bishop of Tours, St. Martin (317–397). St. Martin, born in Pannonia, was the child of a legionary and, despite his early attraction to the hermit life, forced to follow his father into the army. His vocation survived the experiences of the camp, and, once baptized and free of the army (339), he was received into the clergy by St. Hilary, Bishop of Poitiers. For some years afterwards he lived as a solitary, first near Milan and later on an island in the Mediterranean. St. Hilary, banished to the East for opposition to the Arian Constantius II, returned with a new knowledge of monasticism (361); and it was now that, under his direction,

Martin founded at Ligugé, close by St. Hilary's cathedral city, the first monastery of the West—a few huts, one for each monk, grouped round the church in which the monks met for what spiritual exercises they had in common. There was no rule but the mutual good example and the duty of obedience to the superior. St. Martin was still at Ligugé when he was elected Bishop of Tours. The new office made no difference to the man. He continued to live his austere life, to sleep on the bare ground, to wear his old clothes, to fast, to pray as before and, within sight of the walls of Tours, he founded Marmoutier—another and larger Ligugé. Here he lived with his community of eighty monks a life very like that of the Egyptian monasteries of St. Pachomius. Very many of the monks whom this austere life attracted were of noble birth, and from Marmoutier came forth a whole series of bishops—the first monk-bishops in the Church. By an extraordinary paradox this first great monastery of contemplative solitaries became, and almost immediately, the first great centre of that movement to convert the countrysides of Gaul, whose greatest figure is St. Martin.

St. Martin was, however, not an organiser of monasticism, and it was in monasteries founded a little later, in the south of Gaul, that the first monastic legislators of the West arose. Two monasteries in particular must be noticed—Lérins, an island off the coast of Provence, and the abbey of St. Victor at Marseilles. At Lérins, founded by a wealthy patrician St. Honoratus (429), the rule of St. Pachomius was held in great veneration, and although not followed to the letter, it undoubtedly influenced the life there. Lérins too was a nursery of bishops, supplying indeed so many bishops to the sees of southern Gaul that it became a matter of complaint between the clergy and the Roman See. Marseilles had for its founder an Eastern who had travelled much. This was John Cassian. He was born about 350, was a monk at Bethlehem in the early days of St. Jerome's career there, and after several years in Egypt came to Constantinople, where in 403 he was ordained deacon by St. John Chrysostom. Four years later he was in Rome, carrying to Innocent I St. John's appeal against his illegal deposition. Finally, in 414, he was ordained priest at Marseilles and founded there the abbey of St. Victor. The rule's inspiration was Eastern, but modified to suit the very different Western conditions. Cassian, however, did much more than found a monastery. He set down his ideas in two books which were to influence monastic thought and theories of spiritual direction for centuries—his *De Coenobiorum Institutis* and his *Collationes*.

The way of the Counsels—monasticism in the later centuries, the life of the *virgines* and *continentes* in the primitive times—was,

however, the privilege of a minority. This élite was vastly outnumbered by the thousands of believers whom necessity and
choice bound to the life of the world, and of whom the churches
were chiefly composed. To them also, through the Church, the
Spirit spoke. In them, too, ran the same supernatural life, fed
from the same sources which nourished those especially consecrated, and producing in the activities of ordinary human life
the same superhuman fruits. For these Christians, too, the
gospel,—an institution and a belief—was also a way of living,
a code of conduct based on a teaching, and nourished through a
cult.

Conformably to the will of Christ its Founder, the Church
received its new adepts through the visible ceremonial rite of
Baptism. Closely connected with Baptism was the complementary
ceremony of the laying on of hands. St. Justin gives us the earliest
detailed description of the rite which has survived, and fifty years
later Tertullian is evidence that an explanatory and preparatory
ceremonial had already gathered round the primitive nucleus.
The ceremony takes place at Easter. The water with which it is
administered is especially blessed for the purpose. The candidate
makes a previous explicit renunciation of the devil. The baptism
is followed by an anointing with blessed oil and an imposition of
hands. It is the bishop who officiates, and the candidates prepare
for their reception by special prayers and fasts. St. Hippolytus,
Tertullian's contemporary, speaks also of an anointing of the
catechumen before baptism. The heretics, too, had these ceremonies—the Marcionites, for example, and many of the Gnostics
—which points to their being established in the Church before the
heretics broke away, to an origin that is at least as early as the
generation which followed the death of the last apostle.

But the preparatory period was not merely a time of special
prayer. From a very early date indeed those who wished to be
members of the Church were trained in its doctrines and practices,
their sincerity and fervour tested by a long systematic course of
instruction. This was the Catechumenate, and in every church
there came to be a priest appointed for the purpose of instructing
and watching over the Catechumens. The Catechumens had
their special place in the assemblies, and during the time of their
probation they were prepared for baptism by a series of preparatory ceremonies, exorcisms for example, blessings and
anointings. After the baptism and the anointing and imposition
of hands which followed, the newly-initiated received for the
first time the Holy Eucharist.

The minister of these public initiatory rites was, originally,
always the bishop. Later the custom gradually made its way

that the priests, too, assisted at the actual baptism, the bishop blessing the water and the oils but baptizing only a few of the catechumens though still administering to all the rite of anointing and the imposition of hands. Then most of the baptisms fell to the priests. Still later when, in the fourth century, parishes began to be founded outside the cities, the priests in charge of them were allowed to bless the water for Baptism, to baptize all who came to them and to anoint them also, the bishop reserving to himself the blessing of the oils and the final imposition of hands. Such is the Roman practice, at any rate, from the time of Innocent I (402–417).

The centres of the Church's religious life were the weekly assemblies where the bishop presided and at which all the brotherhood assisted. These took place three times each week, on Sunday the weekly feast day, and on the two days of fasting Wednesday and Friday. To Sunday was transferred the ritual importance of the Jewish Sabbath—in the days of the Apostles themselves— and the observance of the two weekly fast days goes back, at all events, to the closing years of the first century.

The services which occupied the assembly were of two kinds. There were first of all the *Vigilia*, celebrated in the hours before dawn. These consisted of readings from the Sacred Books, and homilies delivered by the bishop interspersed with prayers and hymns. In the plan of this service there was nothing specifically new, and the same is true of the first part of the second service— the assembly for the Holy Eucharist.

Here, too, there is a preparatory element which the Christians took over bodily from the synagogue—a service of prayers, hymns, readings from the Sacred Books, and a homily. To this the Christians added readings from their own Sacred Books and made it the preface to their own new liturgy the Holy Eucharist. The origin of this is once more the example and the precept of the Church's Founder, and it is in St. Paul's Epistles and the Synoptic Gospels that we have the earliest description of the rite— in its essentials a special kind of prayer over the bread and wine, a breaking of the bread and a distribution of the "eucharisted" food to those who assisted.

The *Didache*, recalling the obligation of this Sunday reunion for the celebration of the Holy Eucharist, urges the necessity of a good conscience in those who assist, for that at which they assist is the pure sacrifice foretold of old by the prophet Malachi. St. Ignatius is equally explicit, in his witness that the Eucharist is "the flesh of Our Saviour Jesus Christ, the flesh which suffered for our sins, the flesh which the Father in his goodness has raised again." Equally clear is his fidelity to another element of New

Testament doctrine on the Eucharist, namely that it is the symbol
and the source of the Church's unity and peace.

These three fundamental ideas—that the Holy Eucharist is
sacrifice, food, and principle of unity, being the very body and
blood of Jesus Christ—the later writers do but develop and
explain. St. Justin, in his *First Apology*, and in the *Dialogue
with Trypho* too, gives us the earliest detailed account of the
rite which has survived. In it we can see already achieved the
combination of synagogue service and Eucharist around which
the rich diversity of liturgies is later to grow. In St. Irenæus we
have the definite statement that it is by the words of the conse-
crating prayer that the change is wrought, while Clement of
Alexandria uses a phraseology medieval in its concrete realism
"To drink the blood of Jesus is to share in His incorruptibility,"
and Origen speaks of the Christian altars as "consecrated with
the precious blood of Christ." Meanwhile, in the West, St.
Hippolytus composed a treatise *Should the Eucharist be received
daily?* and in Africa Tertullian, and above all St. Cyprian, write,
with a fullness to which nothing is wanting, of the mystery, of its
use, and of its rôle in the general life of the communicants. The
lips with which Christ has been received, shall they turn next to
applaud the brutalities of a gladiator ? the hands which have held
Him proceed to their daily task of making idols ?

Universally, at the Sunday assembly the Eucharist was celebrated. The observance on the fast days varied. The fast remained
unbroken until the mid-afternoon. In Africa, and at Jerusalem
too, the Eucharist was celebrated at the assembly. At Alexandria
and in Rome there was no Eucharist—simply the service of
prayers, readings, hymns and a homily. The next day to receive
a regular service was Saturday, the one-time holy day. By the
fourth century throughout the East, save at Alexandria, there
was on Saturday an assembly with celebration of the Eucharist.
At Rome, however, the development was in the contrary direction.
Saturday became not a new weekly feast but a fast, an extension,
in fact, of the fast of Friday. Another Roman peculiarity was
the fast celebrated in the first week of each of the four seasons—
the fast of the Four Seasons (Quarter-Tense, Ember Week). In
these weeks the unusal fasts of Wednesday, Friday and Saturday
were kept with the additional solemnity of a Eucharistic service
on the first two days and a Vigil and Eucharist on the Saturday.
A fifth specially honoured week centred round the annual commemoration of the death and resurrection of Our Lord. Originally
this was little more than a fifth Ember Week with a feast on the
Thursday to commemorate the institution of the Holy Eucharist.
The commemoration which is the later Easter, goes back to the

Apostles, as the evidence of all parties in the famous controversies of the second century goes to show. Pentecost, celebrating the visible outpouring of the promised Holy Spirit upon the first disciples is just as old a feast and was just as universally celebrated as Easter, but with perhaps less solemnity. The third feast of this cycle—commemorating the Ascension—is of much later origin. The earliest trace of it dates to about 350.

The great annual penitential season which, in English, is called Lent developed from two elements, the fast in preparation for the feast of Easter and the catechumen's preparation for Baptism. The pre-Easter fast was originally very short indeed—one or two days in St. Irenæus—but, to compensate, it was very severe, for no food at all was taken while it lasted. In Africa, in Tertullian's time, it lasted from the Thursday to the morning of Easter Sunday. At Alexandria, a generation later, every day in that week was a fast day. The earliest mention of the fast of forty days in the spring is in the Canons of Nicea (325). Then, and for long afterwards, this fast was primarily directed to the coming baptism of the catechumens; it was a time of retreat, of recollection and special prayers, during which the candidates passed through the final stages of their probation. The discipline of Lent varied. At Rome the Sundays were considered to be outside the season, at Constantinople the Saturdays too. Lent again brought with it liturgical developments. In the East the Eucharist service on the Wednesdays and Fridays disappeared in Lent, but the number of reunions of the "mass-less" type increased. In the West the opposite happened. The number of mass days was increased, until, in the end, on every day of Lent there was an assembly with the celebration of the Eucharist.

Of the many other feasts which, later, were to enrich the calendar of the Church, we have hardly any record earlier than Constantine's conversion. Christmas, for example, was a Western feast originally and the earliest record of its celebration is at Rome in 336. The East had a similar kind of feast—the Apparitions (Epiphany)—commemorating the birth of Our Lord, the coming of the Wise Men, and His baptism, which was kept on January 6. One element in this may go back to a very early date, for about the years 200 the Gnostics kept a feast to celebrate the baptism of Our Lord. Nor are the feasts of Mary the Mother of Our Lord any older. There is no mention of them at Rome before the seventh century, although the feast of the Circumcision, the octave of Christmas, which is an indirect commemoration of her, goes back a century earlier. In this matter the West borrowed from the East where a feast of the Presentation of Our Lord in the Temple was kept at Jerusalem from about 370.

The oldest of all the feasts were the annual commemorations of the martyrs—reunions of the local church, at the tombs of its most distinguished members, those who had testified to the faith with life itself. Of this development the earliest instance on record is the case of the martyred bishop of Smyrna, St. Polycarp, put to death in 155. A practice so natural grew speedily, and though the martyr cults were in their essence local things, some of the more noted of these Christian heroes—St. Lawrence of Rome for example, St. Cyprian of Carthage—soon won a wider renown, and honours in churches other than their own. With the Peace of Constantine the persecution, as a more or less normal incident of Christian life, ended. The heroism which had found its crown in martyrdom now developed in the solitude of the deserts. The new heroes were those who battled in the austerity of the new monasticism; and the next saints to be honoured liturgically after death, their prayers officially besought, were the ascetics, the first of them all in time the great St. Martin of Tours who died in 397.

The religion founded by Our Lord in the Church was then a corporate, social thing, just as truly as it was the sum of the innumerable conquests of the myriad individual souls who made up the mystical body. And from its understanding of its corporate nature there gradually developed its public liturgies, and a Christian art; latest of all there developed an architecture— latest of all, for the first buildings erected for the purpose of containing the Church at prayer, the first churches in the architectural sense of the word, were not built until well on into the third century. Before that time the Christians met for worship in the houses of one or another of the brotherhood. At certain places, in times of persecution, they met in the catacombs—a Christian adaptation and development, on an immense scale, of the underground cemetery system, which, in all probability, they had borrowed from the Jews. This system of catacombs was especially well developed at Rome, where it grew to be a second underground city, *Roma sotteriana cristiana*.[1]

The Roman practice by which great families opened their private cemeteries to their dependants; the sacredness in the eye of the Roman law of the tomb and the cult of the dead; the ancient Roman custom of family reunions at the tomb of its deceased members: all these favoured the development. The Christians, once gathered in their cemeteries were secure, not only from mob hostility, but even from the attention of the police

[1] The title of J. B. de Rossi's classic work (1864–1867): catacombs have been discovered elsewhere too, at Naples, in Tuscany, in Sicily, in Africa, at Alexandria, and in Asia Minor.

during persecutions. These Roman catacombs go back to the days of the Apostles themselves. Still, today, the pilgrim can wander through the miles of their underground galleries and the chambers hewn out of the *tufa* where, nearly two thousand years ago now, the mass was said and the homilies delivered and the neophytes baptized. He can look upon the sites of the tombs of the earliest martyr-popes, and upon the hundreds of funeral inscriptions that tell the names and qualities of these long dead Christians and that attest so many of the doctrines they professed; and he can look upon the earliest Christian paintings, and study, there again, not merely the quality and development of the artistic inspiration, but the beliefs to which the paintings witness and the religious practices of which they are the mute unchanging record.

In the course of the third century, as will be seen, the persecution of the Church changed its character entirely. It was no longer left to the initiative of private malice to unleash the fury of the persecuting laws. All now depended on the emperor; there were emperors who were favourable to the Church as well as those resolved on its destruction; and between the new, most savage persecutions that now took place, there were long intervals of peace when the Church enjoyed recognition as a lawful religion. It was during this peace that, in the third century the first churches began to be built. Traces of these first churches still remain, at Rome for example, below the basilica of St. Clement and the church of S. Martino ai Monti, at S. Anastasia, at SS. Giovannie Paolo, and at S. Sabina. These discoveries of archæology in our own time confirm the witness of the contemporaries who describe this first public appearance of the Church in the public life of the day, whether Christians themselves, like Eusebius of Cesarea, or bitter enemies such as Porphyry.

In all this swarming spiritual activity of Christian life, it is the Church, the whole assembly, which is all important. The newcomer to it is instructed by the Church, and prepared by the common and public prayer of the Church for his reception and baptism, and in the rite itself the collectivity of the life is manifest. It is in the assembly that he makes his progress, and should he fall from grace, his fall is the concern of all his brethren, who assist his penances by their own charitable prayers and good works.

When a Christian marries he is warned to take a Christian for his partner,[1] for there is a Christian law of marriage.[2] The marriage should be with the bishop's consent,[3] or at any rate

---

[1] Tertullian, St. Cyprian, Councils of Elvira (300) and Arles (314).
[2] Athenagoras.
[3] St. Ignatius.

blessed by the Church.[1] Marriage between Christians is indissoluble, even the adultery of one of the partners cannot break the bond.[2] Though Encratites, like Tatian, condemn marriage as mere fornication, and Marcionites forbid it altogether, the Catholic tradition is constant that perpetual continency is not of obligation, that marriage is lawful,[3] —more, that it is a holy thing, since it is the figure of the union of Christ and His Church.[4] Second marriages, which the Montanists condemn altogether, although reproved[5] are tolerated, except in the case of the clergy. A second marriage is also a bar to a man's ordination. Marriage is a holy thing, and the mutual rights and duties of the contracting parties are discussed by these first Christian moralists always with reference to the life of the Spirit which, since Baptism, is the most important factor in every Christian's life.

The primitive tradition that the ruling members of the Church are also the authorised teachers, and the ministers of the Eucharist is faithfully maintained. With these first and essential officers others are now associated; Lectors whose office it is to read the chosen passages of Holy Scripture in the assemblies; Exorcists to whom is entrusted one of the chief functions in the preparation of the catechumen for Baptism; Acolytes who share more closely in the ritual of the Eucharist; and Doorkeepers (*Ostiarii*) whose mission is the very important one of securing that none but members of the Church are admitted to the different reunions. The rite by which all members of the clergy are commissioned and receive their new spiritual powers is still the primitive imposition of hands, its minister the bishop, and in St. Cyprian we note the first appearance of the regulation that for the consecration of a bishop three bishops are required. Marriage is no bar to ordination, although (Councils of Ancyra, 314, Neo-Cesarea, *c.* 314–25) it comes to be the law that the deacon, priest or bishop once ordained may not marry. The prestige of continency is bringing about an association in the mind of the Church between its practice and the ministry. The clerical state, in its higher ranks at least, should not lack the virtue which now adorns so many of the flock. And even in the case of those married before ordination it begins to be suggested that, after ordination, husband and wife should be to each other but as brother and sister. This clerical body, for all its undoubted position apart in the Church, is not, in the first three centuries, a way of life that excludes the

---

[1] Tertullian.
[2] Hermas, St. Irenæus, Tertullian, St. Cyprian, the Council of Elvira and Rome constantly. The Council of Arles is evidence of a less stringent opinion.
[3] St. Irenæus, Tertullian, Didascalia.
[4] Tertullian.
[5] Athenagoras, St. Theophilus of Antioch, Tertullian, Didascalia.

following of a profession. Its members support themselves, as do the faithful to whom they minister, by a variety of occupations. Nor, for the best part of two centuries after Constantine, is there any suggestion of a special clerical dress, any more than there is evidence of what to-day we call, technically, vestments. When the first attempt to introduce a clerical costume was made it met with little favour, and was in fact severely rebuked by the pope of the time (St. Celestine I, 422–432).

How far had Christianity spread by the time of the conversion of Constantine ? The question is much easier to answer definitely than the other question it provokes, how far was the Empire then Christian ? At Rome there had been Christians from within a few years of Our Lord's Ascension, and a Pagan historian speaks of them as "a great multitude" at the time of Nero's persecution. From the second century Rome becomes a great centre of expansion, whence southern and central Italy are evangelised. Northern Italy was a much later conquest. Of Christianity in Gaul, our earliest certain attested fact is the persecution of 177 which reveals at Lyons a well-ordered and flourishing church. A hundred and forty years later, at the Council of Arles, sixteen bishops of Gallic sees were present, among them bishops from Bordeaux, Rheims and Rouen. Spain knew the Church as early as the days of St. Paul who was, seemingly, one of its first apostles. But we know nothing of its Christianity until the persecution of Decius (250–251). Fifty years later the Church there had so profited by the long peace which followed Valerian (259) that, at the Council of Elvira (300), forty Spanish bishops assembled. In Britain, too, there were Christians and organised churches, Christians who gave their lives in the persecution of 304–5 ; and the bishops of York, London and Lincoln sat in the Council of Arles of 314. Of the origin of this British Christianity we know nothing. At the Council of Arles there assisted also bishops from Mainz, Cologne and Treves, the earliest representatives of Christianity among the Germans known to us. Of the conquests of the Church in the lands beyond the Rhine where the Empire never established itself, we know scarcely anything.

The first evidence of Christianity in Africa is as late as 189— the martyrdoms at Scillium. The churches in Africa are, by then, already numerous and well-organised. A few years later and Tertullian has been received at Carthage (c. 194) and can urge as one of his pleas for toleration that the Christians are almost the majority in every town of the province. Certainly in the two provinces of Numidia and Proconsular Africa there were, by the beginning of the third century, seventy bishops.

But the real strength of Christianity lay to the east of the

Adriatic. Greece, Epirus, Thessaly and Thrace were by the end of the second century very well evangelised. Into the Danube provinces to the north Christianity came later, but not too late to produce martyrs under Diocletian. Dalmatia's conversion began with Titus, and it is in the lands evangelised by St. Paul and his lieutenants that we find Christianity strongest three centuries later. While in Palestine, its first home, Christianity had almost disappeared with the destruction that followed the wars of Titus and Hadrian, Syrian Christianity developed amazingly around that most ancient centre of missionary zeal the city of Antioch. Again, in Asia Minor, while Cappadocia remained unconverted until the time of St. Gregory the Wonderworker (c. 230–50), Phrygia and Bithynia were Christian from the end of the previous century. It was, however, the province of Asia, whose chief city was Ephesus, that led all the rest, the one really Christian province of the whole Empire. Egypt, too, was largely Christian. By the end of the third century it had fifty-five bishops, and from what we know of Egyptian Christianity in the first century in which it is known to us (Clement of Alexandria to St Athanasius) it would seem to have been established at a very early date. A list of its bishops is extant that leads back to 61.

Christianity was not, however, confined to the Roman Empire. The buffer State of Edessa was so thoroughly converted in the second century that Christianity became the official religion of the kingdom. Armenia, too, dates its first conversion from about the same time, but the chief agent here was St. Gregory the Illuminator (late third century). He was himself Armenian and under his influence once again Christianity found itself the religion of the State. For all that, the conversion proved superficial. To the south of Egypt lay Ethiopia, and the conversion of Ethiopia counts among St. Athanasius' many titles, to rememberance. From Egypt, too, but a century earlier, came the conversion of Arabia. The most flourishing of all these oriental Christianities was however that of Persia. Persia's first missionaries were from Edessa and they built up, in the century which preceded the conversion of Constantine, a really imposing church. This was the century of the great wars between the Roman Empire and the resuscitated Persia of the Sassanid kings, and the religion persecuted in Rome found, if only for political reasons, a protector in the Great King. Constantine's conversion brought to an end this happy state of things. Christianity, the religion of the Roman Emperor, was henceforth banned in Persia and a century of almost uninterrupted persecution followed in which thousands of martyrs perished.

Although the essential organisation of the spreading Christianity remained the same—the bishop supreme in the local church under the unique hegemony of the Bishop of Rome—two very important new institutions developed during these first three hundred years, the council of bishops and the ecclesiastical province, *i.e.* the permanent grouping of sees round a central *metropolitan* see. The earliest council recorded is that called by the Bishop of Ephesus at the time of the Easter Controversy (189–198). To judge by his letter to the pope the procedure was altogether new, and due entirely to the initiative of Rome. In the next hundred years the institution developed rapidly. Origen records councils at Cesarea in Palestine (230) and in Pisidia. In the same year there is a council at Carthage and in 240 one at Ancyra. In Africa especially was this new organ of government—*L'évêque au pluriel*—made use of, and under a bishop like St. Cyprian, through the council of Africa, the primacy of Carthage developed rapidly. It is, again, through councils that Denis of Alexandria combats the revival of Sabellianism, and that Paul of Samosata, Bishop of Antioch, is convicted of heresy and deposed. The councils secure uniformity of faith and discipline without, as yet, in any way hindering the action of the Roman See, which continues its practice of intervention, even in the case of such great sees as Alexandria and Antioch, intervening always with a tone of authority found nowhere else, commanding as though in no doubt that obedience would be given, holding out sanctions to rebels and the negligent.

The councils, however, even that council of Africa which apparently met every year, were not in permanent session and the new grouping of sees around the metropolitan see—see of the chief city of the province, mother-see very often whence had sprung the rest—supplied a machinery for the co-ordination of every day activity. For all that the bishop is supreme in his own church, the local church is not an isolated spiritual kingdom. Outside bishops have a say in its affairs—in the election of the bishop, for example, and in his consecration—and, for St. Cyprian, this is a tradition which goes back to the Apostles. The system by which the activities of every bishop are subordinated —on appeal—to the collective scrutiny of the other bishops dependent on the same metropolitan see, is already well established by the time of the Council of Nicea (325), whose very important canons do but regulate an already existing institution, adapting it to the new delimitation of provinces accomplished by Diocletian and his successors. Already there is confusion, already rivalry between the great sees. Nicea—with the whole eastern episcopate assembled for the first time—is an opportunity to set all in order.

There is no record of either Antioch or Alexandria as a great central see before the third century, nor is there any regularity or uniformity in the way in which the central sees begin to develop. Rome for example—we are not concerned here with the organisation of its peculiar universal jurisdiction, *potentior principalitas* —is gradually revealed as the metropolitan of all central and southern Italy, Carthage of Africa Proconsularis and Numidia, Alexandria of Egypt and Libya. Antioch, however, for all its civil importance, has nothing like so definite a power over the sees of the East. Asia Minor too is, by comparison with Egypt, Africa and Italy, poorly organised. Ephesus, for example, despite its apostolic origin, and its civil importance as the capital of the province, has an equal and a rival in every other church. Nor is the original grouping based on the civil divisions.

The rise of Antioch is particularly interesting and it is important in view of the history of the fourth century, to notice the failure of this Church to achieve a real local hegemony. From about 250 Antioch begins to show itself the centre of action for a group of sees which finally becomes the episcopate of The East (i.e. the civil diocese of that name). After the death of Constantine, (337) Antioch became the seat of the imperial residence and it continued to be the *de facto* capital down to Theodosius (381). These are the years of the Arian supremacy, and that supremacy and Antioch's predominance went together. It was no matter of ecclesiastical legislation, simply the natural effect of the city's new civil importance increasing the influence of its bishops. But Antioch never drew within its sphere of influence either the province of Asia or Egypt, where Alexandria, during the whole of this period, led the fight for Catholicism—inevitably a fight against Antioch and against the spread of Antioch's influence. It will be seen later how Antioch was the centre of the campaign against St. Athanasius, and how the church of Antioch supplied and consecrated the Arians whom the emperor installed at Alexandria as bishops during St. Athanasius' exile. It is the eternal problem of the East to preserve the Church from this evil of episcopal ambition, so to balance and regulate the relations of sees and metropolitans that no one see shall ever achieve an undue predominance. In its failure to solve that problem, and in the absence of adequate machinery through which the Roman hegemony, functioning continuously, might supply what was lacking to local arrangements, lie the beginnings of the end of Eastern Catholicism. Egypt was organised, Africa and Italy too, while the disorganised East inevitably offered itself to the ambition of first one see and then another. How, finally, Constantinople captured it is what the rest of this history must tell.

The canons of Nicea enact that all the bishops of the province (i.e. the civil province) shall take part in the election of its bishops, that the metropolitan shall have the right of veto; and that, as a check on episcopal misgovernment, the provincial council shall meet twice each year as a court of appeal. But this régime of churches grouped by civil provinces (since Diocletian's reforms these number now ninety-six in all) applies only to the civil dioceses of Asia, Pontus and The East. The council expressly recognises the special and ancient régime which obtains in the (civil) diocese of Egypt—Egypt, Libya, and Pentapolis—where the Bishop of Alexandria himself chooses all the bishops and consecrates them and, if need be, deposes them. His authority is much more than metropolitan, and his authority extends far beyond the civil provinces. They are the same rights, the council recognises, as those which the Bishop of Rome exercises in Italy. Antioch, too, is mentioned by name, but the council again does no more than confirm existing rights "To Antioch and throughout the other provinces, the privileges proper to metropolitan sees." The bishops at Nicea did not innovate; they made no attempt to centralise the organisation of the immense Christianity which stretched from the Euxine to the Red Sea.

CHAPTER VI

THE CHURCH AND THE PAGAN ROMAN EMPIRE

I. THE STATE—HOSTILE AND TOLERANT

THE Roman power, at the time of Our Lord's birth, (4 B.C.), had already nearly reached to what were to be the limits of its geographical expansion. With the exception of the island of Britain, the Romans held the whole of Europe west of the Rhine and south of the Danube, northern Africa from the Atlantic, Egypt, Palestine, Syria and the most of Asia Minor. Claudius (41–54) was to add Britain, Trajan (98–117) Dacia and a great territory to the east of the Euphrates. But except for these later conquests, the Empire which at the beginning of the fourth century saw the conversion of Constantine, was, geographically, the same Empire in which the Apostles had preached.

The conquering power showed to the religions of the conquered peoples a politic tolerance. There was, of course, nothing in the old Roman religion to breed in its adherents anything approaching to a spirit of intolerance. That religion was essentially a private, local, personal relation between an individual, an individual family, an individual city, and its own protecting deity. From the nature of the case there was in such a religion no room for the idea of propaganda, no anxiety that others should share its benefits, no zeal to compel others to come in. The cult of Rome and the worship of the emperor which, later still, was associated with it, was, it is true, universally imposed. But to the syncretist age in which this new State cult developed, the universal insistence that all men should worship the State was no hardship. The new cult—a mere ritual which, like all the rest, involved no new definite belief, prescribed nothing in the way of conduct—was in no way incompatible with the devotee's loyalty to the score of cults which already claimed his attention; and if the State saw in this new cult a means to promote the unity of a world-wide Empire, the means was yet not an artificial thing specially devised by the State for this purpose, but a natural product of the religious spirit of the time.

Two exceptions there were to the Roman State's universal toleration or indifference. No cult would be authorised which was of itself hostile to the State; nor any which was itself exclusive of all others. The basis of these exceptions was, once more, political policy and not any dogmatic zeal. To these exceptions there was again in turn one very striking exception. Judaism was essentially an exclusive religion. No Jew could have any share in any other religion. No Jew could take part in the official worship of the State. Yet the Jewish religion was not only not persecuted, but it was the subject of the State's special protection. The reason for this singular exception is to be found in the coincidence of the religion and the race. Judaism was the religion of a subject nation. The non-Jewish adherents of the sect were so rare as to be negligible, nor did their number really increase. The religion of the Jew was part of his nationality and, as such, the traditional Roman policy, which tolerated all differences in the one loyalty, tolerated the Jew's religion and protected it.

It was in the shadow of that protection that the religion of the Church made its first contacts with the Roman authority, for to the Romans the first Christians they knew were members of a Jewish sect. The differences between the Christians and other Jews were mere quarrels of Jewish divinity, with which the Roman law refused to occupy itself. Naturally enough it was only a matter of time before the Jews who did not see in Jesus Christ the promised Messias, and who were responsible for the expulsion of His followers from the body of Judaism, made it clear to the Roman officials that in Christianity they had to deal with a new, non-national religion. From the moment when the distinction was clear, and the exclusiveness of the new religion recognised, it became for the Roman State an unlawful religion in the technical sense, and the atmosphere thickened with hostility. To this legal suspicion of the Church as a religious conspiracy, there was added very soon the more fruitful suspicion of its members as monsters of depravity, meeting secretly for the performance of rites bloody and unnaturally obscene. A tradition which goes back to the first century itself, credits the Jews with the authorship of these only too successful calumnies.

By the time of the Emperor Nero (54–68) the Christians were known as such in Rome, they were numerous, and they were the objects of popular suspicion and hatred. It is to Nero there falls the horrible distinction of exploiting this hatred to cover up his own misdeeds, and also of setting a precedent in the manner of dealing with the new *religio illicita*.

The circumstances which brought about the persecution under Nero (64–67) are obscure. The terms of the legislation are lost, though it seems agreed that it was Christianity as such that was the object of the law. *Christiani non sint* is its spirit. More certain than the terms of the law are the facts of the terrible scenes in the garden of Nero's palace on the Vatican, where, like so many human torches to light up a festivity, thousands of Christians, clad in garments steeped in pitch, paid with their lives for loyalty to their new faith. Equally certain appears to be the motive which turned Nero's attention to the Christians—the chance of saddling an already suspect people with the guilt of his own recent criminal burning down of Rome. Little is known in detail of this first persecution, though from the first epistle of St. Peter (iv, 12, 15, 16) warning Christians in general to lead good lives so that if condemned for their faith it will be evident to all that their faith is their only crime, it might be argued that the persecution was not confined to Rome.

Nero's criminal insanity was already nearing its term when the Christians fell victims to it. Four years after the Vatican martyrdoms he was dead, slain by his freedman too impatient to wait for the emperor's suicide; and the State, after a century of peace, was once again in all the turmoil of civil war. To Nero, in that year, three different armies gave three successors, all three of whom died violent deaths, the swiftly passing Otho, Galba, and Vitellius. Finally the army of Vespasian triumphed and with his acknowledgment as emperor the Roman world once more had peace. Peace came to the Christians, too, for the persecution had been Nero's personal act. In the reaction which followed his death Nero's laws were annulled, except, significantly, his law against the Christians. Nero had put them outside the State's protection. There they remained, the peace they now enjoyed the accident of circumstances.

Under the Flavian emperors—Vespasian, Titus and Domitian—the restoration necessary after twenty years of crazy rule was systematically carried out in the spirit of the empire's best tradition. How, towards the end of his fifteen years' reign, Domitian (81–96) suddenly turned into a second Nero or Caligula is one of the commonplaces of the imperial story. From his struggle with the senatorial aristocracy a reign of terror developed which involved all the better elements of the population and the Christians with them. Details, once again, are few. There is no record of any new law, and it was, apparently, under Nero's all sufficient edict that the martyrs suffered. They included, at Rome, members of the noblest families, the emperor's own kinsfolk, Flavius Clemens, recently consul, and his wife, and Glabrio, another ex-consul. It is to this persecution, too, that tradition ascribes the martyrdom of St. Clement of Rome, and the passion of St. John the Evangelist before the Latin gate of the city.

Domitian, too, died violently, murdered by his officers before his madness had found the chance to murder them, and before the persecution had lasted long. In his place the officers of the guard installed as emperor the elderly Nerva (96–98) and with Nerva there came in a new tradition of administration and a wholly new spirit. The chronic problem of the "right to the throne" in a State where the chief magistrate was, in the last analysis, supreme because he was the commander-in-chief, where there was no such thing as a principle of legitimacy, and where the army was an army of citizens, this new tradition solved by the principle of adoption. The emperor, early in his reign, chose his successor, adopted him as his son, and secured his recognition as emperor-to-be. For the best part of a century the system worked admirably, and it gave to the empire its golden age of prosperity and peace under Trajan (98–117), Hadrian (117–138), Antoninus Pius (138–161) and Marcus Aurelius (161–180). But Marcus Aurelius chose his own son to succeed him, the worthless and incompetent Commodus (180–192) whose murder was the prelude to a century of civil anarchy in which, more than once, the Empire seemed on the point of disappearing entirely.

With these emperors whose skill in administration, practical wisdom and concern for the welfare of their subjects have made them ever since the very type of the model ruler, Christianity had to face the worst century of all the persecutions. It was to these emperors, moderates like Trajan, cultured scholars like Hadrian, philosophers like Marcus Aurelius, that St. Justin and the rest addressed their reasoned and eloquent pleas for toleration. All in vain. Not only did the Apologists go unheard, but the emperors, by removing the process against the Christians from the unseemly irregularity of lynch-law, not only fixed the State's hostility in their regard, but indirectly provided a recommendation to the zeal of good citizens to discover the Christians and to good magistrates to persecute them: indirectly, for the motive of the first of the new imperial orders was to solve a case of conscience for an administrator anxious to administer the law faithfully and yet perplexed by the consequence that he was thereby sending to torture and death citizens of blameless life.

This administrator was none other than Pliny the Younger and the episode of his correspondence with Trajan throws a great deal of light on the spirit of the persecution under these truly Roman princes, aristocrats, conservatives, inflexible men of law. The administration of the province of Bithynia had lately passed into the emperor's personal charge, and Pliny, his friend and confidant, had been despatched to carry through the necessary re-organisation.

He found a province in which Christians were so numerous, in the countryside as well as in the towns, that the temples were deserted, the public ritual in places abandoned and the traders for whom the sacrifices were a means of livelihood generally impoverished. Denunciations from such interested parties poured in to the new governor, and persons accused of being Christians were hauled before him for judgment. The business was new to him, and in a letter to Trajan he set forth his hesitations, described the course he had taken, and asked for directions. Should he make any distinction on account of the age of the accused ? Should he grant a pardon to those who repented their Christianity ? And in the case of those who refused to abandon it, was it the bare fact of being Christians that should be punished or should they be punished for the crimes which went with membership of the sect ? So far he had questioned the accused, and threatened them with punishment should they admit they were Christians. Those who obstinately refused to deny it he had punished, for, whatever the nature of what they confessed, such obstinacy he thought deserving of chastisement. A vast number had been denounced in an anonymous letter. Those who denied they were, or ever had been Christians, and at Pliny's demand proved it by offering wine and incense before the emperor's statue and by cursing Christ, he had released. Others there were who, once Christians, had now for some years ceased to be. These, too, proved their Paganism in the same way.. From this last class he had obtained strong denials that Christians were bound by oath to a life of crime. Their mutual agreement was rather to avoid theft and robbery, adultery, frauds. Apart from the folly that, on a fixed day, the Christians met before dawn to sing a hymn to Christ as God, he found nothing against them.

Trajan's reply furnished the principle which for the next hundred years determined the procedure. Pliny's action is approved. Christians are not to be hunted out by the magistrates. Those denounced and brought before the tribunals are, however, to be tried. If the accused denies the accusation and supports the denial by taking part in the sacrifices, even though the suspicion was justified, he is to go free. Anonymous denunciations are to be ignored. *Nam et pessimi exempli, nec nostri saeculi est.*

Christianity, then, is very definitely a crime, "an abstract crime," itself punishable. Yet for all its gravity—death is the punishment—it is not the dangerous thing that, say, brigandage is. It is no part of the State's duty to search out these criminals. The situation is an illogical one, as the Apologists were not slow to point out. To punish so savagely, for a "crime" such that it was not worth while tracking down the criminals ! And to free from the penalty his past crime deserves the criminal who will declare that he has lately ceased to commit it ! The procedure before the tribunals was something new. It was not by the testimony of witnesses that the crime was proved, but by the criminal's own refusal to deny it. None sought to convict him, often indeed the magistrate by promises, by threats, by violence sought to prevent his conviction. The law strained every nerve that the criminal might escape the awful penalty which the same law declared to be his just desert. The whole machinery of justice was employed to force, not an admission of guilt, but a denial. In the *acta* of the trials of St. Polycarp (155), of St. Justin (165), of the martyrs of Lyons (177), of Scillium (180), and of others of this century, the whole process can be read in detail.

To this legislation of Trajan the next hundred years add little if anything. And there is to be noted, as the century goes by, a tendency to disregard the prohibition to hunt out the Christians, thanks to the increasing popular hatred of their religion which calumnies inflame, and which the learned apologetic never reaches, and thanks also to the indifference of the officials. During this century, then, the Christian is at the mercy of his Pagan neighbours and acquaintances. Until they move, the law ignores his existence. Once they act, the law must act too. The magistrate is here the servant of any chance spite or hatred. The emperor's sole care is to see that, in the administration of Justice, due order is observed.

With the last of the Antonines, the "roman-ness" of the empire disappeared for ever. Commodus was murdered in 192 and his successor Pertinax, emperor by grace of the imperial bodyguard, a few months later. Didymus Julianus followed Pertinax and, as in 68, the Empire seemed doomed to a long civil war. It was rescued from this by the success of the African soldier who established himself in 193, Lucius Septimius Severus. With Severus there entered into the high places of the State a type hitherto unknown there—the provincial for whom the provinces were more important than the capital, and who had for Rome and Roman ways a simple vigorous contempt. Nor was this all. The wife of Severus, Julia Domna, came of a Syrian priestly family. A woman of talent and highly cultured, the court under her influence became an academy. Galen, Diogenes Laertius and the great jurists Papinian and Ulpian found in her a patron. Thanks to her influence the religion fashionable in the imperial circle, for the next half century, was that philosophical morality which has been described. It was one of this circle of Julia Domna's protégés, Philostorgius, who, at the request of the empress, now wrote the famous life of the chief of the "saints" of the new moral philosophy, Apollonius of Tyana, with its classic pleas for toleration in matters of religion. The old, hard, legalist spirit of the Antonines had indeed disappeared. In its place is this fever of syncretism which finds the old classical polytheism an obstacle to the new aim of a universal, all-embracing, moral religion. Eastern cults, with their ideas of moral purification, expiation for past misdeeds, belief in a future life which is conditioned by present conduct, are a help. One Eastern cult, especially, is patronised—that of the Sun, in which these imperial syncretists see an impersonal symbol for the Monotheism to which they tend. Into this system Christianity could not enter, but thanks to the spirit which inspired it, Christianity was now, for the first time, to experience a certain understanding and even an admiration of its ideals, and to be conceded a legal existence.

Septimius Severus was not himself personally hostile to the religion of the Church, and a Christian was foster-mother to his son and heir, Caracalla. Heliogabalus (217–222) was actually the chief priest of one of the principal Sun-cults at the time of his elevation, and he not only retained the dignity but, to the disgust of his Roman subjects, made no secret that he considered it of more account than his imperial, rank. But the emperor who, more than all the rest, sums up this un-Roman succession of emperors is Julia Domna's great-nephew Alexander Severus. It was to his mother, the Empress Julia Mammæa, that St. Hippolytus dedicated his treatise *On the Resurrection*, and she is remembered, too, as the empress who at Antioch summoned Origen to speak before her on the Christian mysteries. Alexander Severus did not belie his parentage. In him Syncretism is indeed enthroned, more even than was Philosophy in Marcus Aurelius. In his own "oratory," side by side with statues of Orpheus and the more noble of his imperial predecessors, he placed those of Abraham and of Our Lord Himself, and in Our Lord's honour he even planned to build a temple.

Under such princes, and with such a spirit informing the court, some modification of the persecution was inevitable. To that modification the first of the line contributed not at all. Tertullian indeed speaks of his benevolence, but Christians certainly suffered during his reign, notably the famous women SS. Felicitas and Perpetua. There exists, too, the record of an edict which most scholars take as a prohibition against conversions, conversions primarily to Judaism, but also to Christianity—"Under severe penalties it was forbidden to become a Jew (*Iudaeos fieri*), the thing was also enacted regarding Christians." There seems room, however, for the interpretation that the edict of Severus merely forbids circumcision whether practised by Jews or, as was still the case in parts of Palestine, by Christians.

Whatever be the share of Septimius Severus in the new policy of benevolence, that of Alexander Severus (222–235) is beyond all doubt, and this emperor is, in this respect, a more important personage than has been generally recognised. With his reverence for Christian ideals there went some knowledge that their religion was an association ruled by an elected hierarchy, for in his scheme of reforms he holds up the system as an example in reference to the nomination of governors and other high officials. The changes which Alexander Severus introduced into the anti-Christian code were fundamental, for he abrogated the law of Nero which was its basis, granting Christians the right to exist, allowing them corporately to own property, and the right to assemble for worship. Christianity then ceased to be *religio illicita*. The date of this legislation we do not know.

Alexander Severus was but a boy of thirteen when he succeeded his cousin, the fantastic Heliogabalus, and he was still four years short of thirty when Maximin the Thracian murdered him and took his place. With Maximin yet another type of emperor appears—the soldier, born on the frontier, and bred in an army that is less and less a Roman thing, rough and illiterate, the successful recruit who has risen from the ranks, the ex-sergeant-major never at his ease outside the camp. From this class are to come most of the emperors of the next hundred years.

Maximin's policy, in many matters, was the simple one of reversing the policies of his predecessor. His short reign (235–238) saw then a renewal of the persecution, a renewal in which the State set the new precedent of itself taking action against the Christians. The *conquirendi non sunt* of Trajan had fallen along with the *institutum Neronianum* which it had organised. The new fury derived from an edict intended for the whole Empire, and aimed specifically at the Church's rulers. The persecution—in which, among others, both the pope, Pontian, and the anti-pope Hippolytus were deported to the mines in Sardinia—was of short duration, for Maximin's successor Gordian III (238–244) returned to the régime of Alexander Severus, and the next emperor, Philip (244–249) was himself a Christian.

But this short persecution of Maximin had far-reaching results. It set the precedent of State initiative, and the equally menacing precedent of general edicts. No longer was the Christian safe so long as his Pagan neighbours were friendly, or he could find means to hide the fact of his faith. The State was no longer indifferent until provoked to action by private zeal. Maximin had been inspired by hatred of his predecessor, in whose entourage many Christians were to be found, rather than by any interest in Christianity itself. But fifteen years later there came an emperor whom enthusiasm for the old national religions inspired. He copied Maximin's methods and extended them into a plan of simple extermination. This was Decius (249–251).

In Decius it was the spirit of the ancient republic that returned for a few years to the Empire. With Severus, fifty years earlier, a culture hostile to the Roman genius had come to rule the Roman world; with Maximin, Barbarism undisguised; and with these changes, a new and terrifying insecurity for whoever held the throne. Between Marcus Aurelius and Decius (180–250) history counts the names of sixteen emperors, and of them all, one only escaped a violent death. In the thirty years between Decius and Diocletian (251–284) there are eleven emperors more, and of these not one died in his bed. The battlefield claimed of the whole perhaps half a dozen. The rest were murdered, either by the troops who had elected them or by the trcops of their rivals; and if Gallienus continued to rule for eight whole years, there is record during that time, in one province or another, of nineteen rival emperors set up by the different armies.

Decius interrupted this tradition of barrack-square emperors. He came of a Roman family, and he inherited all the cold conservatism and austere reverence for tradition proverbially associated with the Roman. He was a member of the Senate when his predecessor, Philip the Arab, named him as his commissioner to suppress a mutiny of the army. Decius was too successful for his own peace. The troops insisted that he should be emperor. Yet another short sharp civil war, and either the field of battle or the daggers of Decius' supporters removed Philip. The new emperor set himself to undo all the work of the past seventy years. The discontent of the Roman with the domination of the provinces, of the East, of the Barbarian, found in him a leader. The State was to be re-Romanised. Amongst other things the old religion, overshadowed for half a century by the imperial patronage of oriental cults, was to be restored. Christianity was to disappear. A day was appointed by the imperial edict upon which all those whose religious allegiance was doubtful were to appear before a local commission. Each of the suspects was in turn to be bidden to offer sacrifice, to make a declaration denying his faith and insulting its Founder, and finally all were to share in a formal banquet where the wines and food used in the sacrifices were to be consumed. Certificates were then to be issued testifying that the accused had proved himself a good Pagan. Not a town, not a village of the Empire escaped the trial. For those who refused to sacrifice, the penalty was, ultimately, death. But the emperor's intention was not so much the massacre of Christians as their conversion to the old religion. Whence, in the case of the loyal Christians, long drawn out trials which lasted for months and filled the prisons with confessors, repeated interrogations and the extensive use of torture in the hope of gradually breaking down the resistance.

Among the better known victims of this persecution was the Bishop of Jerusalem, Alexander, who had been the fellow-pupil of Origen at the School of Alexandria and was later his protector. Origen himself was imprisoned and subjected to continual tortures. At Rome the pope St. Fabian was executed out of hand, an exception to the general procedure, to be explained perhaps by Decius' own statement after the event that he would rather hear of a rival to his throne than of the election of a new bishop in Rome. The terror inspired by the government was sufficient to keep the see vacant for more than a year.

If martyrs were by comparison few, the number of confessors was huge; and, by the testimony of contemporaries (for example St. Denis of Alexandria), the number of apostates greater still. The penalty of confiscation of all property appears to have influenced many of the better class of Christians, and the connivance of the magistrates countless others. Not so much that there were magistrates who could be bribed, but that very many of them were willing to issue certificates of sacrifice to any Christian who would accept one, whether he had in fact sacrificed or not. Such nominal apostasy often enough satisfied the officials and saved the Christian's property and life. It was one of the chief causes of that crisis which, on the morrow of the persecution, was to occupy the bishops in every province of the Empire. In more than one place the majority of the faithful had, technically at least, renounced their faith.

Decius was slain, bravely fighting the barbarians on the Danube, in 251. He had reigned less than two years. But the persecution had ended even before his death. The emperor apparently realised that he had gained for the State religion merely the feeblest and most worthless of the Christians. He had failed utterly to rally that better element whose falling away from the old ideals he so deplored. For the Church itself the emperor's policy was a rude shock, revealing, as it did beyond all doubt, proof upon proof of the disastrous effects of the long peace upon the quality of its members' spirituality. Origen's general strictures were given an unpleasant particularity.

To Decius succeeded Gallus (251–253) and to Gallus, Valerian, in whom all the best ideals of Decius might seem assured of success, for it was Valerian whom Decius had named as a kind of general superintendent of morality when he appointed him to the restored office of Censor. To the Christians, however, Valerian was at first well disposed, and there were so many of them in his service that St. Denis of Alexandria could say that his palace was almost a church. "He was kind and well-disposed to the people of God, and none of his predecessors, not even the emperors who were openly known to be Christians, showed them more sympathy and made them more welcome than did Valerian at the beginning of his reign."[1] For four years all went well until the influence of his chief adviser, Macrinus, brought the emperor to a renewal of the methods of Decius. The cause of the change, apparently, was the increasingly desperate situation of the Empire, attacked now on all its frontiers at once, the Rhine, the Danube, the Sahara, Mesopotamia and Armenia, while pirates ravaged the coasts of Britain and of Asia Minor. Macrinus, a devotee of the old cults, superstitious, and a responsible official, is thought to have interpreted the disasters as the signs of the wrath of the gods provoked by the toleration of the arch-enemy, the religion of Christ.

There are two phases of the persecution. The first edict—August, 257—was directed against the persons of the clergy and against the reunions of the faithful. The bishop in each town, and his priests, were to be summoned to sacrifice to the gods of the State. Those who refused were to be exiled, and the cemeteries and other places of worship were seized by the State. Christians who persisted in meeting for religious purposes were to be punished with death. A year later, by a second edict, the penalties were increased and the proscription was given a wider field. Not exile, now, but death is the penalty for the clergy who refuse to sacrifice; and it is to be carried out immediately on their refusal. The laity also are brought within the terror. Nobles who admit they are Christians are to lose their rank, their properties and their lives, while those specially attached to the Emperor's personal service—the Cæsariani—are to suffer confiscation of goods and to be reduced to serfdom. The new legislation was rigorously applied. At Rome the newly-elected pope, Sixtus II, was arrested, tried and beheaded within a few days, and his more famous deacon Laurence. At Carthage St. Cyprian, exiled under the first edict, was now recalled and put to death under the second. But, as in 251, a political catastrophe brought the new reign of terror to an unexpected end. An invasion from Persia summoned Valerian to the distant eastern frontier. His armies were overwhelmed and he himself fell into the hands of the enemy, to end his life in chains, to be a public show in every town through which his conqueror passed, and this even after death, for his skin was stuffed and preserved to be an everlasting memorial of the greatest disgrace that ever befell a Roman Emperor.

The new emperor was Valerian's son, Gallienus, associated with him in the Empire since 253. One of his first acts was to end the persecution, and the act by which he did so is extremely important. It was no mere cessation of hostilities but the definite

[1] St. Denis of Alexandria.

restoration of a status once held and recently lost, a recognition once more of the Church's legal right to exist. The "Peace of Gallienus" is a re-affirmation of the policy of Alexander Severus, with the new precedent that the emperor now treats directly with the bishops and restores to them the Church property under sequestration since three years before. Once more the Christian is to be unmolested in the practice of his religion, is to enjoy all his rights as a citizen. It was indeed peace and it endured for forty years.

Gallienus died in 268. Claudius II, Aurelian, Tacitus, Probus, Carus and Diocletian (284–305) succeeded him one after another, and under Diocletian, in 302, the persecution was renewed. About these thirty-four years that lie between the death of Gallienus and the first edicts of Diocletian we have almost no knowledge at all. There is the appeal to Aurelian in 272 on the part of the church of Antioch, embarrassed by the presence of the deposed Paul of Samosata in the episcopal palace. There are allusions to other episcopal dissensions, and that is almost all we know. Aurelian meditated a renewal of the war against Christianity—he even issued the edicts—as a part of his campaign to establish, as the new State religion, the solar monotheism which was his own especial cult. But he was killed before his ordinance could be put into execution and no martyrdom is recorded in his reign. The period is one of unhindered propaganda and of uninterrupted unconcealed activity on the part of the Church. Churches are built everywhere—in Rome alone, by the end of the century, there were more than forty—and to be a bishop is to occupy an envied position, so great is the deference shown by the imperial government, so high and so secure is the bishop's social standing. Christians rise to the chief posts in the administration, even to be governors of provinces, and, in the words of Eusebius of Cæsarea, who grew up to manhood under this happy régime, "The emperors allowed the Christians in their service to make the freedom of the faith almost a matter of glory," even dispensing them from the sacrifices which were part of the routine of official life.

Nevertheless, below the surface, the old Pagan animosity survived. The old calumnies, so scornfully retorted on those who spread them by, say, Tertullian, had perhaps disappeared. Origen and St. Cyprian had found friends and admirers in circles where, fifty years earlier, their very existence would have been ignored. But fifty years later than Origen and St. Cyprian the educated Pagan world is still materialist at heart, sceptical about the life after death, and unhesitating when it feels the attraction of vice. The crowd, despite the philosophers and the centuries of progress in the reformation of religion, is still, in its measureless ignorance, where its ancestors were three, four, and ten centuries earlier—

materialist, sensual, superstitious, its present tolerance easily stirred to cruelty against the demonstrated enemies of the human race. The philosophers have on their side the prestige of the traditional culture. Christianity is still on the defensive, still easily derided as fit only for old women and the abnormally stupid, a butt for wits who continue to make mock of a sect that worships a shamefully executed criminal. In all these manifestations, and they are the ever-recurring theme of the theatre's topical skits, there lurks an active disgusted hostility towards such fools. But most dangerous of all was the reasoned hatred that found its armoury in Porphyry's great work *Against the Christians.* Porphyry himself was, it is true, no advocate of persecution; but his learning, his extensive knowledge of Christianity and of Christians, his specious and effective criticism, were at the service of philosophers less indifferent than himself to the fate of what they attacked. Such a philosopher was the one whom Lactantius describes as a really influential personage of the imperial court, at the moment when the persecution was renewed. This was, apparently, Hierocles. He, too, wrote his book, an address *To the Christians.* It is a reasoned criticism of the Gospels and the Life of Our Lord. The miracles are not denied, but they are set beside the alleged miracles of Apollonius of Tyana to destroy whatever force Christians give to them as proofs of Our Lord's divinity. The book was written in a popular style. Bitter and mordant in its language, it attacks the religion of the Christians as an insult to reason.

As the third century drew to its close the old State religion and the new philosophical deism drew together, in opposition to the object of their common hatred. Popular feeling there was in plenty to exploit against the Christians, a tradition made up of a variety of elements appealing to every rank and class. It needed but the opportunity and the vast coalition would move. That opportunity none could create but the emperor. The moment came when he was won over, and the long peace ended, suddenly, in the greatest of all the persecutions. The emperor was Diocletian.

Diocletian has deservedly a very great name in history. He succeeded in halting the general dissolution of the Empire which had gone on now for half a century, and faulty as many of his measures were, they made possible another century and a half of greater peace and prosperity than the West was to know again until the later Middle Ages. He restored the Roman power by remodelling it: the central administration, the provinces, taxation, the army, the imperial court. The last vestiges of the old republican State disappeared, the *de facto* absolutism that had grown with every generation since Augustus received explicit recognition, and the emperor, even to the trappings and ceremonial, was henceforward that semi-divine autocrat the East had always known, and against which the West had always fought. The truth that the most important region of the Empire was the frontier was emphasised in the most striking way possible. From now on Rome ceased to be the Capital. In all his twenty years of reign Diocletian visited it but twice, and Constantine, the greatest of his successors, hardly more often in a still longer reign. The capital follows the emperors, and the emperors live on the frontiers defending what is now perpetually in danger. The emperors—for, another revolutionary change due to Diocletian, there is no longer but one emperor. The task is beyond any one man's energies, and as well to provide for the State as to lessen the danger from the inevitably powerful subordinate, the imperial task is shared by equals. Diocletian was acclaimed emperor in November 284. On April 1, 285, he made over the administration of the Western half of the Empire to his comrade-at-arms of half a lifetime, Maximian. Eight years later he carried the principle a step further. To each emperor was adjoined a lieutenant, who would ultimately succeed his chief and to whom, meanwhile, there was entrusted with the title of Cæsar the administration of a group of provinces. Thus when the persecution broke out, in 303, four princes ruled the one Empire, Diocletian and Galerius in the East, Maximian and Constantius Chlorus in the West.[1]

Diocletian was as little a lover of Roman ways as Severus had been a hundred years before. He was a provincial, and a none too cultured provincial, with a certain cold surliness of manner that repelled. In religion he had no personal preferences. He was not, for example, like Aurelian, concerned to depress one religion in order to exalt another. But he was notably superstitious. Towards Christianity he continued, and apparently as the obvious policy, the policy official since the Peace of Gallienus. His household was filled with Christians and his wife and daughter were converts to the faith. The persecution when it came was not so much the fruit of long deliberation on his part, as an enormous blunder into which he was tricked to consenting. The real author of the persecution was Diocletian's lieutenant, the Cæsar Galerius, and this time it was undisguisedly the war of one religion on another, a persecution which had for its complement the most elaborate attempt to revive Paganism yet undertaken by the Roman State.

The history of the series of persecutions which began with Diocletian's edict of February 24, 303, and which did not end

---

[1] One feature of Diocletian's reforms should be noted for it had its effect in the history of the Church. This was his subdivision of the existing provinces, and the grouping of the new provinces into dioceses. The dioceses again were grouped into praetorian prefectures. See map.

Diocletian
284–305

Constantine
306–337

Galerius
305–311

Constantius II
337–361

Valens
365–378

Theodosius I
379–395

By the Courtesy of the British Museum

PERSECUTORS AND PATRONS

until the so-called Edict of Milan, ten years later, is far too complicated to be set forth adequately in any chronological summary. It was a persecution differing as widely in its methods as the four princes who ruled the Empire differed one from another, and its history is complicated by the rapid changes in the government which mark these ten years. The Empire is divided, united, divided anew; Diocletian and Maximian resign; Galerius and Constantius Chlorus succeed them, with Maximin Daia and the son of Constantius—Constantine—as their respective Cæsars; Constantius dies in 306 and, although Constantine maintains his hold on the provinces he has ruled as Cæsar, there is a new Western Emperor, Severus. The son of Diocletian's old colleague, Maximian, next makes himself master of Italy and Africa. This is Maxentius. A few years later, and Maximian himself returns claiming the honour he had resigned. Six emperors are simultaneously in the field, and civil war again claims the Empire for its own.

Galerius was, once more, the barbarian soldier in the purple, the typical sergeant-major emperor, a good soldier but by Roman standards hardly civilised, violent, crafty, and greatly influenced by his mother, a superstitious peasant from the Carpathians with whom hatred of Christianity was a passion. The first step was to remove the Christian officers from the army. On the plea that the military discipline was suffering from the neglect of the old religious ritual, orders were issued that the routine sacrifices were to be resumed. Those who refused to take part must abandon their careers. The Christians thereupon resigned by hundreds from the army commanded by Galerius. A little later it was represented to Diocletian, more and more superstitious as he aged, that the presence of unbelievers interfered with the auspices. The augurs were unable to divine the will of the gods while unbelievers were present. The emperor thereupon ordered that all his household, on pain of being scourged, should show their faith by offering sacrifice, and that the soldiers should do the same or leave the army. By the end of 302 the régime of tolerance had so far changed that the army and the imperial service were closed to professing Christians.

In the next few months Diocletian was won round to a plan of general extermination. Again it was with Galerius that the scheme originated. A council of State was summoned to discuss the matter, and the last hesitations of Diocletian were overcome when the oracle of Apollo at Miletus spoke in favour of Galerius. But, still reluctant, Diocletian would allow no death penalties.

The signal was given when on the day the edict was published, February 24, 303, the cathedral of the capital city, Nicomedia, was, by the emperor's order, burned down. The edict forbade the Christians to assemble for worship, the churches were to be destroyed, the sacred books handed over to the police, and all Christians were to renounce their faith. Those who refused were, if nobles, to lose their rank; if citizens to become slaves; and, if slaves already, to remain slaves forever. When, soon afterwards, the imperial palace took fire Diocletian's last hesitations vanished and at Nicomedia blood began to flow in abundance.

New edicts followed. First the clergy throughout the Empire were to be arrested, and be summoned, under pain of death, to abjure. Then (304) the same was decreed for the general body of the Christians. There was now no choice but apostasy or death for millions. The legislation was the most severe so far and the most systematic. A host of new and horrible punishments were devised to terrify the weak into submission. Christians were rounded up by the hundred, summoned to sacrifice, and massacred. In one case at least, in Phrygia, where the whole population was Christian, a whole town was wiped out. A phrase in the authentic acts of one of the victims of this time—St. Philip, Bishop of Heraclea—summarises the spirit of the new savagery. "You have heard the law of the emperor," says the judge, speaking to the accused. "It commands that throughout the world members of your society must either sacrifice or perish." With the resignation of Diocletian and Maximian (305), Galerius and his new Cæsar, his nephew Maximin Daia, developed the inquisition yet further. By the edict of 306 all citizens—not merely suspected Christians —were to be summoned to sacrifice. Heralds in the streets were to call out the heads of families, the army to be paraded for the purpose. It is now, too, that the first evidences show of a decline in the character of the judges who carry out the edicts. A new type of magistrate appears, men as gross as the new emperors themselves, to whom the persecution was an opportunity for loot and for lust, and whose malignity devised new horrors and provoked a new danger for the accused, some of whom—a thing hitherto unknown—threw themselves to death to escape inevitable shame. The persecution went its way unhindered in the East for the best part of eight years. In the West it had never been so violent. Where Constantius Chlorus ruled as Cæsar, in Gaul and in Britain, there had been practically no persecution at all: where the Emperor Maximian ruled, in Italy, Spain and Africa, the Christians had suffered as in the countries directly subject to Diocletian. But in 305 Constantius became emperor; Spain passed under his rule and there the persecution ceased. Africa and Italy passed, first to Severus and then (autumn of 306) to Maxentius; under neither of these princes were the persecuting edicts enforced. When Constantius Chlorus died (July 306) his son Constantine succeeded him and maintained his policy of toleration.

For the policy of Galerius, the successful coup d'état by which Constantine came to the purple was a defeat. The dispossession of Severus, whom he had named to succeed Constantius in the West, was a second; for here again the victor, Maxentius, abandoned the policy of persecution. Far different was the fate of the Christians in the East where the advent of Maximin Daia balanced the gain through Constantine and Maxentius. The new eastern Cæsar was, like his uncle, Galerius, the simple product of the wilds beyond the frontier, tamed a little by the army, but hardly improved from his crude native barbarism. Yet, curiously enough, it was he who planned, and to some extent carried through, a great scheme of reformation by which Paganism should itself at last become a "Church." Temples were restored, new ones built, the priests for the first time organised in a hierarchy with a presiding high priest for each province. The ritual was standardised, and the "magicians," the clergy of Maximin Daia's predilection, promoted to the highest offices of the State. It was in the interest of this new State religion that Maximin Daia continued the persecution, henceforward admittedly the war of one religion on another and not a simple measure of precaution in the interest of the State's security.

This new phase, however, was not of long duration. On April 30, 311, an imperial edict brought the whole persecution to an end, restoring the status of 303. It bears the names of Galerius, of Constantine and of Licinius. Galerius, after eighteen years of Empire, was dying in the horrible agony Lactantius has described. Fifteen days after the publication of the edict he was no more. His share in that edict can have been no more than nominal. It was really the act of Constantine and Licinius, the first stage of the new policy of which the Edict of Milan, two years later, was to be the consummation. The edict of 311 is by no means a pro-Christian manifesto. The emperors are at no pains to hide their scorn for the religion they are reprieving. They refer approvingly to the edicts which inaugurated the persecution, and to the end in view, the restoration of the old Roman life. Those edicts are now annulled because it has been proved that what Christians had returned to the ways of their ancestors had done so simply through fear. The chief result of the persecution had been the creation of a large class who worshipped neither the Roman gods nor the God of the Christians. Before the menace such a feature in the national life presents, the emperors prefer to grant once more a licence to Christianity to exist. *Denuo sint christiani.* They may reorganise their Churches; the prisoners are to be freed. Let them for the future avoid anything which is contrary to the established order, and let them not forget the duty laid upon them to pray to their God for the safety of the State and its princes.

From the new policy Maximin Daia, now in the East the supreme ruler, held himself coldly aloof. As Constantius had never given an effective assent to the edict of 303, so Maximin ignored that of 311. Nevertheless even Maximin yielded somewhat to the new forces, and in a letter to the provincial governors of his Empire halted the persecution. For a moment the Christians breathed easily through all the Roman world.

Licinius was an old friend of Galerius, for years one of his most confidential advisers. Had Galerius been wholly free in the matter, Licinius would have succeeded Constantius in 306, and again Severus in 307. It was not until 308 that he was in fact associated with Galerius in the Empire, and Galerius proclaimed his confidence by naming him Emperor and not Cæsar. He was then heir to the provinces Galerius had ruled, with Nicodemia as their capital, and to whatever he could hold of Galerius' position as the senior emperor. Maximin Daia was overshadowed by a newer power. He did not intend to remain so and with his invasion of the states of Licinius the duel between Paganism and Christianity reopened. It was marked on the part of Paganism by a last supreme revival.

From all over the East petitions from the municipal and provincial councils came in—organised to some extent by the imperial officials—calling for the suppression of Christianity. The petitions and Maximin Daia's replies, into which there has crept a tone of piety that makes them nothing less than Pagan sermons, were inscribed on tablets of bronze and set up in the chief places of the cities—a new and subtle means of anti-Christian propaganda. The calamities which of late years have afflicted the State, war, famine, plague, tempest, all these are the natural effects of the wrath of the gods provoked by the practices of Christian folly. In the loyalty of all good citizens to the ancient religion lies the Empire's one hope. Let the temples once more take up their place in the people's life, the sacrificial fires be renewed. The emperor will himself lead in the pious work, the head and centre of every religious inspiration. For the encouragement of the Pagan, the State organised a campaign of education in the wickedness of Christianity. Placards, pamphlets, lectures subsidised by the State, set before the Pagan the vile thing his Christian neighbours were. Elaborate forgeries alleged to be the sacred books of the Christians appeared, and these blasphemous parodies and caricatures were used as lesson books in the schools. The latest Pagan offensive was at its height and beginning to show results in a revival of Pagan practice when, as Maximin Daia planned to ally himself with Maxentius in Italy—hitherto a usurper in the eyes of the three "legitimate" emperors—against the combination of Licinius and Constantine, the news of news came to him that Constantine had declared himself a Christian.

It was unexpected news, and the occasion of the declaration fitted it—the eve of a battle against Maxentius upon which, following a first reverse, Constantine staked his whole fate.

Constantine had marched from his own States—as yet overwhelmingly Pagan—through Italy, still Pagan too, and was preparing to attack the single army which lay between him and Rome, of all the empire's great cities perhaps the most Pagan. The expedition he had undertaken had no religious significance —its purpose was simply the destruction of the power of a usurper. Constantine himself was not merely a Pagan but, from all his associations and upbringing he belonged to that new school of Paganism from whose scorn Christianity had naturally least hope of recruits. His parents were Pagans, and his father's religion a form of that new moral monotheism, popular with the army, whose symbol was the Sun—Sol Invictus. One form of that cult had seemed destined to high fortunes under Aurelian (269–75). After Aurelian's death Constantius Chlorus was its most eminent supporter. The cult then probably came to Constantine as part of his paternal inheritance, and as he shook himself free of the influence of Diocletian and Maximian (whose son-in-law he was) the young emperor showed himself openly the protector of his father's cult. By the time of his expedition against Maxentius his evolution in religion had gone beyond this. He had abandoned the last traces of a cult of the Sun, and reached the point of a simple belief that there is but one God. The final, decisive step was not the fruit of any further meditation but was due to something which happened to Constantine the very night before the battle at the Milvian Bridge, a mile or two outside the Flaminian Gate of Rome. In a dream the emperor was bidden to mark his soldiers' shields with the sign of God, *cœleste signum Dei*, and go into battle with this as his badge. He did so. In the fight which followed he was victorious, and Maxentius was drowned in the Tiber as he fled from the field. Constantine entered Rome convinced now that the one, supreme God was the God whom the Christians worshipped—Jesus Christ.

From Rome, after receiving the congratulations of the Senate, he proceeded to Milan for the solemnities of the marriage arranged between his sister and his colleague Licinius. At their meeting the two emperors, advancing the policy of the act of two years before, published what has come to be called the Edict of Milan (313, probably February), the final and definitive admission of the

State that the new religion of the Church must survive. Maximin Daia—to anticipate the story by a few months—took advantage of the absence of Licinius in the West and, despite the difficulties of the winter, invaded his States, crossed into Europe, and with his powerful army laid waste the rich provinces which are now the Balkans. There, at Nicopolis, he met, and was defeated by Licinius, returned from Milan in haste; and with the defeat and death of Maximin Daia the authors of the Edict of Milan were masters of the Roman world (May 1, 313).

II. THE STATE DE-PAGANISED

The famous edict of Constantine and Licinius is by no means a charter of rights and privileges. It is a political act, and as such is conditioned by the circumstances of the moment. Both of these emperors had long been agreed that the persecution menaced the future of the State. If one of them was recently converted to a belief in Christianity—and the belief was as yet incomplete— his colleague, however, still remained a Pagan. Constantine himself could have no policy which went beyond the maintenance of a balance between the two religions, and the language of the edict, as far as we can tell, is not that of a Christian at all. In this respect it is very evidently the supplement to the act of 311 and the spirit it breathes is that of the "deistic" monotheism which was the reigning fashion at the court. It is an arrangement prepared by Constantine which his colleague accepts, and which is expressed in tactfully neutral language. The motive for the new policy is no longer the restoration of the old Roman ways but simply "the public good." This is unattainable if due honours are not rendered to "the divinity." That these honours may be rendered, all who honour "the divinity" have leave to do so— Christians with the rest. Thus the edict does not by any means proclaim universal toleration. "To the Christians and to all men we decree there be given free power to follow whatever religion each man chooses, that, whatever gods there be, they may be moved mercifully in regard to ourselves and those over whom we exercise authority"—an insurance devised possibly to comfort the devout Pagan critic against vengeance from the old gods for any apostasy implied in the act. The edict, then, grants once more what Alexander Severus had first granted, and then Gallienus thirty years later. But this time the grant is explicitly built into the law as a fundamental principle of public welfare; and the emperors from whom it emanates are no religious dilettantes, nor weaklings anxious at a crisis to rally a disunited people. They are conquerors, one of them the empire's greatest soldier for generations and a whole-hearted convert to the faith, and the edict is the sign of their conquest. But it does more than restore liberties. A further clause gives the surest of all guarantees that the toleration is no mere matter of form, no political trick of the moment. It decrees the restoration to Christians of whatever property has been confiscated "without any price asked or any transference money . . . without delay and without discussion."[1]

That Constantine's conversion to a belief that Jesus Christ is the one only God was sincere is certain, and equally certain his subsequent loyalty to what he considered to be the best interests of the Church through which the one God chose to be worshipped. But whatever the growth of his knowledge of his new faith and of his attachment to it, he remained, as emperor, faithful to the principles of the edict of 313. Even had he desired to christianise the State, the difficulties before him would have prevented it. The Christians were by no means in the majority. The West especially, his own sphere of operations, was strongly Pagan;[2] and its anti-Christian habits and traditional prejudice survived for the best part of the next hundred years. If there were Christians who, impatiently, demanded a reversal of rôles and repression of the Pagans they found no welcome at the court. Whatever the emperor's personal preferences, he maintained the Pagans in the posts they occupied; and he continued to be the Pontifex Maximus of the Pagan Cults. So bound up with the old religion was the imperial office, that to have abolished the pontificate at that moment would have been to strip himself of vast prestige and authority; to have transferred the office to another would have been almost an abdication. Tertullian had plainly said that no man could become emperor and remain a Christian, and for the next sixty years the Christian Emperor proved him right to this extent, at least, that he retained and exercised the supreme headship of the Pagan Cults. Finally, for the first eleven years which followed the edict, Constantine's colleague was a Pagan, and a Pagan who gradually grew hostile to Christianity.

In 323 there was a breach between the two emperors in which religious differences played their part. Licinius abandoned the policy of 313 and, in the States of the eastern Empire, the persecution raged once more. Constantine's victory at Chrysopolis (September, 323) brought this to an end, and it ended, too, the reign of Licinius. Six months later his death—in which not improbably Constantine had a share—left Constantine without a

---

[1] J. R. Palanque notes, as an important change, that now, *for the first time*, each Christian community, each church, is given legal recognition: previously it had been the Christian religion as such; F. & M. III, 22.

[2] One tenth only of the population Christian: so J. R. Palanque in F. & M. III, 27 note 6.

rival, sole master of the whole Roman world. His new, un-questioned supremacy found expression in a notable change of the form of his language about matters religious. So far he had kept studiously to the neutrality of 313. He had, as Pontifex Maximus, carried through certain reforms—divination in secret was henceforward forbidden, and certain abuses in magical rites. As emperor he had granted the Catholic clergy those exemptions from the burdens of citizenship which the Pagan priests had always enjoyed, he had given the churches the right to receive legacies and he had made the Sunday a legal holiday. In his language he had been as impartial as in his actions, and not a sign escaped to show publicly his increasing contempt for the stupidities of the old polytheism and for its superstitions. But now, victorious over a Paganism lately militant, and master for the first time in the more Christian part of the Empire, he was free to express his personal sentiments. In the proclamation which announced the victory to the bishops of the East, he tells the story of his con-version, describes the atrocities of Diocletian's persecution, speaks of himself as brought to the Faith by God to be the means of the Faith's triumph, and declares that he takes up the govern-ment of his new State "full of faith in the grace which has confided to me this holy duty." There is a like change in his language to his Pagan subjects. The policy of 313 is scrupulously maintained, but he does not hesitate to speak of Pagan "obstinacy," of their "mis-guided rites and ceremonial," of their "temples of lying" which contrast so strikingly with "the splendours of the home of truth."

The convert emperor no longer hides his contempt for Paganism, but he is careful still to distribute offices to Christian and Pagan alike. All are equal, and both religions equal, before the law.

The first breach in this policy of neutrality was the work of his sons. Constantine died in 337 leaving as heirs his three sons, Constantine II, Constantius II, and Constans. The eldest died three years later, and the new law bears the signature of the two younger brothers. It declares the abolition of all sacrifices and threatens dire punishment to those who contravene it (341). Among one section of the Christians its enactment was the oc-casion of great joy. They exhorted the emperors to go further still. Whence so great an uneasiness among the Pagans that, a year later, the emperor in the West, Constans, the vast majority of whose subjects were Pagans, published a new law to reassure them, ordering special care for the historic temples of the old capital. Ten years later Constantius II, now sole emperor, published a new edict which threatened death to those who wor-shipped idols. The temples were to be closed, the sacrifices to cease. No doubt where the thing was peaceably possible the law was enforced. But despite the law the facts show the old religion as still flourishing unhindered throughout the West. All the old feasts were observed at Rome, with all the accustomed sacrifices, in the year which followed this law (354), and in the very year which saw its renewal Constantius II himself, visiting Rome, confirmed the privileges of the different cults, the subsidies of public money granted to them and, acting as Pontifex Maximus, he filled the vacant priestships by nominations of different members of the Roman aristocracy. This contrast between the terrifying threats, and the impotent toleration of those who ignored the threats was characteristic of the general policy of Constantine's vacillating successors. They repudiated their father's policy, and were yet too weak to enforce the repudiation. The chief effect of their legislation was to irritate the Pagans, and to prepare the way for the anti-Christian reaction which followed under Julian.

Julian (361–363), the successor of Constantius II, has gone down to history as Julian the Apostate, but the title is hardly fair, for though Julian set himself to reverse the policy of the previous fifty years and to restore Paganism, it is hard to see that he was ever a Christian at all, and he certainly was never a Catholic. He was a nephew of Constantine and, a child of five at the emperor's death, one of the very few near relations of the new emperors who survived the general massacre designed to remove possible rivals to their succession. For these massacres, in which his father, two uncles, and a brother perished, Julian declared Constantius II responsible, and in this personal hatred of Constantius, which deepened after that emperor's execution in 354 of Julian's only surviving brother, may be found one reason for Julian's fanatical hatred of everything Christian. His earliest education he received under the care of the arch-Arians Eusebius of Nicomedia, George of Cappadocia and Aetius; and once his childhood was past he was deprived of even this pale reflection of Christian truth. In place of Arian bishops and their sterile logomachies, he now had hellenists to tutor him, and in the distant and lonely palaces to which he was exiled, the imaginative boy grew to adolescence and early manhood, dreaming of a revival of the Paganism of the poets and the philosophers. His own religion was little more than a devotion to the classic Greek Culture, a thing intellectual, literary, artistic. His philosophy was the neo-Platonism of the day, something of Plotinus and much more of superstition and magic, a mélange that had in it something of the modern Theosophy cults and Spiritualism, with a veneer of elaborate ritual. The thing he planned to revive had never existed; it was the golden age of every adolescent's dreaming fancy, the past seen through the idealism of literature. But for all his bookishness the shy, reserved, and ascetic young man showed his gifts as a ruler once his cousin named him Cæsar (358), and enough of political ambition once the troops hailed him Emperor (360) to take the offensive against Constantius II. But the sudden death of Constantius (Nov., 361) gave him the mastery of the world without a battle, and for twenty months he ruled supreme. It was too short a time for any permanent accomplishment, and his revival had the ultimate effect of all schemes that plan to ride the skies and fail. It left the prestige of the old religion very much lower than it had found it, left it indeed covered with ridicule.

For the greatest attempt of all was now made to organise Paganism, its cults and its priesthood; to give it a coherent body of doctrine, a fixed and regular liturgy. Its priests, on the model of the Christian clergy, were to be teachers, and schools of Pagan theology were established. The practice of good works was to be a function of the new religion; orphanages, hospitals, asylums to be founded in which the new Pagan virtue of charity would find expression. Nothing was less in keeping with the facts of the old Paganism, nothing less in accord with the Roman tradition, than the new priesthood as Julian planned it, influenced obviously by the desire to defeat Christianity by copying the Christian spirit. The Roman priest had been an important personage in the political and social life of the day. High rank in the priestly college, and high office in the State had always gone together. But Julian's priests were to live like monks, ascetics, carefully avoiding contact with the evil world, given to a life of virtue, and service, prayerful, studious, continent.

The sacrifices were restored and carried out on an enormous scale, Julian himself as Pontifex—against all tradition—actually immolating the victims. The Christian magistrates and officers were replaced. The Christian clergy lost all their privileges. They lost, too, what pensions the State had begun to pay them, and were obliged to restore what they had already received. Even the Christian poor were made to give back the alms which the imperial charity had assigned them. The temples, too, where these had fallen into decay, were to be restored at the expense of the Christians. But the edict most complained of was that which expelled the Christians from the schools. No Christian was henceforth to be allowed to teach or to study the ancient classical authors. "Let them keep to Matthew and Luke," said Julian. Rhetoric, Philosophy, Political Science—to the Christian henceforward these were banned, and with them all hope of a professional career.

All this was but the preparation for a revival of the older persecution of blood—none too easy a matter in 361 with

Christianity strong through fifty years of State favour, and entrenched in all the high places of the State. Julian did not live long enough to launch another frontal attack. Death claimed him before he had the chance to show his quality as a philosophical Decius or Diocletian. But every encouragement was given to the Pagans to attack the Christians. Anti-Christian riots went unchecked, excesses, massacres even, went unpunished. To the Christians who appealed against the indifference of the officials, who stood by while property was destroyed and lives were lost, the emperor mockingly recalled that it was part of their faith to suffer wrong patiently. Martyrs there were as fifty years before, but condemned and put to death now, ostensibly, for rebellion or treason—a new legal trickery intended to rob their deaths of any religious significance.

The persecution ended very suddenly. On June 26, 363, Julian was slain, fighting the perpetual enemy of the East, Persia, testifying with his last breath, according to Theodoret's account, Whom he had fought, and by Whom he was conquered "Galilean, Thou hast triumphed." The army gave him Jovian for a successor and Jovian was a Catholic. Without any elaborate measure of repression, the whole edifice of Julian's "Church" crumbled and fell. The new edict restoring religious toleration, and the statutes of Constantine's régime, was enough. The dead thing lately galvanised into a semblance of life ceased to move, the apostates who had served it returned to Christianity more easily than they had left it. The path to the inevitable Christianising of the State was once more open.

But despite the opportunity a reaction always presents to the victorious reactionaries, the movement to de-Paganise the State halted for another ten years and more. Jovian reigned only nine months and his successor, Valentinian I (364–75), though a Catholic, was as emperor more neutral than Constantine himself. The temples remained open, the oracles were consulted as of old; and if he took from the temples the properties which Constantius II had confiscated to the benefit of the Church, and which Julian had recently restored to the temples, Valentinian did not make them over to the Church once again, but ordered that they should revert to the imperial treasury. As he held himself aloof from the controversy between Catholics and Arians, declaring "I am a layman. It is no business of mine to scrutinise Christian dogma. That is the bishop's affair," so he showed a like indifferent neutrality in the edict which reversed Julian's educational policy; "Whoever is worthy by character and by talent to educate youth shall have the right to open a school or to gather together once more his dispersed scholars." Later in his reign (371) he is even more explicitly averse from any anti-Pagan legislation. "I do not consider this art to be criminal," he declared to the Pagan augurs, "nor indeed any of the religious observances established by our ancestors. The laws enacted at the beginning of my reign are proof of this. They grant to every man the right to follow whatever religion he prefers. I do not, therefore, condemn the auspices. I simply forbid them to be used for criminal purposes."

In the Eastern Empire, where Valentinian's brother Valens ruled (364–378), there was during these years an actual patronage of Paganism. Valens was determined that his Christian subjects should all be Arians. The thirteen years of his rule were for the Catholics of the East a long reign of terror, and in his measures of repression the emperor gladly made use of the Pagans.

Valentinian I died in 375 and with the accession of his son the youthful Gratian (375–383) the religious situation changed immediately, for the new emperor refused to be Pontifex Maximus with the words "A robe such as this does not become a Christian," and abolished the office. The anomaly of the Catholic functioning as the chief priest of Paganism was at an end; and Paganism, the head of the State declining to be its chief priest, may be considered henceforth as "disestablished." It remained to disendow the institution, and this Gratian did seven years later. By an act of the year 382 the privileges and exemptions enjoyed by the Pagan priesthood were abolished, the property of the temples confiscated and henceforward all legacies to temples were null and void.

About the same time the statue of the goddess Victory that stood in the senate chamber at Rome was removed. This statue, to which the senators offered incense as they entered, and through whose presence the goddess herself in some sense presided over the debates of the empire's most venerable institution, had come to be the very symbol of Paganism's official primacy. It had already been removed in the time of Constantius II (357) but, to appease the storm of angry protests, it was speedily replaced. The aristocratic families of the old capital were, in fact—along with the intelligentsia and the half-educated everywhere—the last champions of the cults. Among the first there had developed a new, obstinate ardour about the rites and liturgies; with the men of letters it was an attachment to professional ideals, a dislike for Christianity as the feared foe of beauty and culture, whose triumph would be the triumph of barbarism. What a reality these last oppositions were, and how powerful was their main weapon—scorn—the elaborate constructive apologetic of St. Augustine remains to show, the *De Civitate Dei*. The protestations of the senatorial aristocracy were now renewed and, Gratian being murdered the following year, and the regent for his child-successor—Valentinian II—being an Arian, the Pagans might easily have secured the replacement of the statue once more. That they did not do so was due to the vigorous opposition of the Bishop of Milan, at this time the imperial capital. This was the great man who, until lately, had been governor of the province, one of the last of the Romans, St. Ambrose. He had been Gratian's tutor, as he was now the tutor and protector of the child-emperor. He had been the emperor's adviser in matters temporal no less than spiritual, an ambassador, more than once, where a delicate situation called for the experienced wisdom of the man in whom the Roman administrator and the Catholic bishop were so well combined. St. Ambrose is an augury of what the Middle Ages, at their best, are to be, and in nothing is he more so than in his bold defiance of the Empress Justina in this matter of the statue of Victory. Thanks to his vigour and prudence the policy of Gratian suffered no setback. Upon Paganism it produced the expected result. There was not enough faith in the cults to keep them alive once the revenues went, and with the disappearance of the priestly aristocracy whom those revenues nourished there disappeared, too, the social prestige which was the old religion's chief asset. There was no attempt to punish Pagans for belief or for practice. There was no Christian revenge, and no attempt, as yet, to substitute Christianity for Paganism as the official religion of the State. The Roman Empire was, for the moment, a State in which religion and the republic were things entirely separate. Under Gratian's successor the policy was to reach its logical conclusion. It was Theodosius who first made the State a Catholic thing.

Theodosius (379–395), the one great man the Empire produced in the two centuries which separate Constantine and Justinian, was that phenomenon hitherto rare, an emperor baptised from the beginning of his reign and a convinced practising Catholic. The Catholicism of his regular private life was the mainspring of his public action as the Catholic Emperor. He was not only Latin —almost the first emperor for a hundred and fifty years not born East of the Adriatic—but he came from the most Latin province of all the West, Spain. He had pre-eminently all the Latin virtues; he had a logical mind, an inexhaustible fund of personal energy, a temperament made for prompt solutions, and impatient of half measures. When Valens died, in 378, Gratian had associated Theodosius as his partner and assigned to him the difficult task of restoring the East to something like peace and contentment after half a century of religious disunion that bordered on civil war.

From the beginning Theodosius was definite. The long domination of the little clique of Arian bishops, in whose influence at court lay the real cause of the troubles, came to an end. Catholicism was freed; and security for its future provided in the first code for the repression of heresy. Orthodox Christianity received its first description in civil law as "the faith which the Roman Church has received from the Apostle Peter," it is the faith "professed by the pontiff Damasus and Peter Bishop of Alexandria." The churches of heretics of every sort, Anomeans, Arians, Apollinarians, Macedonians, are to be confiscated and handed over to the Catholics. Heretical assemblies are forbidden and heretics lose all power of making wills or of inheriting. Six times in the next fifteen years these laws are renewed.

Towards the Pagans, on the other hand, Theodosius is much less rigorous. There is a law against apostates from Christianity to Paganism, and all sacrifices to divine the future are now strictly forbidden. Divination of all kinds is abolished. On the eve of his succession to the Western Empire (391) upon the death of Valentinian II, an edict closes all the temples once and for all. Gradually they are given over to other uses. Finally, in the year in which Theodosius becomes master of the whole Roman world (392), the law occupies itself with the domestic religion which was the last refuge of Paganism, as, in Rome at least, it had been the place whence it sprang. All household rites are forbidden, all the domestic shrines are to be destroyed. But with all this anti-Pagan legislation it is to be noted that there is no attempt to compel the Pagan to become a Christian. Christian and Pagan are equal before the law. Honours and office continue to go impartially to the one as to the other. There is no violence offered to persons. The supports of the old religion have been ruthlessly struck away. The structure will soon fall of itself. Pagans remain, and will remain, here and there for a century yet, especially in the country districts. The old cults will, finally, come to be so associated with rusticity that the Roman's very name for a countryman (*paganus*) will for ever describe, and describe primarily, one who worships the old gods. Pagans, countryfolk, living remotely and divorced from the day's life and culture, ignorantly clinging to ancient superstitions and rites, backwoodsmen, there still will be in plenty; and for three centuries after Theodosius the business of their conversion will occupy the Church; but Paganism, with Theodosius, dies never to rise again.

NOTE C

How did the disciples of the Church regard the Roman State which was their persecutor ? From the very beginning there were two schools of thought. The *Apocalypse* speaks of the Roman power in language of unmeasured abhorrence. It is the beast, the great harlot, drunk with the blood of the saints, destined for its crimes to a fearful chastisement.

But in St. Paul there is discoverable a certain pride in the Empire of which he is a citizen, and a faith that its stability and the order it secures are to be, under God, a powerful means of Christian propaganda. The authority which, in some instances, it misuses, is none the less divine in its origin; and whoever resists it resists thereby God Who is its author. To the Christian the prince "is God's minister . . . for good . . . an avenger to execute wrath upon him that doth evil." Obedience, loyalty, the payment of tribute are then obligations in conscience (*Rom.* xiii, 1–7). Nor does the teaching change when, a few years later, Nero's edicts have destroyed the Christian's legal security. It is still his duty to pray "for Kings and for all that are in high station" (*I Tim.* ii, 2), "to be subject to princes and powers, to obey at a word, to be ready to every good work" (*Titus* iii, 1–2). The contemporary writings of St. Peter (*I Peter* ii, 13–15) are inspired by the same ideals, "Be ye subject to every human creature for God's sake: whether it be the king as excelling, or to governors as sent by him for the punishment of evildoers and the praise of the good. . . . Fear God. Honour the King." Such, in the first generation of Christianity, was the Church's general commentary on Our Lord's own direction to "render to Cæsar the things that are Cæsar's."

This theory of the lawfulness of authority, of the State's right to loyal obedience, and of the Christian's political duties as obliging him in conscience, the persecutions by no means destroyed. It is repeated faithfully in the writers of every generation from Nero to Constantine, and, a rooted tradition by the time of that emperor's conversion, it supplied one of the foundations upon which he and his successors were able to build their untraditional novelty of a State-directed Christianity. The epistle of St. Clement of Rome gives a noteworthy testimony to the theory, in the prayer it contains for "our masters and those who govern us on earth" since "Thou, O Lord, has given them sovereign power" and "knowing the glory and honour with which Thou has endowed them, grant us to be submissive and never to rebel against Thy will. . . . Give to them O Lord health, peace, harmony and security, that they may exercise without harm the authority Thou has confided to them."

The martyrs, too—St. Polycarp for example—pray for the emperors in whose name they suffer and for those who are the agents of the imperial power in their death. This religious concern for the welfare of the State is so known an element of the Christian mind that the Apologists can point to it in disproof of the charge that Christianity is a danger to the State; and Tertullian lightly invites the magistrates, "Come good governors, put this soul to the torture while it prays to God for the emperor." Christians, the same bitter spirit insists, have a greater interest than Pagans in the Empire's welfare for it is, in God's providence, the one barrier against all-destroying anarchy and chaos. Nor, he notes, has a Christian ever been found among all the hundred leaders of sedition and revolt.

The Church, then, by no means saw in the Empire a thing evil in its nature, a thing therefore to be destroyed. Nor was there ever any Christian policy in the matter of the persecutions except the heroic policy of patient endurance and prayer for the persecutor until the providence of God should send quieter times.

CHAPTER VII

THE ARIANS, 318–359

THE conversion of the Roman Emperor to Christianity in 312, an event of such proportions that the Christians themselves were staggered thereby for a generation and more, proved in the end to be as important a turning point in the history of the Church's own development as in that of her relations with the State. The century which saw, as an immediate effect of the conversion, the steady de-Paganising of the Roman power, saw also a much more violent sequel to it—the struggle to determine the rôle of the Christian Emperor within the Christian Church. That the autocrat of the Roman world, master of all men's lives, and of the destinies and fortunes of every institution within the world-state, whom millions gladly worshipped as a god, and whom, by formal etiquette, all men treated as semi-divine, that this personification of human might would be, in the Church of Christ, no more than the equal of his subjects, acknowledging there an authority within his State which he did not control, was a consequence of the conversion that the emperor did not realise by any sudden intuition. Nor did the Church as a whole; and before the ecclesiastical mind[1] had come to the clarity of the formulae in which St. Ambrose fixed the matter for all time, the Church had to pass through fifty years of a fight which, more than once, seemed to threaten the death of the traditional faith. Cæsar is no sooner converted than, as the protector of the things that are God's, he threatens to overshadow the hierarchy and its traditional chief. More than any bishop, more than all the bishops, more than the Bishop of Rome himself, Cæsar in his rôle of Faith's defender will determine the course of the Faith's development. When the first Christian rulers appear, of the State in which the Church is born, the Church meets, for the first time, the problem of Cæsaro-Papism that has never since ceased to vex her, of the Catholic prince who wills, in effect, to be pope; the danger that princely benevolence threatens to transform the mystical body of Christ into a department of State.

[1] Some part of the responsibility for the troubles that came of the emperors' failure to understand their true place within the Church must, thinks Palanque, be laid upon the bishops; but he notes well how they were handicapped by the emotions of the sudden revolution in the fortune of religion, the new utterly unprecedented situation, the undoubted enthusiasm—of Constantine especially—for the triumph of the cause of Christ; cf. F. & M. III, 65.

The occasion of the struggle is the renewal of a dispute about a point of doctrine. The point, once again, is fundamental; how far is the Church's founder divine, and therefore how far divine His work in the Church. The disputes spread widely; they are conducted with spirit, with energy and bitterness; and into the arena the whole social life of the time is drawn: not scholars merely and bishops, but the whole lay world, down to the charioteers and market-women. The mobs of the great cities are passionately interested, and play their violent part. The emperor intervenes. There is a council, a decision. The defeated party bides its time; then, through the avenues by which at courts these things are managed, it gradually turns the emperor round. The decision of the council is left intact, but the emperor is worked upon to act against the council's promoters and defenders. There follows a desperate endeavour on the part of the emperor to pacify the State by forcibly imposing the heresy. In the end the heresy disappears, but not even then is the Church's view of Cæsar's rôle wholly victorious. For if, in the East, heresy disappears, it is because an emperor succeeds who is a Catholic. There it is by now a tradition that Cæsar interferes in matters of religion, and that he is a lawful court of appeal. Whence, succeeding the struggle of the Church against Cæsar patronising heresy, a new struggle against the Catholic Cæsar, now fettering the Church with his insistent patronage. The second struggle is not determined for centuries. It only ends with Cæsar's victory and the disappearance of the Church from his State.

Arianism, as a theological doctrine, was the outcome of yet another effort of the Greek mind to reconcile rationally the truths that there is but one God, that the Logos incarnate in Jesus Christ is God, and that the Logos is yet admittedly distinct from the Father. If the Father is God, and if God is one only, and if the Logos is not the Father, how is the Logos God ? The Gnostics of the second century had proposed their solution, and a succession of other theories had continued to trouble the peace of believers through all the next hundred years. All in their turn had been condemned; for, whatever the merit of these ingenious systems, none had produced a satisfactory explanation which yet preserved the traditional faith in its integrity. Praxeas, Noetus, and Sabellius ended by identifying Father and Logos. Theodotus, on the other hand, and the more famous Paul of Samosata, denied that the Logos is truly divine. Of Paul's spectacular disgrace we already know something. With him there fell, too, his friend the priest Lucian, so notorious as heretical in this matter that he lay excommunicated through the reigns of Paul's three successors.

Later, under what circumstances we do not know, Lucian made his peace and, in the persecution of Galerius, gave his life for the Faith, 312. The memory of his martyrdom was still fresh, and his tomb at Nicomedia, the eastern capital, a centre of pilgrimage when, ten years later, Constantine came to rule the East, and the new Emperor's mother, St. Helen, adopted Lucian as her patron saint. Arius was the pupil of Lucian, and Lucian the real father of Arianism.[1]

The theory of Arianism is that "God is One, Eternal, Unbegotten. All other beings are His creatures, the Logos the first of them. Like other creatures the Logos was created from nothing and not from the divine substance (*ousia* in the Greek). There was a time when the Logos did not exist. His creation was not necessary, but due to the will of the Father. The Logos, God's creature, is in turn the creator of all other creatures and his relationship to them is a kind of justification of his being called God. God adopted him as Son foreseeing his merits, for the Logos is free, subject to change and determined to good by his own will. From this adoptive sonship there does not result any real share in the divine nature, any true likeness to it. There cannot be anything like to God. The Holy Spirit is the first of the creatures created by the Logos. He is even less God than the Logos. The Logos became flesh in this sense that in Jesus Christ he took the place of the soul.".

Arius, at the time of Constantine's conversion, was a priest in Alexandria known for his ascetic life, with a great following, among the clergy and, especially, the consecrated virgins whom he directed in the higher way. He was also a preacher of talent, and he began a few years later to fill his church with a popular exposition of Lucian's theory (318). The novelty had all a novelty's success until it was officially brought to the notice of the Bishop of Alexandria. There followed the usual procedure of enquiry and consultation, and it was decided that Arius' explanation was not in accord with the traditional belief. Arius was called upon to abandon it. He refused, and thereupon, with his adherents, he was excommunicated. So far the dispute was on the smallest possible scale—an obscure priest and his bishop. But the priest had travelled, had made friends, and some of these were powerful. The most powerful of them was an old class-fellow of the days when, at Antioch, Arius had followed the lectures of Lucian. This was Eusebius, now a bishop—bishop indeed of the imperial city Nicomedia, and related to the new imperial family. When, after his condemnation, Arius set himself to write

[1] The full detail of the theories of St. Lucian of Antioch is not known; they were certainly strongly tainted with subordinationism; *cf.* BARDY in F. & M. III, 72.

"to all the bishops," in writing to Eusebius of Nicomedia he was writing to an assured ally. The Bishop of Alexandria, too, wrote to the other bishops—more than seventy letters in all, among them one to the pope—an official notification of the heresy and the condemnation, to ensure that Arius, who by this time had fled, should find himself condemned wherever he halted.

Arius, however, found a welcome among his friends at Nicomedia, and set himself to organise a body of supporters. Letters, pamphlets, and popular songs embodying his doctrine, poured from his pen. His bishop replied, the other bishops took sides, and soon all the East was ablaze with the controversy—Egypt condemning Arius, the bishops of Asia, led by Eusebius, supporting him. The dispute was still unsettled when, in the September of 324, Constantine defeated the Eastern Emperor Licinius and became, at last, sole master of the Roman world. To him the disputants turned.

His first action was to send to Alexandria the bishop who most possessed his confidence, Hosius of Cordova. It was possibly from this meeting of Hosius and Alexander of Alexandria that there came the idea of submitting the matter to a council that would not be local merely, as all councils up to now had been, but would gather in all the bishops of the Church. Whatever the origin of the plan, Constantine made it his own. It was in his name that the bishops were invited; he provided the travelling facilities which alone made its meeting possible; and he chose the place where it should assemble, Nicea, a city of Bithynia, close to his capital. The council opened in the June of 325. Estimates differ as to the number of bishops present. Traditionally they were 318, but the creed bears the signatures of 220 only. They were almost all from the eastern half of the Empire, fourteen only from Europe and of these fourteen eleven were from European Greece.[1] The Bishop of Rome was absent; his age forbade his making the journey, but two of his priests represented him. Hosius presided.

To the bishops who assisted at the magnificent festivities with which the council opened, the whole affair must have seemed incredible. Most of them had suffered for the Faith, some very recently indeed, in the persecution of Licinius. They had seen their colleagues die atrociously in its defence. Many of them, blind and lamed, still bore in their bodies eloquent testimony of their own fidelity under trial. Now all was changed, and the honoured guests of the power which so recently had worked to destroy them, escorted by that soldiery the sight of whose arms must still provoke memories at which they shuddered, the Catholic

[1] There was one bishop from Africa, one from Spain, one from Gaul.

bishops were come together with all possible pomp to regulate their differences before the face of the world.

The minutes of the Council of Nicea have long since disappeared. Apparently the procedure followed by the Roman Senate, and already traditional in councils, was adopted. Each bishop who wished to speak stated his opinion, and then followed the general discussion. The parties soon showed themselves. For Arius there was a tiny fighting band of seventeen, led by Eusebius. Of the rest, one large party was against any innovation in the traditional Faith or in the manner of its exposition, opposed indeed to the idea that any investigation was necessary. Others were for examining every detail of the tradition before re-affirming it.

Arius was given his chance. He stated his doctrine in all its bald simplicity. The bishops agreed to condemn it. It was a more difficult matter to agree on the form the condemnation should take. A test-formula was needed which would express the traditional Faith precisely as it differed from the heresy, and thus bar out the new doctrine's adherents. Eusebius of Nicomedia had one ready. It was rejected, because it was so ambiguous that Arians could sign it as easily as Catholics. His namesake, Eusebius of Cesarea,—"the Father of Church History," one chief source for many earlier matters, down to 324, and who, also, from a Lucianist education, favoured Arius—proposed a better. It was however, even so, too ambiguous to suit the Council. Something more precise, a phrase which could not possibly be interpreted in an Arian sense was needed; and finally, to express the fullness of the Son's divinity in relation to that of the Father, the term *homoöusion* (i.e. consubstantial, of the same substance) was proposed. It met the case admirably, and it was accepted. But not without much discussion, hesitation and, even in the end, reluctance. Quite apart from the Arianisers, whom such a close definition would force into the open as innovators and drive out of the Church, there were Catholics also who disliked this fashion of defining faith in new terms not to be found in the Scriptures. Again this particular term had, for Easterns, unhappy heretical associations. Paul of Samosata, it was remembered, had used it fifty years earlier, not it is true to express the idea that Father and Son are of the same nature, but with the meaning that they are identical in person. Sabellius, too, had used it to convey a like notion. Paul's theory had been condemned and with it the term he used, as he used it. On the other hand, with the meaning now given it, the term had long been in use in the West. It was Tertullian's *consubstantialis* translated, and Rome had given this use an orthodox consecration in the settlement of the disputes about Denis of Alexandria's orthodoxy now nearly seventy years ago. In favour of the term *homoöusion*, then, there was the great advantage that it exactly met the need of the moment as did no other term; and there was good warrant for its being so used. In this acceptance by Easterns of a term they disliked but which had Roman use to support its orthodoxy, we can perhaps discern a trace of Roman influence at the Council; the test clause of the formulary it adopted was Roman. That formulary is the famous Creed of Nicea. It deserves to be cited as the council proclaimed it.

"We believe in one only God, the Father, Almighty, maker of all things visible and invisible; and in one only Lord, Jesus Christ, the Son of God, the sole-begotten of the the Father, that is to say of the Father's substance, God of God, Light of Light, true God of true God; begotten not made, consubstantial with the Father (*homoöusion to Patri*), by whom all things were made; who for us men and for our salvation came down, became incarnate, became man, suffered, was raised again on the third day, ascended back to heaven and will come again to judge the living and the dead; and in the Holy Spirit. As for those who say 'There was a time when He did not exist; before He was begotten He did not exist; He was made from nothing or from another substance or essence; the Son of God is a created being, changeable, capable of alteration,' to such as these the Catholic Church says Anathema."

With two exceptions all the bishops signed, whatever their real beliefs, whatever their doubts as to the prudence of the defining word. Eusebius of Nicomedia at the solicitation of his patron Constantia, Constantine's sister, the widow of Licinius, signed with the rest. The two recalcitrants were promptly exiled, and the Emperor's orders were sent to Alexandria to secure the acceptance of the council's decision and the removal of dissidents.

Here the history of Arianism should have ended. But now, for the first time in the history of the Church, a heresy was, after its condemnation, not only to survive, but to survive within the Church, to be protected there and maintained, and to be a cause of disorders whose bitter fruits are with us still; and all this was because now, for the first time, there remained to the condemned heretics the resource of appealing against the condemnation to that new element in the Church, the Christian Emperor. A new untraditional procedure is to begin to function; the new circumstance of Cæsar's being a Christian is to be made to tell. It is the condemned who will attempt it, and their success will not only create a precedent for future condemned heretics, but initiate Cæsar into the exercise of new unlawful power, create in him a taste for it, and habituate him to its exercise.

The first attempt to reopen the question ended badly for those who organised it. Some of the dispossessed Arians from Alexandria came to court to plead their case. Eusebius and a neighbouring bishop—Theognis of Nicea—supported them, but too enthusiastically. The appellants were dismissed and the two bishops exiled. In exile they remained for three years.

It is with the return of Eusebius in 330 that the next chapter in the story begins. Eusebius was no mere theorist concerned only to expound his unorthodox views, but a cool and capable leader who must, in order to retain his influence and position, either capitulate to the forces which had defeated him in 325 and exiled him in 327, or now, in his turn, drive them out. He realised that a frontal attack on the Council of Nicea would fail. Constantine was too attached to the council and to its definition as his own achievement to tolerate, where these were concerned, any other attitude than obedient submission. It was, however, another matter to attack the men responsible for the definition. To force these into exile, and then, with a new personnel in the highest ranks of the hierarchy substitute an Arian interpretation of Nicea might be possible. Eusebius could count on sympathy within the imperial family; he could use against those who stood by the letter of the *homoöusion* the numerous bishops who, though they believed what it expressed, disliked the term and suspected those who imposed it. The council had long ago dispersed: Eusebius remained, Bishop of the Capital, the emperor's natural adviser in religious matters, ready and able at every opportunity astutely to suggest what he was now too wise to propose, and at every turn able to show himself as the emperor's obedient servant.

Slowly, gradually, after the return of the exiles, the controversy re-opened, its central point shifted now to the expediency of using the critical "*homoöusion*". Was the term really orthodox ? Was it not as heretical as Arius himself ? Not of course Arian, but, perhaps, Sabellian ? In the meshes of this subtle dispute Eusebius caught his first victim the bishop of the second chief city of the East, Eustathius of Antioch. Eustathius accused the Bishop of Nicomedia of betraying the faith of Nicea. Eusebius replied that the Bishop of Antioch was a Sabellian. At Antioch, the city where Lucian had taught, where Arius and Eusebius had learnt their heresy, there was a strong pro-Arian faction. Eustathius had done his best to drive them out. Here was their opportunity. A council was summoned, at which Eusebius played his part, and Eustathius was deposed, 331. There were riots and, lest

Eustathius should become a perpetual provocation by his presence, Constantine followed up the council's sentence by a second sentence of exile. This henceforth is to be the normal procedure with deposed bishops.

In place of the deposed Eustathius there was elected one of the few bishops who, at Nicea, had gone so far as expressly to defend Arius—Paulinus of Tyre. He died, however, in a matter of months, and in the election of his successor the emperor took a hand. He congratulated the Antiocheans on their expulsion of Eustathius—"they had cleared the ship of its bilge"—and he recommended as their new bishop either of two candidates for the orthodoxy of whose faith he pledged his word. Inevitably one of the imperially nominated was chosen, Euphronios. For the first time in history the civil power has interfered in the election of a bishop; the novelty is the work of a faction; they will make over to the civil power one prerogative after another, if only they can thereby destroy that orthodoxy by whose existence they stand condemned.

The events at Antioch were a pattern for susequent Eusebian procedure. One city after another saw them repeated, and bishop after bishop who had fought Eusebius was deposed, exiled, and provided with a Eusebian successor. The machinery of this ecclesiastical revolution was consistently the same—orders and directions from the emperor himself.

The next stage was to install a Eusebian in the greatest of all the Eastern sees, Alexandria. The bishop who, years ago now, had condemned Arius and assisted at Nicea's ratification of that condemnation, was dead. In his place there had been elected one of his principal advisers, his companion at Nicea, the deacon Athanasius. With him there enters into the story its greatest figure. He was able, he was learned, he was orthodox. His life was irreproachable. He was to his people a model bishop, and for tenacity of purpose, the inflexibility bred of a clear grasp of principle, no hero of Church History has ever surpassed him. Eusebius attacked, in a letter inviting Athanasius to open his church to the friends of Arius. The Bishop of Alexandria explained that since they all lay under the anathema of Nicea the thing was impossible. Whereupon there came to him a further letter, this time from the emperor, "You know my will. Whosoever wishes to re-enter the Church is to be given all facilities. If I hear that you have forbidden to enter anyone who wishes to return, I shall speedily send someone with power to depose you by my order." Athanasius, undismayed, protested ever more clearly that "there can be no communion between the Catholic Church and a heresy which fights against Christ."

Athanasius had on his hands, at this time, a more domestic anxiety—the Meletian schism. Three of the schismatics went to the capital to lay complaints of a civil nature against him. Eusebius welcomed them, advised them, and Constantine, though he was not sufficiently convinced to have the affair formally dealt with, summoned Athanasius to reply in person. He cleared himself without difficulty and, apparently, quite won over the emperor. But, twelve months later (334), the trouble began again. New accusations of the same nature, with this in addition that he had murdered a bishop, were made and this time it was before the emperor's brother, residing at Antioch, that Athanasius had to clear himself. Again, without difficulty, he was successful, producing the supposedly dead bishop as convincing answer to the charge ! But this time Eusebius had been certain that his opponent was finished. So certain indeed that with other bishops of his party he was already *en route* for the East, to a council to be held at Cesarea, which would make an end of Athanasius, when the emperor ordered him home. To Athanasius Constantine wrote once more, expressing his confidence in him.

Constantine had twice turned from Eusebius to his calumniated opponent. But when Eusebius, a third time regained it, his hold on the imperial mind was to be permanent. The council forbidden at Cesarea in 334, was allowed to meet in 335. The place chosen was Tyre. With Athanasius came forty-nine bishops from Egypt. They were refused admission. The jury was already carefully packed, Arians to a man, Eusebius at their head ; and behind this Eusebian conspiracy lay the prestige and power of the Court. An imperial official was the Council's president. "How can anyone dare to give the name of synod to this assembly over which a count presided ? It was the count who spoke, the members of the synod were silent, or rather they took the count's orders. He gave his orders and the soldiery put us out. In reality it was Eusebius and his friends who gave the orders. The count was there to carry them out. What kind of a synod was it, which, if such were the prince's good pleasure, might end with a sentence of exile or death ?" So the Egyptian bishops protested in later days. It was indeed a new kind of council, the first of its kind, but destined to be the pattern of imperially organised councils under the Cæsaro-papist emperors. The old accusations once more made their appearance, and along with them new ones of the same type. Athanasius, yet again, cleared himself of the first, and as to the newer charges the council named a carefully chosen deputation to investigate them on the spot. That they made the investigation so carefully as never to examine the principal witnesses, and with such discretion that they never officially knew even of their existence, surprised no one. Not truth was their aim but a report which would help on the work of the council. Athanasius understood—none better—and he left the council to lay his case in person before the emperor.

In his absence the Eusebians carried out the appointed programme only the more easily. They condemned him, deposed him, forbade him to return to his episcopal city. They had not yet separated when from Constantinople came letters from the emperor. Athanasius and his sovereign had met—casually, in a street of the capital, as the court returned from its hunting. Constantine would have ignored him but the bishop held firm, coldly stating his one simple desire—to meet his enemies face to face in the emperor's presence. Constantine agreed and the bishops, fresh from sentencing Athanasius, were ordered to the captial to justify their proceedings. The heretics had called in Cæsar to redress the balance of the orthodoxy so heavily weighed against them. Now Athanasius had made a like appeal—none too wisely. It was his first—and last—reliance on the princes of this world. The provincial council was arranged. It was very brief, for Eusebius had found a new charge, that the Bishop of Alexandria had schemed to hold up the capital's corn supply. The mere accusation drove Constantine into one of those fits of fury to which he was liable. Without further ado Athanasius was exiled, banished to the very end of the world, to Treves and the distant Moselle (335).

Eusebius might rest content. The last out-and-out leader of the homoöusion party, the most uncompromising of the survivors of Nicea, was driven out at last. The victor returned to the East, to Jerusalem, whither the bishops from Tyre had gone to celebrate the consecration of the new basilica built by the magnificent imperial generosity over the site of Our Lord's tomb. Thence, in a synodal letter, he proclaimed his victory to the Christian world. Arius and his associates have now given pledges of their orthodoxy to the emperor. He exhorts us peaceably to receive them back into the Church whence unseemly envy has lately expelled them. He stands guarantee for their good faith. The formula the Arians were to sign as the condition of their restoration, and which Eusebius and his bishops at Jerusalem accepted as proof of their orthodoxy, follows the imperial letter as an appendix. It is the creed of Nicea with the critical phrases carefully omitted. The term *homoöusion* does not appear at all, and instead of the affirmation that Jesus is the Son "begotten of the Father," it is merely stated that as God the Logos He existed from all time. The Nicean definition is not explicitly repudiated, it is simply ignored. In its place is an equivocal compromise, which Arians can subscribe as well as Catholics, and which Arian ingenuity has devised to obscure the distinction between Nicea and the theories there condemned. In ten years, Arius, thanks to the astute pertinacity of his "fellow-Lucianist" Eusebius, and despite Nicea, is back in the Church. The bishops at Jerusalem have sanctioned the new practice of finding substitutes for definitions of faith in order to rally dissidents. This, too, is a precedent that henceforward every condemned heretic will most carefully strive to follow.

To complete the triumph, it only remained for Arius to be received back into the Church with all the apparatus of public ceremonial. But Alexandria would have none of him. Its bishop might be in exile, but the people stood loyally by him. The riots were so violent, so continuous, that the scheme was abandoned, and Arius was summoned to Constantinople, charged with the responsibility of the disorder. There, too, his arrival divided the city into hostile factions. The bishop, no Arian but perplexed, hesitated. The prelates of the Council of Jerusalem were by this time, most of them, in the capital, enthusiastic to see their decisions imposed as law. Constantine lent his aid. The Catholics of the city stormed heaven with supplications that the catastrophe might be averted. In vain, apparently, for the day was fixed and the church chosen. But on the very eve Arius himself suddenly died (336). A few months later Constantine, too, was dead (May 22, 337). The Eusebians had lost, in the very moment when their triumph seemed complete.

The figure of the historical Constantine later ages overlaid with legend. Under this softening influence he becomes the model of Catholic princes, a first pattern St. Louis for all succeeding ages. The truth is very different.[1] In his manners he remained, to the end, very much the Pagan of his early life. His furious tempers, the cruelty which, once aroused, spared not the lives even of his wife and son, are not only disproof of the legend but an unpleasing witness to the imperfection of his conversion. That conversion was indeed sincere. The emperor certainly believed that Christ Our Lord had appeared to him, had promised him victory. Victory had in fact followed and thenceforward Constantine's faith had been proof against all doubt. He gave himself to Christ, and broke from the official polytheism incompatible with his new allegiance. But there he halted. He was not received into the Church, even as a catechumen, until the very end. Nor, possibly, did his knowledge of

[1] Cf. Palanque in F. & M. III, 29, for whom Constantine is " un passioné . . . téméraire . . . un impulsif . . . esprit puissant mais confus . . . superstitieux . . ." who combines " une mystique sincère " with " une ambition démesurée ".

his new religion ever advance beyond this simple belief that Christ is the One and Only God. Uninstructed, a politician, concerned to safeguard at the same time the welfare of the Church of Christ and the public order, expediency inevitably determined his decisions; and in the oligarchy of court prelates such as Eusebius of Nicomedia this disposition found every encouragement. Constantine was the greatest military leader the Empire had known for nearly a century, and as an administrative reformer he was only surpassed by Diocletian. That such a man should be indifferent to the internal life of the Church, to its controversies and the intense movement born of them would have been impossible. His intervention was inevitable, and it had its limits. It was, in his own conception, as the servant of Christ's religion that he intervened, to protect the faith defined—but never himself to define it. It was his misfortune, rather than his fault, that Christ's religion was to him the religion of Eusebius and his associates. To their influence was due the most serious flaw in all his ecclesiastical policy—his practical neglect of the Roman primacy, which he treated as non-existent. Later legend told how the Emperor, struck with leprosy, visited the pope, and how, St. Sylvester baptizing him in the Lateran, the leprosy was healed as the baptismal water cleansed his soul. The truth is far other. "The Roman Church—Constantine's generous presents apart, and the presence of two of its priests at Nicea—has no history between the council of 313 under Pope Miltiades and that of 340 under Julius I. The Papacy, one may say, seems with Sylvester to pass through a quarter of a century's retirement." In place of the traditional court of last appeal, Constantine was guided by the oligarchy whose head was the bishop of his capital city. This novelty was to show all its mischievous consequences in the reign of his son Constantius II (337–361). Not only would the emperor then "protect the faith, but he would himself decide what faith merited his protection. And if, with all his advantages, the son did not succeed, his failure would be owing very largely to the fact that the Bishop of Rome, carefully excluded from effective power in the East, continued in his traditional authority in the West, and binding the West in a firm resistance, rallied what remained of orthodox Catholicism even in the carefully disciplined eastern hierarchy.

These things, in 337, no man could foresee, neither the aggression of Constantius II nor the amazing sudden re-appearance of the Papacy, fully armed, with St. Julius I (338–352). The great emperor was dead, and he had died as a Christian should, sorrowing for his sins and begging God's mercy, pledging himself most solemnly as he received the white robe of the newly-baptized to live what rest of life God granted him in more seemly accord with the Faith he professed. It was, however, no Catholic who thus initiated him with the sacraments but an Arian, no less an Arian in fact than Eusebius himself.

Constantine did not lack for relatives to inherit his Empire. He had three surviving sons, he had brothers, he had nephews. His death was the signal for a family massacre in which, to the profit of his sons, his brothers and some of the nephews perished. There were left as almost the only survivors of the descendants of Constantius Chlorus, the three sons of Constantine, Constantine II, Constantius II and Constans. The vast heritage was once more divided. To Constantine II went the dioceses of Spain, Gaul and Britain; to Constantius II those of Thrace, Asia, Pontus, Egypt and the East; to Constans Africa, Italy, Rome, Dacia and Macedonia. Three years later, in a civil war with Constans, Constantine II met his death and, his heritage passing to the victor, of the two surviving brothers Constans was master easily of the greater part of the Roman world, and the predominant partner. The fact played an important part in ecclesiastical affairs, for, while Constantius II in the East was a decided Eusebian, though not even a catechumen, Constans was a Catholic, and was even baptized. His health unfortunately was poor, and with this continual debility went a disinclination for action. Nevertheless, he was strong enough, so long as he lived—he died in 350—to make any Arian aggression in the West impossible, and to exercise some restraint upon anti-Catholic violence in the East.

Two events marked the beginning of the new régime after the death of Constantine the Great (337). St. Athanasius was allowed to return to Alexandria, and Eusebius succeeded, in defiance of Church law, in capturing for himself the see of Constantinople. A renewal of the conflict in the East was already in sight.

It began with an attempt to install at Alexandria an Arian rival to Athanasius. The Eusebians revived the memory of the sentence passed on him long since at Tyre (335) but never confirmed. Each of the three emperors was approached, and an embassy sent with a like mission to Rome. The Western Emperors dismissed the envoys; Constantius II welcomed them, and promised support. Rome acted with the traditional formality, observance of the canons which governed appeals. The pope—Julius I—. knew the men with whom he was dealing. They had already planned to trap him into an implicit disavowal of Nicea when they sought confirmation for the Arian competitor of St. Athanasius, suppressing the fact that, excommunicated himself, he was ordained by an excommunicated bishop. Now, presented with

the minutes of the Council of Tyre, the Pope wrote to St. Athanasius, enclosing the accusing documents, bidding him summon a
synod before which he should clear himself and to report its
decision. The synod was held. The Bishop of Alexandria, once
more going through all the ancient charges once more cleared
himself, and the council sent its decision to Rome.

Meanwhile, the Eusebians had written again to Rome. This
time they asked the pope to judge between them and St. Athanasius.
The emperors held aloof. After all these years of imperial protection the normal procedure was once more to have its chance—
the Bishop of Rome deciding an appeal of one bishop against
another. But before the appeal was heard, the situation at
Alexandria suddenly changed. Constantius sent orders that
St. Athanasius was to be expelled, and in his place another
enthroned as bishop—Gregory of Cappadocia, a notorious
Arian, a lieutenant admittedly of Eusebius. This was indeed
imperial confirmation of the sentence manufactured at Tyre.
It revealed Constantius as an Arian, and that Eusebius was able
to play in the new reign the part he had played in the old.

St. Athanasius, expelled but not a whit thereby dismayed,
blazed out in an encyclical of protest, to which the pope replied
by summoning him to the council shortly to be held at Rome,
the council for which the Eusebians had asked, where all should
be reviewed. To this council there came in, from all parts of the
East, bishops who had been the victims of the Eusebian treachery,
expelled by his manœuvres, hailing the unhoped for boon of an
ecclesiastical council free from imperial influence. But the
Eusebians now would have no share in it. To the pope's notification—since they had chosen him as judge, he now informed them
when the council would meet and that should they not appear
they would be judged accordingly—they replied in a manifesto full
of threats and sarcasms, refusing to accept his jurisdiction in the
matter. Unless the pope will recognise the sentences of Tyre and the
other depositions they have decreed, they will not, for the future,
hold communion with him. The manifesto was the product of a
council held at Antioch, and it bears the signatures of a variety
of bishops. It strikes a new note in the history of the relation
between Rome and the other sees. It is the first open denial of
her primacy, the first occasion when the Bishop of Rome has
been threatened with rebellion to coerce his jurisdiction (341).

For the moment the pope ignored the letter. The council
held its sessions. The deposed and exiled bishops stated their
cases. The case of the Bishop of Alexandria was given especial
consideration. The council thereupon decided that all had been
unjustly condemned, and the pope summed up the decision in a

letter to the Easterns. As one reads this letter one understands
the reluctance of the Eusebians to appeal to Rome, the long
years during which they kept Rome out of the quarrel, and the
instinct which prompted them to refuse her jurisdiction once
they realised it had begun to operate. It is not merely that the
letter has all the easy Roman serenity, that the charity which
inspires it is itself such a condemnation of their own misdeeds.
But there is present, throughout, that Roman consciousness of
universal authority, which, informing the precedents that St.
Julius quotes against the incipient schismatics, makes the letter the
most notable of papal contributions to the century's long debate.
The pope is astonished that his own charitable letter has provoked
such a bitter and scornful reply. He would have preferred not to
publish it, had in fact held it back until the last, hoping against
hope that the arrival of the Easterns, returned to a better frame
of mind, would cancel what they had written. "That he whom
you chose to write it thought it an occasion to make a show of
eloquence moves us not at all, for in ecclesiastical matters the
important thing is not to parade one's eloquence but to observe
the apostolic canons, and carefully to avoid whatever may give
scandal." The Easterns now deny that the decision of a council
(i.e. Tyre in 335) can be revised by a second council. They are
reminded that they themselves petitioned for the second council,
and "even had your envoys not themselves demanded that
council, had it been myself who sought it as a means whereby
the appeal of those complaining of injustice might be heard, my
intervention would have been just and praiseworthy because in
accord with ecclesiastical practice and agreeable to God." Nicea
itself had passed judgment in matters where previous councils
had already judged, and in so doing Nicea itself had merely followed ancient precedent. "Your claim is then unjustifiable, for
a custom once established in the Church, and confirmed by
councils, is not to be abolished by a chance group of individuals."
As for the intruded Gregory of Cappadocia, whom this faction
asserts to be the lawful Bishop of Alexandria, "what ecclesiastical
canon, what apostolic tradition empowered them, at a time when
there was peace in the Church and when Athanasius was so
generally recognised, to send this Gregory, ordained by them
at Antioch and escorted thence to Alexandria, not by priests and
deacons of his church, but by soldiery?" The church of Alexandria and the bishops of the province alone had the right to decide
the matter. Supposing there had been some real ground of complaint against all these bishops—Athanasius, Marcellus of Ancyra
and the many others who had come to Rome to make appeal—
the ecclesiastical rule should have been observed. "Your duty

was to write to all of us so that in rendering justice we might all of us have shared. For it was a question of bishops and churches more than usually important since they had, in times past, had the Apostles themselves for rulers. Are you ignorant that the usual thing is to write first to us, and that thus justice may be rendered from here ? Those then who, far from this, have acted without reference to us, in this arbitrary fashion, would then like us now to signify approval in a case where we have no knowledge? This is not according as Paul commanded, nor as the tradition of the Fathers. This is a procedure wholly foreign and new. I beseech you, allow me to say it thus. I write what I write in the common interest, and what I write to you is what we have received from the blessed apostle Peter."

The protest fell on deaf ears. The emperor who mattered—the emperor of the East, Constantius II—ignored it, and St. Athanasius with the rest could only resign himself to the exile. Constantius was one with the arianising Easterns, and the bishops of the court faction, later that same year (341), assembled at Antioch with others to the number of a hundred for the dedication of the basilica, picked up the challenge of the letter of Pope Julius and replied with an implicit denial of his claims. They confirmed Gregory of Cappadocia as bishop of St. Athanasius' see; they denied that they were Arians although they acknowledged that they had received Arius once more into the Church. As an exposition of Catholic teaching in the matter of the divinity of the Logos they preferred to the Nicean creed a creed attributed to Lucian; it expressed the same truth but, they explained, in more suitable language. More truly the new creed sacrificed that truth because it sacrificed the one term which unmistakably expressed the precise deviation of the heresy Nicea had condemned. The new equivocal phraseology was a deliberate confusing of issues clarified these fifteen years, and the new confusion was introduced in the interests of the heresy. This council, *In Encaeniis*, of 341 inaugurates the new strategy of finding synonyms for the technical terms used in conciliar definitions, synonyms designed to betray the truth already decreed and to ensure the condemned heretics their place within the Church. The precedent now set will be followed faithfully in every crisis of heresy for the next two hundred years. It will, almost always, gain the emperor—for it is the high water mark of ecclesiastical expediency in matters doctrinal. It will often rally to a lowering of the standards of orthodoxy that orthodoxy's recent defenders, for it promises to gain the heretic while maintaining truth. It will always find in the last resource a resolute opponent in the Bishop of Rome, if nowhere else. His opposition will reject such compromise, at the cost of no matter what measure of peace, ecclesiastical or civil.

It was in the emperor's presence that this council met, Eastern bishops, heretics all, banded with their emperor against Rome. So will it be, again and yet again, until with their emperor they work themselves free of the Bishop of Rome and the Church of Christ.

The council of 341 has another interest, for it marks a change of tactics on the part of the bishops who led the movement. They are anxious to dissociate themselves from Arius, dead now this five years, and from his radically exposed ideas which only a few extremists defend. To be a self-acknowledged Arian was no recommendation anywhere outside that narrow circle. Hence, with a last salute to the memory of the dead heresiarch, they put out a series of formulæ of calculated vagueness to indicate the difference between their own orthodoxy and the universally reprobated heresy. It was not Arius, nor was it Nicea: it was Lucian. Its present defenders claimed it as the traditional Catholic faith; the Catholics signed it because there were defenders of the *homoöusion* who were Sabellian; and the Council went on to condemn, yet once again, the heretics who failed to make the proper distinction between the Father and the Son: Sabellius, that is to say, Paul of Samosata, and Marcellus of Ancyra. The first two were dead long since. The third, however, was not only alive but, driven from his see like Athanasius for opposition to the Eusebians, at this very moment in Rome. More, the famous letter of St. Julius had expressly mentioned his case, had publicly proclaimed him as a protégé of the Roman See so that, as has been said, that letter marks an alliance between Julius, Athanasius, and Marcellus of Ancyra. Now, unhappily, Marcellus was looked upon with suspicion throughout the East. He was a true opponent of Arianism, and perhaps his intentions were orthodox. But his language was certainly tricky, and there was only too much justification, in the terms he used, for the charge of Sabellianism made against him. When the council of 341 made the charge, and condemned him, it promised to do more harm to the Roman-led defence of Nicea than any frontal attack could have done, for it not only condemned this apparent heretic, but also "all those in communion with him." The council proclaimed the chief defenders of Nicea as themselves suspect of heresy in the eyes of the Catholics in the East who still held out against Eusebius.

Eusebius himself died this same year, 341, the fruitful result of his sixteen years of episcopacy a divided Church, East and West drawn up the one against the other. It was a lamentable state of things indeed, and before it should harden into permanency the pope turned to a last effort of reconciliation. Through his own emperor, the Catholic Constans, he approached the sovereign of the East. After one or two failures the negotiations succeeded thus far that the two emperors agreed to call a council of bishops of the two empires. It was to meet at Sardica, the modern Sofia, a city of the Western Empire but close to the frontier of the East.

At Sardica then the council met in the autumn of 342 or 343 (authorities dispute the date). There were, in all, a hundred and seventy bishops, seventy-six of them from the States of Constantius II. Hosius of Cordova once more presided and the pope was represented by two priests of the Roman Church. The Easterns arrived with their minds made up. The council's task would be the simple one of registering what they had already decided. Before they would consent to take their places in the council, the council must ratify the condemnation of St. Athanasius and Marcellus—accept, that is, without discussion, the Eastern view on two of the points to discuss which the council had been called. Hosius, of course, rejected their ultimatum, and the Easterns thereupon, that same night, left Sardica, leaving behind a lengthy protestation. In this they renewed their condemnation of St. Athanasius and Marcellus, denied the right of the West to revise the decision of an Eastern council, and, laying upon the West the blame for this new breakdown, they excommunicated Hosius and the pope with him. They ended with a statement of belief characteristically ambiguous. Meanwhile at Sardica, the council proceeded with its work—the stale re-examination of the ancient often-exploded charges against St. Athanasius and those against Marcellus too. St. Athanasius once more they cleared. As to Marcellus he, too, was cleared, the council accepting an explanation that what had provoked criticism in his exposition of faith had been, in his intention, theory merely and hypothesis. The bishops unlawfully intruded by the emperor into the different sees of the East were excommunicated and, with them, the leaders of the recent schism from the council. It was suggested, too, that the council might issue a new statement of belief, but, thanks to St. Athanasius, the wiser course was followed of re-issuing the adequate, unmistakable creed of Nicea.

The Council of Sardica, failing to unite the divided episcopate, served only to stabilise the division. But although it failed completely in the purpose for which it had been summoned, it left behind it a memorable series of disciplinary canons in which, seeing how the root of the trouble lay in the civil power's usurpation of ecclesiastical jurisdiction, it proposed, by strengthening previous legislation regarding the relative rights of bishops, to set a barrier against the new aggression. These canons recall and re-enact the old law that a bishop consecrated for one see is not, on any pretext, to pass therefrom to any other see. Bishops are not to receive clergy excommunicated by their own bishop, nor are they to invade the sees of a neighbouring (civil) province unless duly invited. Bishops whom a necessity of private affairs calls outside their sees are reminded of the rule that no bishop is to be absent from his see for more than three Sundays, and that outside their own sees they are to respect the rights and liturgical prerogatives of the bishop in whose see they find themselves. Useful legislation, this, to check the episcopal *vagabondage* which had so assisted the Eusebian faction's growth. The clergy's right of appeal from their own bishop to the bishops of the province is recognised, and where the bishop himself is accused, the old law is still maintained that he is not to be judged by his own subjects. Such cases the council of the bishop's province must decide. From the provincial council such a bishop, should he be condemned, can appeal and the appeal is to the Bishop of Rome. The Bishop of Rome may himself decide the case or order a new trial, and at this the judges are to be the bishops of a neighbouring province. The Eusebian Council of Antioch (*In Encaeniis*) of 341 had decided that sentences passed on a bishop by the unanimity of a provincial council were irrevocable; and that where the provincial council was divided, the metropolitan should associate with his own bishops those of a neighbouring province and, whatever the new decision, it should be final. This attempted destruction of a bishop's right of appeal to Rome had been the Eusebian reply to Pope Julius I's council in Rome and its re-habilitation of St. Anthanasius. The canons of Sardica were a riposte to the Eusebian innovations. They re-affirm and implement what St. Julius had affirmed in his letter to the Easterns, namely that a case could be re-judged, and that the usage is that Rome is consulted first so that "judgment may be done from here." But Sardica did more than merely re-affirm existing rights. In its turn it innovated, when it prescribed the course of action which the Bishop of Rome judging an appeal should follow. This innovation the papacy ignored. The appeal-procedure does not appear ever to have functioned in the detail prescribed by Sardica, nor does Rome's over-riding of the council in this respect appear to have provoked any protest.

Finally the council reported to the pope in a formal synodal letter "since it seems right and truly most suitable that in what concerns each and everyone of the Lord's provinces bishops should act with reference to the head, that is to the see of Peter the Apostle."

Constantius II's reply to the letter of the Council of Sardica was of the practical order. He forbade the bishops it had rehabilitated, under pain of death, to return to their sees, and the two bishops of his Empire who had gone with the Council were sent into exile. None the less, new efforts were again made to heal the breach, and as a result delegates met at Milan in 345. But since the Catholics continued to demand a repudiation of Arius and his teaching, while the Arians refused to accept the definition of Nicea, the negotiations were without result. The Arians clung, also, to their demand that Marcellus should be condemned, and although the Catholics were willing to condemn the undeniably heretical opinions of his disciple Photinus, Bishop of Sirmium, they still refused to accept the Arian view of Marcellus. St. Athanasius, however, increasingly suspicious of Marcellus the better he came to know him, now definitely broke with him. Also, in 346, thanks to a sudden change in court favour, St. Athanasius was allowed to return to Alexandria. His second exile had lasted seven years.

So, in a kind of deadlock, the next few years went by; St. Athanasius at Alexandria but isolated from the Easterns (Palestine, Syria, Asia Minor and Thrace); the Easterns cut off from Rome and the West; while Photinus, whom all condemned, still reigned at Sirmium since no emperor had concerned himself to execute the sentence passed upon him. The assassination of Constans on January 18, 350 brought the deadlock to an end, for his heir was his one surviving brother, Constantius II, who now became sole emperor of the whole Roman world. His Arian sympathies no one could doubt, nor his willingness to act on them, and though the circumstances of his brother's death involved him in three years of civil war, the heirs of Eusebius immediately began their preparations for another attempt to capture Alexandria for Arianism by driving out St. Athanasius, and, also, to end the scandal of Photinus' hold on Sirmium.

For the moment they were powerless against St. Athanasius, for Constantius held firmly to his promises of protection. But the next year, 351, found Constantius in residence at Sirmium and at a council called there by him, and held in his palace, Photinus was deposed. This council followed a curiously novel procedure which made very evident the extent to which the new emperor was prepared to stretch his assumed ecclesiastical prerogative. By his orders a theological debate was arranged in which Photinus was allowed to expose and defend his theories. As opponent there was assigned to him the successor of his old master Marcellus, the new Bishop of Ancyra, Basil. The debate was conducted in approved scholastic fashion, official stenographers took notes for the emperor's benefit, and as judges Constantius nominated eight high officials of the Court. To complete its work the assembly at Sirmium added yet another to the series of indeterminate creeds which, by suggestion, repudiated Nicea, while Photinus—condemned as Sabellian—was given a successor of proved Arian orthodoxy.

The civil war came to a close with the victory of Constantius, on August 10, 353, over the usurper who had murdered his brother. Its vicissitudes had suggested to the Arians a new pretext by which to revive in Constantius his old opinions of St. Athanasius. The Bishop of Alexandria, they urged, had had his share in the attempt of the Western usurper on the peace of the empire. Day by day more bishops were rallying to him. He considered the Arians heretics, enemies to be rid of as soon as possible. Could he be really loyal to the emperor who was their patron ? Moreover, there was a new pope. Julius I had died in the previous April (352). He had been the staunch champion of Athanasius. With his successor, Liberius, Arian intrigue might be more successful.

The new pope suggested to Constantius the convocation of yet another council, at Aquileia, to take up the work unfinished at Sardica ten years before. Constantius was at the moment at Arles. Instead of the council asked for, he summoned one to Arles, to which the bishops of Gaul were convoked. Assembled (353) they first of all desired to express their belief in the definition of Nicea. But the emperor would not allow this, nor indeed any discussion on the faith. Instead, he presented the assembly with an edict condemning to exile whoever would not condemn Athanasius. It was the West's first experience of the policy which had made the Eastern Church Cæsar's, and it succumbed. Paulinus of Treves stood firm and was exiled. The rest, to a man, signed—and with them the legates of Liberius.

The effect upon the pope of this betrayal by his legates should be carefully noted, for of all the popes Liberius is the one in whose case contemporary calumny has had most lasting effect. Discouraged truly, but by no means despairing, Liberius replied to this new tactic of breaking St. Athanasius by isolating him from the West as well as from the East, with a new request for a council. Constantius, whose violent language in his regard had certainly reached Liberius, made a show of entering into the plan. The pope chose new legates and in 355 the suggested council met, this time at Milan. At Arles, the bishops, incredibly ignorant of the history of the previous twenty years in the East—it was the first time some of them had even heard of Nicea[1]—had acted in fitting deference to requests from "the most Christian emperor."

[1] E.g. St. Hilary of Poitiers.

Their acquiescence had been a victory for the emperor's prestige as the son of the great Constantine. At Milan there was, from the beginning, no attempt to cloak the violence under such formalities. Arian bishops dragged the pen from the hand of the Bishop of Milan as he prepared to sign the creed of Nicea in token of orthodoxy. The council became a riot. The mob invaded the church to defend its bishop, and the council's next meeting took place in the palace. In this more favourable *locale* the imperial will had its way more easily. Once more, as at Arles, the bishops signed—all save a handful among whom, alas, were not the papal legates. The little band who resisted, Paulinus of Treves, Lucifer of Cagliari, Eusebius of Vercelli and Denis of Milan, were summoned to a special audience. "The emperor," it is St. Athanasius who describes the scene, "having summoned the bishops, ordered them to sign the condemnation of Athanasius and to receive the heretics into communion. They protested against this innovation in Church discipline, crying out that such is not the ecclesiastical rule. Whereupon the emperor broke in 'My will is canon law! Bishops in Syria make no such objections when I address them. Obey me or . . . exile.' The bishops, astounded at such language, lifting their hands to heaven, with great boldness opposed to the emperor that his kingly power was not his own, that it was in fact God's gift to him, and that he should fear God Who could, and suddenly, strip him of it. They reminded him of the last day and its judgment. They advised him not to throw church affairs into utter confusion, not to confuse the civil power with the Church's constitution and not to open the Church of God to the Arian heresy." Constantius, undersized and bandy in the legs, a poseur who flattered himself that his very gaze struck terror where it fell, who cultivated a deep voice and an oracular manner, listened patiently enough. Then, brandishing his sword, he ordered the bishops to instant execution, only to countermand his sentence immediately and substitute one of exile.

There were, of course, many bishops in the West who had been unable to make the journey to Milan. To reach these absentees, couriers were now sent to one town after another, and by the means used at Milan yet more signatures were obtained to the condemnation of Athanasius. Once again Liberius had been duped. This time something more was required of him. He too must sign. One of the emperor's confidential eunuchs was despatched to ask his assent. He made show of the valuable presents Constantius sent. Liberius replied fittingly. The eunuch next deposited them at the shrine of the Apostle. Liberius, learning of it, had them thrown into the street. "If the emperor is really anxious for the peace of the Church let us have a truly ecclesiastical council, away from the palace, where the emperor will not appear, nor any of his counts, nor judges to threaten; for the fear of God is sufficient, and the teaching of the Apostles, to enable the Council to secure the Church's faith such as it was defined by the Fathers of Nicea." There, for the moment, the matter of Liberius' signature was allowed to rest.

The Arians turned their attention to Alexandria. Plots were laid to entice the bishop, quietly, away from the city; but he knew his enemies too well to be so easily taken in. Finally they resorted to force. On February 8, 356 the imperial troops broke into the church where St. Athanasius was presiding at the night office. Their arrows flew right and left—more than one of the congregation was slain—and with drawn swords they made for the bishop. Despite his efforts to meet death, as centuries later St. Thomas of Canterbury, his attendants managed to get him away. From that moment the city knew its bishop no more. He simply disappeared from view, while the imperial troops hunted for him from one end of Egypt to the other. In Alexandria itself the churches were seized and handed over to the Arians—the Catholics always resisting to the end—and Constantius, fresh from legislating terrible penalties against the Pagans, now called in the Pagans themselves to assist in the forcible enthronement of yet another successor to Athanasius. It was once more a Cappadocian, and, like his predecessor, ordained at Antioch for his new post, a certain George whose chief claim to notoriety hitherto had been his skilful mismanagement of the imperial finances. Under George of Cappadocia the Catholics of Egypt were to suffer for the next few years as half a century before Catholics had suffered under Diocletian and Galerius. Once more the mines were filled with Catholic convicts, bishops, priests and laity alike, condemned for their loyalty to St. Athanasius.

The most outspoken defender of Nicea was now, and finally it seemed, driven out; and with him disappeared orthodoxy's last spokesman. For by this time Hosius was a prisoner and Liberius, also, far away from his see in exile.

Liberius, indeed, the emperor had not dared to silence in his own city; and, fearing riots, should he attempt openly to arrest the pope, he at last had him kidnapped by night. He was carried to the imperial court (357), and between him and his captors there took place an interview whose detailed record, preserved by Theodoret, is one of the golden pages of the history of the Roman See. With hardy courage Liberius recalled to the emperor himself the facts of the case, that the so-called trials of St. Athanasius by the different imperial councils had been so many mockeries, and that before pursuing further the Bishop of Alexandria, Constantius should proclaim his own belief in the creed of Nicea and recall the exiled bishops to their sees. The emperor, for a reply, could do no more than revile St. Athanasius as his personal enemy and demand that the pope should join in the "universal" condemnation. It was on this note that the scene came to an end. The emperor: "There is only one thing to discuss . . . choose the side of peace, sign and you will return to Rome." Liberius: "I have said farewell to my brethren in Rome. Ecclesiastical law is more important than living in Rome." The emperor: "You have three days to decide. Should you choose to sign you will return to Rome, if not think over to what place you would prefer to be exiled." Liberius: "Three days will not alter my decision. As for exile, send me where you will." Two days later the place was notified to him—Beroea in Thrace. Before he left, the emperor offered him money for his expenses, the empress also. Liberius refused. The eunuch Eusebius—the same who had two years before proffered bribes in Rome, and who had played a sycophant's part in the famous interview—came forward also, offering a bribe. To whom Liberius suggested that before attempting to tip the pope it would be as well first to become a Christian !

The Arian triumph was complete in this, at least, that the Catholics were all completely muzzled and gagged. Not a single bishop was left in possession of his see who dared refuse to condemn Athanasius. But there the triumph ended. The cowed episcopate was very far from being in its heart anti-Nicene, and if no one dared openly defend the *homoöusion* and its champion, no Arian on the other hand dared openly disavow it. The triumph would only be complete when the bishops who had been forced to renounce Athanasius were brought to renounce Nicea too. To this, then, the Arian energy next turned itself.

The old theological discussions were renewed and presently (357), there appeared a new statement of belief drawn up by the bishops in residence at the court at Sirmium. This is the so-called Second Formulary of Sirmium. Its teaching is Arian, and its manner of expression the most radically Arian so far. Not only does it not declare the Son to be of the same substance as the Father—the Catholic teaching—but it states definitely that the Son is unlike the Father. The plan of those who drew it up was that it should be sent round the episcopate to be signed by each individual bishop. But its first effect—when the collection of signatures began—was to turn the divergent tendencies among the heretics into so many hostile sects. From the beginning the really radical Arians, in the theological sense, had been very few. More numerous, but still a minority, had been the political Arians, ambitious place seekers, who saw in the trouble a chance for their own advancement, and who had "managed" the party since Nicea. The vast majority of the Arian bishops were what the majority of a new party so often is, enthusiastic, and confused in their enthusiasm, driven as much by the hope of avoiding what they feared as by zeal for anything positive: their only definite characteristics their suspicion of the *homoöusion* and their docility to the ruling emperor. From this section had come the support for that succession of vague, ambiguous creeds which gradually deprived the faith of all definite meaning for those who adopted them.

The publication of the Second Formula of Sirmium, suddenly reviving the most radical kind of Arianism—patent anti-Nice-anism—as the creed of the party, forced into joint action the vague and hitherto fluctuating body of middle opinion which, although suspicious of the *homoöusion* as a definition of the traditional belief, was yet Catholic in mind and willing to express the relation between Father and Son as one of *likeness* of substance (*homoiousion*). St. Cyril, Bishop of Jerusalem, was one of the chiefs of this section, but its real leader was Basil of Ancyra. The split between radical Arians (Anomoeans), and these so-called Semi-Arians (*homoiousion* party), bred in the group of Politicals a new subtlety. In their endeavour to keep the party together they grew ever more carefully vague, proffering finally as a basis of agreement the formula that the Son is like to the Father (*homoios*—whence the name of Homoean sometimes given them). It is round the manoeuvres of these three sections to capture the favour and interest of the Court that the history of the next three years turns (357–360).

The Anomoean formula provoked criticism throughout the scarcely tamed West. It also, in their hour of victory, split the Arians. Immediately the prestige of the Anomoeans fell, and Basil of Ancyra became in Constantius' mind the all-important bishop of the day. The Second Formula was withdrawn. In its place Basil proposed one of his own fashioning—the Third Formula of Sirmium—a provisional statement designed to gain the support of the Nicene West, to be the basis of an alliance between the Westerns and those Easterns who, if they differed from the West as to the wisdom of the term *homoöusion* and as to its suitability to express their common belief, agreed in that belief none the less. The moderate Arians in the East whom the sudden revelation of Anomoean aims and strength was driving slowly back towards Nicea would, it was hoped, come in too. Before such an alliance—and with the imperial favour which Basil enjoyed—Arianism would be ended for ever.

The new formulary was sent round and signatures began to come in. Its crucial point was its use of the word *homoiousion* where Nicea had used *homoöusion*. To say the Son is of like substance with the Father as a way of denying that He is of the same substance, is of course to deny Nicea. But to make the assertion in opposition to the Anomoean teaching—that the Son is not like to the Father—is to use *homoiousion* in an orthodox sense. It was, so those who presented the formulary for Catholic signatures explained, as against the Anomoeans that the new term was used, and to avoid the misunderstandings which the Nicene term had bred.

For the complete success of Basil of Ancyra's scheme the signature of Liberius was essential. The formulary was presented to him and, in the sense in which it was offered, he signed it, adding to his signature a kind of appendix in which he made clear the meaning of his signature by condemning all those who say that "the Son is not like to the Father in substance and in all things." This appendix Basil accepted and he himself also signed it. The rout of the Anomoeans was complete. The real Arians were defeated now, in 358, as they had been defeated at Nicea thirty years before. A general council would fittingly sum up the whole affair and celebrate the new reunion, and where more fittingly could it meet than once again at Nicea ?

At this moment, however, Basil fell out of favour with Constantius II; the Anomoeans and the Politicals came back. The council Basil had asked for was not abandoned. It would meet—but a dual council, one section for the West at Rimini, the other for the East at Seleucia in Isauria—and under Arian auspices; its work would be the imposition, not of the Third Formulary of Sirmium but of yet another of the vague Arian creeds that were a betrayal of Nicea. In the formulary proposed there was no mention at all of "substance," only the simple ambiguous declaration, "We declare that the Son is like the Father in all things as the Holy Scriptures say and teach." Under the circum-stances this equivocal creed was an indirect denial of Nicea.

To Rimini (359) there came four hundred and more bishops, eighty of them professedly Arian, the remainder Catholic. The pope was not present, nor did he send a representative. The bishops voted against the proposed betrayal, but the imperial commissioner had instructions from Constantius that they were to be kept at Rimini until they signed one and all. The weary business dragged on then all through the year, negotiations, promises, threats, until, with what mental reservations to accom-modate the contradiction between their thoughts and their actions we know not, all the bishops signed. At Seleucia there were fewer bishops—150 only, of whom only a mere handful were enthusiastic for the Nicene formula—and the emperor's difficulties were less. The majority—105—readopted the Eusebian creed of Antioch (341). Thirty-two of the remainder signed a creed vaguer still. It was like to that adopted at Rimini, and it was this which was destined to triumph.

Delegates from both councils met at Constantinople. Those from Rimini made common cause with the Arian minority of Seleucia. Pressure on the delegates of the Seleucia majority did the rest. A joint council, at Constantinople, in the first week of January 360 published to the world their lamentable unanimity. Not the *homoiousion* of Basil of Ancyra had triumphed, in whatever sense one took it, nor the radical Arianism of the Anomoeans whom he had ousted. The victory had gone, once again, to the Politicals, to the section which opposed all attempts at precision in the hope of stabilising a happy permanent confusion where all parties, even the most contradictory, should find their place in the Church. Of their victory, and the surrender of the bishops, St. Jerome commented in words which have become famous, "The whole world groaned to find itself Arian." Liberius judged more truly of the surrender's value, writing of the Western bishops' action as a simple surrender to external pressure.

Whatever the next development which the Politicals had planned, it never matured for, within a few months, the power on which the party depended had vanished. The joint Council at Constantinople was held in the January of 360. In the May following, Constantius' cousin Julian, hitherto ruling Gaul as Cæsar, was, at Paris, proclaimed Emperor. The West at any rate was delivered from Constantius and the Politicals. Eighteen months later (November 3, 361) Constantius himself was dead, and Julian sole emperor of the Roman world. In the new emperor's councils, bishops, no matter how "political" would count for little. As in 337, an unexpected change of ruler had delivered the Catholics, in the very moment when their cause seemed utterly and for ever lost.

CHAPTER VIII

THE CATHOLIC RESTORATION. 359–382

JULIAN's reign was of short duration. With his death the unity of rule disappeared once more, and under the dyarchy of the brothers Valentinian I and Valens the sequel to the débâcle of Rimini-Seleucia was, in West and East, widely different. Valentinian (364–75) was a Catholic and his return to the religious policy of the Edict of Milan put no hindrance to the restoration of Catholicism in the States he governed. "The heads that had been bowed were raised, movements once more became natural." Liberius had indeed judged more accurately than St. Jerome when he described the action of the bishops at Rimini as a material surrender to external pressure. The advent of Julian removed that pressure, and spontaneously the West returned to its old allegiance to Nicea.

The Arian victory at Rimini was the culminating point of the policy which, for thirty years, had ignored the Roman primacy, had attempted to substitute for it the patronage of the Christian Emperor. It is not surprising that the reaction after Rimini produced strong and explicit declarations of the special prerogative of the Roman Church and, in St. Ambrose, the first theorist of the relations between the Church and the Christian State. "My will is Canon Law," Constantius had told the Gallic bishops at Arles, and henceforward while, in the East, Cæsar continued to rule the Church until his interference became an accepted institution regularly obeyed, there developed in the West—thanks especially to St. Ambrose—a clear understanding of the relations between Church and State, and a clearer appreciation of the role of the Roman primacy. For seven years (353–360) the West, unwillingly, had borne the yoke of Cæsaro-papism. Its liberty once restored, it rebuilt its strength in a more conscious adherence than ever to the authority of the Bishop of Rome, recognising in loyalty to his teaching rather than to the password of any council howsoever sacred, the touchstone of true faith and membership in the Church.

St. Ambrose, however, a young man of twenty, was as yet only a catechumen when the *coup d'état* of Julian's army emancipated the Latin churches from the Arians of the East. The first leaders of the restoration in the West are the three bishops Eusebius of Vercelli, Lucifer of Cagliari and Hilary of Poitiers, who were

exiled under the late régime for their loyalty to Nicea. The first
place where the reaction dared to make a public demonstration
was, naturally enough, Paris—Julian's late capital. Here in 360
a council of bishops, led by St.

Hilary, excommunicated Saturninus
of Arles, Constantius II's ecclesiastical henchman, and sent a
letter of sympathy to the deposed Catholic bishops in the East,
the victims of the policy of Rimini-Seleucia, in which they confess
their late error of tacitly ignoring the testword—*substance*—
of the whole dispute. A similar feeling showed itself in Spain and
in Africa, but in the Danubian provinces, thanks to the convinced
Arianism of the leading bishops, the régime of 359 still held.
In Northern Italy, too, the Arians were still in possession of the see
of the imperial city, Milan, which remained theirs for yet another
fifteen years, the Western Emperors during this time being either
Pagan or, Valentinian I, liberally unconcerned with church disputes
and so in no way to be relied on to coerce unorthodox prelates.

In 362 Julian's mischievously inspired amnesty to the exiled
bishops began to bear fruit. Liberius had issued a formal condemnation of what had been done at Rimini, and he had sent out
to all the provinces regulations concerning the bishops who had
there betrayed Nicea. His policy—the policy also of St.
Athanasius in Egypt—was that the bishops who disavowed the
signatures extorted by force should retain their sees. With the
sudden return from the East of Lucifer of Cagliari the peaceful
carrying out of this policy was at once disturbed. Lucifer, one
of the three bishops who had bravely withstood Constantius to
his face at Milan in 355, was by nature an extremist. His exile he
had spent in writing furious tracts against the Emperor. Their
titles throw some light on his methods, *No Peace With Heretics*,
Apostate Princes, *No Mercy for God's Enemies*. He came back,
fresh from his unhappy and uncanonical interference in the
domestic troubles of the Catholics of Antioch,[1] to campaign
against the laxity of the Roman settlement and presently, preaching
that the Church had ceased to exist except in his own diocese,
he retired to Cagliari.

St. Hilary of Poitiers had all Lucifer's courage and all his gift
of blunt, direct speech. With him Catholicism in the West comes
for the first time to a clear understanding of the nature of the
Church's independence of the Christian State—and this within
less than fifty years of the Christian State's first coming into
existence. It is the State which is the new thing, the State which
creates the problem. The solution lies in the traditional belief that
the belief is essentially a tradition. The Faith begins to be in
danger, St. Hilary writes, as soon as "definitions of the Lord's

[1] vid. inf. 225-6.

teaching are enacted by a human judge, by the prince." In his book, *Against Constantius*, he breaks out violently against the emperor, exposing the novelty of his usurpation and its danger, painting for all time the picture of the Cæsaro-papist prince who allows himself to define the faith, to distribute sees right and left to whom he chooses, to call councils and override their decisions with his soldiery, while at the same time his munificence covers the churches with gold, his piety embracing the bishops and humbly bowing before them for their blessing, inviting them to his table, and showering privileges upon them.

St. Hilary died in 367. It was not until eight years later that the writer who turns these controversial protestations into a consistent theory was consecrated Bishop of Milan. Nor certainly, in 367, had the thought of being St. Hilary's continuator ever come to St. Ambrose who was then in the early stages of his chosen career in the imperial civil service. It had been his father's career too, and in it, at the time of St. Ambrose's birth, his father had risen to the highest post of all under the emperor—Pretorian Prefect of the Gauls, with Britain, Gaul and Spain under his jurisdiction, and his residence at Treves. Hence it was that the Roman Ambrose was himself born in the distant provinces. He was, however, educated in Rome, and by 374 he had risen to be Governor of the Province of Emilia-Liguria. When the old Arian Bishop of Milan at last died in that year, the Governor, a Catholic but as yet a catechumen only, foreseeing the inevitable riots which the election of a successor would cause, took personal charge of the policing of the ceremony. It resulted, through the accident of a child's acclamation and the mob's instant appreciation of a rare suitability, in his own election. He accepted, was baptized, consecrated, and immediately set himself to the acquirement of his office's technique. Ruler and diplomat he was already by nature, and by the training of long experience. In the twenty-three years that remained to him he showed himself of the first rank as the Catholic bishop—preacher, writer, poet, ascetic, and such an unfearing rebuker of evil-doing in high places as to be ever since the very type and pattern of the heroic virtue of episcopal courage.

Since Valentinian I's accession the court once more resided at Milan, and on Valentinian's death (375) the new bishop found himself the guardian and tutor of the two young sons who succeeded, Gratian, aged sixteen, and Valentinian II, a child of five. In this, as in his presence at the emperor's council and in his frequent employment as an ambassador, St. Ambrose sets yet another precedent for the coming new age, creating the familiar rôle of the patriot prelate, statesman and diplomatist. But his independence survived the atmosphere of the court and the complications of his high civil importance. When in 384, after Gratian's death, the Pagans, still a force in Rome, demanded the restoration of the idol of Victory to the Senate House, and hoped easily to win it from the Arian empress-mother now the regent, St. Ambrose held firm. While the court hesitated the bishop was urgent that the matter lay beyond its jurisdiction, being a matter of religion—*causa religionis est*. In such the Church must be heard.

Two years later, the petition of the Arians of Milan that one of the churches of the city be granted to them gave St. Ambrose yet another opportunity to demonstrate the duty of episcopal independence of the State. He refused to make over the basilica they sought, and, cited before the court, was bidden remember that the emperor was but using his rights since all things were in his power (*eo quod in potestate eius essent omnia*). He agreed; but insisted on the exception that what belonged to God was beyond the emperor's jurisdiction (*ea quae sunt divina imperatoriae potestati non esse subiecta*), and in a sermon shortly afterwards he developed the theme for his people, summing up the whole matter in one of his own beautifully cut phrases *ad imperatorem palatia pertinent, ad sacerdotem ecclesiae* (palaces are matter for the emperor's concern, but churches belong to the bishop). The next stage in the affair was a summons to Ambrose to appear before the council to answer for his refusal to hand over the basilica. Once again his reply was a refusal, and in a letter to the emperor he explained his reason. In matters of faith bishops alone have authority to judge. That laymen, in such a cause, should sit in judgment on a bishop is a thing unheard of. "In cases where matters of faith are in question it is the custom for bishops to judge emperors when the emperors are Christians, and not for emperors to judge bishops." Bishops who allow laymen to trample under foot this right of the episcopate (*ius sacerdotale*) are, as the emperor will one day realise, rightly considered contemptible. This astonishingly outspoken letter the bishop followed up by yet another sermon in which he explained to his people the latest phase in the struggle. He was not acting in ignorance of the imperial practice where episcopal independence was inconvenient to the State. He remembered, and in his sermon and letter recalled, the tyranny of Constantius II. Valens, dead only eight years, was a more recent memory still. None the less the bishop personifies Christ, and "in the imperial council Christ should be the judge, not the prisoner at the bar." To Cæsar, by all means, the things that are Cæsar's—the bishop will pay the taxes levied on the Church's property, and if the State should confiscate its property he will not resist. But the basilica is God's.

No temple of God can belong to Cæsar. Then, two wonderful phrases which cover all the differing mentalities which are already preparing the schism between West and East, and which point unerringly to the origin of all the mischief, "The emperor is within the Church, and not above the Church" (*imperator enim intra Ecclesiam, non supra Ecclesiam est*): it has been the crime of the Arians, the crime which stamps them as the worst of all heretics, that "they were willing to surrender to Cæsar the right to rule the Church" (*Isti imperatori volunt dare ius Ecclesiae*). The emperor abandoned his project.

Valentinian II was a minor in whose name the Arian empress-dowager ruled. He was barely past the years of tutelage when, in 392, he was murdered, and Theodosius who had ruled the East since 379 and, only a year before, had restored to Valentinian the states which Maximus had usurped, was left sole ruler of the Roman world. Theodosius was, as emperors went, an exemplary Catholic. But the Bishop of Milan continued to claim from the mature and experienced Theodosius the same complete independence, the same autonomy and authority in spirituals, for which he had fought in the time of his child predecessor.

Even before Theodosius succeeded to the rule of the Empire in the West he had had experience of the saint's limitless and courageous solicitude for the rights of religion. In distant Osroene a synagogue had been destroyed in a riot. Theodosius ordered that it should be rebuilt at the expense of the local bishop, and the news of this reaching Ambrose he immediately protested. Once more he is concerned that, in a matter which concerns religion, the emperor should act without the advice of his bishops. And since it touches the emperor's conscience, and therefore his soul's salvation that he should act in these matters as God directs, charity demands that the bishop should instruct and warn him —privately first, as by this letter, but, should it be necessary, publicly before all the Church. The emperor ignored the letter, and Ambrose, true to his word, made the affair the subject of a sermon. Theodosius he compared to David, set by God in the place of the worthless Saul (Valens). God had sent Nathan to rebuke David when, in turn, he, too, promised to be faithless. So Ambrose spoke to Theodosius. And Theodosius present at the service heard the rebuke. As the bishop came down from the pulpit the emperor stood in his way. The bishop insisted. If the emperor would not withdraw his order that Christians should rebuild a house of impiety, the bishop would not offer the sacrifice. Theodosius submitted.

Twelve months later a still graver matter produced a second crisis. A serious riot at Thessalonica, in which a high official had been murdered, had been punished, on the emperor's orders, by an organised massacre. Ambrose waited, resolved, at the last extreme, to do what hitherto no bishop had dared, to threaten the Roman Emperor with expulsion from the Church. As before he first of all wrote to Theodosius. The emperor is only a man. He has sinned. Sin is not taken away but by tears and penance. Until the emperor acknowledges his wrong-doing and submits to penance, in no church, while he is present, will the holy sacrifice be offered. Once more religion triumphed, and Theodosius, his insignia laid aside, publicly confessed his crime and asked God's pardon.

St. Ambrose is, very literally, an epoch-making figure. Thanks to his personality, to the accident that made the very centre of the world's affairs the stage on which his personality was displayed, to his gifts as writer and speaker, his life set the pattern for all the next thousand years of the relations between the Catholic bishop and the Catholic prince. In these few years at Milan he laid the foundations, in his careful demarcation of the rights of *religio* and *respublica*, of all the public law of the *respublica christiana* of the coming Middle Ages. Theodosius, though neither emperor nor bishop realised it, was to be the last emperor to rule effectively all the lands between the Atlantic and the Adriatic. Slowly increasing and inevitable chaos was to descend upon that vast heritage. One of the few things to survive was the Catholic episcopate, and it survived formed in the mould of Ambrose of Milan.

He has, however, another and more particular importance from his rôle in the restoration of Catholicism in the Arian-ridden Europe of the years after Rimini, an importance deriving from action once again, and, still more, from his clearly expressed teaching on the nature of the Church, and on the Church's relations to its own rebellious subjects, be they rebels against its government—schismatics, or, like heretics, rebels against its teaching. In 379 St. Ambrose had to preach the funeral sermon of his own brother Satyrus. He recalled, in testimony of the dead man's Catholicity, how a few years earlier, shipwreck had thrown him on to the coast of Sardinia and how, being thought near to death, Satyrus had sent for the local bishop to baptize him. But for Satyrus not any baptism could suffice. He must assure himself that the bishop was truly of the Church. "He made diligent enquiry," the preacher explained, "whether the bishop was in agreement with the Catholic bishops, that is to say with the Roman Church." Satyrus knew about the schism of the fanatical Lucifer of Cagliari, understood that though Lucifer's belief was in accord with Nicea, nevertheless—and for this St. Ambrose commends him—"he did not think he could find the Faith in a schism" (*non putavit fidem esse in schismate*). Accord with Nicea was not of itself sufficient to make a Catholic. The root of Catholicism lay elsewhere, in the approval of the Roman Church.

Two years after this sermon the Council of Aquileia gave St. Ambrose a better occasion still to repeat that teaching. It was a council of the bishops of the civil diocese of Italy, and though the pope—Damasus I—was in correspondence with St. Ambrose regarding the council's business, he was not represented at its meetings. Of that council St. Ambrose is the inspiration and its synodal letter to the Emperor Gratian is his work. The council, the emperor is informed, has just tried and deposed the two last survivors in the West of the Arian bishops. The prospects of unity and harmony are improved. The bishops assembled at Aquileia beseech the emperor therefore to be on his guard against the intrigues of Ursinus, the anti-pope, "lest the Roman Church, the head of the whole Roman world, be troubled and its most holy apostolic faith, since it is from Rome that the right to communion flows to all the rest." Ursinus had been a trouble in Rome since the pope's very election. Riots, deaths, and a criminal suit against the pope, from which he emerged, acquitted, had marked the struggle. Ursinus had been condemned and exiled. The bishops still fear his resources and hope to anticipate his wickedness. How literally their declaration of the nature of the Roman Church's importance was meant to be taken, and was in fact understood, we can gather, curiously enough, from an attack on the council, in which that declaration is criticised, by one of the two bishops whom the council had deposed—the solitary protest of "a prisoner under sentence cursing his judges." This was Palladius, Bishop of Ratiaria. In his attack he denies that the Bishop of Rome has any rights other than those common to all bishops, and claims that every bishop is as much Peter's successor as the pope, that Peter himself had no superiority over his apostolic colleagues. Therefore he condemns the council for its connivance at Damasus' assumption that he is "The prince of the episcopate" (*princeps episcopatus*)—Damasus who has not even deigned to attend the Council !

The Catholic reaction in the West is then associated with the direct activity of the popes, with Liberius until 366, and Damasus after him, with renewed assertions of the Church's independence of the State and with renewed recognition of the Roman See's peculiar function as the touchstone of orthodox Christianity. The popes, during this time, are personally overshadowed by the genius of St. Ambrose, the greatest ecclesiastical personality the Church in the West has so far produced; but the whole effort of that genius is given to strengthening the tradition of Rome's hegemony—*potentior principalitas*—to a more explicit reference

CHRISTIANITY TRIUMPHANT

The Fourth Century mosaic in the apse of S. Pudenziana, Rome

of it to the practice of ecclesiastical life, and to the demonstration in word and in act of the Christian theory of the State. Such a personality the East never knew, and the tradition of the Roman Supremacy, lacking as yet any systematic organisation of detailed control, was to suffer there accordingly.

In the East the new sacrosanct autocracy created by Diocletian, baptized in Constantine, Catholic at last with Theodosius, was related to instincts too deeply rooted in the oriental mind for any Eastern, even the Catholic bishop, not to reverence it as a thing half divine, against which even criticism partook of sacrilege. Where, in the West, the Church, in closer relation with the Roman See, clung desperately to the tradition of its self-sufficiency and independence of Cæsar, in the East it tended little further than the ambition of securing Cæsar's orthodoxy. Granted an emperor who was Catholic in faith, the Church in the East was always willing to trust its destinies to his direction. Should such an emperor prove anti-Roman, the Eastern episcopate, fascinated by the fact of the semi-divine's acceptance of Christ, would follow him—logical result of its abandonment of the tradition for the novelty of the imperial patronage—would follow him in all his patronage of heresy, and into schism itself. How often this happened, and how regularly it was to the intervention of the Roman Primacy—lacking every resource except the belief in its traditional authority—that orthodoxy owed its salvation, the next few chapters must tell.

To the Church in the East the death of Julian the Apostate (June 26, 363) and the accession of Jovian brought not only its first experience of the rule of a Catholic prince, but, for the first time almost in sixty years, real peace. Those sixty years (303–363) had been for Catholicism in the East years of continual, breaking strain—strain mercifully spared to the Church in the West. There had been the terrible years of the Great Persecution —in the West a matter of months only. There had been the insecurity of the reign of Licinius, ending in a renewal of the persecution and civil war. Constantine's victory had been followed only too speedily by the thirty years of Arian disorders; and, after Rimini-Seleucia, the East had had to bear the brunt of Julian's sour hatred of the faith. The harvest of those years was an indescribable anarchy in every church, good men desperate at the sight of the disorder, a chaos from which the memory of normal, peaceful, Christian life and its tradition of ordered administration had almost disappeared. The Church in the East, at that moment, was as a battlefield from which the armies have scarcely yet retired.

Then, just as the Church, uneasily, dared to breathe once more, Jovian died, after a reign of seven months (364). Valentinian was hardly named in his place when he made over the East to Valens; and Valens, an Arian, proceeding to show himself another Constantius II, inaugurated yet another stage in the agony of Catholicism in the East. Not indeed that Valens was an Arian of intimate personal conviction. His support of Arianism, thorough indeed, was in itself simply political. The East was in a state of incredible confusion. Half a dozen schools of thought battled for recognition as the true Church; everywhere rival bishops claimed the same see; and beyond the main division of this unhappy Christianity, there were, inevitable legacy of the last forty years of trouble, local schisms, local religious feuds whose interaction on the main complications sometimes made the same combatants simultaneously adversaries and allies. To Valens, a soldier, vigorous in decision, brutal in manner, successful, where successful, through a policy of violence and force, it was an obvious policy to make one of the contending theories his own, and impose it on all. The theory he adopted was not the Catholicism of Nicea but the vague political Arianism which had triumphed at Rimini. It was the religion of the reigning bishop of his capital see—a fact which no doubt determined its adoption. For all the rest, for the supporters of Nicea in particular, bad days were in store, a renewal of the days of Constantius II.

An incident of the very first days of the new reign revealed the spirit that was to guide its religious policy. In the repression which followed the Council of Rimini-Seleucia, the party of Basil of Ancyra had suffered equally with the avowed defenders of the Nicene formula. The death of Julian and the succession of the Catholic Valentinian encouraged them to ask for a Council. Leave was given, and at the council—held at Lampsacus—they issued a condemnation of what had been done at Rimini, and republished, with a Nicene interpretation, their homoiousion formula. By this time Valens was in command in the East. It was to him that the council's delegates had to report, and not to Valentinian. He simply ordered them to come to an agreement with the Bishop of Constantinople—with one of the chief supporters of the Council they had just condemned. A few months later, in 365, an edict appeared reviving all the sentences of exile enacted under Constantius II. From one see after another, accordingly, the anti-Rimini bishops were tumbled out. The Church in the East was again where it had been at the accession of Julian, at the mercy of the Arians.

For the moment, however, Valens had more urgent problems than this of ecclesiastical uniformity. First the defeat of a rival to the throne, installed in Constantinople itself, and then a critical phase of the never-ceasing war with Persia, occupied all his energy. Meanwhile the bishops of the Council of Lampsacus, defeated at home, looked to the West for aid. Valentinian I, indeed, ignored their appeal like the liberal Gallio he was. From the pope—Liberius still—their delegates had a better reception. They gave the pope satisfying assurance that they accepted the creed of Nicea, and rejected the Council of Rimini. Whereupon Liberius received them into communion and wrote to the sixty-four bishops in whose names they had come. The delegates returned to the East after a series of encouraging receptions from the Catholic bishops all along their journey. All now promised well for the desired union with those Easterns who had never, even nominally, rejected Nicea. A new council was planned to meet at Tarsus which would seal the re-union. But once again Valens, inspired from Constantinople, intervened. The council was forbidden.

By 370 Valens, free of his wars for the moment, was in a position to impose the planned religious uniformity. As in his predecessor's reign, the sacred formula was taken round from town to town by imperial commissioners. The bishops were called on to accept it and to sign. Where they refused, sentences of deposition and exile rained down plentifully, and their churches were taken from them and handed over to the docile conformists. Often there was a spirited resistance, whence often, also, sieges of the churches, sacrilege, and massacre. The temper of the new tyranny showed itself when, upon the emperor's nomination of yet another Arian to Constantinople (370), a deputation came to protest against the new bishop. Its members were ordered into exile, and as the ship on which they sailed, eighty-four of them, passed into the open sea, the crew, under orders, fired it.

So the new desolation spread through Asia Minor and Syria and, after the death of St. Athanasius (May, 373) through Egypt too. Even Valens had not ventured to match himself against the aged saint's prestige, but once he was dead, the Alexandrian churches were witness of horrors that recalled the worst days of George of Cappadocia. In all the Eastern Empire one see alone, where the bishop remained firm, was spared. This was Cæsarea in Cappadocia, the see of St. Basil.

Thanks to the number of his letters that have survived we know much more about St. Basil (329–379) than the mere facts of his career. When elected Metropolitan of Cæsarea he was just forty years of age. He came of a distinguished family which had suffered for its faith under the last Pagan Emperors, and he could pride himself that it had been equally constant through all the years of the Arian troubles. His fine mind had enjoyed every chance of cultivation that the time offered, and at Athens, with his friend

Gregory of Nazianzen, he had had for a class fellow Julian the Apostate. His studies finished, Basil had turned to monasticism, and he had come to be familiar with the ascetic life in all its forms. He had travelled much, and it was his wide experience of monasticism in different lands which went to make him, what he remains to this day, the Patriarch of monks in the East as St. Benedict is of monks in the West. Inevitably he was drawn into the theological controversies of his time. He was the friend of Basil of Ancyra, and friendly always to the group of Homoiousians whom scruples whether its test word was expedient alone separated from a simple acceptance of Nicea. Of his own full and loyal acceptance there was never any question and when in 360 his own bishop, through fear, accepted the ambiguities of Rimini, Basil broke with him. With the next Bishop of Cæsarea he was on better terms, and was the real ruler of the diocese. With St. Athanasius, too, he was in high favour, and his appointment to Cæsarea in 370 was hailed in Alexandria as an important gain for Catholicism in that East where Constantinople had, for forty years, been in Arian hands and Antioch was at the mercy of schism.

Basil was of the type with whom to exercise authority is second nature. Thinker, organiser, man of action he ranks with St. Ambrose and St. Leo as one of the bishops whose influence did much to mould all subsequent Catholicism. Inevitably he came into conflict with Valens. He met the aggression with all his own firmness, yet with tact; and with so overwhelming a display of personality that the savage Arian for once was halted. More, the emperor even assisted at the offices in Basil's cathedral, and munificently eased the strain of the bishop's extensive charities —for all that Basil, to his very face, denounced his impiety and faithlessness unsparingly. Characteristically so great a mind and heart did not rest content with the measure of peace secured for his own see. The desolation of the East called imperatively, and from the first days of his episcopate he set himself to the work, to unite the broken and dispirited faithful and to bring them something of aid and comfort from the West and Rome. The task occupied all the life that remained to him. Its pursuit brought him the greatest sorrows his life knew, and he died, prematurely at fifty, his end still unachieved.

The insurmountable obstacle was the schism which divided the adherents of Nicea in the see of Antioch and which, because of Antioch's ecclesiastical primacy in the East, reacted upon every stage of ecclesiastical development there. Antioch, ever since Eusebius of Nicomedia had procured the deposition of its Catholic bishop of 330, had been ruled by Arians of one school or another.[1]

[1] Cf. sup. page 194.

When the see fell vacant in 360, by the translation of its Arian titular to Constantinople, the bishops in whose hands the election lay, chose as his successor Meletius, Bishop of Sebaste, a Homoiousian of the school of Basil of Ancyra. It was a brave demonstration of Nicene sympathy to make on the morrow of Rimini; and within a month Constantius II had expelled the new bishop, exiled him, and installed an Arian of satisfying type in his place. Meletius returned with the rest of the exiles whom Julian recalled in 361; he was again exiled by Valens in 365, and exiled yet a third time two years later. This last exile lasted until 378. Thus of his first eighteen years as Bishop of Antioch, Meletius spent twelve in exile for the faith of Nicea. Whence, throughout the East, he won a great name as a confessor and, titular of the East's ecclesiastical capital, he ought to have been the rallying point for Catholics in the period of restoration.

Unhappily not all Catholics would acknowledge him as Bishop of Antioch; many, despite St. Basil's guarantees of his perfect Nicene orthodoxy, continued to suspect him—the elect of bishops themselves none too orthodox—as an Arian. The chief of these anti-Meletians was the Bishop of Alexandria, first St. Athanasius, and then, and with even greater zeal, his successor Peter (373–383). A more serious consequence still was that, in this matter, Alexandria influenced Rome; and for the popes too, Liberius and Damasus I (366–384) Meletius to whom the Catholic East, St. Basil at its head, looked as to its primate, was simply an heretical intruder.[1]

The uncanonical interference of a Western bishop, Lucifer of Cagliari, in 362, made matters worse; and however right Rome and Alexandria may have been in the matter of Meletius, when they accepted the fruits of Lucifer's illegal action they put themselves, on that count, as much in the wrong in the eyes of the East, as Meletius and St. Basil were in their own. What Lucifer had done was this. There had always been at Antioch, ever since the deposition of the last undoubtedly Catholic bishop in 330, a tiny minority who refused all contact with his Arian successors and with the Catholics who tolerated them. At the moment of the election of Meletius, the leader of the group was a priest Paulinus. He refused to accept Meletius as his bishop because of the Arian antecedents of his electors, and because

---

[1] For a very different account of this involved affair cf. G. Bardy's summary in F. & M. III 173–4, according to which Meletius had allied himself with the more political type of Arians, the so-called Homoeans, who favoured and promoted equivocal substitutes for the homoöusion; and although his own belief may very well not have been so unorthodox, there was good reason for the suspicion aroused by his conduct and by his choice of allies, e.g. George of Alexandria and Acacius of Cæsarea.

his consecration had an heretical pedigree. It was a renewal of the ancient condemned theory that heresy in the minister, invalidates the sacraments which he gives. It was Lucifer's great fault that, without any authorisation beyond his own impulse, and without the assistant bishops whom custom and law required, he consecrated Paulinus as Bishop of Antioch. It was Paulinus, in turn, thus unlawfully consecrated whom Alexandria recognised as Bishop of Antioch; and if Rome hesitated to be equally explicit, it was yet Paulinus who acted as Rome's man of confidence for what related to the Catholic East. A greater tragedy, in the circumstances, and a more complicated one, it is hard to imagine.

From the first year of his appointment to Cæsarea, St. Basil set himself to reconcile Rome to Meletius, and Meletius to Athanasius. To the East, if peace were ever again to be its good fate, Rome was necessary. Basil's letters express this clearly. "One solution alone do we wait for, that your mercy would consider a little our terrible plight." Rome should send someone with authority who, taught by actual knowledge of Eastern conditions, would realise the need to recognise Meletius and realise also the need for Rome to be more explicit in her condemnation of the heresies into which some of her Eastern allies had fallen during the fight with the great common enemy. Here we touch on yet another complication in the story. Rome's supporters in the East had, in more than one case, fallen under suspicion as heretics, and the Arians had not neglected to profit by the misfortune. So, for example, it had been with Marcellus of Ancyra thirty years before. So too, now, Apollinaris Bishop of Laodicea, while orthodox on the point at issue with the Arians, was teaching erroneous novelties on the relation between the human and the divine in Our Lord. So Paulinus; and so, too, Rome's latest messenger, Vitalis, whom neither Meletius nor Paulinus would accept and who had therefore launched yet a third anti-Arian claim to be Bishop of Antioch.

St. Basil's solution was simple. Meletius was orthodox— none more so. His election was according to form, therefore he was the Bishop of Antioch. Rome should declare for him, and, condemning explicitly the allies whose company had done so much to lessen her influence, rally all the Eastern Catholics to Meletius. Then, and then only, would the restoration really begin. At Rome the pope was willing enough to condemn the new heresies as he was to condemn again the old. But he refused to condemn by name the alleged heresiarchs before they had been tried. And, in 375, he recognised Paulinus as Bishop of Antioch.

St. Basil had written to Rome as to an ally—a most powerful ally, and, truly enough, an ally of superior rank. The reply was that of authority instinctively conscious of its own power. Community of faith, he was told, was not by itself sufficient condition for intercommunion. Canonical observance was just as necessary; in other words submission to the Bishop of Rome with whom it lay to decide who was Bishop of Antioch, and who should not be asked simply to ratify a *fait accompli*. Meanwhile, *nominatim*, Apollinaris was condemned. The decision was a bitter one for St. Basil. Before he could renew his appeals with the knowledge experience was bringing him of Rome's wider cares, death came to him—January 1, 379. It came at a moment when he promised to be of greater usefulness to the Catholic cause than ever. For Valens had pre-deceased him, slain in battle with the Goths (378). The new emperor, Theodosius, was enthusiastically Catholic. A restoration of Catholicism, imperially aided now, was certain; and since, despite Rome's recognition of Paulinus, the East adhered to Meletius, the restoration, now that St. Basil was dead, would be guided by this bishop whom Rome would not recognise but who was now, none the less, in the eyes of the East and its new Catholic sovereign, Nicene orthodoxy's greatest champion.

Events moved quickly. In the autumn of 379 Meletius gathered a great council of his bishops at Antioch—a hundred and fifty-three of them—and on his suggestion they accepted the profession of faith lately published by the Roman council of Pope Damasus. In February, 380, Theodosius, by imperial edict, ended the State's connection with Arianism. The test of Catholicity was to be acceptance of the Faith "given to the Romans by the divine Apostle Peter . . . the faith clearly taught by the pontiff Damasus and by Peter, Bishop of Alexandria." All other beliefs are heresy, and heretics are to suffer as the law directs. The State, for fifty years at the service of Arianism, was now for the first time to be at the service of Catholicism. The restoration so long over-due had come at last. But political power was to be its foundation. The circumstance was calamitous, and calamitious, too, the surely related circumstance that Rome was not consulted in the procedure adopted; and also that Meletius of Antioch was the president of the Council summoned by the emperor to carry into effect his good will towards the Church. The council which met at Constantinople in 381, and over which Meletius presided, was hardly likely to be enthusiastically concerned with any practical acknowledgement of the primacy of Pope Damasus. Nor was it favourably predisposed towards that other see, which, Rome's ally through all the disastrous half century which was closing, had been rewarded for its unshaken fidelity to the Roman *homoöusion* by all Rome's confidence, and which had become the pope's natural adviser for all matters oriental. The council was not more likely to over-exalt the power of Alexandria than it was to over-proclaim the primacy of Rome.

The Arian bishops who had accepted the invitation, there were thirty-six of them, repelled all the attempts, whether of the Catholic bishops or of the emperor, to persuade them to an acceptance of Nicea and, faithful to their heresy, left the city before the council began.

When finally, in the May of 381, the Council opened, its first business was to elect a Bishop of Constantinople to supply the place of the Arian who, rather than conform, had gone into exile. Gregory of Nazianzen, Bishop of Sasimos, the life-long intimate of Basil, friend and ally of Meletius, was chosen. Within a few days Meletius himself died and it now lay within the council's power to end the schism by electing Paulinus in his place. Such would have been the solution preferred by St. Gregory, now the council's president. But the anti-western spirit was too strong. If the East had returned to the faith which the West had never lost, it still preferred to settle matters of discipline as though the West did not exist. So St. Gregory notes and laments. The council left the election to the bishops of the civil diocese whose capital Antioch was. They chose, to succeed Meletius, one of his priests, Flavian. The next crisis arose with the arrival of the Bishop of Alexandria. He protested against St. Gregory's election to Constantinople, citing the ancient canon, a living thing in Egypt and the West, though by now a dead letter in the East, which forbade episcopal translations. The council which had elected St. Gregory failed to support him. The emperor, too, was silent. Gregory resigned. In his place, both as bishop and as president, they chose a retired dignitary of the civil service, Nectarius, an old man of blameless life indeed but not as yet baptized.

The council had no difficulty in framing a statement of the faith upon which, as a basis, the bishops proposed to restore Catholicism throughout the East. After fifty years of controversy and discussion they ended where they had all begun, with the unamended formula of Nicea, the much disputed, much criticised, and altogether necessary *homoöusion*. And, following for once the precedent of western-inspired councils, they refrained from publishing any new creed, any gloss on the invaluable talisman they re-accepted. But the canon which expressed their allegiance went on to condemn severally the various types of Arianism and the heresies into which more than one opponent of Arianism had tripped—Anomoeans, Pneumatomachi, Marcellians, Photinians, and Apollinarists alike.

The council's next work, with an eye to the future peace, was the stricter regulation of the bishop's extra-diocesan activities. Except the imperial interference in church matters nothing had been so productive of lasting mischief as the interference of bishops in the spiritual affairs of neighbouring sees and neighbouring provinces. Legislation which would confine episcopal zeal to its own well-defined territory should stave off, for the future, one of the plagues which had most grievously affected the past. Henceforward, then, so the council decreed, the bishops of each civil diocese were to confine their activities within its limits; nor were they to interfere in the affairs of any other civil diocese unless specially invited to do so. The canon goes on to explain in detail what this means for each of the five civil dioceses which made up the Eastern Empire: the bishops of the East[1] have authority over the churches in the East alone (while the privileges of Antioch which Nicea recognised are to be preserved); the bishops of Pontus have authority over the churches in Pontus only, those of Asia and Thrace over the churches of Asia and Thrace alone; for Egypt there was the special arrangement that the competent authority was not the bishops of the diocese of Egypt but the Bishop of Alexandria—a recognition of the special character of that see's Egyptian hegemony; and his authority was limited to Egypt only. Furthermore, the Nicene rule was recalled that the affairs of each province were subject to the control of the bishops of each province.

Never again, if the new rule is observed, will bishops rich in Cæsar's favour wander about the Empire, a peripatetic council, deposing at will whoever opposes them. Against that, a remedy is provided in the equilibrium of these five autonomous, self-contained groups. But whatever chance there might be of this new arrangement's success as an antidote to the civil influence of any one particular leading see, the council in its next canon sanctioned an innovation which, in effect, was to neutralise that arrangement. This is the famous third canon, which runs "The Bishop of Constantinople should have the primacy of honour after the Bishop of Rome because Constantinople is New Rome." The canon, though it tacitly admits the new unheard-of-principle that the honour should be according to the civil importance of the see-city, offers, it is true, no more than a title of honour. It does not make any exception for Constantinople in the matter of jurisdiction as settled by the preceding canon. For all his new honour the Bishop of Constantinople remains, in jurisdiction, the simple suffragan of the Metropolitan of Heraclea, with no authority beyond the limits of his own see. The council had merely done for him what Nicea had done fifty years earlier for

[1] The civil diocese called *Oriens: cf.* the map which follows the index.

Jerusalem. But for the Metropolitan of Heraclea it had created
the embarrassment that one of his suffragans was now, in honorific
precedence, not only his own superior but the superior of every
other bishop in the Church save the Bishop of Rome. And the
embarrassment, inevitably, was to affect a very much wider
sphere than the province of Heraclea. Two of the chief causes
of the fifty years chaos in the East, now happily ending, were
the continual interference of the emperor in church affairs, and
the hardly less continual interference of the Bishop of Constantinople in matters outside his own jurisdiction. The basis
of this new uncanonical, ecclesiastical thing was the mere accident
of Constantinople's civil importance. Now, in the council called
to organise the Catholic restoration, that accident was given
legal recognition; the uncanonical novelty, whence had come so
much mischief already, was built into the very foundation of the
new régime. The primacy of honour was bound to develop into
one of jurisdiction.

The work of the council completed, the bishops sent an official
report to the emperor, praying him to confirm and seal all they
had accomplished. Whereupon an imperial edict published
officially the formula of orthodoxy, and indicated for each civil
diocese the bishop, communion with whom was to be, for the
officers charged to return church property, the proof of a bishop's
Catholicism. "Facing the West whose disciplined unity has been
in these last years the envy of the East, the Council of 381 has set
up an East, harmonious and organised: Theodosius has succeeded in imposing upon the Easterns, in appearances at all
events, a quasi-western discipline. Are not the Easterns, in return,
turning their backs upon the West?"[1] The council, which itself
made no claim to be a general council, made no report to Rome.
There, as late as Chalcedon (451), its canons were still unknown.
But, thanks to the energetic protestations of St. Ambrose the
East was to give a sign of its fidelity to the tradition, real enough
if only made at the eleventh hour. An embassy of high officials
was sent to the pope to announce the election of the new Bishop
of Constantinople and to ask letters of communion in recognition
of it.

[1] Batiffol. *Le Siège Apostolique*, p. 141.

CHAPTER IX

ROME AND THE CATHOLIC EAST. 381–453

I. THE PRIMACY OF HONOUR. 381–419

To anyone who had understood the forces which blighted Catholic life in the East all through the fourth century, the evolution of Constantinople's new primacy would have seemed merely a matter of time; and just as much matter of time the resulting conflict between Rome and Constantinople. The fifty years between the Council of 381 and the next of the general councils—Ephesus—are in fact filled with the din of that strife, and the fight ranges round one of the greatest personalities of all church history, St. John Chrysostom, Bishop of Constantinople from 398 to 407.

Nectarius, the elect of the Council of 381, died on September 27, 397. More than one candidate was put forward for the vacant see, and at last, to put an end to the intrigue and the tumult, the emperor—it was Arcadius, for Theodosius had died two years before—named the new bishop. His choice fell on John, a monk of Antioch, a man of saintly virtue, learned, and reputed the greatest preacher of his time, whom after ages were to call the Golden-tongued—Chrysostomos. At the time of his consecration he was close on fifty years of age. He had been a monk—a solitary—until his first patron, Meletius, called him into the clergy. The successor of Meletius, Flavian, ordained him priest, and at the time of his election to Constantinople he was one of the outstanding personalities of Eastern Catholicism. His appointment was, none the less, an imperial appointment. His early associations, too, were with that imperial Catholicism which had shaped the re-organisation of 381. His nomination represented, even more than that of Nectarius, an Antiochian gain at Constantinople. One of the candidates whom the appointment ruled out had been supported by Antioch's great rival Alexandria, whose bishop was now Theophilus (382–412) a proud man, able and unscrupulous, a sinister figure indeed, in whom there seems re-incarnated something of Egypt's ancient dark mystery. John's election was a defeat for Theophilus—a defeat which, no doubt, he resented all the more, in that he was compelled to submit by threats of a criminal prosecution for his misdeeds.

The new bishop was to secure from Rome recognition of the

successor of Meletius. The succession of Paulinus had died out. His followers had accepted Flavian; and St. John's intervention removed the last trace of the long unhappy schism. Rome, Alexandria and Antioch, the three chief sees, were once more in communion—the first time for nearly seventy years. With St. John Chrysostom the bishop remained the monk. He showed himself as zealous in reforming evil as, in his days as priest at Antioch, he had been eloquent in denouncing it. And since much of the evil he wrought against was the affair of those in high places, he soon made powerful enemies.

Nor was his zeal confined to his own city or province. From the beginning of his reign he followed the custom his predecesor had inaugurated of using the prestige of the primacy of honour to settle disputes which, by the strict law of the Council of 381, really lay outside his competence. So he crossed into the neighbouring civil diocese of Pontus, in 398, to depose the Bishop of Nicomedia and, despite opposition from the populace, appointed his successor. More seriously still, a year later, on the authorisation of a handful of bishops whom chance accident brought together in the capital, he undertook to judge between two bishops of the neighbouring civil diocese of Asia. Nectarius had similarly broken through the canon of 381 when, a few years earlier, with the tacit consent of Alexandria and Antioch, he had judged a case between two bishops from Arabia. The ingenious machinery which would secure order in the East without reference to Rome was already ceasing to function. Three years later it broke down altogether, under the weight of the two-fold plague which still oppressed the Eastern Church—imperial interference and unrestrained episcopal ambition. It is to be noted that all sides tolerated, were willing to use, invited and welcomed the imperial intervention; and that, turn by turn, all the great sees of the East were guilty of these manifest usurpations of jurisdiction. The difference in kind between the jurisdiction they ambitioned and usurped, and that which, turn by turn, they acknowledged or disobeyed in Rome—none denied it—is, once more, equally evident.

The aggressor this time was Alexandria, the victim Constantinople; the means of the aggression was the imperial hold on ecclesiastical obedience, bought now by Theophilus at a great price. Theophilus had never loved St. John, and disappointed to see Antioch installed at court in his person, the Egyptian had filled the capital with spies who might, it was hoped, furnish matter for its bishop's trial and deposition. In the calumnies spread by the wretches whom St. John's reforms had exposed and dislodged, the spies found of course a wealth of material.

Towards the end of 401 there appeared at Constantinople a number of monks expelled from Egypt by Theophilus for, as he alleged, their heretical opinions. They came to appeal to the emperor against their bishop, and they sought the patronage of St. John. Without prejudging the case, he charitably wrote to Theophilus to intercede. For reply Theophilus despatched some of his clergy with a wealth of "evidence" against the alleged heretics. The newcomers were, in turn, accused of calumny by the monks, convicted and, the bribes of Theophilus alone saving them from the executioner, sent to the mines. Then followed, at the demand once more of the alleged heretics, the first steps in a suit against Theophilus himself.

The emperor, since the accused was a bishop, refused to judge the case himself. He named as judge the Bishop of Constantinople, and sent a summons to Theophilus to come, and to come alone, for his trial. Theophilus obeyed, but brought with him twenty-nine of his suffragans and the ever-useful Alexandrian gold, and he came, as he said in his farewells to Egypt, "to get John deposed." His trickery, his gold, and the mentality of Eastern Catholicism assisting him, he was successful.

St. John, most correctly, had refused the emperor's commission to judge the Bishop of Alexandria. That, by law, was a matter for the bishops of Egypt. Theophilus, three weeks later, was asking the emperor for leave to judge St. John—accused, it appears, of all manner of wickedness. The Bishop of Alexandria, whose three weeks at court had been usefully employed, was by now in residence across the Bosphorus, at Chalcedon, in the summer palace known as The Oak. There, in July 403, with his twenty-nine suffragans and half a dozen other bishops, fortified with the imperial favour, he opened what, impudently enough, he called his council and summoned St. John to appear and take his trial. St. John is to suffer from that very imperial usurpation which he had himself refused to use against the man now wielding it. All is done by virtue of it, and in its presence Church law, even the canon of 381, is null—and all the bishops concerned are Catholics and the emperor too. Under such a régime how is religion more safe than under Arian princes? Now, as then, it is the emperor's bishop alone who is secure.

St. John once more behaved admirably. He refused to acknowledge the usurpation of Theophilus by appearing. "It is not right that bishops from Egypt judge bishops from Thrace." The emperor insisted, but the saint stood to his resolve. In his absence he was at length "condemned," deposed, and by imperial edict ordered into exile. Three days later, through a city whose excited populace looked only for a sign from him to raze all to the ground, he obediently followed his escort to the waiting ship and the distant coast of Bithynia.

The emperor was a weakling. The excitement in his capital shook him from his opposition to St. John, the exile was recalled; while the clerics whose malevolence had functioned at The Oak, took to flight, Theophilus at their head. The emperor next made a show of revising the iniquities, but within a couple of months the old intrigues were once more at work, and finally, thanks to Theophilus and the gang of like-minded bishops whom he led, the emperor, at their petition, confirmed anew the sentence of 403 and ordered St. John's arrest. This time the exile was definitive, and distant. First to Nicea, thence to Armenia, and further still, the saint was harried until, worn out by privation, he died at Comana on September 14, 407. Theophilus was revenged for the election of 398, Alexandria had prevailed against the creation of 381. Clerical disorders in the capital, the intrigues of the disaffected, intrigues of bishops come to the capital from heaven knows where, the corruption of the court, the chance whims of the emperor, "I leave you the lot," cried St. Epiphanius to the bishops who bade him good-bye on his last visit in 403, "the city, the court, the whole hypocritical farce." They were still in the East, these things, what they had been for three generations, what they were to be more than once again, an important engine of ecclesiastical government.

Happily for the Church in the East the supreme authority lay elsewhere. This last great treachery of eastern bishops was to reveal that authority's different nature in very striking fashion. Rome's first news of the new crisis was through Theophilus whose messenger simply announced to the pope that "John has been deposed." This was, apparently, towards the end of May, 404, nearly a year after the "council" at The Oak, and in the last weeks of the semi-imprisonment in his own palace which preceded St. John's exile. Three days later came St. John's messengers— four bishops with a letter for the pope, a letter sent likewise to the bishops of Milan and Aquileia.

Here the whole story is told, the "trial," the exile, the recall. Theophilus and his set are blamed for the outrage, there is not a word against the emperor, and the letter ends with the request for a declaration that the acts of the "council" at The Oak are null and that its bishops have broken the law. To a properly constituted court St. John will gladly submit the proofs of his innocence.

The pope—St. Innocent I (401-417)—replied to both the bishops. He condemned the "council," of The Oak, and acquiesced in St. John's request for an impartial council of bishops from West and East. The reply had hardly been sent when, from Theophilus, there came a fuller account of the transaction with the minutes of his "council." The pope answered with a renewal of his proposal for a general council. Then came, from the bishops faithful to St. John, the news of the second banishment, the news too, of the imperial edicts threatening with deposition any bishop who supported the exile and with confiscation of goods whoever sheltered such bishops. Once more from the East the tide of refugees began to flow in to Rome.

The pope's reply to the edicts was to write to St. John assuring him of support, and to write in the same sense to the bishops who had remained faithful. He wrote also to the clergy and people of Constantinople—a refusal to acknowledge the bishop set up in St. John's place, a strong reasoned protest against the uncanonical proceedings which had driven him forth, and, once more, a plea for a general council to clear the whole affair. At the pope's petition his own sovereign the Western Emperor, Honorius (395-423), joined him in the demand to Arcadius for a joint council of East and West. An embassy of bishops and clerics conveyed the imperial request, but no sooner did they cross the frontier of the Eastern Empire than they were arrested and their papers taken from them. They refused to be bribed into a recognition of the new bishop, and thereupon, were summarily deported. The refugees who had returned in their company were exiled (April, 406).

Once more the East had bidden the West leave Eastern affairs to Easterns. Before Rome passed to the only measures of protest left to her—the excommunication of Theophilus, of the new Bishop of Constantinople, Atticus, and of all their supporters—St. John was dead. It had been a quarrel between Easterns and a quarrel on a point of discipline; Rome had intervened, and was to stand by her decision until the unwilling East submitted. Theophilus stood out to the end, and refusing the amends to St. John's memory on which Rome insisted, was still outside her communion when he died (Obtober 15, 412). At Antioch when the new bishop Porphyrios, who had accepted the communion of Atticus, wrote to Rome, too, for letters of communion, the same Roman intransigence refused them. Porphyrios' successor in 413 restored St. John's name to its place among the recognised bishops commemorated in the Mass, and the pope thereupon restored him to communion. "I have made diligent search," the pope wrote, "whether all the conditions in this case of the blessed and truly religious bishop John had been satisfied. Since what your envoys affirm accords in every particular with my wishes, I have accepted to be in communion with your church. . . ."

And he makes the Bishop of Antioch his agent for the reconciliation of the other bishops of the East.

Atticus made more than one attempt to obtain recognition, but so long as he refused to comply with the pope's conditions it was refused. Again St. Innocent's authoritative phrases give life to the routine formality. "Communion, once broken off, cannot be renewed until the person concerned gives proof that the reasons for which communion was broken off are no longer operative, and that what is imposed as a condition of peace has been fulfilled. We still await a declaration from Atticus giving us assurance that all the conditions which at different times we have laid down have been fulfilled. We are willing to renew our communion with him when he makes fitting petition therefor, and when he proves that he merits the favour." In the end Atticus, too, complied with the pope's demand and was received back into his communion.

Last of all Alexandria humbled herself, the successor of Theophilus—his nephew Cyril—submitting in his turn.

In the East whether the bishops are Catholic or heretic, saints or courtiers, the emperor's good pleasure is law for them. Rome, whatever the civil prestige of the city, remains mistress of herself, and to Rome's primacy even the state-ridden churches of the East ultimately bow, rather than lose that communion which is hers uniquely.

II. EPHESUS. 427–433

The crisis of 403–408 had centred around questions of ecclesiastical discipline. All those concerned in it, Theophilus, St. John, Atticus, St. Innocent I, had been united in Faith. There had been no repetition of discussions such as those which the Council of 381 had closed. But within twenty years of the death of St. John, and when all the personalities of that crisis had passed away, the peace of his see was troubled more violently than ever by far-reaching discussions on a fundamental point of faith. In the fourth century Arius had striven against the tradition that the Logos is truly God. Now the discussion shifted to the question of the relations between the Divine and the Human in Jesus Christ. Was there, for instance, a real distinction between the Human and the Divine, or had the Divine absorbed the Human? If the Divine and the Human are really distinct in Him what was the nature of His earthly activities? Was it God acting, or the Man mysteriously and wonderfully united to God? or was the activity sometimes divine and sometimes human?

The practical effect on Christian life of divergent reasoning here cannot, of course, be exaggerated. If the activity is not divine then the gospel loses its chief claim to a hearing, the *ecclesia* its one claim on the absolute attention and obedience of mankind. It becomes straightway nothing more than the masterpiece of human idealism, in life and in moral teaching. If the Divine and the Human are distinct how can the activity be divine ? And if the Divine absorbs the Human how can our vitiated humanity be reintegrated by the mysterious Incarnation of the Logos ? Such reintegration demands a full complete humanity in Him Who is thus to restore it. Such a full complete humanity there cannot be in Our Lord if, in Him, the Human is not distinct from the Divine.

One school of theologians, concerned to safeguard the all important truth of the real distinction between the Human and the Divine, pressed the distinction so far that in Our Lord they were inclined—some of them—to see two realities, united truly enough, and harmoniously one in action, but united with a union that was no more than a moral union. This was the teaching of the so-called school of Antioch.

The Alexandrians, approaching the problem from its other pole, anxious above all to safeguard along with the Divinity of Christ the unity of His activity, and especially of course the Divine character of His action as Saviour of mankind, stressed the union of Human and Divine in Him, until in some cases, the two seemed for the thinker united in such a fusion that the Human reality ceased to be real. In God the Son incarnate, they urged, there was but one incarnate *physis*.

This, in words at any rate, was flat contradiction of the thesis of the Antiochians, for the Antiochians used this very term *physis* to describe each of the realities whose real distinction they were so concerned to defend. In Christ, they taught, there were two *physes*—the Human and the Divine. *Physis*, for this school, meant what the Latin theologians were to call *Nature*; while the same word, with the Alexandrians, was equivalent to the Latin *Person*. Both schools thus used the one term *physis*, and they each used it to express a different reality. The matter of the debate was, then, fundamental. More fundamental matter of debate between members of the Church there could not be. Those who debated it were only too well aware of their subject's vast importance. Each school had worked out its theory as a defence of truth against a particular heresy—and as the heretics differed, so the viewpoint of the defenders differed too. Hence high feeling and passion in the polemic. Again they were debating the matter for the first time, and without an agreed technical terminology to express even their common ideas, much less their individual differences. Hence, not infrequently, misunderstandings and confusion. A final point to note is that the disputants were, almost all of them, Easterns; Greeks by culture, Egyptian or Syrian by blood, subtle of speech with a subtlety far beyond that of anyone then bred west of Alexandria, and endowed with a tropical luxuriance of rhetoric in the expression of their passionately held ideas, which sometimes did little to help on the work of agreement.

Another factor, too, quite untheological this, played its part in the event, influencing the circumstances of the great decisions if it left the decisions themselves untouched. This was the rivalry now traditional between the three great sees of the East. Alexandria, until the unhappy exaltation of Constantinople in 381, had been unquestioned leader of the East. Her bishop it was who, for nearly half a century, had held fast to Catholicism while Antioch and Constantinople had fallen to the Arians. Then, at the council which organised the restoration of orthodoxy, Alexandria had seen her prestige sacrificed to the profit of Constantinople, parvenu see as parvenu city, creature of the Court, heretic and Catholic by turn as the emperor chose. But the council's decision was law for the East, and Alexandria had had to bow to the *fait accompli*. And as the years went by after 381 another interesting development had revealed itself. The predominant influence in the new imperial see was Antiochian. From Antioch, and not from Alexandria, were its bishops taken, and Antiochian theories rather than Alexandrian usually guided its teachers. Alexandria, for the fifty years that followed the restoration council of 381, was, despite its ancient prestige, its services to orthodoxy, and its wealth, decidedly out of the fashion.

In the history of the next two general councils all these elements play their part. The traditional faith is asserted,—each time by the see which, ever refusing to philosophise, reserves to itself a rôle of decisive authoritative teaching—but asserted after a strangely complex exhibition of passionate contending humanity. The story is simple enough, so long as the traditional faith and the traditional procedure for resolving doubts are alone in question. The story only begins to be involved when there enter in these extraneous elements, rival systems of theology, hereditary rivalries of the great sees, the novelty of appealing to Cæsar to assist the settlement—this last above all, for as a result of such appeals, Cæsar is fast becoming to the Church in his dominions as omnipresent and paralysing as was ever the old man of the sea.

Atticus, the intruded successor of St. John Chrysostom, died in 425, his peace with Rome made long before. To him succeeded

Sisinnius who reigned only for a year and ten months. Whereupon, to cut short the intrigues of interested parties in the capital itself, the emperor, Theodosius II (408–450), decided, like his father Arcadius in 397, that the new bishop should be chosen from outside. And once more, as in 397, it was a priest of Antioch who was elected. His name was Nestorius and already he had made a name for himself as a man of ascetic life and a notable preacher. He was a pupil of the most celebrated of all the Antiochian theologians, Theodore, now ending his life as Bishop of Mopsuestia.

Theodore, a friend of St. John Chrysostom, had with the saint been the pupil of Diodore of Tarsus (394) whose ideas he had developed, making for himself a name that quite eclipsed his master's. Diodore had been in his time a mighty controversialist. His especial foe was Apollinaris, the Alexandrian Bishop of Laodicea (360–377). Apollinaris, a powerful opponent of Arianism, insisting on the unity of Our Lord's salvific activity, and its divine character, had resolved the main difficulty in the way of his theory by teaching that the humanity which the Divinity associated to itself was incomplete—a true human body indeed but lacking a human soul. Against these theorisings, condemned often, and condemned most solemnly at Constantinople in 381, Diodore insisted on the truth they denied, namely that in Our Lord there are two natures, really distinct, complete, true natures. Unfortunately he so isolated them that a duality of nature, as he conceived it, was not compatible with any unity of personality. Theodore, Bishop of Mopsuestia (392–428), developing his master, speaks of the two natures as though they were each complete persons, failing, like Diodore, to understand all that is implied in the notion of "one person," and that a duality such as he constructs is not compatible with that unity.

Nestorius was not so clear as his master. Like Theodore, while he admits in theory the unity of person, he speaks of the two natures as though these were two independent persons. Again, for Nestorius, the one person is not conceived as the active divine person of the Logos associating with itself the created humanity, but the personality is taken as the result, the effect, of the union of the divinity and the humanity. The Logos and the humanity, anterior to the union, have each their proper person; in the union there is still but one person—the person of Christ, to which the person of the Logos and the person of the humanity are in a kind of subordination.

Such intricate and involved theorising might have gone the way of much other like speculation had not Nestorius worked it out to the practical conclusions of everyday spirituality, and attempted to impose it as the true tradition of faith upon his clergy and people. What brought the Bishop of Constantinople to this, was the need, now become urgent, to provide in a popular way, some refutation of the many heresies about the divinity of Our Lord that troubled the peace of the capital, and especially a revival among the Arians and Apollinarians. Constantinople was indeed, at the moment, full of militant heretics. Nestorius had had much to say about this in the inaugural address that followed his appointment to the see in 427. One result of his zeal was a new imperial law against heretics (May 30, 428) and a great campaign to convert them or drive them out. In that campaign the truth of the faith was to be set out cleared of the misrepresentations of it circulated by its enemies. And so it came about that one of the bishop's intimates, the monk Anastasius, announced the "new theology" of the Incarnation in a popular sermon on the Mother of God. "Mother of God" she had always been to the ordinary faithful. It was a title consecrated by long usage and it expressed succinctly the traditional belief that He whose mother she was, was not merely man but also truly God. But the monk, Anastasius, explained that this title "Mother of God," *Theotokos*, should only be used with the greatest care, had better in fact not be used at all. Mary was "Mother of Christ" rather than "Mother of God." The ambiguity of the new teaching, its implication that somehow Christ was not fully divine, were not lost on the audience. A tumult began, a noisy appeal to the bishop to depose the preacher. Nestorius, however, not only refused to do this but took the opportunity himself to preach against the traditional cult. The monks and many of his clergy objected and he excommunicated them, deposed them, even had some of them scourged and imprisoned. Whereupon they appealed to the emperor (428).

But before the emperor acted another power had intervened. This was the Bishop of Alexandria, St. Cyril. Among the excommunicated at Constantinople were monks. Egypt was still the centre of monasticism and its chief bishop the patron and protector of monks wherever found. The news of the excommunications and of the novel teaching in whose name it had been inflicted was, then, not slow in reaching Alexandria. It roused against the unhappy Nestorius the great man of the day. It was not merely that St. Cyril, like his uncle and predecessor Theophilus, disposed of vast material resources, and a highly organised and well-disciplined following of bishops, nor merely that he was a capable organiser gifted with tremendous energy. He was the most powerful theologian the Greek-speaking Church had yet known, a thinker whose subsequent effect on the definition of doctrine was to be greater than that of any other eastern, except perhaps his predecessor at Alexandria, St. Athanasius.

St. Cyril, informed of the difficulties, studied the whole matter systematically and wrote to Nestorius (February, 430). He wrote also to the emperor and the empress. He wrote, in the third place, to Rome (Easter, 430). To the pope he communicated the whole dossier of the case: the sermons of Nestorius, his own letters to him, a catalogue of the alleged errors, another of extracts from the Fathers that bore on the matter, and a Latin translation of all these. "The ancient custom of the Church" he wrote "admonishes us that matters of this kind should be communicated to Your Holiness." The matter was too grave for him to act on his own authority. "We do not openly and publicly break off communion with [Nestorius] before bringing these things to the notice of Your Holiness. Deign therefore to prescribe what you feel in the matter, so that it may be clearly known to us whether we must hold communion with him, or whether we should freely declare to him that no one can remain in communion with one who cherishes and preaches suchlike erroneous doctrine."

Rome's reply was startling, not in its acceptance of the appeal, but in the peremptory arrangements it made for judgment. The pope, St. Celestine I (422–432), already knew something of the controversy. Nestorius himself had sent him some of his sermons; and one of the deacons of the Roman Church, Leo, had had them examined by John Cassian. Only one verdict was possible. The new theories were not in accord with the traditional faith. When the dossier from Alexandria arrived, the pope called a synod and the whole matter was carefully considered: not only St. Cyril's letters, but also the letters which Nestorius himself had sent to the pope enclosing extracts from his sermons to illustrate his theories. After which the pope wrote to all the parties concerned —to Nestorius, to St. Cyril, to the other eastern patriarchs and to the church of Constantinople: but to the emperor, from Rome, not a word. Nestorius was told that St. Cyril's faith was in accord with the tradition, that St. Cyril's remonstrance should have been a warning to him. This was his last. Should he not, within ten days of being notified by St. Cyril, renounce his impious theories, St. Cyril had it in charge to dethrone him. The Catholics of Constantinople were congratulated on the stand they made against the heresy, consoled for the persecution Nestorius had inflicted on them, and bidden to trust in Rome, always the refuge for persecuted Catholics. All the sentences of Nestorius were annulled, and finally it was announced that since, in so grave a matter, the pope himself must judge, and since the distance forbade his personal presence, "we have delegated our holy brother Cyril in our place."

To St. Cyril himself the pope sent detailed instructions. Acting in the pope's name he was formally to summon Nestorius to recant, and, should he not do so within ten days, to excommunicate and depose him. All these letters were sent through St. Cyril. The emperor the pope had ignored, or overlooked. A decision in a matter of faith, a dispute between bishops was, by all Roman traditions, matter for episcopal action exclusively. But east of the Adriatic another tradition held. Nestorius had appealed to Cæsar, and on Cæsar's action much would depend. Much also would depend on the manner in which the Roman commission was executed by Rome's Alexandrian commissioner.

The Emperor Theodosius II was still a young man, thirty years of age, cultured, pious, amiable and vacillating, his judgment always very much at the mercy of his last adviser. The monks and clergy excommunicated by Nestorius had appealed to him. St. Cyril had written from Alexandria in the same sense. But in the end it was Nestorius who prevailed; and before St. Cyril's ulti-matum had arrived—what delayed it all this time, August to November, 430, we shall see presently—the emperor had decided that the whole affair should remain untouched pending the meeting of a general council which he now[1] convoked to meet at Ephesus on the Whit-Sunday of the following year 431. This council, Nestorius wrote to Pope Celestine, would deal with a number of charges brought against St. Cyril and his administration. Had Nestorius, by now, heard something of the Roman reaction? We may well think it, for in this letter he begins to qualify his objection to the expression *Theotokos*.

The imperial couriers carrying to Alexandria the announcement of the forthcoming council crossed a deputation coming thence *en route* for Constantinople, and Nestorius. They were four of St. Cyril's suffragans, deputed, by the synod he had called, in November 430, to carry to Nestorius the letters of Pope Celestine as from the pope's commissioner.[2] St. Cyril had chosen, before acting, to summon a council of his suffragans and to give the papal decision the setting of their support. Whence, from the bishops of Egypt, a synodal letter admonishing Nestorius, and attached to it twelve propositions for him to sign and accept. Whence a certain delay, and, because of these twelve propositions, a new source of discord. At the outset let us note that for the consequences which followed from the accidental setting in which Rome's ultimatum was presented, none is to be blamed but the author of that setting, not St. Celestine but his commissioner.

The twelve propositions were the work of a skilful theologian

---

[1] November 11, 430.
[2] The four bishops arrived at Constantinople on December 7, 430.

drawn up to provide against any chance of equivocation on the part of the man who was to sign them, and whose sincerity was naturally suspect. Whatever hope Nestorius might have had of retaining both his see and his heresy by a simple acceptance of Pope Celestine's demands, would not survive his reading of this formidable requisitory. Unfortunately, with all their wealth of detail and distinctions, and despite their evident usefulness for nailing down a slippery opponent, they were an addition far beyond what the pope himself had demanded. Nestorius might be well within his rights in ignoring them. More seriously still, as compromising the pope's action, they presented the papal decision about the faith in St. Cyril's own special terminology, a terminology which could be explained in an heretical sense as well as in a Catholic sense, a terminology very like what had been condemned in Apollinaris[1] and what was again to be condemned in Eutyches, a terminology by no means beyond criticism and one to which no Antiochian, Catholic or not, was likely to give assent. That the Roman decision should have been presented in what appeared as the trappings of party theology, at the very moment when party feeling ran so high, was a great misfortune. Rome apparently knew nothing about the twelve propositions. St. Celestine never mentions them. They were designed as a personal test for Nestorius, and for that only. Unfortunately they raised the whole Antiochian school against their author, the Bishop of Antioch leading the denunciation of St. Cyril as himself a heretic—an Apollinarian who believed that in Our Lord there is but one nature. At the request of John of Antioch another great man took up his pen to criticise the twelve propositions, Theodoret, Bishop of Cyrrhus, a greater scholar than St. Cyril and almost as great a theologian.

So the winter passed and the spring (November, 430–May, 431). The pope agreed to the council (beginning of May, 431) and appointed legates to represent him. They were the bishops Arcadius and Projectus, and the priest Philip; and the pope, in their credentials, wrote to the emperor that the legates would explain his decision, to which he made no doubt the council would adhere. The legates themselves he instructed to co-operate with St. Cyril and to follow his lead throughout. To St. Cyril himself, who had written asking, logically enough, whether Nestorius was to be considered already excommunicated since the ten days of grace had long since run out, the pope wrote a reminder that God wills not the death of the sinner but his repentance. It

---

[1] Its crucial phrase, which everyone at the time ascribed to St. Athanasius, was in fact of the mint of Apollinaris himself! It is one of St. Cyril's favourite formulae to express his teaching, " *one incarnate* physis *of God the Word*."

is the salvation of Nestorius that now concerns the pope. Let not Cyril be numbered with those of whom Sacred Scripture speaks "swift to shed blood."

The council was summoned for Pentecost, June 8, 431. Nestorius had arrived, with his supporters, by Easter. St. Cyril came just before the feast, accompanied by fifty bishops from Egypt; the shifty Bishop of Jerusalem five days later. They sat down to wait for John of Antioch, whom the emperor had appointed to preside, and the bishops of his "patriarchate." They waited a full fourteen days—two weeks for both sides to organise, and for their supporters to battle in the streets of Ephesus—and then, thanks to St. Cyril's urgency and despite numerous protests, on June 22 the council opened with something like 159 bishops present. St. Cyril presided, no doubt in virtue of the commission of 430 deputing him to judge Nestorious. After a formal protest, from the Count who represented the emperor, against the council's meeting before the arrival of the Antiochians, the assembly passed immediately to the business of Nestorius and his theories. The notaries read the charges and Nestorius was formally summoned to appear, summoned three times as custom required, and, of course, he refused. The council proceeded without him. The creed of Nicea was read and hailed as the profession of orthodox faith. St. Cyril's letter to Nestorius[1] was read too, and approved as conforming to the creed of Nicea. It was then the turn of Nestorius' reply to St. Cyril. This too was read out, and when the question was put "Whether or not it accorded with Nicea?", the bishops, by acclamation, unanimously anathematised the letter and its author. Next, at the demand of the Bishop of Jerusalem, Pope Celestine's letter to Nestorius was read out, the letter of St. Cyril to Nestorius which contained the twelve propositions, and the report of the four bishops sent by him to Nestorius. Extracts from earlier writers to show the orthodoxy of the term *Theotokos* were presented, and after them the passages from Nestorius to illustrate his theories. Finally the council "urged thereto by the canons and by the letter of our most holy Father and colleague Celestine, Bishop of the Roman Church," declared Nestorius deposed for his contumacy, and for the errors publicly proclaimed in his sermons, his letters, and his speeches even here at Ephesus. A report was drawn up for the emperor, and the bishops dispersed to their lodgings, escorted by the enthusiastic populace, through a city illuminated in honour of the victory of truth over heresy, of the Theotokos over her would-be traducer.

But the history of the council does not, by any means, end

[1] i.e. cf. February, 430, cf. supra p. 241.

with the story of its first laborious session. Nestorius, for example, appealed from its sentence to the emperor, alleging that the council should not have begun while so many of the bishops had not yet arrived. And the emperor, irritated by the bishops' independence of his lieutenant, the Count Candidian, lectured them for their disregard of his orders and ordered the council to sit once more and not to disperse until it was unanimous in its judgment (June 29). This perhaps was a reference to the hitherto absent Antiochians, who had arrived (June 24) two days only after the great opening session, and before even the report of this had gone in to the emperor. Upon hearing what had already taken place these bishops had straightway formed themselves into a council apart; the Count Candidian, reporting the events of June 22, renewed his protest before them; and the bishops excommunicated the other council and its president: the council for proceeding in their absence, St. Cyril for his twelve "heretical" propositions. So far had events progressed when, finally, there arrived the legates from Rome. They joined themselves to St. Cyril and on July 10, in their presence, the second session of the council opened—nearly three weeks after the first. There were present the bishops who had assisted at the first session and those only, St. Cyril still president, still "holding the place of the most holy and venerable archbishop of the Roman Church Celestine."

It was the Roman legates who now took the initiative. They demanded that there be read the letter of Pope Celestine to the council, the letter of May 7 which narrates the pope's decision and invites the council to adhere to it. More, when the bishops broke into acclamation of the agreement the legates were careful to interrupt them and to stress the point that, less important than the fact of the pope's decision being in agreement with that of the council, was the pope's demand that the council should execute his decision. The council having reached that conclusion in its first session, it remained only for the legates to confirm what it had done. First of all they must examine the minutes of its proceedings; and the council adjourned to give them the necessary time. It reassembled for the third session the next day, and one of the legates, the priest Philip, in a striking speech notable for the assumption of the Roman primacy that underlay it, declared the proceedings of the famous first session valid and good in law. The minutes were then formally read, and the sentence decreed against Nestorius.

A report of this new session was sent to the emperor, and, an effect no doubt of the more independent Roman spirit, it contained no reference to his recent edict, no apology for the flagrant contravention. Five days later, after repeated unavailing summonses to John of Antioch and his followers to appear before the council and explain their conduct, the council excommunicated them also; to the number of thirty-four. And once more they sent to the emperor an official report, and to the pope an account of all that had happened since June 22.

The emperor in his reply took a truly unexpected line. He declared his approval of the condemnation of Nestorius, and also of the sentence passed by the Antiochians on St. Cyril. To assist in the restoration of unity he now sent one of his Ministers who could explain to the bishops "the plans our divinity has in mind for the good of the faith." The day that saw the new functionary arrive with this letter[1] saw also the arrest of the excommunicated leaders—St. Cyril as well as Nestorius was in prison. John of Antioch had called in Cæsar, and Cæsar had acted.

The history now becomes a confusion of protestations and counter protestations, of intrigues at the court, of backstairs influence and bribes to officials. St. Cyril knew the court, knew the only means which at times influence those whose influence in such places is paramount. He had the means to influence the influential: he made lavish use of them. The emperor slowly gave way. In a joint conference at Chalcedon (September 11, 431) he received delegates from the two councils, and although he refused St. Cyril a hearing, he refused equally to listen to suggestions that the famous twelve propositions were anti-Nicene. He accepted moreover the deposition of Nestorius and he allowed the return of St. Cyril to Alexandria. The council he declared at an end, the bishops might now return to their churches. Nestorius was to go into exile.

But between the rival deputations the division was as wide as ever. The Antiochians the emperor had been powerless to win over, yet "because before us none has been able to convict them" he would not condemn them. The council ended, then, with Nestorius condemned and isolated, but with a new division between Alexandria and Antioch and the bishops of the two "patriarchates". "For all the tactlessness of Cyril, and the obstructions of John of Antioch, it was with the solution which Rome had from the beginning prescribed that the conflict came to its end. It was the Roman See, and that alone, which came through the violent and confused crisis that we call the Council of Ephesus with its prestige undiminished, nay even greater than before."[2]

But far more than to the mistakes of St. Cyril and John of Antioch, the responsibility for the confusion is to be laid to

---

[1] Early in August.
[2] Batiffol, Mgr. Pierre, *Le Siège Apostolique*, p. 393.

the general willingness of the Easterns to make Cæsar the arbiter in the things that are properly God's. The monks and clergy persecuted by Nestorius appeal to him, and Nestorius appeals too. The simple ecclesiastical procedure of the Roman See, the traditional procedure for charges against high ecclesiastics, is disregarded again by the emperor, when, to settle between the contending parties, he summons the council. Again he intervenes —at the demand once more of a bishop, John of Antioch—to quash the council's proceedings and to order a re-hearing (June 28, 431) and if, at the end, he accepts the solution first proposed by Rome, his acceptance is no more than an act of grace. The emperor's interference had simply increased the confusion and magnified the bitterness in which the affair was conducted, and his interference had been sought and welcomed by all the ecclesiastics concerned, turn by turn, excepting, only and always, one, the Bishop of the Roman Church.

With the meeting between the emperor and the delegates at Chalcedon, in the September of 431, the history of the council ends. Not so, however, the history of the relations between Alexandria and Antioch, and of the theories associated respectively with each. When Pope Celestine replied to the synodal letter of the council he necessarily made reference to the council's condemnation of John of Antioch. He is most anxious that John, too, shall subscribe to the council's decision, although he evidently looks upon him as a Nestorian in his views. He does not, however, endorse the council's excommunication, that matter being too weighty for any authority less than his own to decide. But before Pope Celestine could proceed further with regard to the Antiochians he died, July 27, 432. His successor, Sixtus III, was however of the same mind and, in a letter to the Orientals, he insisted on their submission, since it was to a decision of the Apostolic See that submission was demanded. John of Antioch was not a Nestorian, but he looked askance at the Cyrillian terminology in which the orthodox faith offered for his acceptance was formulated. Before he could accept St. Cyril as a fellow Catholic, St. Cyril and he must mutually explain themselves. In a happier atmosphere than the antechambers of any council could have provided explanations were made and an accord reached, both parties signing the formulary which expressed in terms acceptable to each the faith they had always held in common. John, the formulary signed, accepted the definition of Ephesus, the orthodoxy of the term *Theotokos*, and the deposition of Nestorius (433).

The celebrated formulary was the work of Theodoret. It is important because it sets out the points of the faith both parties held in common, and is evidence of the sacrifices of individual preferences in terminology, sacrifices made mutually for the sake of peace. The sacrifices were chiefly on the side of St. Cyril. His favourite phrase, "*one incarnate nature of God the Word*," disappears, and in its place he consents to use the Antiochian term, "*the union of two natures.*" Also, by this time, he had explained away the difficulties occasioned by his twelve propositions, especially the phrase "a natural union" used to describe the union of the Divine and Human in Our Lord. Theodoret had criticised this especially, for it seemed to leave loopholes for the theories which considered the union as an absorption of one nature by the other. St. Cyril explained that "natural" was used in the phrase in contradistinction, not with "person," but with "moral" or "virtual." Nestorius had taught that the Divine and Human were, practically, distinct existences, only united morally. To make his heresy clear St. Cyril, in the third of the propositions, asked him to say the union was real, not moral merely. The word to which Theodoret objected was simply chosen to express the union's reality. It has to be allowed to Theodoret that St. Cyril did not make very clear the distinction he drew between "nature" (*physis*) and "substance" (*hypostasis*), and while what St. Cyril called "a natural union" was, in his mind, something very different from an Apollinarian and Monophysite use of the words would have conveyed, there was certainly room for misunderstanding.

For the moment, however, misunderstanding was at an end, although Theodoret seems never to have been convinced in his inner man of the sincerity of the Alexandrian explanation, or, to speak more truly, of the Alexandrian terminology's being patient of such explanation. St. Cyril as long as he lived could explain to objectors, and decide between the rival interpretations of his terminology, and he could keep his own followers loyal to the agreement of 433; as long as he lived there was peace. He died in 444. John of Antioch had predeceased him, as had Pope Sixtus. Of the chief actors in the drama of 431, three alone were left, the emperor at Constantinople, Theodoret in his great diocese of Cyrrhus, and, away in the distant oasis of the Thebaïd, almost at the limits of the known world, Nestorius his friend. The peace endured yet three years longer, and then, in a fiercer heat than ever, the old rivalries flamed yet once again.

III. CHALCEDON. 446–452

In the theological crisis of 448–451 which draws to a head in the Council of Chalcedon, the rivalry of Alexandria and Constantinople again plays its part. For the third time in less than forty years the Egyptian primate is to sit in judgment on the "primate of honour." But while the Alexandrian is, this time, as much in the wrong as was Theophilus in 407, the issue is not merely personal. As in 431 it is a question of the faith, and it is the successor of Theophilus and St. Cyril who now patronises the heresy.

This time it was the Bishop of Constantinople who was the Catholic, and when, worsted, and obstinate to the last in his heresy, Dioscoros of Alexandria fell, his people, save for a tiny minority of court officials and imperialists, chose to follow him out of the Church. Not that they would so describe their action, nor Dioscoros himself. *They* were the Catholics, the rest were Nestorians, and Nestorian too that Council of Chalcedon which condemned Dioscoros; while, for the orthodoxy of their faith, the Egyptians appealed to the theology of St. Cyril ! The story of the events of which the Council of Chalcedon in 451 is the centre, offers many points of very high interest. Its definitions brought to a finish the debate on the fundamental theology of the Trinity and the Incarnation, and the council's proceedings were the occasion of the clearest testimony to the Roman Primacy as a primitive Christian tradition, which the collective eastern episcopate, acting freely, ever made. On the other hand, the circumstances in which the definition was adopted by the council produced effects which reacted on the relations between Church and State for centuries. The last long stage now began in the struggle between Rome and the Catholic Emperor for the control of the Church within the Empire—the struggle which only ended with the destruction of the Church there, with its transformation into a State institution from which, actually, Rome was excluded. Chalcedon is incidentally an important stage in the long road that leads from the Council of 381 to the schism of 1054. We can note, once more, in the history of the intrigues and debates which preceded, accompanied and followed the council, all the features that appeared twenty years earlier at Ephesus. Not one of them is missing: the innovator with his theory, the bishops' condemnation, the appeal to the emperor, the court's policy of expediency, the pope defining the Faith, the definition disregarded so long as the court bishops are in the ascendant; finally comes the council—which is not a means of the pope's choosing, but of the emperor's—and, resulting from the accidental circumstances of the council, a long aftermath of religious feud and civil disorder.

At Ephesus St. Cyril had been the great figure. Twenty years later that rôle fell to his one time adversary Theodoret, Bishop of Cyrrhus. Theodoret has his place in ecclesiastical history and a great place again in the history of Catholic theology. Theodore of Mopsuestia had been his tutor, as he had been the tutor of Nestorius, but Theodoret had revised his master's theories, expurgated them of their errors and heretical tendencies, and if ever he had leaned to Nestorianism he was by this time most assuredly Catholic. His terminology, judged by the more exact use of later times, is, like that of all these pioneer thinkers, loose and faulty. But he was a more exact scholar than St. Cyril, and if he lacked St. Cyril's intellectual power and depth, he was a useful counterbalance to the Alexandrians, as he was also a barrier against the heretical tendencies of some of his own associates. He was, too, a great bishop, a true shepherd to the vast diocese he ruled for so long, a model of pastoral zeal and charity. St. Cyril's death in 444 left Theodoret the greatest personality in the Eastern Church.

Such was the man whose opposition a monk of Constantinople, Eutyches, now drew down on himself. Eutyches was himself a highly influential person in the religious life, not of the capital only but of all the Eastern Empire. He was the head of one of the city's largest monasteries—it counted three hundred monks —and by reason of his great age, and the repute of his ascetic life, a kind of patriarch of the world of monks, while at the court the all-powerful official of the moment was his godson, the eunuch Chrysaphius. Eutyches, then, had the means to impress his ideas on a very large world indeed and in theology his ideas were Apollinarian. Whence bitter opposition to Theodoret and all who shared his opinions, and a long campaign of mischief-making throughout the East designed to undo the union of 433, to destroy the remaining chiefs of the Antiochian school and to impose on all, not only the Alexandrian theology as alone patient of an orthodox meaning, but also the heresy that Our Lord was not truly a human being. To this Theodoret replied in a work—*Eranistes* (The Beggar-man)—in which, in dialogue form, without naming Eutyches he exposed and attacked the peculiar form of Apollinarianism he professed. At the same time the Bishop of Antioch, Theodoret's superior, appealed to the emperor to suppress the new heresy.

How great was the influence of Eutyches at court was revealed immediately. An edict appeared snubbing the Bishop of Antioch for his intervention, while Irenæus, Bishop of Tyre, another of the party, was deposed and ordered to resume his lay status— an unprecedented usurpation on the part of the State; whereupon, heartened by these signs of imperial patronage, the intrigues spread ever more widely. One of the most notable of the Antiochian survivors of the crisis of 431 was the Bishop of Edessa—Ibas. He, too, had been a pupil of Theodore of Mopsuestia and a friend of Nestorius. He had turned from Nestorius in irritation and disgust, upon his refusal to accept the

Theotokos unreservedly, but, true disciple of Theodore, Ibas, while himself orthodox enough, remained the sworn enemy of the Alexandrian mode of theologising in what concerned the Incarnation. Towards Ibas, too, the intrigues were then directed, as they were directed, once more, against Theodoret and against the bishop who was their superior and the nominal leader of their party, Domnus of Antioch.

In this new offensive Eutyches found a powerful ally in the new Bishop of Alexandria, Dioscoros. Dioscoros comes down to us painted in the darkest of colours, a kind of ecclesiastical brigand and blackmailer, to whom no crime came amiss if it furthered his immediate ambition and greed for money. When, later, Flavian of Constantinople died as the result of the injuries received at the council where Dioscoros presided, tongues were not lacking to say that he died at the patriarch's own hands ! Be that as it may, he had already, in the four years since he succeeded St. Cyril, won a name for carrying things with a high hand, with a cruelty and unscrupulousness that seemed to show a complete absence of heart. For some time, now, this sinister personage had been in close relation with Eutyches. The monk had done him good service at court. Now it would be for him to return the obligation; and how eagerly he welcomed the opportunity !

He began by an imperious letter to Domnus questioning the orthodoxy of Theodoret, and that of Domnus for tolerating Theodoret. Theodoret received an order from the court to confine himself in Cyrrhus. Everything seemed to threaten a crusade of Eutyches against the Catholics of Syria and Asia Minor. Eutyches had even taken the step of seeing what Rome would do for his party, representing his Catholic victims as Nestorians, of course, when (November 8, 448) the whole situation suddenly shifted. Eutyches was formally denounced to his own bishop, Flavian, for the heretic he undoubtedly was. The tables were turned. The hunter was now himself in the toils.

But a much more anxious man than Eutyches was the Bishop of Constantinople! He had much to fear if he betrayed the faith, but more—in this world—if he condemned the all-powerful monk. So far, all through the crisis, he had striven to ignore the crisis. Now he must act, particularly since the denunciation was the work of the bishop who had been the first to denounce Nestorius, and who made every sign that, once again, he would hold on, Eusebius of Dorylæum.

Eutyches was cited to answer to the charge. He refused to come, repeatedly. His health, his age, his vows, his holy rule, all were alleged in turn, and when at last he did appear it was with a letter of protection from the Emperor and with the highest officers of the court for escort. He refused to give up his theory. There were not, in God Incarnate, two natures, for a humanity such as ours Christ Our Lord had not. And he quoted as his defence the formula dear to St. Cyril "One incarnate nature of God the Word." He had taken this formula in its monophysite sense, and had developed it in his own way, for whatever the consequences of St. Cyril's use of the term *physis*, the substantial error of Eutyches is his own. It finds no warrant in St. Cyril, nor did the Egyptians who, after Chalcedon, broke away in the name of St. Cyril claim Eutyches, too, as a patron. They were indeed as anxious to condemn him as was Chalcedon itself.

Flavian's council—thirty-two bishops in it—made short work of Eutyches once they had forced him into the open. Since he would not consent to admit the two natures they deposed him, from his office and from his orders, and declared him excommunicated. Given the circumstances it was an act of very high courage. Flavian was to pay for it with his life.

Eutyches of course appealed, first to Alexandria and then, the emperor also writing on his behalf, to Rome. Dioscoros acted immediately. Without even the formality of an enquiry, beyond the reading of Eutyches' exposition of his belief, he declared the sentences passed on him null and received him into communion. With the court, too, Eutyches' good favour continued. He petitioned for a council to try his appeal, the emperor consented. The council was summoned (March 30, 449) to meet at Ephesus for the following first of August. Dioscoros was summoned to it, and the pope was invited also.

It was the good fortune of the Church that at this moment the Roman See was ruled by one of the only two of its bishops whom all later history has agreed to style "the Great." This was St. Leo I. He had, at this time, been pope a matter of nine years and was a man close on fifty years of age. He was gifted in the handling of men, and possessed of a vast experience. For years before his election he had been employed in important diplomatic missions by the emperor as well as by the popes. He was the traditional Roman character at its best, the natural instinctive ruler, and he added to this the less usual happy circumstance that he was a skilled theologian, and for knowledge of the merits and the history of this latest question in no way dependent on the learning of others. But here, too, the Roman genius showed itself in his leaning towards simple formulæ to express what could be expressed, and in his silence about matters which lay beyond human powers of elucidation. It is also worth recalling that St. Leo wrote a Latin of singular strength and clearness in which the whole man is admirably mirrored. Of Eutyches he had already some knowledge, from the attempt to trick him into patronising the heresy in the preceding year. Now he had the monk's account of the trial, and the emperor's recommendations too. Finally, but very tardily, as the pope reprovingly noted, he received a report from Flavian.

St. Leo fell in with the emperor's plan for a council and appointed three legates to represent him. To them he entrusted a series of letters (June 13, 449). To the emperor he wrote that in a letter to Flavian he was going to expound "what the Catholic Church universally believes and teaches" on the matter. To Flavian he wrote the dogmatic letter ever since famous as the *Tome* of St. Leo. It is written with all his own vigorous clearness, and marked by that consciousness of his office that is so evident in every action of his twenty-one years' reign. Our Lord, it states, is only one person but possesses two natures, the divine and the human. These natures are not confused, not mixed, though the singleness of personality entails a communion in the acts and properties of each distinct nature, the only Son of God having been crucified and buried as the Creed declares. There is, in this historic document, nothing whatever of speculative theology, nothing of ingenious philosophical explanations to solve difficulties. The pope shows no desire to explain the mystery, none at all to discuss rival theories. He makes a judgment, gives a decision, re-affirms the tradition, and all in his own characteristic style which fitted so well the office and the occasion.

The council met—a week late—and in the same basilica which had seen the condemnation of Nestorius in 431. There were a hundred and twenty bishops present, and, by command of the emperor, Dioscoros presided. St. Leo, to judge from his letters, although he had consented to take part in the council had not expected very much from it. But there developed immediately such a transformation that in the end the pope could not see the council for the episcopal bandits who composed and directed it— *in illo Ephesino non synodo sed latrocinio* to quote his own lapidary phrase. And as the *Latrocinium*, the den of thieves, of Ephesus it has gone down to history.

The *Latrocinium* lasted a fortnight, the second session being held on August 22. The first move of Dioscoros was to exclude forty-two of the bishops, some because they had been judges in the previous trial of Eutyches, others because they were suspected of being unfavourable to his theories. What little opposition threatened to show itself Dioscoros quelled with terrible threats of punishment to come, deposition, exile, death; and to give the threats reality paraded the soldiery placed at his disposal. The pope's letters were ignored, the legates, Julius of Pozzuoli weakly making no protest.[1] Next Eutyches was allowed to make a vague profession of faith in which there was no sign of his heresy. His accuser was not allowed to speak, and the sentences on Eutyches were all annulled. He was rehabilitated and restored to his monastery. Finally there came what might be called the trial of Flavian. It could only end in the way Dioscoros and Eutyches had planned when they worked the summoning of the Council. He was deposed, condemned and marched off to prison. All the bishops present signed the acquittal of Eutyches and the sentence on Flavian, except St. Leo's legatees. In the second session it was the turn of the Antiochian theology. St. Cyril's famous propositions, which had slept since the peace of 433, were brought out once more, and confirmed and officially accepted as Catholic doctrine. Ibas and Theodoret, like Flavian, were deposed and excommunicated—in their absence, for, needless to say, they had been most carefully kept away from Ephesus. Luckily for themselves, perhaps, for such was the ill-treatment to which Flavian was subjected that he died from it. The legates managed to escape.

Once more in the East, then, heresy was supreme, the heresy of a faction, of a small minority, and it was supreme because the heresiarchs had the emperor's ear, and because that influence seemed to a group of bishops themselves not heretical (as yet) an instrument for the subjection of a rival group. The days when Eusebius of Nicomedia "managed" Constantine seemed for the moment to have returned.

There remained, however, Rome, and St. Leo. Flavian, before he died, had managed to draw up an appeal. Theodoret also wrote one in truly magnificent style as became the great stylist of his time. There was, too, the report of the legates when, ultimately, they had made their way back. St. Leo did not lack for details. This was his opportunity to write to the emperor, October, 449, protesting vigorously against the mockery of the recent council, "an insult to the faith, a blow to the entire Church," and demanding a truly general council in which bishops from all over the world should sit, and in which Flavian's appeal could be heard. He wrote also to the sister of Theodosius, the Empress Pulcheria. From the emperor, two months later even, the pope had had neither reply nor acknowledgement. At Christmas therefore he wrote once more, and in the February of 450, at his urgent request, the emperor's western colleague Valentinian III wrote, too, and Valentinian's mother the Empress Galla Placidia. Finally, March 17, St. Leo himself wrote yet again, and once

---

[1] The legates had no Greek—the language, of course, in which the business was being transacted.

more to Pulcheria. In April the emperor at last replied. His letter is a defence of what was done at Ephesus, pointedly ignoring the fact of the appeals from its victims to the pope, ignoring, too, the reminders of Valentinian III's letters that the Roman See is supreme in all matters of religion. Theodosius more or less suggests that the East can regulate its own disputes in these matters. Let the most revered Patriarch of Rome—a new title he coins for the Roman Bishop—keep to the things that really concern him.

Meanwhile a "successor" to Flavian had been appointed, one of the Bishop of Alexandria's henchmen, and had sent to St. Leo notice of his election. It gave the pope a last opportunity to plead with Theodosius. The pope explained that he could not enter into communion with "him who now presides over the Church of Constantinople" until he is satisfied of his orthodoxy. Such satisfaction he can give by notifying his assent to the letter recently sent to Flavian—the *Tome*. The two bishops who bear the letter will receive his submission. This letter bears the date of July 16, 450. Whether or not it would have had any more success than the previous appeals no one can say, but before the two bishops reached Constantinople the long deadlock was ended. Theodosius II was dead, killed by a fall from his horse.

The situation changed immediately. The new ruler was the devotedly Catholic Pulcheria, and the man she married shortly afterwards and associated with herself in the Empire, Marcian, was Catholic too. The exiled bishops were immediately recalled, the body of Flavian brought back to Constantinople with all manner of solemnity. Eutyches was placed in retirement, and gradually, one by one, the bishops of the *Latrocinium* went back on their acclamations and votes. In all they had done, they now explained, they had yielded only to fear. The council for which St. Leo had pleaded, a truly universal council, would be summoned and St. Leo was asked himself to preside (August to November, 450). The edict convoking the council is dated May 17, 451, and the place and date are Nicea for September 1 following. St. Leo had already decided how the servile bishops of the *Latrocinium* should be dealt with. The rank and file were to be received back on easy terms, if they acknowledged their wrongdoing. The case of the leaders, Dioscoros notably, he reserved to himself. Now, accepting the plan of a new council, St. Leo named four legates to represent him. One of the legates is to preside. The council is not to discuss the matter of faith involved. It is simply to accept the letter to Flavian and the definition of faith it contains.

There were the usual delays. There was a change in the place

of meeting. The council finally opened at Chalcedon on October 8,
451, with between five and six hundred bishops present—so far as
mere numbers went it was easily the greatest council of antiquity,
and the greatest of all councils until that of the Vatican fourteen
hundred years later. Among the members of the council the
Roman legates had the first place. With them lay the initiative.
They led the council. But the actual presidency was in the hands
of a body of eighteen high officials of the court. Upon them lay
the responsibility for maintaining order within the Council.
They were, compositely, the Speaker of its discussions. The
council's first care was to revise the proceedings of the *Latrocinium*.
Dioscoros was removed from the seat he occupied as Bishop of
Alexandria, and, as one of those to be judged, placed in the
middle of the floor. Theodoret, reinstated by St. Leo's orders,
was next introduced and his appearance gave rise to the council's
first "scene." Curses and execrations from the Alexandrians,
cheers and acclamations from his own supporters, greeted him as
he took his place. Then the minutes of the *Latrocinium*, amid
further demonstrations of emotion, were read out by the notaries
and the question being put by the presiding officials the council
declared Flavian's condemnation of Eutyches in 448 to have been
in accord with the traditional faith, and its own.

But the emperor's representatives were not content with this.
They asked the council for a new declaration of faith. Upon
which the bishops declared that the *Tome* of St. Leo was sufficient.
The *Tome* was then read, in company with the creed of Nicea
and St. Cyril's two letters to Nestorius. The bishops cheered and
cheered again the successive declarations, and the perfect accord
between the two theologians, Roman and Alexandrian, between
the *Tome* and the definitions of Ephesus 431. When the *Tome*
itself was read their enthusiasm broke all bounds. "Behold the
faith of the Fathers! the faith of the Apostles! So do we too, all
of us, believe, all who are orthodox believe the same! Anathema
to whoever believes otherwise! Thus through Leo has Peter
spoken!"

Dioscoros, in the next session, was tried and deposed. He
had protected the heretical Eutyches, had suppressed at the
Council of 449 St. Leo's message to the council, and, latterly,
had excommunicated St. Leo himself. St. Leo had left it to
the council to sentence Dioscoros, and the council now left it
to St. Leo's representatives. "Then, Paschasinus, with his fellow
legates, Lucentius and Boniface 'holding the place of Leo the most
holy and blessed Patriarch of Great Rome and Archbishop'
solemnly recited a summary of the crimes of the Bishop of Alexandria and concluded: 'Wherefore the most holy and most

blessed archbishop of great and elder Rome, by us and the present most holy synod, together with the thrice-blessed and praise-worthy Peter the Apostle, who is the rock and base of the Catholic Church, and the foundation of the orthodox faith, has stripped him of the episcopal and of all sacerdotal dignity; wherefore this most holy and great synod will vote what is in accordance with the canons against the aforesaid Dioscoros.'" [1]

In 431 Rome had deposed the Bishop of Constantinople, and a General Council had carried out her decision. Now, twenty years later, Rome had similarly deposed a Bishop of Alexandria and a second General Council had once more, unanimously, accepted the decision because of the see whence it came.

The fifth session was marked by a striking protest against imperial interference in matters of Church discipline. "We are all of the same opinion," the council made known to its lay presidents "that government of the Church by imperial edicts must cease. The Canons are there. Let them be followed. Upon you lies the responsibility."

The work of the council was now finished, the *Tome* of St. Leo solemnly accepted, the outrage of 449 made good, the chief criminal punished. The bishops might have dispersed, but the emperor still wished for a declaration of faith, a new creed, a new rule by which to measure orthodox and heretic. To this the council objected; the *Tome* of St. Leo, the bishops declared, was a sufficient statement of the true doctrine. As for the legates, it was in their instructions that they were not to consent to a re-opening of the discussion about the point of faith. But the emperor's representatives insisted, and a profession of faith was drafted, and put to the council at its sixth session, October 22, 451. Most of the bishops liked it well enough, but the bishops of the East—the Antioch group—protested; so, also, did the papal legates. The draft had, in fact, omitted all reference to the *Tome* of St. Leo, and in place of the Roman formulary, "in two natures", it contained the ambiguity favoured by Dios-coros, "of two natures". The new creed was, seemingly, as carefully ambiguous as all the creeds of State manufacture since the days of Constantine. It was designed no doubt as a statement of Catholic doctrine, but designed also to avoid any provocation of Monophysite[2] opposition, a creed which Catholic

---

[1] *cf.* H. J. Chapman, O.S.B., *Bishop Gore and the Catholic Claims*, 1905, p. 91, quoting *Mansi*, VI 1048.

[2] By Monophysite is not meant an adherent of the peculiar tenets of Eutyches, but one who held that St. Cyril's terminology was alone orthodox, that Theodoret and all his school were actually Nestorians (whether they knew it or not) and (after Chalcedon) that the *Tome* of St. Leo was just as heretical. These first Monophysites held indeed the Catholic doctrine about the relations between the divine and human

and Monophysite might sign together. St. Leo's legates would have none of it. Either the *Tome* of St. Leo—or they would go back to Rome, and another council there would decide the matter. Whereupon a tremendous eagerness to conciliate the legates, and a commission to arrange a compromise. Finally there came forth a lengthy formulary indeed. The creeds of Nicea and Constantinople (381) to begin it, then an acceptance of the letters of St. Cyril to Nestorius so that no Alexandrian could say that Chalcedon in condemning the heresy of St. Cyril's successor had condemned St. Cyril himself, and finally, for the theological dispute which had occasioned the Council, an explicit acceptance of the *Tome* of St. Leo, now declared to be "in harmony with the confession of the great apostle Peter, a barrier against all evil thinkers, the bulwark of orthodox faith." Then followed the formulary stating the faith—it was in the terminology of St. Leo's letter.

Rome then, in St. Leo, had triumphed once more, the faith over heresy, thanks to Rome; and it was in the clarity of the Roman phraseology that the belief was proclaimed. But this had not been achieved easily, nor was the majority in the council wholeheartedly enthusiastic about the last part of the business—which involved the victory of a non-Alexandrian manner of speech over the terminology dear to St. Cyril. The greater part of the bishops had been, for a lifetime, too sympathetic to St. Cyril's way of describing the mystery to accept another way easily or wholeheartedly—even though they accepted that it was a true way of describing it. Already during the very council, in this spirit in which so many of the bishops accepted the formulary of the faith, the dissension was evident that was presently to inaugurate two centuries of acute disturbance and the loss of whole races to the Church. It was only at the emperor's insistence, that these bishops had finally consented to promulgate, in a terminology so repugnant to them, the faith which they held in common with the rest. Had it not been for the emperor, the question would never have arisen; the doctrinal work of the council would have ended—as the pope intended—with its acceptance of the *Tome* as the Catholic faith.

In a lengthy letter to St. Leo the council gave an account of its work. Our Lord, they said, had commissioned the Apostles to teach all nations. "Thou then hast come even to us. To us

---

in Our Lord, as truly as did St. Cyril or St. Leo. But because St. Leo expressed that doctrine otherwise than in St. Cyril's language they regarded him as a heretic, and because Chalcedon had accepted and used St. Leo's terminology they rejected it as an heretical council.

thou hast been the interpreter of the voice of the blessed Peter, to all thou hast brought the blessing of his faith." Five hundred and twenty bishops were met in Council; "Thou didst guide us, as doth the head the body's limbs." Dioscoros has been fitly punished. Who more criminal than he, who, to the wickedness of reinstating Eutyches, "dared in his folly to menace him to whom the Saviour made over the care of His vineyard, Your Holiness we mean, to excommunicate him whose charge it is to unite the Church's body."

St. Leo had seen orthodoxy vindicated and the privilege of his see proclaimed as never so strikingly before. But not all the council's proceedings were likely to please him. And the council knew it. The council had, once more, following the unhappy precedent of 381, set itself to heighten the prestige of the see where now the imperial capital was established. To the famous "primacy of honour" voted Constantinople in 381 Chalcedon recognised considerable extensions. By its ninth, seventeenth and twenty-eighth canons the council gave legal consecration to all the jurisdiction which had accrued to Constantinople, since 381, though the illegal usurpations of its bishops. The bishops of Constantinople had for seventy years been the spiritual pirates of the Eastern Church. One after another the different metropolitan sees had seen their rights of jurisdiction invaded and captured. Now Chalcedon ratified all that had been done, blessed the spoiler, and gave him, for the future, the right to spoil as he would. The new rights, too, would develop; and to Constantinople would accrue, on this unecclesiastical principle of the city's worldly importance, such an importance in the Church that, by the side of it, the ancient traditional apostolic prestige of Alexandria and Antioch would be as nothing, and the Roman See, in appearance, hardly be more than an equal.

It had clearly been law since 381 that suits between a bishop and his metropolitan should be judged by the primate of the civil diocese in which the litigating prelates lived. The innovation was now made that the judge was *either* the primate or the Bishop of Constantinople. This was to hold good for the three (civil) dioceses of Thrace, Pontus and Asia. The "primacy of honour" was now recognised as one of jurisdiction in all those regions where the perseverance of the capital's bishops had already established this as a fact.

The twenty-eighth canon begins by confirming the canon of 381. It goes on to say that Rome owes its traditional primacy to the city's one-time civil importance, and that Constantinople being now the imperial city, to that see too certain privileges are due. Wherefore the council grants to the see of Constantinople the right to ordain the metropolitans of the (civil) dioceses of Pontus, Asia and Thrace, and of all the missionary bishops depending on them. Constantinople is to be in these regions what Alexandria is in Egypt, what Rome is in the West, the effective supervisor of all the other sees. The Roman legates protested, but the council approved, and in its synodal letter to St. Leo made a special request for the confirmation of the novelty. The emperor wrote in the same sense, and the Bishop of Constantinople too.

But St. Leo held firm. In a series of letters to the emperor and to the empress, to the Bishop of Constantinople too, he complained sadly of the spirit of ambition which bade fair to trouble anew the peace of the Church, and suggested that the Bishop of Constantinople should be content that his see, "which no power could make an apostolic see", was indeed the see of the empire's capital. The new canons are contrary to the only rule the pope knows, that of Nicea, and he will not consent to any innovation so injurious to the rights of ancient, undoubted apostolic sees such as Antioch and Alexandria. Let the Bishop of Constantinople obey the Law as he knows it, or he too may find himself cut off from the Church. The innovations then are void, of no effect and "by the authority of blessed Peter the Apostle, in sentence altogether final, once and for all, we quash them."

Nor was this the end of the pope's protests. To safeguard ancient rights against further encroachment on the part of the parvenu authority at Constantinople, and to keep himself informed as to the reception of the faith of his *Tome* throughout the East, St. Leo now installed at the imperial court a permanent representative. This was Julian, Bishop of Kos, skilled in both Latin and Greek, Italian by birth, Roman by education, Bishop of a Greek see.

Finally March 21, 453, St. Leo replied to the synodal letter of the council. He notes the work accomplished by the council as twofold. First of all the acceptance of the defined faith and the revision of the outrages of 449. This was the purpose for which the council had been called and to the council's proceedings in this respect the pope gives all possible confirmation and praise. But the council had gone further, taken upon itself to make other decisions and regulations. Now no matter what the authority invoked to sanction these proceedings, no matter what the council, anything in them that contravenes the canons of Nicea is null and void. Of these canons as implying a derogation from the rights of his own see, there is not in all these letters a word: not a hint that St. Leo so construed the innovations. But such innovations are inspired by worldly ambition, and this, if not checked, must open the way to endless new troubles among the bishops. Therefore St. Leo stands by the old order, the traditional rule. The emperor assented, and finally, by a disavowal of his own share in the measure, and by a letter which implied submission to the papal ruling, the Bishop of Constantinople, too, made his peace. "Better certainly had the Bishop of Constantinople said plainly 'We'll say no more about the decision of Chalcedon which the Apostolic See will not confirm.' He does not say it. He contents himself with the protestation that he has done nothing in this matter to deserve the reproach of insincerity or ambition. St. Leo believed the cause safe for which he had battled so gallantly, so tenaciously: he asked nothing more, neither of the Bishop of Constantinople whose disavowal seemed to suffice, nor of the emperor whose sincerity was beyond doubt."[1]

[1] BATIFFOL, MGR. PIERRE, *Le Siège Apostolique*, p. 381. *Cf.* also G. BARDY "L'équivoque a plané sur cette réconciliation, qui ne résout aucun problème et laisse subsister le canon tant discuté " in FLICHE ET MARTIN IV, 266 n. 2.

CHAPTER X

THE TRADITIONAL FAITH AND THE IMPERIAL POLICY

I. THE AFTERMATH OF CHALCEDON. 452–518

IN the twenty-eighth canon of the Council of Chalcedon were sown seeds of dissension destined to bear an immense fruit in centuries yet to come. The more immediate trouble was born of the circumstances in which its definition of faith was framed. Here the terminology of St. Cyril had yielded to that of St. Leo, and there were regions in the East too accustomed to St. Cyril's language to take the change easily. Just as there were Catholics after Nicea who dreaded the possibility that the Arians would interpret the *Homoöusion* in a Sabellian sense and exploit the misinterpretation against the defenders of the defined doctrine, and, more recently, Catholics after Ephesus who suspected the Apollinarian possibilities of St. Cyril's technical phrases, so now there were to be Catholics uneasy lest Chalcedon might be construed as a posthumous rehabilitation of Nestorius.

The first element to consider, in the resistance to Chalcedon which now began to show itself, is the opposition of those who cannot see truth except through the terminology they have inherited from St. Cyril. Nowhere, it is interesting to note, is Eutyches defended. These "Cyrillians,"[1] so to call them, condemn Eutyches equally with the council, but they will not condemn him as the council condemns him, since to do so is, they consider, an indirect condemnation of St. Cyril. Thus far the resistance is an academic affair, the conflict of theologians over terms, and its chief importance is perhaps that it explains the lukewarmness of many Catholic bishops in the East in the next few years. At Chalcedon they had whole-heartedly condemned Eutyches as they had whole-heartedly acknowledged St. Leo's claim to define the truth; but it was only after Rome's gesture of authority that they had consented to the definition in the terminology they suspected.

There was, however, another source whence trouble was

[1] It is a dangerous thing to coin new names. I retain this unfortunate example in order to correct it, by saying that " ultra-Cyrillians " would have been nearer the fact (for St. Cyril assuredly would have disowned them—they are the " wild men " of his party with whom he had his own difficulties after the settlement of 433). Actually these are the Monophysites of the first generation.

much more likely to come. This was in the resentment, which it is hardly incorrect to call national, felt by the people of Egypt at the condemnation of their patriarch. Dioscoros, whatever his misdeeds, was Patriarch of Alexandria, and to the newly-reviving race consciousness of the Egyptians he was the head of his nation. For nearly a century and a half a succession of great personalities had filled that see, and for half a century one of them, backed by his people, had defied successfully all the efforts of the hated power at Constantinople to depose him. The later victory of Theophilus over St. John Chrysostom and that—admittedly a very different affair—of St. Cyril over Nestorius had also been, for the Egyptians, the triumph of Egypt over the Empire. In 449, at the Latrocinium, Dioscoros had gained just such another triumph in his deposition of St. Flavian. Now, in 451, his own degradation was felt in Egypt as a national calamity. Well might the bishops of Egypt, prostrate before the great council, beg and implore with tears to be excused from signing the condemnation of their patriarch. They knew their people, knew that in this matter forces far less judicial than those which ruled theological discussions, were moving. If they returned home, and the news spread that they had assented to the condemnation of Dioscoros, their lives would not be worth an hour's purchase. It needed but the interest of the few genuine Monophysite heretics to exploit this immense reserve of anti-imperialist feeling—and organising it as the cause of St. Cyril they would secure the benevolent neutrality of the "Cyrillian" bishops—and Egypt would be roused against Chalcedon even more easily than it had been roused for Nicea. The imperial government understood well enough what the immediate future might hold, and it gathered troops to protect the defenders of Chalcedon when the emergency should arise.

It was in Palestine that the trouble began, and the pioneers were people who feared neither Government nor council, the innumerable army of monks and solitaries. The news of its bishop's vote reached Jerusalem long before that prelate, with his new dignity of fifth patriarch, had returned. The cry went round that the faith was in danger, that in Dioscoros St. Cyril had been condemned. The whole city rose, monks and solitaries pouring in by thousands, at the head of the insurrection no less a person than the Empress Dowager, Eudoxia, widow of Theodosius II, and delighted in her exile to find this means of embarrassing the imperial sister-in-law whom she so little loved. New bishops, it was urged, must be chosen not for Jerusalem only but for all Palestine, to replace those who at Chalcedon had betrayed the faith, and the new Patriarch returned to find his city in the hands of half-mad fanatics, murder and outrage the order of the day. Order was not restored until the monks had been defeated in a pitched battle.

There were revolts of the same kind throughout Syria, and in Cappadocia too, but the scene of the fury at its worst was naturally Egypt. Here the first practical consequence of the council was the meeting to elect a successor to Dioscoros, and at the mere announcement the mob rose. Dioscoros was still alive, therefore still bishop. There could therefore be no need of a new election. Once again the troops had to fight the mob and the monks before the formalities could be gone through and the new bishop elected. Still the fighting in the streets continued, the troops were driven into the great temple of the old religion—the Serapeion—and held there until with the buildings they perished in the flames. The imperial government must evidently fight for its own existence. All Egypt was placed under military law and the pro-Dioscoros bishops everywhere deposed. So a certain external order was at last obtained. It lasted for an uneasy five years.

Its first shock was the news (September, 454) that Dioscoros had died in his distant captivity, when it took all the efforts of the government to prevent the Monophysites from electing a "successor" to him. When, three years later, the emperor Marcian followed Dioscoros into the other world the tumult broke out irrepressibly. Marcian had been orthodoxy's chief supporter. Chalcedon was his council, and to repress the Monophysite faction had been for him an elementary necessity of practical politics. Pulcheria had pre-deceased him, and in his place the army and officials installed the tribune Leo. The Monophysites did not wait to learn that the change of emperor meant a change of policy. They elected their successor to Dioscoros, Timothy surnamed the Cat, while the mob once more held the city and the Catholic bishop was murdered, his body dragged through the streets and savagely outraged. For the best part of a year the Monophysites were masters, deposing the Catholic bishops everywhere and re-instating the partisans of Dioscoros while the government looked on indifferently. From Rome St. Leo did his utmost to rally the new emperor to the support of Chalcedon, and finally the government made up its mind. Bringing in more troops, it deposed the Monophysite bishops and deported Timothy the Cat. Once more there was the peace of repression and it endured this time for sixteen years.

When the Emperor Leo I died in 474 he left as his successor a baby grandson, Leo II, and the child's father, Zeno, acting as Regent, was associated with him as Emperor. The baby died, another claimant to the throne, Basiliscus, appeared, and he was so successful that presently Zeno was an exile, and Basiliscus reigned in his place at Constantinople. (January, 475).

One of the first acts of the usurper was to recall the Monophysite exiles. Their chief, Timothy the Cat, was still alive and at the news of his return the Catholic bishop fled from Alexandria and Timothy took possession without opposition, while the remains of Dioscoros were solemnly set in a silver shrine. To Antioch also there returned its Monophysite bishop, Peter called the Fuller, and the new emperor, hoping to establish himself securely on the basis of a re-united people, issued what was to be the first of a long series of edicts designed to undo the work of Chalcedon without express disavowal of the faith there defined. Monophysites and Catholics alike would sign the formula proposed and the religious disunion be at an end. This was the aim of the *Encyclion* of Basiliscus. It condemned Eutyches and it condemned Chalcedon, it approved Ephesus and it approved the *Latrocinium*. All the bishops were to sign it under pain of deposition, and laymen who opposed it were to suffer confiscation, of goods and be exiled.

The success of the measure was instantaneous. Almost every bishop in the East signed without difficulty—Catholics because it condemned Monophysitism in condemning Eutyches, and because, if it condemned Chalcedon too, there was much in the terminology imposed at Chalcedon to which they objected. On the other hand, the Monophysites had never ranged themselves as supporters of Eutyches since the *Latrocinium*. They were delighted to have an opportunity, in once more condemning him, of affirming the orthodoxy of St. Cyril and of their own claims, and of course, of the orthodoxy of their own opposition to Chalcedon. For the Monophysites the future was now full of promise. They held the two chief sees of the East, and, thanks to the *Encyclion*, Monophysitism was no longer a bar to the promotion of yet more of the faction. Their one and only obstacle was the Patriarch of Constantinople, Acacius. He had refused to acknowledge Timothy the Cat when the exiles were recalled, and had locked the churches of the capital against him. Now, almost alone of the hundreds of bishops in the Eastern Empire, he refused to sign the *Encyclion*. His constancy, or obstinacy, would no doubt have brought his term of office to a speedy conclusion, but the short reign (twenty months) of Basiliscus ended as unexpectedly as it had begun.

In the September of 476 Zeno returned with an army and re-established himself. Basiliscus had seen defeat coming, and in a last wild hope of rallying the capital—where Monophysites were few—he had cancelled the *Encyclion* by the edict called the *Anti-encyclion*, and the versatile Eastern episcopates signed this as easily as they had signed its forerunner, excepting always the Monophysites. Timothy the Cat's brief triumph was over, and the deposition of Acacius to which he looked forward as the fitting sequel to the Alexandrian defeat of 451, a fourth condemnation of Constantinople by Alexandria in fifty years, was not to be. Chalcedon was once more in the ascendant, and only the old man's death (July, 477) saved him from arrest and further exile. Secretly and hurriedly his chief lieutenant, Peter Mongos[1] was consecrated in his place and, consecrated, immediately went into hiding to avoid the coming storm. The Catholic bishop came out of the monastery where he had buried himself since 474 and, if the government would only put its troops at the disposal of orthodoxy, the Catholicism of Chalcedon might once more hope for peace.

The recent crisis had proved one thing very clearly. In the whole East the great council had scarcely a friend prepared to suffer in its defence. The bishops, evidently, would vote "yes" or "no" as the government bade them. Twenty-five years after Chalcedon it was on the Patriarch of Constantinople alone that, in the East, the defence of orthodoxy depended. Acacius was its sole bulwark against the energy and determination of the Monophysites. And now, whether from fear on his part that the task was hopeless, or whether the emperor, weary of the repression and turning to other means, won him round, Acacius changed his policy.

The occasion was the death in 482 of the Catholic bishop of Alexandria. As his end drew near this defender of Chalcedon grew more and more anxious that an equally zealous Catholic should succeed him, and that the government should not, upon his death, end the trouble by recognising the Monophysite, Peter Mongos, as the lawful bishop. He therefore despatched to the court a trusted member of his clergy, John Talaia, to urge the matter. Talaia chose his intermediaries badly—high officials themselves under suspicion of treason—and compromised his cause accordingly. However, the promise was made that the new patriarch should be a Catholic, and Talaia had in return to promise that he would not seek his own election. But when in the June of 482 the Bishop of Alexandria died, and Talaia was elected in his place, he ignored his engagement and accepted. The emperor, already planning some scheme of reunion, refused to acknowledge him, and, since no Catholic bishop could expect to live in Alexandria once the imperial government ceased to uphold him, Talaia fled to Rome. The government meanwhile had found its formula. Its officials sought out the Monophysite successor of Timothy the Cat and offered him official recognition

---

[1] *i.e.* The Stammerer.

as Patriarch if he would sign it and admit Catholics to the sacraments. Peter Mongos accepted and signed. This document is the *Henoticon*, and its author was the Patriarch of Constantinople Acacius.

The *Henoticon* is more subtly drawn than the *Encyclion* of Basiliscus which inspired it. It takes the form of a letter from the emperor to the bishops, and it proclaims his faith to be that of Nicea, of Constantinople, of Ephesus (431). It repeats the condemnation of Eutyches, and it accepts the theology of St. Cyril's famous twelve propositions against Nestorius. Of Chalcedon there is no mention at all, nor is there, in the reference to Eutyches, any mention of the *Tome* of St. Leo which is the official form of his condemnation. In the circumstances, and in the light of all that had happened since Chalcedon, the *Henoticon* was a jettisoning of the faith there defined, an implicit acknowledgement that Chalcedon was unimportant and henceforward not to be imposed, an equivocal surrender of St. Leo, without whom Chalcedon is a mere pageant and against whom all the Monophysite bitterness of thirty years had been directed. There was nothing in the document which a Catholic could not approve, but to approve the document at that time and in that place was undoubtedly to surrender the controverted point of faith. The issue of the *Henoticon*, whatever the hopes of its authors, was a triumph for the Monophysites.

Nevertheless it had a very mixed reception. In Egypt Peter Mongos accepted it, but the Monophysites generally refused it, as equivocal, and called for the logical term of its reasoning— an explicit condemnation of Chalcedon. Once more there were riots, and from the deserts an army of 30,000 monks converged on Alexandria to enforce the demands. The Monophysite Patriarch of Antioch too, Peter the Fuller, accepted, thereby winning recognition; and the Monophysites in Syria, generally, accepted it. The same thing happened in Palestine. The situation of 475 was repeated with this difference that the leader of the movement now was the very man who then had been the head of the orthodox opposition. The whole of the East had ceased to fight for the definition of Chalcedon, and on a basis of "silence where we differ" the Catholics there had received into communion those who declared that the definition meant heresy.

There remained Rome. It was the action of the pope St. Leo which in 458 had saved Catholicism in the East from Timothy the Cat, and when that personage returned in triumph seventeen years later the pope—Simplicius now—had immediately protested and called for his re-exile. He had been no less insistent, in 482, in his opposition to the emperor's acknowledgement of

Peter Mongos as Patriarch, and had pressed Acacius to use all his influence to prevent that acknowledgement. Acacius ignored the letters, but before Simplicius could proceed further in the matter he died (March 10, 483).

His successor, Felix III, was once again the classical Roman, simple, direct, courageous, a man of action. Talaia had arrived in Rome while Simplicius lay dying and had laid a formal accusation against Acacius. The new pope thereupon sent an embassy to Constantinople with instructions to summon Acacius to answer the charges made against him by the exiled Catholic patriarch. When the legates arrived Acacius confiscated their papers and procured their arrest. They were put to the torture and presently went over to the side of Acacius. They, too, signed the *Henoticon* and assisting publicly, in their official capacity as the pope's legates, at the liturgy when Acacius pontificated, crowned his tortuous betrayal of the faith of Chalcedon with the appearance of the papal sanction. There was, however, one small group of faithful Catholics in the capital who guessed the truth—the monks known, from the continuous character of their offices, as the "Sleepless" (*Akoimetoi*). They found means to inform the pope and when the legates returned their trial awaited them. In a synod of seventy bishops the pope judged both the legates and Acacius. They were condemned and deposed, and Acacius excommunicated for his betrayal of the faith. With him were excommunicated all who stood by him, and as the whole of the East that was not Monophysite supported him, the effect was a definite breach between Rome and the Eastern Church. It was to last for thirty-five years, and history has called it the Acacian Schism.

Acacius died, intransigeant to the last, in 489 and two years later Zeno died too. He left no heir and his widow, influential as the Augusta, designated as his successor Anastasius, an officer of the civil service. The contrast between the two emperors could not have been greater. Zeno was the rough, uncultured product of a province where the only influential citizens were brigands, and he was the most notorious evil-liver of his Empire. Anastasius, already sixty-eight years of age, was the trained official, scholarly, scrupulous, so pious that in 488 he narrowly escaped election as Patriarch of Antioch; he had a pronounced taste for preaching, and he was an ardent Monophysite. The schism therefore suffered no interruption from the change of emperor. In Egypt the régime of the *Henoticon*, interpreted as hostile to Chalcedon, continued. In Syria, under the same régime, the bishops were pro-Chalcedon and the monks divided. At Constantinople, outside the court circle, Monophysites were rare and the new patriarch was as much a supporter of Chalcedon as he dared be, which was too much for the new emperor, and therefore he was soon replaced.

Felix III, too, died in 492. His successor, one of the great popes of the early Middle Ages, was Gelasius I and he continued his predecessor's policy in his predecessor's spirit. Constantinople must acknowledge the sentence on Acacius before it can be restored to communion. The successor of Gelasius, Anastasius II (496–98), used a somewhat gentler tone. He died before he was able to see what fruit this would bear, and the immediate result was a schism, at Rome itself, on the part of the more intransigeant of his own clergy, and the beginnings of a legend concerning Anastasius that grew with the Middle Ages and won the peace-loving pope a place in the *Inferno* of Dante. With Symmachus, elected in 498, the party of Gelasius was again in control, but hampered for the next ten years by schism arising from a double election. The situation, after twenty-five years of the breach, was unchanged, except that the East was becoming accustomed to live in hostility to Rome; and then, in 511, change came. From the Catholic point of view it was change for the worse and its author was the emperor, still Anastasius and by this time close on ninety years of age.

The *Henoticon* had never been a success. It was one of those compromises which satisfy none. It pleased the radical Mono-physites as little as it pleased the Catholics, Anastasius the emperor as little as Anastasius the pope. The emperor then, in 511, resolved on a more definitely anti-Chalcedonian policy, the imposition of Monophysitism generally throughout the Empire. His greatest difficulty lay in the fact that only Egypt was sufficiently Monophysite to welcome the policy whole-heartedly. But his purpose was stiffened, and his arm strengthened, by the appearance at this moment of the man who was destined to make a church of the Monophysite party, and to found it so thoroughly that it endures to this day—the monk Severus.

Severus was a man who had suffered much for his opposition to the *Henoticon*—opposition, of course, because that document, he considered, conceded too much to Catholicism. The business of an appeal to the emperor had brought him to the capital at the very moment when Anastasius was planning how best to depose its Patriarch for his anti-monophysite activities. The presence of Severus, whose most remarkable learning, and sufferings for the cause, had made him the leading personality of the party, gave new life to the dispirited Monophysites of the capital. The Patriarch, Macedonius, was deposed and a Mono-physite installed in his place. Heartened by this victory the emperor turned next to purify the sees of the East. In Syria the monks were his willing agents and Severus the chief organiser. Within a few months the deposition of the Patriarch of Antioch, too, had been managed and in his place there was elected Severus himself. The bishops of Syria went over, almost in a body, to the strictly Monophysite interpretation of the *Henoticon*. At Jerusalem, however, Severus was refused recognition, and to reduce this last stronghold more summary measures still were adopted. The patriarch was deposed, banished and provided with a Monophysite successor by a simple order from the emperor. But, for all its appearance of completeness, the policy was far from successful. Monophysites did indeed occupy the chief sees, and the other bishops had accepted the Monophysite version of the faith. But in many cases it was only a nominal acceptance; the convinced Monophysites among them were a minority; the dissident radical Monophysites of Syria still held aloof; and at Constantinople the opposition of the Catholics— still of course divided from Rome and the West by schism—to the whole Monophysite movement was as active as ever. The religious chaos after seven years of the new Monophysite offensive was greater than before. Affairs were going steadily from bad to worse when the death of the aged emperor (July 9, 518) suddenly changed the whole situation.

The new emperor—the commandant of the guard, who had profited by his position to seize the vacant throne—was not only a Catholic, but, what had not been known for a century and a half, a Latin. With the accession of Justin the end of the schism could only be a matter of time. Events, indeed, followed each other rapidly. Anastasius died on July 9. Six days later mobs were parading the streets calling for the acknowledgement of Chalcedon and St. Leo, and the condemnation of Severus. On the 20th a council of bishops reversed all the policy of forty years and more, recognising Chalcedon and St. Leo's teaching, and decreeing Severus' deposition and excommunication. More they were unable to do for, like a wise man, he was already flown. Everywhere, except in Egypt, the superiority reverted to the Catholics, and on August 1 the new emperor re-opened communications with the pope, Hormisdas.

It was not until the following March (519) that the legates arrived to execute the formalities which would bring the schism to an end. They were simple enough, and strict. Each bishop must sign the formula sent by the pope, and in this he acknowledged the indefectibility of the faith of the Roman Church, condemned Nestorius and Eutyches and Dioscoros, made explicit recognition of the decisions of Ephesus and Chalcedon, accepted the *Tome* of St. Leo and finally condemned along with Timothy the Cat, Peter Mongos and Peter the Fuller, Acacius too and all who had supported him. Furthermore, the bishop promised never "to associate in the prayers of the sacred mysteries the names of those cut off from the communion of the Catholic Church, that is to say those not in agreement with the Apostolic See." The formula was not drawn up in view of the present reconciliation. It had been devised in Spain, during the schism, as a means of testing the orthodoxy of visiting prelates from the East. Rome now made it her own.

Justin asked for a Council to discuss the matter, but the legates were firm. They had come for one purpose only—to gather signatures to Pope Hormisdas' formula. They had their way. The patriarch signed and the other bishops, too, amid scenes of great enthusiasm. But outside Constantinople things did not go so smoothly. To begin with, there was an unwillingness to condemn the patriarchs since Acacius, especially those who, for their opposition to the Monophysites, had been deprived by the Monophysite emperor. At Thessalonica and at Ephesus especially was there resistance on this account. At Antioch, Severus having been deposed, there was once more a Catholic patriarch. He signed, and with him a hundred and ten out of the hundred and fifty bishops of his jurisdiction. The monks, however, held firm and nothing short of a wholesale dissolution of their monasteries and a general rounding up of hermits and solitaries reduced their opposition. This necessary work was entrusted to the army. Its immediate result was to loose on the East thousands of convinced, and none too instructed, apostles of the heresy, destined now to wander over the East for another twenty years preaching resistance to the bishops and to the Council of Chalcedon. Their sufferings at the hands of the imperial soldiery naturally added not a little to their eloquence and zeal. In Palestine the change had not been too difficult, but it promised to raise such storms in Egypt that the government, for the moment, left that province untouched; and to Egypt there began to flow in the full tide of the persecuted and dispossessed from all the rest of the Empire. Nor was Severus idle. From his hiding place he still directed and encouraged the whole vast movement, and to take the place of the priests and deacons now reconciled with the pope, wholesale ordinations were arranged and a new Monophysite clergy came into being whose pertinacity no power would ever shake.

II. JUSTINIAN. 527–565

The old emperor, Justin I died on August 1, 527, and his nephew, Justinian, who throughout the reign had been the chief adviser and the real ruler, succeeded. The uncle had been one of those rough, hardy Illyrians who had more than once shown themselves such capable administrators, endowed with a hard practical common sense and a natural shrewdness that compensated for their native illiteracy. But the new emperor added to what practical abilities he inherited, a wide and extensive culture, and—sure menace for the newly-restored peace in things ecclesiastical—a pronounced taste for theological speculation. Justinian, like his uncle, was a Catholic. He had played an important part in the negotiations which ended the schism, and in the measures taken since to dislodge the Monophysites from the vantage points they had come to occupy during those thirty-five disastrous years. His Catholic subjects were now once more in communion with their chief the Bishop of Rome, but the subsequent measures of repression, of deposition, and confiscation had by no means reconciled the Monophysites of the eastern provinces. At heart they still remained bitterly hostile to the Catholicism of Chalcedon, and the new conformity was very largely a conformity in name alone. One of the first tasks before Justinian was to transform this nominal submission into a submission of fact.

From the new emperor the Catholic Church had everything to hope, but he was not the only figure with whom it had to reckon. Justinian was married, and the new empress, Theodora, a personality indeed, was no mere consort but associated as Augusta with her husband's new rank. They were a devoted couple, and the imperial ménage a model to all their subjects. It had not always been so; and long before the time when Justin's unexpected accession had raised Justinian too, Theodora had been already famous, notorious even, as a comedienne, for her feats of impudicity in the capital's less distinguished places of amusement. But whatever her origins, and however true the stories that circulated about her, Theodora had long since broken from it all; and she was already living in decent obscure retirement when Justinian, heir-apparent, found her, loved her, and, despite the opposition of the emperor, his uncle, married her. Like him, she was now a Catholic, but her own religious inclinations, less theological than those of Justinian, drew her to monasticism; more especially, it is suggested, to monasticism as it displayed itself in feats of unusual austerity. And the most celebrated of these spiritual athletes were, often enough, not orthodox. From

JUSTINIAN

The Contemporary Mosaic in S. Vitale, Ravenna

their ill-instructed and undisciplined ardour, heresy and rebellion against ecclesiastical authority had drawn in the recent past only too many champions; and as Theodora's association with the monks she preferred increased, so, too, did her inclination to support and encourage the recently defeated Monophysites.

Her great influence brought it about that, in 531, the sentences of banishment were revoked; and the thousands of exiles, bishops, priests, and above all monks, now made their way back, none the less fervid in their hatred of Chalcedon and its teaching for the pain they had had to suffer in its name. They came even—five hundred and more of them—to Constantinople itself. Theodora procured them a common house and a church, and, blessed by her patronage, their church speedily became a centre for the capital's fashionable devotees. Justinian, ever perplexed by a religious division which, for the first time in the empire's history, was making the imperial rule a foreign thing in the chief provinces of the State, set himself, along theological lines, to find a reconciling formula. Under his auspices conferences were held between Catholic bishops and Monophysite bishops and, yet once again, the complicated discussion took up its ancient round.

To all the Catholic explanations the heretics made the old reply, that Chalcedon had reversed Ephesus, that its supporters were Nestorians. At all costs, then, if the dissidents were to be argued back to conformity, Chalcedon must be cleared of this charge. To make clear, beyond all doubt, the opposition between what was approved at Chalcedon and what was condemned at Ephesus, a new formula expressive of the Catholic doctrine was therefore prepared. If it was Catholic doctrine, in accord with the faith of Chalcedon, to say, "One of the Trinity suffered in the Flesh", no Monophysite could truthfully assert that Chalcedon had canonised the heresy condemned at Ephesus; for no Nestorian would ever assent to such a proposition, any more than he would accept the term *Theotokos*. Then, again, this formula would show that Catholics and St. Cyril were of one mind on the great question, that Chalcedon had in no way condemned the saint in whose name the Monophysites justified their dissidence, for the formula was St. Cyril's very own, devised by him for the very purpose of exposing Nestorius and used in the twelfth of the celebrated propositions of 430. It was as good Cyrillian theology as the most Cyrillian Monophysite could wish for. If it were officially announced as orthodox Catholicism, what further delay could prevent the Monophysite from accepting Chalcedon?

It was not the first time that, in Justinian's own experience, this formula had been suggested. The Akoimetoi monks had sought approbation for it from the legates of Pope Hormisdas in 519. To the legates it had too novel a sound to be welcome, and they were inclined to frown down a suggestion which promised to open new controversies at the very moment when the old ones were about to heal. Justinian was of the same opinion. The monks seemed wanton disturbers of the peace. Nor was the pope, to whom the legates referred the matter, anxious to decide, and despite the endeavours, at Rome, of a deputation from the monks, the matter went no further until Justinian, converted now to the monks's view of the formula's usefulness, made its adoption a matter of State policy. The monks, while in the West, had enlisted the support of a group of African bishops, exiled to Sardinia by the Vandals, among whom was St. Fulgentius reputed in the West the greatest theologian of the time. When in 534, then, the question was, in much changed circumstances, put to the Apostolic See the pope, John II, after consultation, approved it, quoting in his declaration both St. Cyril and St. Leo in support of his approval and once more condemning *Nestorius insulsus* along with *impius Eutyches*.

While Justinian drew up schemes for reunion, evolving formularies of reconciliation which should clothe the decision of Chalcedon in a terminology which the Monophysites could accept, showing that on the points at issue St. Leo and St. Cyril were at one, Theodora was left to deal with the more congenial business of ecclesiastical personalities. In 535 the Patriarch of Alexandria died—a Monophysite elected years before, in the time of the Emperor Anastasius, whom Justin I had found it wiser to leave undisturbed at the time of the great change over. His people were violently divided, though Monophysites all, between the rival systems of Severus and Julian of Halicarnassus. Whence a double —Monophysite—election. There was no thought of a Catholic candidate, but thanks to Theodora the government influence secured the election of Theodosius the candidate of the milder, Severian, school.

The noise of the riots amid which Theodosius was installed had not yet died down when the Patriarch of Constantinople died too. Once again it was Theodora who decided the election. The new patriarch, Anthimos, was one of her own confidants, a man of ascetic life, who, though Bishop of Trebizond, had for long lived at court, and who was known to be a concealed Monophysite. At this moment, ending the resistance of years, Severus himself consented to come to the capital to assist, from the Monophysite side, at Justinian's theological conferences. The first result of his presence was the explicitly declared conversion to the heresy of the capital's new patriarch. It seemed as though the old days of heretical domination were about to return. The two chief bishops of the East known as heretics, and supported with all the prestige of the empress, while the arch-heretic himself lived in her palace as chief adviser, and director-general of the new restoration ! What saved the situation for orthodoxy was the accidental presence of the pope, Agapitus I, in Constantinople, and his energetic action.

It was no ecclesiastical business which brought the pope to Constantinople. He came as the ambassador of the Gothic King in Italy, in a vain attempt to stave off the impending imperial re-conquest of the long-lost western provinces. But the recent changes in the personnel of the great churches, and the new doctrinal positions they implied could not but be the main subject to occupy Pope Agapitus. The new patriarch, whatever his beliefs, had been translated to his present high position from the see of Trebizond, and translations were contrary to canonical usage. Hence the pope's first hesitation to recognise Anthimos. The emperor pressing the point, the pope asked next for satisfaction in the matter of the patriarch's orthodoxy. Upon which the patriarch took the simplest of all possible ways out of the approaching difficulty and disappeared. A priest of irreproachable orthodoxy was found to fill the vacancy, and on March 13, 536, the pope himself gave him episcopal consecration.

For the Catholics of the imperial city it was already a great encouragement to see their heretical bishop deposed and a Catholic in his place. Heartened thereby, they now demanded the expulsion of the other prominent Monophysites, and especially of Severus. The pope gave his own strong support to the requests and, though he died, suddenly, before the defeat of Theodora and her protégés was complete, it was only a matter of four months before an imperial edict ordered the writings of Severus to be destroyed, and himself and his associates once more to be banished.

That Theodora's plans had been brought to nought was due, chiefly, to the vigorous action of Pope Agapitus and to the amount of popular support which that action found because it was the action of the pope. For the success of any future schemes to reconcile the Monophysites the empress must in some way enlist the pope's good will. What better way could be found than by securing the election as pope of one of her own ? And Agapitus dead in the moment of his victory, what more suitable moment to install a pro-Monophysite successor than the present ? No emperor had, as yet, dealt so imperially with the first of all the sees, but the new policy should be the more easily carried out since, for nearly half a century, there had been a succession of scandals and innovations in the episcopal elections at Rome. In 498, for example, at the death of the conciliatory Anastasius II, there had been the scandal of a double election in which, while partisans of the deceased pope's milder policy in the matter of the schism of Acacius had elected their candidate, the more powerful majority of his critics had elected the more generally recognised Symmachus. The tumults of this unhappy beginning troubled the whole of this pope's six years' reign. They were only appeased by the election of Hormisdas (514) who thus appeared as the healer of a schism at Rome itself before he achieved the greater task of arranging the schism between East and West.

Hormisdas died in 523; his successor, John I, more tragically three years later. He had been despatched to Constantinople by the Gothic king, Theodoric, who ruled Italy since 493, to plead the cause of the king's Arian co-religionists in the capital. Their churches had recently been confiscated and the Arians forcibly converted. The mission failed, and on his return the pope was thrown into prison and died there. Theodoric speedily followed him into the other world but not before he had had time himself to give the Roman Church its new bishop, Felix IV: *ex iussu Theodorici regis* says the *Liber Pontificalis*. Felix IV, pope through this startling innovation, proceeded to introduce into the system a second innovation more startling still, for, as the end of his life approached he named to his clergy as his successor one of his deacons, Boniface. Felix died on September 22 , 530. Immediately there was trouble from those of the Roman clergy who held the late pope's nomination invalid. They were in the majority and they elected, at St. Peter's, the deacon Dioscoros, while at the Lateran the late pope's nominee was likewise consecrated and enthroned. Luckily for the peace of the city Dioscoros died within the month, and his supporters recognised his rival. Boniface II now proceeded to imitate the unhappy precedent set by Felix IV, but more solemnly. In a synod at St. Peter's he, too, named the one who was to succeed him, the deacon Vigilius. The clergy agreed; but some time later, under what circumstances we do not know, the pope came to regret what he had done and, just as publicly, he revoked it as an action beyond his powers. Boniface II reigned for even fewer years than his predecessor, and when he died (532) the troubles broke out once again. Once more there were rival candidates, faction spirit running high, bribes from the interested parties till the treasury was exhausted, and a vacancy, long for the time, of four months. With the new pope, John II, came a wholesome decree against the abuses which had marked the recent interregnum and three years' peace. To him in 535 succeeded that Pope Agapitus whose death in Constantinople has been recorded.

Given the history of the papal elections during the previous forty years, Theodora's plan of interference had then, nothing more than usually shocking about it. Nor was any choice of hers likely to be disregarded. Her choice fell upon that deacon Vigilius who, as the nominee of Boniface II, had so nearly become pope in 532. Since then he had risen to be the archdeacon of the Roman Church, the leading cleric after the pope himself. As such he had accompanied Agapitus on his diplomatic mission, and he was still in Constantinople when that pope died. The news of the pope's death travelled to Rome more quickly than Vigilius, and he returned home to find the successor of Agapitus elected, consecrated, and in function, Silverius. Vigilius, with the assistance of the imperial officials, set himself to oust the pope as the necessary preliminary to his own election. The critical situation of public affairs soon gave him his opportunity.

The war of restoration was by this time in full swing, and for five years now the armies of Justinian had been marching from one victory to another in the desperate endeavour to win back for the imperial government the provinces of the West, lost to it in the disastrous fifth century. The Vandal kings had been dispossessed in Africa, and Sicily; the Goths driven from their hold on Southern Italy. Rome itself had become once more a "Roman" city when, at the moment of Vigilius' return from Constantinople, the Goths turned to besiege in Rome the victorious imperial army and its general Belisarius. Pope Silverius, summoned to an interview with the general, was suddenly accused of treasonable correspondence with the Goths. He was immediately stripped of the insignia of his office and, clad in a monk's habit, secretly shipped from Rome that same night. To the Romans nothing more was announced than that the pope had embraced the monastic life and that the see was therefore vacant.

The clergy were assembled to elect his successor. Belisarius presided, and, despite considerable opposition, Vigilius was elected. He had been privy to the forgeries that cost Silverius his place, and he had been the pope's sole companion in the momentous interview with Belisarius. Now, at last, he was pope himself—at any rate pope in possession. The unfortunate Silverius did, it is true, thanks to the bishop appointed to guard him, succeed in lodging an appeal against his violent deposition. Justinian ordered his return to Italy and an enquiry into the whole affair. But Belisarius was still in charge, and through his wife, who dominated him, the empress maintained her protégé. Silverius was once more condemned, and banished to the little island of Palmaria off the Neapolitan coast, and there soon afterwards he died of hunger.[1]

For the next six years all the religious troubles slumbered while Justinian, Theodora, and in Italy Vigilius, found all their energies absorbed by the terrible Gothic war. It was in a province far removed from the seat of that war, Palestine, that the disputes re-awakened. And the question around which they developed was not Monophysitism but the more ancient matter of the orthodoxy of certain theories attributed to Origen. Among the monks of certain Palestinian monasteries there had, for some time, been a revival of interest in these theories, in the old heresy of the pre-existence of souls and a quasi-pantheistic teaching about the last end of man. The old theories daily found new disciples, and the "new theology" found, of course, a host of zealous opponents. Whence through the early part of Justinian's reign (530–540) an ever-increasing disorder in Palestine which was by no means confined to the peaceful solitudes of the monasteries concerned. When in 541 a great synod met at Gaza to enquire into certain serious disorders in the local churches and to try the chief person accused, the Patriarch of Alexandria, it was inevitable that the bishops and dignitaries present should discuss the new trouble and plan a common course of action. One of these dignitaries was the permanent ambassador (*apocrisiarius*) of the Roman See at Constantinople, the deacon Pelagius, an intimate friend and confidante of Vigilius. Pelagius did all his chance allowed to strengthen the abbots in their opposition to the Origenists, and he worked in the same sense upon the mind of Justinian. He was so successful that, in 543, there appeared an imperial edict condemning the theories, and promulgating a new profession of faith in which they were repudiated. This all bishops and heads of monasteries were now obliged to sign.

Justinian was not, of course, unaware of the trouble until the moment when Pelagius intervened. More than one deputation from the rival disputants had already appeared in the capital. One of these deputies, the Origenist Theodore Askidas, had found in his temporary mission the beginning of a new career. He was named bishop of the important see of Cæsarea in Cappadocia, and, his learning gaining him a place in Justinian's confidence, he contrived to live on at court after his consecration. But now, great as the favour he enjoyed, he saw the emperor influenced

[1] His feast is kept as Pope and Martyr on June 20.

against the Origenist theories, and his own prestige somewhat lowered through the action of Pelagius. To keep his place he signed the formula: and set himself to prepare a counter-stroke which would dislodge Pelagius.

It was never difficult to interest the theologically-minded emperor in religious matters, and where these touched a question of civil peace less difficult still; where they concerned the reconciliation of the Monophysites least difficult of all. The plan which Askidas now proposed was just such another as Zeno and Anastasius had attempted. But it was more subtle, in this, that it did not suggest even a tacit repudiation of Chalcedon, but merely the condemnation of three allies and friends of Nestorius, two of whom Chalcedon had re-instated. It would be yet another proof to the Monophysites that Catholics were not Nestorians if Catholics condemned these old opponents of St. Cyril, proof again that Chalcedon had not undone what Ephesus had settled. The proposed condemnations were of Theodore of Mopsuestia —the master of Nestorius—and all his writings; of those writings of Theodoret of Cyrrhus which had been directed against St. Cyril during the controversy about Nestorius; and of the letter which Ibas, Bishop of Edessa, wrote to a Persian bishop, Maris, telling, from his point of view, the story of the Council of Ephesus. These three items of the proposed condemnations are the Three Chapters which have given their name to the subsequent controversy. It was to drag on for a good eighteen years and more, to involve the most curious of all the general councils, and finally to issue in a miserable schism that divided Italy for a generation.

The three persons concerned had been dead now nearly a century, Theodore for longer; but then Origen had been dead longer still, and yet condemned only this very year. Askidas in his turn prevailed and in 544 the edict appeared, to the dismay in particular of the Apocrisiarius. Pelagius refused to sign it, and upon his refusal the Patriarchs of Constantinople, of Alexandria, and of Antioch would only sign conditionally, the condition being that the pope, too, should sign. Here truly was a difficulty. Chalcedon, more than most, had been the pope's council, and Chalcedon had reinstated both Theodoret and Ibas in their sees upon their express repudiation of Nestorianism. It had then, for the ordinary man, cleared them of any charge of heresy. More, the letter of Ibas, now imperially condemned, had been read at Chalcedon and the Roman legates there had declared that "his letter having been read we recognised him to be orthodox." Were the pope now to condemn Theodoret at least and Ibas, for heresies they had renounced or heretical expressions which they had explained satisfactorily, it might easily seem, given the circumstances of the condemnation, that repudiating those whom Chalcedon had gone out of its way to protect he was inaugurating a policy that would end in the repudiation of the council itself. All eyes then turned to the pope. All would depend on his action—and the pope with whom lay decision, in this tricky attempt to conciliate the Monophysites, was the creature of the pro-Monophysite Theodora. Truly her hour had come at last, as the emperor's commands went westwards to Vigilius; and, as Askidas saw the dilemma preparing for the Roman author of his own recent trouble, he, also, may have felt a like satisfaction.

Vigilius hesitated. For a time the pre-occupations of the Gothic War gave him an excuse for temporising; Totila, the Gothic king, had now taken the offensive and was preparing to besiege Rome yet once again. But finally, as the pope celebrated the feast of St. Cecilia (November 22, 545), he was carried off from the very church by Theodora's orders and shipped to Sicily and thence, after a stay of some months, to Constantinople, where he arrived in the January of 547. During those months in Sicily the pope had learnt of the violent opposition to the emperor's edict which was gradually showing itself throughout the West. He himself adopted the same attitude, and when the emperor refused to withdraw the edict Vigilius broke off relations with the unlucky Patriarch of Constantinople who had led the way in signing it. Little by little, however, the explanations of the court theologians had their effect. By the summer of 547 the pope was once more in communion with the patriarch, and had signed a private condemnation of the Three Chapters. This, of course, was insufficient for Justinian's purpose, and the pope pleading the dignity of his see against the attempts to wring from him a public declaration, he was allowed to assemble at Constantinople a council of bishops to give his new condemnation of the Three Chapters an appearance at least of freedom. At the council, alas, the eloquence of a young Latin bishop defending Ibas was so effective that Vigilius broke up the assembly. Private interviews between the various bishops and the emperor brought them all to a striking unanimity, however, and one by one they sent in to the pope their written opinions in favour of the condemnation. Finally, on Holy Saturday, 548, Vigilius issued his public condemnation, the so-called *Iudicatum*. Its text has perished, but we know that, in condemning the Three Chapters, it made such reservations to safeguard the essential teaching of Chalcedon that, so far as concerned the Monophysite reunion, it might just as well never have been issued.

However, issued it was and, despite its reservations, promptly misconstrued in the West, raising storms of condemnation wherever it was known. The whole of the West—what West remained after the devastations of war—deserted the pope. A council in Africa excommunicated him as the betrayer of the faith of Chalcedon, and in Rome his own deacons led the opposition and gave the lead in the furious war of pamphleteering which now broke out.

The West, evidently, did not understand. Had not Vigilius himself needed to come to Constantinople to be educated in the complex question ? How natural that Latin bishops, too much occupied for a century in saving the elements of civilisation to be worried with such subtleties as those presented by the leisurely Monophysite East, should also fail to understand. A general council at Constantinople might smooth away all the misunderstanding. Meanwhile both the edict of 544 and the *Iudicatum* would be withdrawn. So it was arranged between pope and emperor. Both pledged themselves to silence on the question until the council met; and Vigilius, privately, bound himself by oath to Justinian that he would at the council do his utmost to bring about the desired condemnation.

This was in the August of 550. The council did not meet for nearly three years more. The interval was filled with crises. First of all the emperor broke his pledge of silence and, in 551, urged by Askidas, issued a new edict condemning the Three Chapters. The pope protested energetically and excommunicated Askidas, and then, Justinian planning his arrest, he fled for safety to the church of St. Peter. Thither a few days later Justinian sent troops to effect the arrest; at their heels followed the mob of the city. The doors were forced, soldiers and mob poured in. The clerics who endeavoured to protect the pope were dragged out and the soldiery then laid hands on Vigilius himself. He clung desperately to the columns of the altar, until, as the struggle heightened, these began to give way, and to save themselves from injury the soldiers released him. So far the mob had watched, scandalised, at the outrage on the old man who, Latin though he was, was yet the chief bishop of their religion. Now, as the altar and its columns fell in a roar of dust, they turned on the troops who fled for their lives. That night the pope—marvellous feat for an ancient of eighty years—escaped over the roofs of the city to a waiting boat and crossed the Bosphorus. His new refuge was Chalcedon, and, of all places, the basilica where, just a hundred years before, the famous council had sat around whose decision still raged these violent animosities. From his retreat he issued a well-written encyclical describing the recent events, denouncing the forgeries put into circulation in his name, and excommunicating definitely Askidas and his associates.

Justinian had overshot his mark and he knew it. The excommunicated bishops were sent across the straits to make their submission. Processions of monks and influential citizens serenaded the pope with prayers that he would return. A kind of peace was patched up, the edict of 551 was withdrawn, Vigilius gave way and preparations for the council were resumed. They consisted chiefly, on the emperor's part, in eliminating from the bishops who were to come from the West all those who had given signs of opposition to his policy. As the council drew nearer and nearer the pope's perplexity increased. It was increasingly evident that, at this council which was to educate the western bishops and guarantee the condemnation against all chance of misunderstanding, the West would have scarcely any representatives at all. Vigilius would have preferred an Italian city for its meeting place. The emperor insisted on the capital, and as the bishops arrived, all from the emperor's own Greek East, the pope's anxieties grew. One day he seemed willing to take part in its proceedings, and then he would refuse even to speak of the matter. In the end he made it known that although he would not interfere with the Council he would take no part in its deliberations. His decision would be given independently. And so there opened, on May 5, 553, in the new Sancta Sophia, the strangest of all the general councils.

The number of bishops present varied. At the first session there were a hundred and fifty. At the last, a hundred and sixty-four. Save for the picked few from Africa, and a handful of Italians, all were Greeks. The first session was taken up with the solemn reading of the documents to be condemned. In the discussion which followed, the only difficulty before the Fathers was to choose sufficiently vigorous epithets to express their abhorrence. Vigilius meanwhile, with the assistance of Pelagius, was hard at work on his own decision. On May 14 it was ready for the emperor— the *Constitutum*. It contained a detailed condemnation of the errors of Theodore of Mopsuestia, but his person the pope did not condemn, alleging the traditional ecclesiastical usage that left heretics once dead to whatever judgment then befell them. The writings of Ibas and Theodoret, since they were approved at Chalcedon, could not now be condemned without such condemnation involving that Council.

Justinian refused to receive the *Constitutum*—Vigilius having already condemned the Three Chapters and having sworn to maintain the condemnation, any more recent retractation on his part was naturally not welcome. The *Constitutum* then was not presented to the Council. Instead, at its seventh session, Justinian laid before it all the documents in which Vigilius had condemned the Three Chapters, and a decree ordering the pope's excommunication for the way in which, ever since, he had shifted and changed, and for his refusal to attend the council. The Fathers obediently approved. One week later the council came to an end (June 2, 553) with a long final condemnation of "the wicked Theodore and his wicked writings," his supporters, defenders, and apologists. Likewise, "if anyone defends the wicked writings of Theodoret against the first Holy Council of Ephesus, against St. Cyril and his twelve anathemata, and all the things he wrote on behalf of the wretched Theodore and the wretched Nestorius . . . and does not anathematize these things . . ." he is henceforward himself anathema. Still more definitely, "if anyone defends the letter which Ibas is said to have written to the heretic Maris the Persian . . . and does not anathematize it and all its defenders, and likewise all those who say it is right or right in part, and those . . . who presume to defend, in the name of the Holy Fathers or of the Holy Council of Chalcedon the letter or the impiety it contains . . . let him be anathema."

The good work done, the bishops dispersed. There still remained Vigilius. Vigilius unconvinced, the council's work was incomplete. Whence a new siege of the unhappy pope. It was eight months before the emperor won him over. But in the end he yielded completely and on February 26, 554, in a second *Constitutum*, solemnly recognised the condemnation. Then, at last, the pope was allowed to return to his see, from which he had been absent now nine years. He was, however, destined never again to see it, for he had only travelled as far as Syracuse when death claimed him, June 7, 555. He was fortunate in his death in this, at least, that it spared him the inevitable trouble which awaited at Rome whoever had had hand or part in the alleged condemnation of Chalcedon.

Justinian determined that Pelagius should be the new pope. He was undoubtedly the ablest of all the Roman clerics, and for a good fifteen years now had been the pope's chief adviser. To pass over such ability and such experience would, in the then state of Italy, have been foolish in the extreme. Who could do more as pope for the new imperial re-organisation of the West, and especially for the reconstruction of Italy wasted by twenty-five years of savage war ? Who, indeed, could do as much ? There was this difficulty to overcome that Pelagius had been the very soul of the dead pope's resistance to the council. It was with his strength that Vigilius had armed himself in the conflict that followed the withdrawal of the *Iudicatum*, and the *Constitutum* of 553 had been his very handiwork. The council over, Pelagius found himself separated from the pope—as, moreover, were all the rest of the pope's advisers—and in a monastic prison. From that prison nevertheless he had contrived to conduct a violent literary campaign against the council's condemnations, and the news that Vigilius had submitted drove him to write only the more violently. Vigilius, he explained, to the scandalised uncomprehending West, was old, senile, isolated from his advisers, the victim yet again of the imperial tyranny. That the leader of such an opposition would retract while the air around was still dry with the bitter violence of his polemic might seem the least likely finale of all. Yet so it happened. Under circumstances of argument or blandishment of which we know nothing, Pelagius withdrew his opposition and accepted the council's condemnation. Then, as the emperor's nominee, he set out for Rome to be there consecrated as its bishop.

A more unwelcome successor to Vigilius could hardly have been found, and, popularly considered to have surrendered his opinions as the price of his appointment, the new pope was more or less universally boycotted. In all Italy there could not be found more than two bishops to officiate at his consecration. A priest had to supply for the third. There was no attempt to elect another pope in opposition to him, but simply a cold sullen hostility. Pelagius was left to make the first move. He did it in the profession of Faith made on the day he was consecrated. He announced his faith to be the faith of Chalcedon, of St. Leo, and of all St. Leo's successors down to the last pope but two, Agapitus. All those whom they had held to be orthodox he, too, held as such, and especially did he hold to be orthodox . . . Theodoret and Ibas. In the whole statement there is not a reference to the recent council, nor to Vigilius, nor to the transactions between himself and the emperor which had resulted in his nomination.

For all its careful omissions the statement, none the less, availed little to help Pelagius. Nowhere did he ask the western bishops to acknowledge the council, nor to condemn what the council had condemned. The utmost of his demands was recognition of his own election, acknowledgement that he was the lawful pope. In his own metropolitan district he had scarcely any difficulty in this. But "Lombardy" and "Venetia", to speak more accurately the bishops of the great sees of Milan and Aquileia with their suffragans, would not enter into communion with him. Pelagius was helpless, for the imperial officials were little disposed to lend the troops for which he clamoured, and when the inevitable pamphleteering began now in Italy, he met with scanty success indeed, refuting as pope the position he had maintained so vigorously as a deacon. From Gaul there came a request that he should satisfy the bishops as to his orthodoxy. The declaration he sent, again made no mention of all the recent happenings that were the source of the anxiety, and as his classic writings against the council were now beginning to pass from one bishop to another in the West also, Pelagius wrote a final appeal for peace and unity. "Why all this recrimination? When I defended the Three Chapters was I not in accord with the majority of the bishops? I have, it is true, changed my opinion, but changed it along with the same majority. Did not St. Peter yield to the brotherly correction of St. Paul? Did not St. Augustine, too, write his *Retractations*? I was mistaken I allow. But then I was only a deacon and it was my duty to follow the bishops. Now the bishops have decided. Africa, Illyricum, the East, with its thousands of bishops, have condemned the Three Chapters. It would be extremely foolish to ignore such high authority and to follow in preference the guidance of these propagators of forgeries."

Scholars of a later age, studying at their leisure the detail of these ancient dissensions, can perhaps distinguish easily between Chalcedon re-instating Theodoret and Ibas in their sees upon their giving guarantees of their orthodoxy at that moment, and the Council of 553, a hundred years later, deciding the wholly different question as to the orthodoxy of their writings at the time when, twenty years before Chalcedon, they were admittedly among the chief supporters of Nestorius. Chalcedon's approval, and the condemnation of 553, though affecting the same personages, were concerned with realities wholly distinct.[1] Between the two councils there is no contradiction. But the Latin bishops, hot and angered with ten years of controversy, always impatient of the theoretical subtleties in which their eastern brothers were so much at home, were in no mood to listen to such distinctions at the time. Hence, on the part of some, a refusal to acknowledge Pelagius, and a schism which lingered for another century, and on the part of others a suspicion of Pelagius which lasted as long as he lived.

Better than any other incident of Justinian's long reign does the story of the Council of 553 illustrate his conception of the emperor's rôle in religious matters. But it was no isolated incident, and to realise its full importance we must see it against the background of the Christian State as, under Justinian, this was conceived and ordered. Constantine's disestablishment of Paganism, the recognition by Theodosius of the Catholic Church as the State's religion, now receive further development. The emperor now lays claim to an initiative in Church policy, patriarchs

---

[1] As Pelagius endeavoured to make clear.

and bishops are his lieutenants in religious affairs as his generals are for the army, his silentiaries for the civil administration. Justinian's chief title to fame is his work of legal reform, the careful collection of his predecessors' laws, their "codification" and the elaborate official provision for the study of Law. It is a work that still influences the everyday life of the world. Like all the great emperor's undertakings, this, too, bears the impress of his piety and of his concern to be faithful to conscience in the high state to which God has called him. "Nothing," he declared in the collection of his own laws, "should escape the prince to whom God has confided the care of all mankind," and he legislated for churchmen and the Church as instinctively and as carefully as he legislated for everyone else in his world state. Church and State were but two aspects of the one reality, that Roman Empire conterminous with civilisation, over which Justinian, the divine vice-regent, presided. The system had its advantages. It furnished, perhaps prematurely, what had hitherto not yet developed in the Church itself, a system of continuous day to day control by which the religious life of the whole Church was centralised, with the minimum of local departure from an enacted common practice. Nor was the system either bred of servility in ecclesiastics or the inevitable begetter of such servility. For all the emperor's un-relaxing control there were never lacking Patriarchs of Constan-tinople—to say nothing of popes—who resisted him steadfastly when principles called for resistance. Nevertheless the system was extraneous to the Church. It did not spring from the Church's life and it could not live by what gave life to the Church.

Between the system—even supposing the emperor a Catholic and friendly—and the life it aspired to control there must in-evitably be friction. The Church would either escape from the system or die under its oppression. History was to show the Church escaping from it as the empire rapidly ceased to be conterminous with the Church's world, while in what survived of the Empire the system remained, grew to perfection, and, under it, the Church disappeared.

The Roman Emperor, then, was now very definitely a Catholic, and an imperial policy in religious matters a duty of conscience for him. Pagans for example, were henceforward excluded from civil office; they lost all power of inheriting. Their last intellectual centre was destroyed when, in 529, Justinian closed the schools of Athens, and in the next twenty years an official mission to convert the Pagans was organised. Occasionally there is a record of executions under the law, and, more often, of mob violence lynching those known to be Pagans. In 546 an edict commanding Pagans to be baptized completed the code. The penalty for refusal was loss of goods and exile, whence, inevitably, a number of nominal conversions and, thereafter, clandestine reunions of these crypto-pagans, with floggings and executions for the participants when they were discovered. To the Jews and to the Samaritans Justinian was equally hostile. Synagogues were forbidden, the Jews lost all right of inheriting, the right to bring suits against a Christian or to own Christian slaves. A succession of bloody revolts, bloodily suppressed, brought the Samaritans almost to extinction and under Phocas (609) thousands of them were baptized by force. Heretics were pursued no less violently, Montanists, for example—still after four hundred years awaiting at Pepusa the second coming—Novatians, Marcionites, Macedonians and, once Theodoric's power was ended, Arians too. To convert the Pagans outside the empire missions were organised, the State taking the initiative and the emperor, often enough, standing sponsor for the Pagan kings and chiefs who were baptized. These missions were not of course without their political importance. The State's attachment to religion is shown yet again in the insistence on the religious character of, for example, the great war with Persia. For the Roman Emperor it was, in part, a crusade against the Sun Worshippers, and the Persian kings were no less clear in their antagonism to Christianity. So Chosroes II, in 616, replied to the ambassadors of Heraclius petitioning for peace, "I will spare the Romans when they abjure their crucified criminal and worship the Sun."

The newly-enthroned Justin I, through whom in 519 Rome regained the obedience of the Churches in the East, was, it should be borne in mind, the heir to a line of highly successful emperor-popes. For a good forty years before him the emperor's word had been law in matters of religion all through the empire. When, sixteen years after the reconciliation of 519, Justinian's generals conquered the Vandals in Africa and the Ostrogoths in Italy, what, in theory, was the restoration of imperial rule in those provinces, was, in reality, the annexation of Italy and Africa to Byzantium. The new régime was no restoration of what had obtained before 476, but the introduction into the West of the uses—Byzantine by now—of the mid-sixth century East. The papacy, for example, had been independent of the old empire of the West in the days of Gratian and St. Ambrose, of St. Leo and Valentinian III, while in the East, during these last hundred and fifty years (381–536), Cæsar had been supreme, and the four eastern patriarchs little better than his officers in spirituals. Italy now annexed to Byzantium, the pope came into the imperial system as a fifth, and senior, patriarch, to enter, despite protestations and re-minders, on a new rôle of *de facto* subordination. There was of course no denial of Rome's primacy in the universal church, nor of its traditional prerogatives. These were indeed fully and explicitly acknowledged. The new Code described the pope as "chief of all the holy priests of God", and Justinian's own laws spoke of Rome as "the source of all priesthood," and decreed that "the most holy pope of Old Rome shall be the first of priests." But henceforward the emperors rudely assume that the primacy is as much at their disposal as the political loyalty of those to whom it is entrusted. Whence, inevitably, two hundred years of recurrent friction until the popes are set free.

Rome, then, is now to be broken in, as Constantinople has already been broken in. It is now that the bishop of the imperial city comes fully to the heights of his place in the Church. When, two hundred years before, Constantine transformed Byzantium into Constantinople its bishop was a mere suffragan of the Metropolitan of Heraclea. The rôle of the bishop in the Arian troubles (330–381) gave the see a new importance. The Councils of Constantinople (381) and Chalcedon (451) recognised that importance officially, and, the Monophysites having by the time of Justinian's accession destroyed the Catholicism of Egypt and the East, Constantinople enjoyed, henceforward undisturbed, a very real primacy east of the Adriatic. Alexandria and Antioch had fallen below the capital in jurisdiction as well as in honour, and it was the Patriarch of Constantinople who now consecrated the bishops of these more ancient, apostolic sees. As the sixth century developed, Alexandria and Antioch lost steadily in real importance, Catholics were few, Monophysites many in the territories subject to them; and so while Constantinople kept all the fullness of Catholicity in the provinces immediately subject to her—thirty metropolitans and four hundred and fifty bishops in all—the Patriarchs of Antioch and Alexandria shrank to mere titularies resident at the court, without flocks, without clergy, without suffragans. Legend, finally, forged for the see of the capital a pedigree of apostolicity. The first Bishop of Constantinople, it was now discovered, was St. Andrew.

The Byzantine bishop is a man of many occupations. He has a place and duties, because a bishop, in the hierarchy of the civil administration. He is already responsible for the care of vast church properties, responsible for the numerous monasteries, for the hospitals and charitable institutions. He is the ordinary judge in all suits to which clerics, monks, and nuns are parties, and in all suits where both parties are willing to take him as judge. Hence a whole legislation *de vita episcopali* in Justinian's *Code* and the *Novellae*. Qualifications for elegibility are minutely laid down, age, condition and character. The bishops are still elected, but only the better class are allowed a say in the proceedings, and these have only the right to present a list of three names. It is for the metropolitan, or the patriarch, thence to choose the new bishop. In practice it is the emperor who chooses, for the imperial candidate is never rejected. Rome is a notable exception to this "reform." The election of the popes remains free, but it is subject to the emperor's ratification, and it is a testimony to the prestige of Eastern Catholicism in the sixth and seventh centuries that for seventy-five years almost every one of the popes was Greek or Syrian.

The civil law requires bishops to live in their dioceses, it orders an annual provincial synod, and it forbids bishops to come to court unless they have, in writing, the permission of their superior —the bishop of his metropolitan, the metropolitan of his patriarch. Each patriarch is represented at the court by a permanent ambassador, the Apocrisiarius. In practice there is, of course, always a crowd of bishops at court, a more or less permanent synod whose personnel is continually changing. This, the so-called *synodus endemousa*, was an important, extra-constitutional, engine of the politico-ecclesiastical government.

As the law regulated the life and conduct of the bishops, so it provided for the clergy, and for the monks who flourished in the sixth century as never before. It was perhaps the golden age of monasticism in the Eastern Church. Since the reforms of St. Basil monasticism had grown to be an immense power in the empire's religious life, perhaps the greatest force of all. Whoever had the monks on his side had the people too. Hence the close alliance between the ecclesiastical princes of Constantinople or Alexandria and the heads of the vast religious congregations. Hence, too, the repeated occasions where the monks have been the principal means of the defeat of Catholicism. They played a great part in the scandal of the *Latrocinium*, and ever since Chalcedon their adherence to the patriarch there condemned, and to his successors, had been the very life of the Monophysite party. But although so many of the monks had gone over to heresy, they accepted the decrees of Chalcedon in sufficient numbers for monasticism to continue to be the main driving force in the religious life of the Catholics too. Monasteries abounded. In 536 there were no fewer than 108 in Constantinople and its suburbs and, apart from the army of Cenobites, the solitaries were still numerous. Each monastery was autonomous. Nowhere, except in the convents descended from the foundations of St. Pakhomius, is there trace of a religious order in the later western sense. All monasteries were, moreover, since Chalcedon, subject to the diocesan bishop. Exceptionally—by the imperial favour

—they are directly subject to the Patriarch of Constantinople. The law fixes the duration of the novitiate at three years, and the Cenobite is forbidden to leave the monastery for which he is professed, whether it be to join another community or to become a wandering monk. With the Mohammedan conquests of Egypt and Syria, in the early seventh century, the number of solitaries diminished notably, and henceforward the hermit was very much the exception. The rule that the monk or nun shall never leave the enclosure of the monastery became ever more strict, and the bishops of the great synod of 692 insisted, too, that the monk should be decently clothed, and that the scandal of the bedraggled beggar monks of the cities should cease.

One abuse of monasticism is familiar to every student of the political history of these times. The monasteries offer a convenient solution for the victorious usurper embarrassed by the survival of his predecessor. More than one emperor—to say nothing of lesser dignitaries—escapes death by taking the monastic habit, as others are despoiled of their chance of a return to power by being forcibly ordained and consecrated. The monks again were the popular preachers and spiritual directors, and from their ranks came most of the great bishops and the ecclesiastical writers.

III. BYZANTINE CATHOLICISM. 565–711

Justinian died, an old man of eighty-two, in 565. In the half century or so during which he had ruled the Roman world he had been amazingly successful in his ambition to restore the imperial authority in the lost provinces of the West. Rome, Ravenna, Carthage were once more the seats of Roman government. Italy, Dalmatia, Africa, the islands of the Mediterranean, the southern half of Pannonia, the south of Spain had been recovered. If much remained to be won, much had been won already.

But the cost had been too great. It had exhausted the resources of the treasury and it had exhausted the emperor himself. Nor was the reconquest in any sense final. Huns, Slavs and Avars continued to raid the recovered Illyricum. Thessalonica, and the capital itself, more than once were threatened, and the hordes only bought off by the pledge of an annual pension. To Italy, in 568, there came the last, and worst, of her plagues—the Lombards, and by the end of the century they had wrested from the imperial officials three fourths of the peninsula. On the eastern frontier the war with Persia was almost a habit of life. In all Justinian's long reign there were scarcely ten years of peace, and less than ten in the thirty years which followed his death. To carry through successfully this war, which must be waged simultaneously on every frontier, and to maintain the complex administration of the empire was more than ever an impossible task for the one man with whom, as the superhuman autocrat, all initiative traditionally lay. It is little wonder that after eight years of the strain Justinian's successor, Justin II, lost his reason. Nor that, within half a century of the great emperor's death, with Constantinople beset simultaneously by Avars and Persians, the empire's last hour seemed at hand. It was a general from Africa, Heraclius, who staved off the end and after years of patient and laborious effort—reconstructing the administration, restoring the finances, rebuilding the army—finally dictated peace to the Persians in their own capital (628).

In those sixty years of crisis and calamity which separate that victory of Heraclius from the death of Justinian (565–628), the Monophysites are still one of the main problems of domestic policy. More than ever is it important that Egypt and Syria shall remain loyal, now that the empire is faced with this renaissance of Persia. And loyal they can never be so long as between them and the emperor there lie those decisions of Chalcedon which to the East register a Greek imperialist victory over Syrian and Egyptian. Whence, after a hundred and fifty years, it is still the great aim of the imperial policy to find a reconciling formula which, without repudiating the definition of faith of 451, shall convince the Monophysites that St. Leo is there in agreement with St. Cyril, and that the supporters of the great council are not Nestorians. Whence also, with each scheme for reunion, new trouble between the emperor and the Catholics, and, since one such scheme is based on a new theological theory which conflicts with the tradition of faith, very serious trouble with the Roman See.

Justinian's immediate successor, Justin II, was friendly to Monophysitism and so, too, was his wife, a niece of the old empress, Theodora. The exiled bishops were recalled, the old business of conferences and discussions was resumed. Once more it was the emperor who offered concessions, and this time he offered everything short of an implicit repudiation of Chalcedon. The Monophysites, themselves rent by now into hostile factions, could not agree. Nor, even if the bishops had been able and willing to accept, would their monastic allies have supported them. The fanaticism of the Monophysite monks was proof against all the imperial diplomacy and at last, after six years of fruitless negotiations, the emperor returned 'to the policy of coercion. Two years later and the policy changed again. Justin II was now out of his mind (574) and the new ruler, Tiberius II, brought the persecution to an end. The Monophysites took advantage of the truce to elect a new Patriarch of Alexandria—

there had been none for ten years—and the new patriarch, in preparation for future emergencies, consecrated, at once and in the one ceremony, seventy new bishops (576).

For the remainder of the century the persecution was intermittent, and although the Monophysites fought continuously among themselves—divided, united, then divided yet more bitterly—they all of them held firmly to their refusal to accept Chalcedon, and with every year the chances of reunion grew fainter. With the new century came the murder of the Emperor Maurice (582–602) and the rule of the worthless Phocas (602–610). It was now that the Persian offensive began under the great king Chosroes II (590–628). Syria, Egypt and Asia Minor were overrun. Antioch fell in 611, Damascus in 613, Jerusalem—after a siege where 57,000 were killed—in 614, Alexandria in 617. The Monophysites did not indeed, play the traitor. But they were antiimperialistic, and the Catholics, identified by the invaders as the party of the emperor, were dispossessed to the profit of the Monophysites. By 620 Chalcedon had not an adherent in the whole of the eastern provinces which had fallen to the Persians. Also, an unlooked-for coincidence, the Monophysites now patched up their own quarrels, the Copts of Egypt and the Jacobites of Syria combining. When, ten years later (629), Heraclius was once more master of Egypt and the East, he was faced immediately with the necessity of reuniting these provinces, still lost to him by the more fundamental division of religion, provinces where a century or more of religious persecution had bred a tradition of hatred for Constantinople, for its emperor as for its patriarch.

Along with the political restoration Heraclius, then, had no choice but to attempt something in the way of religious restoration too, nor would coercion serve any longer.

Once more the theological subtlety of a Patriarch of Constantinople came to his assistance. He devised a new exposition of the eternal problem. It had the merit that, from the new point of view, it involved neither St. Leo nor St. Cyril, nor did it mention Chalcedon. The Monophysites shrank from contact with the Catholics because these, so they alleged, divided Christ as Nestorius had done. The Patriarch of Constantinople, Sergius, offered as new proof that Catholics were just as anti-Nestorian (and therefore in the Monophysite sense as orthodox) as the Monophysites themselves, their belief that in Our Lord there is only one source of action (*energeia*). To his own Catholic people this could be explained as in conformity with Chalcedon, since action is of persons and therefore the singleness of the source of action in Jesus Christ derived from the single Person—the Logos—active in the two natures. Ephesus, defining the singleness of

Person, Chalcedon defining the duality of nature, and the Monophysites protesting against any division of Christ, were, then, all three here conciliated. On this basis, which satisfied everyone, reunion could now go forward. As with the faculty of action so was it with other faculties, for example, the faculty of choice, the will. Catholics, it was explained again to the Monophysite critic, did not consider Christ to be two beings mysteriously united, for they believed that in Christ there was but one will. The application of the new theory to the question of the will gave it its most popular development, and also the name—Monothelism—by which the whole movement is, somewhat loosely, known.

It was while the East still lay in the hands of the Persians that Sergius elaborated his theory, and it was only after the reconquest that it passed into politics. By then Heraclius had been won over to it, and the Monophysite, Cyrus of Phasis, recently (631) elected to fill the long vacant (Catholic) see of Alexandria (617–633), adopted it as an instrument of negotiation with the Monophysites. The conferences, for once, ended in agreement, and in 633 an Act of Union was signed at Alexandria which ended, after a hundred and eighty years, the feuds and divisions of the Christian East. The discovery of their common agreement in Monothelism had revealed to Chalcedonian and anti-Chalcedonian alike the unimportance of the details which had kept them too long apart. But unfortunately if, for the Monophysite, the new theory was simply an extension of what he had always professed, the Catholic's acceptance of it was not merely a surrender of the point, so long debated, that, whoever refused to acknowledge Chalcedon was out of accord with the Tradition, but it involved recognition of yet another heresy. The theory was simply a radical form of Monophysitism in another guise. And there were Catholics, more acute mentally than Sergius, or perhaps less preoccupied with the hopes of political peace which the theory presented, who saw this from the beginning and who urged their objections. One such critic was the monk Sophronius.

Sophronius was one of the most learned men of the century, and he had an equally wide reputation for holiness of life. He had travelled much, was well known through the East, in Rome, too, which he had visited, and especially well known in Alexandria where he had lived for many years. He was now eighty years of age, but still vigorous in mind as in body and he knew the detail of the long controversy with the Monophysites as perhaps no one else knew it. He was in Alexandria when the Union of 633 was signed, and immediately he set himself to point out its implications to those responsible. Cyrus refused to be convinced, and took shelter behind the authority of Constantinople, where-upon the ancient Sophronius set out for the capital. There, too, he found little but polite obstruction, Sergius giving him no more than an explanation in writing of the reason for his action. Palestine, where Monophysites were fewer, and where the political preoccupations of Alexandria and Constantinople did not exist, was the monk's next objective, and thither, with Sergius' letter, Sophronius then went. He arrived to find the see of Jerusalem vacant. He was himself elected Patriarch.

This sudden and surprising election changed immediately the nonchalance of Sergius towards his critic—and towards a more important personage still, the pope. So far, the whole business of the reunion, with its tacit abandonment of Chalcedon, had been carried through without any reference to Rome. Now, obviously, Rome would hear it all from this new Athanasius unexpectedly become Patriarch of Jerusalem. Sergius determined to forestall him. He wrote to Rome himself, and with his letter he sent the explanations he had given to Sophronius. In his letter he gave his own account of the reunion, and of his discussion with Sophronius, and he ended by the suggestion that further dis-cussion as to whether there were one or two "energies" was impolitic; silence was now the wisest course.

The reply of the pope, Honorius I (625–638), is curiously interesting, because he fails utterly to grasp the point of the patriarch's letter. Sergius had before him the Monophysite contention that since Catholics repudiated the Alexandrian phrase "union in one nature," they must believe that in Christ there are two beings united by a moral union. To disprove this he urges that Catholic belief accords to Christ Our Lord one only faculty of action. This point the pope wholly overlooks or, more truly, misunderstands. Not the singleness of the faculty, but the unity in action between the divine and the human, is the subject of the pope's reply. Certainly, Honorius answers, Christ always acted with the two natures in harmony, no conflict between them being possible, the unity of action being perfect. As to the number of ways in which He acted no man can count them, much less say they were one or two. Questions of grammatical subtleties should be left to grammarians, and he agrees with Sergius that the discussion should be left where it stands.

Obviously Sergius and Honorius are at cross purposes. They are not discussing the same thing at all. But the consequences of the misunderstanding could hardly have been more serious. How far Honorius was from approving the new theory can be gathered from what he wrote to Sophronius. The new Patriarch of Jerusalem, following the custom, wrote to the other patriarchs and to the pope a letter—the synodal letter—notifying his election and testifying to his acceptance of the traditional faith. The synodal letter of Sophronius is a long and elaborate criticism of the new theory, which it exposes and refutes as a development of the heresy condemned at Chalcedon. The pope thereupon wrote to Constantinople, to Alexandria and to Sophronius. The first two letters are lost, and of the third only fragments survive. We do, however, possess an earlier letter to Sophronius, written before the latter's synodal letter had been received. Three things definitely emerge from the pope's letter and the fragments. The pope deprecates all discussion as to whether there are one or two "energies," for, whichever expression is used, misunderstanding is certain. We must, however, hold that Jesus Christ, one in person, wrought works both human and divine by means of the two natures. The same Jesus Christ acted in His two natures divinely and humanly. Finally—again the fatal *ignoratio elenchi* —we must acknowledge the unity of will, for in Jesus Christ there is necessarily harmony between what is divinely willed and what is humanly willed. That Honorius held and taught the faith of Chalcedon is clear enough, despite the muddle. It is equally clear that he failed to grasp that a new question had been raised and was under discussion; clear, also, that he assisted the innovators by thus imposing silence alike on them and on their orthodox critics; and clear, finally, that he definitely said, in so many words, that there is but one will in Christ. It was a patronage of heresy no less effective because it was unconscious.

The next move lay with the emperor, and in 638 appeared an edict, the *Ecthesis*, which put forward the teaching that in Our Lord there is but one will as the Church's official doctrine.

Sophronius died that same year; Honorius, and Sergius too. A few months later Heraclius died, in 641, and Cyrus of Alexandria in 642. The principal actors in the controversy were gone then within four years of the appearance of the *Ecthesis*, and in those same few fateful years there had disappeared too—and for ever—the provinces whose pacification had been the original cause of all the trouble. It was in 629 that Heraclius had triumphed over the Persians, and, while the ink was still wet on the treaties, the power was already preparing which was to destroy both victor and vanquished. The new religion of Mahomet, slowly developing in Arabia for the last thirty years, was about to begin its epic conquest of the East. In 633 Damascus fell to it, Jerusalem in 637, Alexandria in 641. The actors gone, the provinces gone, it might be thought that, necessarily, the whole wretched business of this imperial patronage of dogmatic definition was at an end. Alas, the real fury of the Monothelite heresy had not even begun. The dogmatic question once raised must be settled. Honorius, failing to see the point raised, had set it aside. Sooner or later there would come a pope who, more understanding, could not follow that precedent. Rome must teach, and definitely. On the other hand the imperial prestige was bound up with the new theory. If Rome condemned it the emperor must either submit or fight. No emperor yet had surrendered his patronage of heresy at the bidding of a pope. All the emperors who had once adopted heresy had died ultimately in the heresy of their choice—Constantine and Valens in Arianism, Theodosius II compromised with the Monophysites, Zeno and Anastasius in actual schism. Now it was the turn of the family of Heraclius, and once again, heresy, for forty years, finds in the Christian Emperor its chief and only support, while the traditional faith is proscribed and the faithful persecuted.

The first sign of opposition from Rome came when the envoys of Honorius's successor reached the capital, with their petition that his election should be confirmed. Presented with the *Ecthesis* and asked to sign it, they would not do more than promise to present it for signature to the newly-elected, Severinus. Shortly afterwards (August 12, 640) this pope too died; and in his place was elected the equally short-lived John IV (640–642). To John IV, Heraclius did indeed write, in the last months of his life, disclaiming all responsibility for the *Ecthesis*, and naming Sergius as its author. Nevertheless it was not withdrawn and John IV wrote vigorously to Heraclius' successors, Constantine III and Heracleonas, demanding its revocation. At the same time he protested against the use of Honorius' name in support of the heresy. Honorius, he recalls, had written to Sergius that "in our Saviour there can by no means be two contrary wills, that is in His members since He was free of those weaknesses which result from Adam's fall. My aforesaid predecessor, therefore, teaching on this mystery of Christ's incarnation, declared that there were not in Him what is found in us who are sinners, to wit conflicting wills of the spirit and of the flesh. This teaching some have twisted to suit their own ends, alleging Honorius to have taught that there is but one will to His divinity and humanity which is indeed contrary to truth."

John IV died in October, 642. His successor, Theodore (642–649), continued the policy of protest, condemning the *Ecthesis* anew, and sending to the Patriarch of Constantinople a declaration of the true faith to be posted in its place. The patriarch refused, protested the orthodoxy of his attitude and invoked Honorius among his patrons. Finally, in 646, the pope declared him deposed. The sentence was never carried out. Instead, on the patriarch's proceeded no further with his mission. Four years later arrived another envoy of a different stamp (653). The pope, a great sufferer from gout, foreseeing trouble, had his bed carried before the high altar of the Lateran and there the troops found him when they broke in. The envoy brought an imperial decree notifying him that he was deposed and ordering him to be arrested and despatched to Constantinople. Another pope was to be elected in his place. The pope forbade any attempts at resistance and, surrendering to the officers, was straightway carried off.

It was more than a year before he reached the capital, and during all that length of time he suffered greatly from the brutality of the soldiers. When, finally, the convoy arrived at the quays of the imperial city the old man, helpless and confined to his bed, was left on deck for the best part of a day to be the butt of the populace. Then for three months he lay in the dungeons until, on December 19, 654, he was brought before the Senate to be tried for, of all things, treason. The cruel farce of a State trial, with the usual apparatus of trained official perjurers, dragged on and the pope was found guilty. They took him next to a balcony of the palace, and, to the acclamation of the mob, went through the ritual ceremony of degrading the pope, stripping him of his vestments and insignia. Then, half naked and loaded with chains, he was dragged through the streets to the prison reserved for wretches awaiting execution, the executioner, bearing a drawn sword, marching before him. This sentence, however, was not carried out. Constans II, who had enjoyed, from behind a grille, the scene he had so carefully arranged, went from his triumph to recount it in detail to the patriarch, ill at the time and thought to be nearing his end. The recital struck terror into the prelate. "Alas, yet another count to which soon I must answer," was all he could say, and it was at his earnest entreaty that Constans commuted the sentence for one of exile. Three months later (March, 655) the unhappy pope, half dead with his privations and sufferings, was shipped off to the Crimea where new hardships speedily put an end to his life (September 16, 655).

St. Martin I, in whom the incompetence of Honorius was so gloriously redeemed, was not the only martyr to Constans II's barbarity. The abbot Maximus, a one time secretary to Heraclius, and two monks, one of them the pope's late ambassador to the imperial court, were likewise put on trial. The skill of the one time secretary had no difficulty in stripping the trial of its pretences and in forcing an admission that the real cause was loyalty to the Roman decisions. The three were exiled, horribly tormented, mutilated even, and in the end, like the pope they had defended, they, too, died from the results of their ill-treatment.

advice, the Emperor Constans II (642–668), issued a new e
in place of the *Ecthesis*. This was the *Type*[1] promulgated in (
The *Type* was not merely a profession of faith, as the *Ecthesis* h
been, but an edict forbidding, under heavy penalties, all discussi
of the subject. Whether the Monothelites were right or wron
the pope and those who stood by him must be content to k
silent. Bishops and clerics who defy the law are to be degradec
monks to be expelled from their monasteries, laymen to b
stripped of their property if nobles, and the ordinary citizens to be
flogged and exiled, "in order that all men, restrained by the fear
of God and respect for the penalties rightly decreed, may keep
undisturbed the peace of God's holy Churches." It was a warning
against interference. Was it meant for Rome too? Events were
shortly to show. Pope Theodore died about this time (May 14,
649), and the responsibility of decision fell to his successor,
Martin I .

No better choice of pope could have been made. Martin
had been his predecessor's ambassador at Constantinople, and
had been entrusted with the delicate task of warning and excommunicating the patriarch three years before. He knew the problem
thoroughly and he also knew well the personalities opposed to him,
the Patriarch Paul and the young Emperor Constans II. The new
pope made no attempt to obtain the emperor's confirmation of
his election, but, planning a courageous defiance of the *Type*, he
summoned a synod of bishops to meet in the Lateran basilica
for the October of 649. One hundred and five bishops answered
the summons, and the sessions occupied the whole of the month.
All the correspondence and documents of the twenty years'
controversy were read, the complaints of the persecuted and their
protestations. Finally, in a series of canons, the *Type* and its
promoters were condemned, and an official declaration given
that in Jesus Christ Our Lord there are "two natural wills the
divine and the human, and two natural operations the divine and
the human." Nor did Pope Martin rest content with his great
council at Rome. Its decisions were transmitted to every part of
the Church, to missionary bishops in Holland and Gaul as well as
to Africa and Constantinople. Local councils were to be organised
to support and to accept the Roman decision.

The emperor replied by action. A high official arrived in Rome
with instructions to force an acceptance of the *Type* on the pope
and all the bishops. He could not, however, rely on the loyalty of
the soldiery. Pope and clergy and people were too united for
intrigue to have any chance of success, an attempt at assassination
failed and finally he came to an understanding with the pope and

[1] τύπος περὶ πίστεως : i.e. outline of the faith.

One very unpleasant feature of this episode is the attitude of the Roman clergy to their persecuted bishop and his supporters. It is also illuminating testimony to the hold which, in this new Byzantine Catholicism, the emperor had managed to gain even on the clergy of the supreme see. Before St. Martin had been tried, before even he had arrived at Constantinople, the wretched Roman clergy had obeyed the imperial order and given him a successor. Hence, in his prison at Constantinople the old pope waited in vain for help, for even the support of friendship from his own Roman people. The election of Eugene was a sad disillusioning of the valiant soul who had expected that something of his own spirit would keep his clergy loyal. Worse still was the news that the ambassadors sent by Eugene to petition for the emperor's confirmation of his election had gone over to the heretics, and, if they had not accepted the *Type*, had fraternised with them to the extent of concelebrating with the patriarch. This was one of the new facts thrown in the teeth of St. Maximus as he protested that he had for his warrant the teaching and practice of the Roman See. In desperation he turned to prayer that the divine mercy would somehow make manifest the gift of truth with which It had enriched the see of Peter.

He had not long to wait. The new pope, Eugene—really pope since Martin's death—was already, by 656, a source of anxiety to those who had contrived his election. The new patriarch at Constantinople had sent to Rome the synodal letter announcing his election. It was read with the wonted ceremony at St. Mary Major's before a great assembly of clergy and people, and its language on the crucial point of "energies" was considered too obscure to be orthodox. Cries of opposition broke out. The pope tried diplomatically to calm the tumult, but was forced to promise that he would never acknowledge as patriarch the author of the letter. Then, and then only, was he allowed to proceed with the mass. At Constantinople the news of this rejection of the new patriarch roused the official world to new fury, and one of St. Maximus' judges referred to the incident "Know this, Lord Abbot, as soon as the Barbarians leave us a breathing space we shall treat as we are treating you this pope who dares now to raise his head, and the rest of those folk in Rome who cry out so loudly, and your own disciples with them. We shall bury the lot of you, each in his own place, as we did for Martin." However, Eugene I died before the emperor's hands were freed (June 2, 657), and his successor, Vitalian, made his peace and recognised the new patriarch unasked.

Six years after Vitalian's election political affairs brought Constans II to Rome, the first emperor to appear in the ancient capital for more than two centuries. Whatever the orthodoxy of his belief, he was the sovereign, the pope was his subject, and pope and clergy headed the citizens in the demonstration of loyalty which greeted the tyrant who had sent St. Martin to his death not ten years before. From Rome the emperor went south and he was still in Sicily when (668) the dagger of an assassin put an end to his life. His sudden death so far from the capital seemed likely, for the moment, to be the prelude to civil war. That his son, Constantine IV (668-685), succeeded peaceably was due in no small measure to the activity of Pope Vitalian, and, possibly in gratitude for the pope's service, with the new reign the *Type*, though not disavowed, disappeared into the lumber rooms of history. There was henceforward a kind of peace, but neither of the popes who succeeded Vitalian—Adeodatus 672-676, and Donus 676-678—were recognised by the patriarchs at Constantinople, nor were the patriarchs John V (669-675) and Constantine (675-677) recognised at Rome. It was the initiative of the emperor which brought the estrangement to an end, and from his letter to Pope Donus asking him to send representatives to a conference, there developed the sixth general council of 680-1 (Constantinople III).

Two years of delays followed the imperial invitation. To begin with, the pope to whom it was addressed died before the letter arrived. Then his successor Agatho (678-681) decided, before he replied, to consult the western episcopate generally. His acceptance should go to Constantinople bearing the signatures of as many Latin bishops as possible. There was at Rome the usual council of the pope's own immediate suffragans, in which an English bishop, Wilfrid of York, took part. There was a council at Pavia, and other councils, apparently, elsewhere, following the procedure of St. Martin I in 649. As his principal legate the pope would have liked to send the Greek monk who at the time occupied the see of Canterbury, Theodore of Tarsus. The difficulties which prevented this, delayed the mission yet further. Finally, in the September of 680, the delegates reached Constantinople and an emperor who had almost despaired of seeing them. They were eleven in all: two priests and a deacon representing the pope himself, three Italian bishops—the emperor had asked for twelve—a priest of Ravenna and, as the emperor had desired, four monks chosen from the Greek monasteries of Southern Italy.

The legates presented to the emperor a letter from the pope, the three bishops the profession of faith which the western bishops had signed—a hundred and twenty-five of them. On November 7 the delegates came together under the presidency of the emperor.

The project had grown since he wrote to the pope, and with the mission from the West there were present the bishops of the Patriarchate of Constantinople, and what could be gathered to represent the three other patriarchates where, thanks to Monophysitism and the fifty years of Mahometan occupation, Catholicism as an organised thing had practically disappeared. In all one hundred and seventy-four bishops were present.

The sessions of the Council—eighteen in number—did not end until the following September (681).[1] The Monothelites were allowed to state their case, the whole vast literature of manifestoes and synodals was read, with the acts of the previous councils on which the Monothelites based their new claim to orthodoxy.

Agatho's letter to the emperor was read to the council. Like the *Tome* of St. Leo, two centuries earlier, it is a simple statement of the belief as traditional that in Christ Our Lord there are two wills and two operations. As St. Leo at Chalcedon, so now Agatho, was acclaimed as Peter's successor "Peter it is who speaks through Agatho." In the eighth session the emperor intervened and demanded that the two patriarchs should give their opinion as to the doctrine of Agatho's letter. The Patriarch of Constantinople declared it to be the Catholic faith and the immense majority of the bishops agreed. His colleague of Antioch —a patriarch *in partibus* these many years—held firmly to his Monothelism. Sergius, Cyrus, Sophronius, and Honorius, dead now half a century, came to life again in the debates. Sophronius was hailed as the defender of the true faith, the rest condemned; Sergius as the pioneer of the heresy, Cyrus and the successors of Sergius as his supporters, all of whom, the decree notes, have been already condemned by Agatho, "the most holy and thrice blessed pope of Old Rome in his suggestions to the emperor." To this list, sent on from Rome, the council added the name of Honorius "because in his writings to Sergius he followed his opinions and confirmed his impious teaching." The emperor accepted all the council decreed, he presided at the closing session, and by an edict gave the definitions force of law.

The council, following immemorial tradition, wrote also to the pope, begging him to confirm what had been decreed. At the moment the Roman See was vacant. Agatho had died (January, 681) before the council was half way through its labours, and his successor, Leo II, was not elected until nearly a year after the council had ended (August 17, 682). To acknowledge its synodal letter and to send a reply was one of his first duties. This he did in a letter to the emperor. The pope confirms the decrees, and

[1] Forty-three bishops were present at the opening session; 174 signed the final act.

re-echoes the condemnations of his predecessor, and in even more indignant terms, he makes his own the council's condemnation of Honorius "who did not make this apostolic Church illustrious by teaching in accord with the apostolic tradition, but on the contrary allowed its spotless faith to be sullied by a sacrilegious treachery." He used a similar hard phrase in a letter to the King of the Visigoths. But it is in a further letter to the bishops of Spain that this pope, in a sentence, most clearly describes the fault for which Honorius merited these condemnations: "Honorius who did not extinguish the fire of heretical teaching, as behoved one who exercised the authority of the apostles, but by his negligence blew the flames still higher." The condemnation of Pope Honorius does not seem greatly to have moved those who witnessed it. It was recorded in all solemnity in the *Acta* of the council, it appears in all the correspondence which notifies the decision of the council to the rest of Christendom. In the archives where these rested, his memory, too, slept until, centuries later, controversial archæologists, straining every resource to embarass the champions of the Roman primacy, turned to the record of the sixth general council and with more ingenuity than good faith tried to put on the decrees a meaning they were never meant to bear. Much more singular than the inclusion of the negligent and misunderstanding Honorius among the condemned of 681, is the entire absence of any reference in the council's proceedings to the memory of the story's heroic figures, St. Martin I, St. Maximus and the rest. The ingenuity of Constans II, condemning for treason where he dare not proceed on a cause of faith, was successful to the end. No council, no pope, under this Byzantine régime, would glorify the criminal convicted for treason, any more than it would condemn the emperors who had fostered and encouraged the heresy, opposition to which was the martyr's real crime. The memory of Heraclius and of Constans II was officially undimmed, while that of St. Martin and his companions remained officially infamous.

In the council of 680 Rome and Constantinople came together after a breach of relations that had lasted thirty-five years. The acknowledgement of the Roman primacy then made was as full, and as spontaneous, as at the time of Hormisdas, or at Chalcedon, two hundred and thirty years before. Nevertheless in those two hundred and thirty years a new world had slowly been coming to birth. It is always difficult to draw the dividing lines of historical periods, but certainly by the end of the seventh century the world into which the Church had come had definitely given place to another. That world had been a civilisation, Roman politically, Hellenistic culturally, imposed on and adopted by a score of peoples, overlaying, in East and West alike, older cultures still. By the time of the Council of 680 the West had long since slipped from the grasp of the one-time world State. For nearly three centuries now, Gaul, Spain and Britain had been outside its boundaries. Italy, too, which Justinian had recovered, was by 680 once again "barbarian", save for Sicily, Calabria and a few scattered vantage points along the coast. Africa had recently (695–698) fallen to the Arabs, who, as has been noted, had, sixty years earlier made themselves masters of Egypt and the East. The Slavs were now established south of the Danube. The State, which had not been a Roman empire for three centuries, was by this hardly an empire at all. More and more it was become a Greek-speaking nation, whose strength lay in the peasantry of Asia Minor; and if it still retained in Constantinople a European capital, it was to the East that its capital looked for inspiration, to the lands and the traditions of those ancient cultures whence had derived that non-European conception of the semi-divine despotic ruler whose influence, since Diocletian, had done so much to make the Empire a new thing. The lands had vanished, the culture had changed, the inspiration of life was other, and it was in a world already changed that this last great controversy between the Roman See and the Roman Emperors was fought out. Nevertheless, since the affair of the Monothelites is the last chapter of the history which begins with the Edict of Milan it is best told here in order to complete that history. To show in what degree the world in which the controversy ended was a different world, and how truly a new age had begun with Constantinople's pride of place reinforced by the consciousness of its cultural and even "national" superiority to Rome—a consciousness now characterised by deep anti-Roman feeling—it remains to say something of another council at Constantinople, summoned twelve years after the council of Pope Agatho and Constantine IV. This is the famous synod in Trullo[1]—so called from the place where it met, the great domed hall of the imperial palace at Constantinople.

It was summoned by the son of Constantine IV, the youthful Justinian II (685–95, 705–711). This emperor's reputation has left him the very type of that treachery and sadistic cruelty which, for so long, was all that the world "byzantine" conveyed to western minds. He was, however, no friend to the defeated Monothelites, and he needed little encouragement to busy himself, after the pattern of his great namesake, with the Church's internal discipline. It was represented to him that neither of the last two general councils (553 and 680) had occupied itself with questions

---

[1] Also called *Quini-Sext*, because intended to supplement (by canons about discipline) the Fifth and Sixth General Councils (i.e. those of 553 and 680–1).

of discipline, and to supply what was wanting Justinian called the Council of 692.

It was a purely Byzantine affair. The pope was not invited, and there was no East to invite. Two hundred and eleven bishops attended, and the papal ambassadors at the imperial court were present too. The council did little more than publish once more, in collected form, laws which had come down from earlier councils. There were, however, some new canons and, bearing in mind the emperor's aim of elaborating in this council a common ecclesiastical observance for the whole empire, their anti-Roman character is very significant. The famous 28th canon of Chalcedon is, of course, re-enacted, and the eastern discipline in the matter of Lent and of clerical marriage is extended to the whole Church in language designedly insulting to the Roman See. Equally significant of a new, aggressive anti-Roman spirit was the fact that, among the avowed sources from which this code was drawn, were councils which Rome had never recognised, and others which Rome had definitely rejected. The code went through, however, without a protest, and the pope's ambassadors to the imperial court signed with the rest.

It remained to be seen what the pope himself would do, and so much importance did Justinian attach to his signature that six copies of the decrees were sent to Rome. Each of the patriarchs, as well as the emperor, should have his autograph copy of the papal submission. The pope, Sergius I, was himself an oriental, Syrian by blood though Sicilian by birth. He refused the council all recognition.

Straightway the old tyranny began to function, officials coming from Constantinople with an order to drag the pope in chains to the capital. But it was not so easy now as it had been fifty years before in the time of St. Martin. The troops mutinied, the mob drove the high officials out of Rome with appropriate indecencies, and shortly afterwards a revolution at Constantinople drove out Justinian too—his nose slit in the latest fashion of mutilation. Ten years later, wearing a new nose of gold, he returned and, once securely established, his thoughts turned again to the decrees of his council still lacking the pontifical signature. Once more this half-crazy fanatic addressed himself to the task. The pope, John VII, was asked to note the canons to which he objected, and to sanction those he approved. The poor man was not only himself a Byzantine but the son of an official of the imperial service. Obedience to the emperor was in his blood, and yet he was pope. Something of the tradition triumphed despite the "human frailty" of which the *Liber Pontificalis* speaks. He did not dare to pick and choose, but sent back a kind of vague and general approbation. Justinian found it lacking, and sent orders for a fuller and more definite assent. Pope John was dead by this time. It was his successor, Constantine, who had to face the difficulty and an order to proceed himself to Constantinople. The pope was received everywhere with the utmost ceremony and reverence. The emperor too, most astonishingly, threw himself at his feet, begged the privilege of assisting at his mass and receiving Holy Communion from his hands. And thanks to the diplomatic skill of the future Gregory II the affair of the Council of 692 was left as it was. The emperor asked no further approbation. The pope abstained from further condemnation. To this day the place where the pope's name should show is blank. After which happy ending to what had promised to be so tragic, the pope was allowed to return to Rome. Two months later the mob rose once again, and this time the emperor and his son died in torments at its hands (December, 711).

Here ends the story of the Church and the world into which it was born. But the régime of Byzantinism under which the Church's ruler had been so oppressed, continued still. It was to last—so far as it affected the popes—just something short of fifty years more. Then a liberator came, in the person of the Catholic king of the barbarian Franks. He beat off from the nominally imperial lands the Lombards who menaced St. Peter, and "for love of St. Peter and the remission of his sins" made over his conquests to the pope (754). St. Peter is thenceforward no longer the subject of the successor of Augustus and Constantine. The alliance of the Papacy and the Franks has most momentously begun. It is a warning, if warning is needed, that the Middle Ages are upon us, that the Roman Empire is already a matter of history. Just two hundred years had passed since Justinian's re-conquest of Italy. For so long, and for no longer, had Cæsar imprisoned the Papacy in his Byzantine State.

BIBLIOGRAPHICAL NOTES

The few pages which follow do not profess to do more than offer some guidance for further reading. The books recommended are, almost all of them, the work of specialists and based directly on the actual sources of our knowledge. They may serve as the intermediary between an introductory work, such as this, and the only finally satisfying study—the reading of the sources themselves. I have, to the best of my ability, avoided the recommendation of works whose usefulness is lessened by the learned author's enslavement to his own hypothetical reconstruction of the past—a not uncommon tendency, and indeed a very natural tendency, in dealing with a subject whose source-material is, so often, a thing of shreds and patches.

Since the first object of this list of books is to provide a means by which the reader can make a speedy direct contact with the sources, no works are included which do not offer—by way of notes, for example—some authority for the statements and views expressed in the text. This will, perhaps, explain such a striking omission as that of all reference to the great Cambridge histories. These contain, of course, many masterly studies by leading authorities and long lists of sources and modern works accompany each study. It is surely nothing less than tragic, from the point of view of the studious reader, that the studies are—on principle—divorced from the sources; and so sixty massive volumes of historical scholarship are set before him without a single note offered in evidence of the assertions, or in justification of the weighty reflections, of some of the greatest scholars of our time.

That the great work of Mgr. Duchesne,[1] so often referred to in these notes, is still on the Index is true, but it is none the less true that in the right hands and critically used, it cannot but be of the very highest service to all students of Church History.

The most notable item of bibliography during the twelve years since this book was first published, is the appearance of the first seven volumes of a new General History of the Church, planned to run to twenty-four volumes in all. Its editors are MM. Augustin Fliche and Victor Martin, and the collaborators include the whole corps of the French specialists in Ecclesiastical History: Lebreton, Zeiller, Amann, Bardy, de Labriolle and Bréhier, among others. The first volume *L'Eglise primitive* is already translated into English.[2] In this work there is a competent discussion of the sources used and continual—and of the modern works also—reference is made to them. Every aspect of Christian Life is studied, and the expansion of Christianity in the lands outside the Roman Empire.

Before coming to the detailed special inventory of works according to the order of this book, I may perhaps be allowed to refer to some of the classic standard works which, from various points of view, cover the whole field of this volume, more or less: e.g. ALBERT DUFOURCQ, *L'Avenir du Christianisme* (t. i, 9th edit.; t. ii, 8th edit.; t. iii, 8th edit.; t. iv, 9th edit.;) retains all its value as the most stimulating work that a serious student could desire; but it presupposes a certain familiarity with the history.

[1] *Histoire Ancienne de l'Eglise*, 3 vols; *L'Eglise au VIme siècle* is a different, later work.
[2] By E. C. Messenger Ph.D., in two volumes, Burns Oates.

J. P. KIRSCH, *Kirchengeschichte*, t. i. *Die Kirche in der antiken grieschich-römischen Kulturwelt*, Freiburg-im-Breisgau, 1930.

B. KIDD. *A History of the Church to A.D.* 461. Oxford 1922, 3 Vols. (Anglo-Catholic).

H. M. GWATKIN. *Early Church History to A.D.* 313. London 1909. 2 Vols. For the ecclesiastical writers, who are a principal source during all this period *cf.*

OTTO VON BARDENHEWER. *Geschichte der Altchristlichen Literatur.* 5 Vols. 1913–23; a most impressive piece of scholarship, untroubled by subjective hypotheses.

P. DE LABRIOLLE. *Histoire de la littérature latine chrétienne.* 2nd edit. Paris 1924.

A. PUECH. *Histoire de la littérature grecque chrétienne depuis les origines jusqu'à la fin du IVe siècle.* 3 Vols. Paris 1928–30.

More elementary introductions to the ecclesiastical writers are these four works, all translated into English, viz.

BARDENHEWER. *Patrology.* 1908 (translated from the 2nd German edition).

TIXERONT. *Manual of Patrology.*

BARDY. G. *The Christian Latin Literature of the First Six Centuries.* 1930.
    id.   *The Greek Literature of the Early Christian Church.* 1929.

There are two extensive series of English translations of the early writers (1) *Library of the Fathers* edited by Newman, Pusey and others, 45 volumes (from 1832 onwards); (2) *The Ante-Nicene Christian Library*, 24 volumes, 1866-1872. For most purposes the general student will find all he needs in the matter of texts in the four handbooks published by Herder, viz.

DENZINGER, H. *Enchiridion Symbolorum Definitionum, et Declarationum de rebus Fidei et Morum;* contains all the canons and decrees of popes and councils concerning faith and morals down to our own times.

KIRCH, C. *Enchiridion Fontium Historiae Ecclesiasticae Antiquae*; a collection of the principal texts, from popes, councils, and ecclesiastical writers around the discussion of which church history as a science has developed.

ROUËT DE JOURNEL, M. J. *Enchiridion Patristicum*; a collection of texts from the ancient ecclesiastical writings (the Didache to St. Gregory of Tours, who died 593-4) to illustrate theological teaching.

ROUËT DE JOURNEL, M. J. and J. DUTILLEUL. *Enchiridion Asceticon :* a collection of texts to illustrate.

B. KIDD has edited a collection of English translations of various texts in *Documents Illustrative of the History of the Church.* 2 Vols. London 1920, which cover the history down to A.D. 461.[1]

H. J. SCHROEDER. *Disciplinary Decrees of the General Councils.* London 1937, gives the text, a translation (which is sometimes a summary paraphrase—and stated to be such) and a commentary on the decrees.[2]

It remains to explain the few abbreviations used.

E.T.—there is an English translation of the work.

D.A.C.L.—*Dictionnaire d'Archéologie Chrétienne et de Liturgie.*

D.H.G.E.—*Dictionnaire d'Histoire et de Géographie Ecclésiastique.*

D.T.C.—*Dictionnaire de Théologie Catholique.*

F. & M.—*Histoire de l'Eglise depuis les origines jusqu'à nos jours*, publiée sous la direction de Augustin Fliche et Victor Martin.

[1] Published by the Society for the Promotion of Christian Knowledge; *cf.* this Society's catalogue for the many handy modern editions of classic ecclesiastical writings and translations of them.

[2] The standard work on the Councils is Dom. H. Leclercq's translation and re-edition of Hefele *L'Histoire des Conciles.*

CHAPTER I.—THE WORLD IN WHICH THE CHURCH WAS FOUNDED

I. THE ROMAN IMPERIAL UNITY

ROSTOVTZEFF, M., *A History of the Ancient World*, Oxford, 1926.
CHAPOT, V., *The Roman World*, London, 1928.
DE BURGH, *The Legacy of the Ancient World*.

II. THE PAGAN RELIGIONS OF THE ROMANO-HELLENISTIC CULTURE

DUFOURCQ, A., *L'Avenir du Christianisme*, Vol. I, *Les Religions paiennes et la religion juive comparées*, 9 ed., Paris, 1932.
LEBRETON, J., *Histoire du Dogme de la Trinité*, 7 ed., Paris, 1929, I, 1–99. E.T.
TIXERONT, J., *Histoire des Dogmes*, 9 ed., Paris, 1931. Vol. I, ch, 1, § 1. E.T.
HUBY, J., *La religion des Grecs*, in *Christus, Manuel d'Histoire des Religions*, 4 ed., Paris, 1923, pp. 434–85.
MARTINDALE, C. C., *La religion des Romains*, in *Christus*, pp. 486–542; and *The Religion of Ancient Greece; The Religion of Early Rome; The Religion of Imperial Rome*; in *Studies in Comparative Religions* edited E. MESSENGER (London, Catholic Truth Society, 1934).
FESTUGIÈRE, A. J., *Le monde greco-romain: Le milieu spirituel*, 1936.

III. THE RELIGION OF THE JEWS

SCHÜRER, E., *Geschichte des jüdischen Volkes im Zeitalter Jesu Christi*. 4 ed., 1907–11. 3 Vols. and index.
LAGRANGE, M. J., *Le Judaisme avant Jésus-Christ*. Paris, 1931.
NIKEL, J., *La religion d'Israel*, in *Christus*, pp. 813–910.
BARTON J. M., *Patriarchal and Mosaic Religion; The Religion of the Hebrew Prophets; The Religion of Post-Exilic Judaism* in *Studies in Comparative Religions* (ut supra).

IV. TENDENCIES IN THE RELIGIOUS WORLD OF THE FIRST CENTURY A.D.

DUFOURCQ, *op. cit.*, Vol. II, *La Révolution Religieuse*.
TIXERONT, I, ch. 1, §§ 2, 3.
DE GRANDMAISON, *Jésus-Christ*, Bk. II. E.T.
LEBRETON, *op. cit.*, I, pp. 142–52, 168–97, 249–53; and in F. & M. I., 26–62. E.T.
BEURLIER, *Le Monde Juif au Temps de Jésus Christ et des Apôtres*, 6 ed., Paris, 1907.
BONSIRVEN J., *Les idées juives au temps de Notre-Seigneur*. Paris, 1936.

CHAPTER II.—THE FOUNDATION

I. THE FOUNDER

D'ARCY (ed.) *The Life of the Church*, London, 1932, Part I.[1]
TIXERONT, I, ch. 2, §§ 1 and 2.
BARDY, G., *Le Sauveur*. Paris, 1937.

[1] This is an English translation of pp. 954–1302 of *Christus*, i.e., Ch. XVI. *La religion chrétienne* by P. Rousselot, J. Huby, A. Brou and L. de Grandmaison.

LEBRETON, *op. cit.*, I, 253–341; also F. & M. I, 63–126.
   id.   *La Vie Chrétienne au premier siècle de l'Eglise*, Paris, 1927.
   id.   *La Vie et l'enseignement de Jésus-Christ, Notre Seigneur*, Paris, 1931. E.T.
DE GRANDMAISON, *Jésus-Christ, esp.* Bks. I. II, III.
PRAT, F., *Jésus-Christ, sa vie, sa doctrine, son œuvre*, Paris, 1931.
LAGRANGE, M. J., *L'Evangile de Jésus-Christ*, Paris, 1928. E.T.
LEMONNYER, *The Theology of the New Testament*, London, 1930.
MARTINDALE, C. C., *Jesus of Nazareth* in *Studies etc.* (ut supra).

THE NEW TESTAMENT
KIRCH gives the celebrated texts from Josephus.

II. THE FIRST GENERATION

BATIFFOL, *L'Eglise Naissante et le Catholicisme*, 7 ed., Paris, 1919, ch. 1, 2, 3. Eng. Tr. *Primitive Catholicism.*
PRAT, *La Théologie de S. Paul*, Paris, 1920–3. E.T.
LEBRETON, *Hist. du dogme de la Trinité*, Vol. I, pp. 379–540; also in F. & M. I.
TIXERONT, I, ch. 2 (§§ 3, 4, 5, 6), 3.
DUCHESNE, *Histoire Ancienne de l'Eglise*, 6 ed., Paris, 1911, Vol. I, ch. 1–7, 10. Eng. Tr. *History of the Early Church.*
CATH. ENCY., *Church*, §§ III, IV—*Judaizers—Paul—Apostles—Peter*, § IV—*Clement of Rome—Hierarchy in Early Church.*
BARDY, G., *L'Eglise à la fin du premier siècle.* s.d. (? 1930)
MARTINDALE, C. C., *The Apostolic Church* in *Studies etc.* (ut supra).
KIRCH, for Texts from the Didache, St. Clement of Rome, Epistle of Barnabas, St. Ignatius of Antioch.

CHAPTER III.—THE FIRST CONTACTS WITH THE PAGAN RELIGIOUS WORLD

I. THE RELIGIOUS WORLD OF THE SECOND CENTURY

LEBRETON, *op. cit.*, II, Livre I *La religion paienne au IIme siècle*, pp. 1–93, an excellent survey.

II. THE FIRST APOLOGISTS

TIXERONT, I, ch. 5.
DUCHESNE, *H. A.*, I, ch. 12.
LEBRETON, *op. cit.*, II, (1928), 395–516; and in F. & M. I.
CATH. ENCY., *Justin Martyr.*
BARDY, G., *The Greek Literature of the Early Christian Church*, London, 1929.
   id.   art. *Justin* in *D.T.C.*
DE JOURNEL for Selections from the Apologies of Quadratus, Aristides, St. Justin, Tatian, Athenagoras, St. Theophilus of Antioch, Tertullian.

III. THE GNOSTICS AND THE CHURCH

LEBRETON, *op. cit.*, II, 81–122; and in F. & M. II
DUCHESNE, *H. A.*, I, ch. 11, is very good indeed.
TIXERONT, I. pp. 173–206.
CATH. ENCY., *Basilides.*
BAREILLE, G., *Basilide*, in *D.T.C.* II (1905), cols. 465–75.
   id.   *Gnosticisme, ib.* VI (1920), 1434–67, especially 1463–7.

IV. ST. IRENÆUS OF LYONS

BATIFFOL, *op. cit.*, ch. 4.

LEBRETON, *op. cit.*, II, Livre VI, *S. Irénée*, pp. 517–617; and in F. & M. II.

TIXERONT, I. ch. 6, passim.

VERNET, F., *Irénée*, in *D.T.C.* VII (1922), cols. 2394–2533, especially cols. 2410–40.

KIRCH, for Selections (pp. 62–81), from St. Irenæus, also Hegesippus.

DE JOURNEL, Selections from St. Irenæus (pp. 79–105), also Hegesippus, Papias, St. Polycarp, the II Epistle of St. Clement of Rome.

V. MARCION—MONTANISM

TIXERONT, I, ch. 4, §§ 5 and 7.

DUCHESNE, *H. A.*, I, ch. 2, pp. 182–6 and ch. 15, pp. 270–85.

BATIFFOL, *op. cit.*, pp. 122–31.

CATH. ENCY., *Marcionites—Montanists*.

AMANN, E., *Marcion*, in *D.T.C.* IX (1926), cols. 2009–2032.

BARDY, G., *Montanisme*, *ib.* X (1928), 2355–70.

LEBRETON, J., in F. & M. II.

DE LABRIOLLE, P., *La Crise Montaniste*, Paris, 1913.

IV. THE CRISES OF THE THIRD CENTURY

I. THE EASTER CONTROVERSY

BATIFFOL, *op. cit.*, pp. 267–74.

DUCHESNE, *H. A.*, I, ch. 16.

LEBRETON, J., in F. & M. II.

KIRCH gives Polycrates' reply to St. Victor I and the letter of St. Irenæus to the same, with the account from Eusebius.

II. THE MONARCHIANS—SABELLIUS—ST. HIPPOLYTUS

DUCHESNE, *H. A.*, I. ch. 17.

TIXERONT, I, pp. 337–8, ch. 9 and pp. 390–418.

CATH. ENCY., *Monarchians*.

BARDY, G., *Monarchianisme*, in *D.T.C.* X (1928), 2193–2209.

AMANN, E., *Hippolyte*, *ib.* VI (1920), cols. 2487–2511.

D'ALÈS, A., *La Théologie de S. Hippolyte*.

KIRCH gives St. Hippolytus' version of the early career of the pope St. Calixtus I.

DE JOURNEL gives selections from St. Hippolytus against Noetus.

III. THE PENITENTIAL CONTROVERSY—ST. CALIXTUS I.

BATIFFOL, *op. cit.*, ch. 6.

DUCHESNE, as for § II; also pp. 394–6.

TIXERONT, I, ch. 10, pp. 361–8 (for the controversy), and (for Tertullian) pp. 333–4 and ch. 12 passim.

CATH. ENCY., *Calixtus I—Tertullian*.

VACANDARD, E., *Confession*, in *D.T.C.* III (1908), 838–861.

VERNET, F., *Calixte Ier*, *ib.* II (1905), 1333–42.

D'ALÈS, A., *L'Edit de Calliste* (1914).

GALTIER, P., *L'Eglise et la remission des péchés aux premiers siècles*, (1932).

LEBRETON, J., *Tertullien* in F. & M. II, 161–185.

D'ALÈS, A., *La Théologie de Tertullien*, (1905).

DENZINGER, the "Edict " of Calixtus, i.e. from Tertullian's *De Pudicitia.*
KIRCH, for 34 pages of selections from Tertullian, including the " Edict "
in its context.
DE JOURNEL, for 30 pages of selections from Tertullian.

IV. THE SCHISM OF NOVATIAN

BATIFFOL, *op. cit.*, pp. 420-39.
DUCHESNE, *H. A.*, I, pp. 323-6, 407-18.
TIXERONT, I, pp. 369-377.
CATH. ENCY., *Novatian.*
AMANN, E., *Novatien: La Crise Novatienne*, in *D.T.C.* XI (1932), 829-841.
D'ALÈS, A., *La Théologie de Novatien*, (1925).
DENZINGER, for the important clauses of the letters of St. Cornelius I to
St. Cyprian and to Fabian of Antioch.
KIRCH, for the letter of St. Cornelius to Fabian.
DE JOURNEL, for extract from letter of St. Cornelius to St. Cyprian and the
last clauses of that to Fabian: a long extract from Novatian *On the Trinity.*

V. ST. CYPRIAN AND ROME

BATIFFOL, *op. cit.*, ch. 8.
DUCHESNE, *H. A.*, I, pp. 397-431.
TIXERONT, I, ch. 8 and 12, passim: for the baptismal controversy ch. 11.
CATH. ENCY., *Cornelius—Cyprian.*
D'ALÈS, A., *La Théologie de S. Cyprien*, (1922).
LEBRETON, J., in F. & M. II, 186-210.
BÉVENOT, M. *The De Unitate of St. Cyprian*, (1935).
BAREILLE, G., *Baptême des hérétiques (controverses relatives au)*, in *D.T.C.*
(1905), cols. 219-233.
DENZINGER, for the decree of St. Stephen I extracted from St. Cyprian.
KIRCH, for many valuable extracts (25 pages) from St. Cyprian: the *Acta*
of his martyrdom: the anti-Roman letter of Firmilian.
DE JOURNEL, for a selection (12 pages) from St. Cyprian, with the text of the
decision of the Council of Carthage (256): a further extract from the
letter of Firmilian.

VI. THE SCHOOL OF ALEXANDRIA—ORIGEN

DUCHESNE, *H. A.*, ch. 18, 27.
BATIFFOL, *op. cit.*, ch. 5 for Clement of Alexandria, ch. 7 for Origen.
id.   *La Paix Constantinienne et le Catholicisme* (9 ed., Paris, 1925),
pp. 142-52 for the anti-Christian aspect of Neo-Platonism.
TIXERONT, I, ch. 7, § 1 for Clement of A., § 2 for Origen.
LEBRETON, J., in F. &. M. II, 225-248.
BARDY, G., *Clément d'Alexandrie.* Textes et commentaires, (1926).
BOUSSET, W., *Jüdisch-Christlicher Schulbetrieb in Alexandria and Rom.* Göt-
tingen, (1915).
CATH. ENCY., *Origen.*
WESTCOTT, F., *Origen* in *Dict. Christian Biography* IV, 104-27.
LEBRETON, J., *Origène* in F. & M. II, 249-94.
BARDY, G., *Origène* in *D.T.C.* XI (1932), 1489-1565.
PRAT, F., *Origène, le théologien et l'exégète*, Paris, 1907
DE FAYE, E., *Origène, sa vie, ses œuvres, sa pensee*, 3 vols. Paris, 1923-30.
KIRCH, for selections from Clement of A. (pp. 83-8), and Origen (144-153)
two quotations from Porphyry showing his anti-Christian use of the
New Testament.

DE JOURNEL, for selections from Clement of A. (pp. 146–62), and Origen (pp. 163–197).

IX. DENIS OF ALEXANDRIA—PAUL OF SAMOSATA

BATIFFOL, *op. cit.*, pp. 393–6.
DUCHESNE, *H. A.*, I, ch. 23 (pp. 475–90), for St. Denis of A., ch. 22 (pp. 465–74), for Paul of Samosata.
TIXERONT, I, pp. 482–91 for the affair of the two St. Denises: pp. 462–7 for Paul of Samosata.
CATH. ENCY., *Denis of Alexandria—Paul of Samosata.*
BARDY, G., *Paul de Samosate.* 2 ed. Louvain, 1929.
    id.   id.   in *D.T.C.*
DENZINGER, for letter of St. Denis of Rome on the Trinitarian Controversy.
KIRCH, for selections from St. Denis of A., the Council of Antioch's denunciation of Paul of Samosata (269) to the pope St. Denis, the account (from Eusebius) of Aurelian's intervention.
DE JOURNEL, Fragment of St. Denis of A. on the Trinity.

CHAPTER V.—CHRISTIAN LIFE

DUCHESNE, *H. A.*, I. ch. 4, 25, 26: general account, for which see also
LEBRETON, J., *La Vie Chrétienne au premier siècle* (ut sup.) and in F. & M. I, 259–74, 357–67; II, 65–85.
ZEILLER, J., in F. & M. I, 397–418; II, 429–456.
LECLERCQ, H., *La Vie Chrétienne Primitive.* Paris, 1928 (with 60 plates).
POURRAT, *La Spiritualité Chrétienne*, Paris, 1926, Vol. I, ch. 1, and
PRAT, *op. cit.*, II, 81–90, 375–426, for the New Testament basis of the Ascetic Ideal.
POURRAT, *op. cit.*, I, ch. 2 for the cult of virginity.
    ib.   ch. 3 and
BATIFFOL, *Etudes d'Histoire et de Théologie Positive*, 6 ed., Paris, 1920, 45–57 for Encratites.
DUCHESNE, *H. A.*, II, ch. 14, and
POURRAT, *op. cit.*, ch. 4–6 for Primitive Monasticism; see also
DE LABRIOLLE, P., in F. & M. III, 299–370 (a masterly study);
LECLERCQ, H., *Monachisme in D.A.C.L.*
DUCHESNE, *Origines du Culte Chrétien*, 5 ed., Paris, 1925, and
BATIFFOL, *L'Arcane* and *L'Agape* in *op. cit.* for Primitive Ritual, Feasts, Catechumenate, etc.
TIXERONT, I, ch. 4, § 4, ch. 6, § 6, ch. 12, § 5, and
BATIFFOL, *L'Eucharistie*, 8 ed., Paris, 1920, for primitive Sacramental Theology.
CATH. ENCY., *Asceticism—Monasticism—Catechumens—Diocese*, §§ I, II—*Egypt*, § V—*Persia*, § III.
BATIFFOL, P., *Arcane*, in *D.T.C.* I (1903), cols. 1738–58.
VERNET, F., *Catéchuménat, ib.* II (1905), cols. 1968–87.
DE PUNIET, art. *Catéchuménat*, in *D.A.C.L.*
VAN DEN EYNDE, D., *Les normes de l'enseignement chrétien* (1933).
VACANDARD, E., *Célibat du Ier au IVme siècle*, in *D.T.C.* II, cols. 2068–77.
DELEHAYE, H., *L'Origine du culte des martyrs* (2 ed., 1933).
CABROL, F., *La Prière des premiers chrétiens*, Paris, 1929.
    For the expansion of the Church, see the excellent résumés of
ZEILLER, J., in F. & M. I, 279–88, 387–96; II 123–144.
DUCHESNE, L., *Autonomies ecclésiastiques: églises séparées* (2 edit., 1905), E.T.

HARNACK, A., *Die Mission und Ausbreitung des Christentums in den ersten drei Jahrunderten* (4 ed. Leipzig, 1924), E.T.
ZEILLER, J., in F. & M. I, 373–86; II, 387–428 for organisation *ante* 312.
id. *L'Empire romain et l'Eglise*, Paris 1928.

CHAPTER VI.—THE CHURCH AND THE PAGAN ROMAN EMPIRE

I. THE STATE—HOSTILE AND TOLERANT

ALLARD, *Le Christianisme et l'Empire Romain de Néron à Théodose*, 9 ed., Paris, 1925.
BATIFFOL, *La Paix Constantinienne et le Catholicisme*, 3 ed., Paris 1914., ch. 1 and 3.
DUCHESNE, *H. A.*, Vol. I., ch. 8, 12, 13, 19; Vol. II, ch. 1.
ALLARD, *Dix Leçons sur le Martyre* (English translation *Ten Lectures on the Martyrs*, pub., Kegan Paul).
CATH. ENCY., *Martyrs*.
DE LABRIOLLE, P., *La réaction paienne: Etude sur la polémique anti-chrétienne du Ier au VIme siècle*, Paris, 1934.
ALLARD, *Le Christianisme, etc. (cf. supra)*, gives the passages from Tacitus, and Suetonius referring to Nero's persecution; Dion Cassius on that of Domitian; Pliny's letter to Trajan with Trajan's reply; the rescripts of Hadrian, Marcus Aurelius, Septimius Severus, Alexander Severus; a specimen of the certificates of apostasy issued under Decius; passages from the *Acta* of the trials of St. Cyprian; the rescripts of Gallienus and of Aurelian; the several edicts of the final persecution.
KIRCH, The same extracts from Tacitus; the passage from Suetonius describing the persecutions of Nero and Domitian; the Pliny-Trajan correspondence; Hadrian's rescript; extracts from the *Acta Proconsularia* of the martyrdoms at Scillium (180), of SS. Carpus and Comp., of St. Cyprian, St. Denis of A.; numerous extracts from Eusebius of Cæsarea, from writings on martyrdom of Tertullian and St. Cyprian; specimen of the certificates issued by Decius.

II. THE STATE DE-PAGANISED

ALLARD, *Le Christianisme, etc.*, pp. 145-287.
BATIFFOL, *La Paix, etc.*, pp. 188–201, 216–228 for Constantine's religious development down to 313, and pp. 229–67 for the *Edict of Milan*.
DUCHESNE, *H. A.*, Vol. II, ch. 2, 9, 17.
CATH. ENCY., *Constantine*.
BAYNES, N. H., *Constantine the Great and the Christian Church*, London 1931.
PALANQUE, J. R., *Constantin* in *Hommes d'Etat*. Paris 1936.
ALLARD, *op. cit.*, gives in the appendix the passage from Lactantius with the Edict of Milan.
KIRCH gives the text of the Edict from Lactantius, with that from Eusebius also; the account of Constantine's vision from Lactantius, and from Eusebius; Constantine's laws regarding Christians from the Theodosian Code.

CHAPTER VII.—THE ARIANS

General Account

BATIFFOL, *La Paix, etc.*, ch. 6–9.
DUCHESNE, *H. A.*, Vol. II, ch. 4–8.
CATH. ENCY., *Eusebius of Nicomedia, Semi-Arians, Liberius*.

LE BACHELET, X., *Arienisme*, in *D.T.C.* I (1903), 1779–1863.
   id. *Athanase, ib.* I, 2143–2178.
BARDY, G., *Lucien d'Antioche, ib.* IX (1926), 1024–31 (critical of Duchesne's account).
   id. *S. Lucien d'Antioche*, Paris 1936.
CHENU, M-D., *Marcel d'Ancyre, D.T.C.* IX, 1993–98.
AMANN, E., *Liberius, ib.* IX, 631–659; good account of the modern controversies, summing up against, e.g., BATIFFOL and the account as given in this book.
   id. *Lucifer de Cagliari, ib.* IX, 1032–44.
   id. *Mélèce d'Antioche, ib.* X, (1928), 520–31.
LE BACHELET, X., *Hilaire de Poitiers, ib.* VI, (1920) 2406–09 (for Liberius).
AIGRAIN, R., *Arius*, in *D.H.G.E.*, IV
BARDY, G., *Athanase, ib.* IV.

Theological Aspects

TIXERONT, Vol. II, ch. 2, 3.
BARDY, G., in F. & M. III has written what is the best general account of Arianism—a critical and well documented statement.
DENZINGER gives the Creed of Nicea.
KIRCH gives Alexander of Alexandria's synodal letter denouncing Arius; Arius' letter to Eusebius of Nicomedia; one of the Arian street-songs; the synodal letter of the Council of Nicea to the Egyptians; Constantine's edict against Arius; St. Athanasius' account of the death of Arius; Eusebius of Cæsarea's account of the calling of the Council of Nicea, and of Constantine's baptism and death; the Canons of the Councils of Antioch (341), and of Sardica, with its synodal letter; all the texts concerning Liberius.
DE JOURNEL gives the fragments of Arius' exposition from St. Athanasius; and a passage from his letter to Alexander of Alexandria; 40 pages of extracts from St. Athanasius.

CHAPTER VIII.—THE CATHOLIC RESTORATION. 359–382.

General Account

BATIFFOL, *Le Siége Apostolique*, ch. 1, 3, 2 ed. Paris 1924.
DUCHESNE, *H. A.*, Vol. II, ch. 10, 11, 12.
CATH. ENCY., *Basil, Ambrose*.
PALANQUE, J-R., *S. Ambroise et l'empire romain*, Paris 1933.
BARDY, G., and PALANQUE, J-R., in F. & M. III, 237–298.

Theological Aspects

TIXERONT, Vol. II, ch. 2, § 7, ch. 3 and 4.
DENZINGER gives the condemnations of the General Council of 381 and its creed.
KIRCH gives the two Canons of the Council which referred to hierarchical precedence, and the Council's synodal letter.
DE JOURNEL gives (pp. 331–63) a varied selection of extracts from St. Basil; from St. Gregory Nazianzen (pp. 364–82) and St. Gregory of Nyssa (pp. 382–400).

CHAPTER IX.—ROME AND THE CATHOLIC EAST 381–453.

I. THE PRIMACY OF HONOUR. 381–419

General Account

BATIFFOL, *Le Siége, etc.*, ch. 5.
DUCHESNE, *H. A.*, Vol. II, ch. 16, Vol. III, ch. 2, 3.
CATH. ENCY., *John Chrysostom*.
BAUR, Chr., *Der heilige Johannes Chrysostomus und seine Zeit*, Munich 1929–30.
BARDY, G., in F. & M. IV, 129–162.
KIRCH gives St. John's *Appeal* to Innocent I, pp. 421–432.
DE JOURNEL, pp. 421–69, selections from St. John's works which illustrate the activity of his many-sided genius.

II. THE COUNCIL OF EPHESUS. 427–433

General Account

BATIFFOL, *op. cit.*, ch. 6.
DUCHESNE, *H. A.*, Vol. III, ch. 9 and 10, whose view of St. Cyril, however, can no longer be wholly accepted since
LEBON, J., *Autour de la définition de la foi au Concile d'Ephese* (431), *in Ephemerides Theologicae Lovanienses*, t. viii. July, 1931, 393–421.
CATH. ENCY., *Nestorius—Ephesus, Council of—Cyril of Alexandria*.
AMANN, E., *Nestorius*, in *D.T.C.* XI (1932), 76–157.
D'ALÈS, A., *Le dogme d'Ephèse*, Paris, 1931.
BARDY, G., in F. & M. IV. 163–210 .

Theological Questions

TIXERONT, Vol. III, ch. 1 and 2 who gives the text of the Act of Union of 433.
DENZINGER gives the important clauses of the speech of Philip, the papal legate and the text of St. Cyril's XII *Anathemata*.
KIRCH gives the important passage of the pope's letter of August 11, 430, summoning Nestorius to retract; the account (in St. Cyril's letter to his people) of the deposition of Nestorius; Nestorius' twelve counter-anathemata against St. Cyril; Socrates' account of the controversy from his *Historia Ecclesiastica*.
DE JOURNEL gives three short extracts from the sermons of Nestorius, and a passage from his memoirs, the *Liber Heraclidis*, which explain his teaching; texts from Cassian refuting the heresy; a varied selection from St. Cyril's writings (pp. 642–72) including passages from the *Adversus Nestorium*, and from the letter of 433 to John of Antioch; a selection (pp. 674–84) from Theodoret.

III. THE COUNCIL OF CHALCEDON 446–452

General Account

BATIFFOL, *op. cit.*, ch. 8.
DUCHESNE, *H. A.*, Vol. III, ch. 11.
CATH. ENCY., *Dioscoros—Eutyches—Ephesus, Robber Council—Chalcedon*.
BATIFFOL, P., *Léon I*, in *D.T.C.*. IX (1926), 218–301.
JALLAND, T. G., *The Life and Times of St. Leo the Great*. 1940.
BARDY, G., in F. & M. IV, 210–240, 259–270.

Theological Questions

Tixeront, *op. cit.*, Vol. II, ch. 4 and 5 (Apollinaris), Vol. III, ch. 3, with text of the Council's profession of faith.

Denzinger gives the defining clauses of the *Tome*, the text of Chalcedon's definition of faith, the passage from its synodal letter acclaiming the Roman primacy.

Kirch gives Flavian's appeal to St. Leo against the *Latrocinium*; St. Leo's protest to the Emperor against the 28th canon.

De Journel gives selections from the *Eranistes* of Theodoret.

CHAPTER X.—THE TRADITIONAL FAITH AND THE IMPERIAL POLICY

I. THE AFTERMATH OF CHALCEDON

General Account

Duchesne, *H. A.*, Vol. III, ch. 12 takes the story down to the Schism.
Duchesne, *L'Eglise au VI Siècle*, Paris, 1925, ch. 1 and 2 complete it.
Cath. Ency., *Eutychianism—Monophysites*.
Salaville, L., *Hénotique*, in *D.T.C.* VI (1920), 2153–77.
Amann, E., *Hormisdas*, ib. VII (1922), 161–176.
Lebon, J., *Le Monophysisme sévérien*. Louvain 1909.
Bardy, G., in F. & M. IV, 271–320.
Bréhier, L., *ib.* 423–436.

Theological Aspect

Tixeront, Vol. III, ch. 4.
Denzinger gives extracts from letters of Pope Simplicius to Acacius and to the usurper Basiliscus with reference to the *Encyclion*; the Formula of Hormisdas.
Kirch gives the text of the *Encyclion* and *Henoticon*.

II. JUSTINIAN

General Account

Duchesne, *L' Eglise au VI Siècle* ch. 2–7.
Pargoire, P. J., *L'Eglise Byzantine de 527–847*, 3 ed., Paris, 1927, ch. 1.
Vancourt, R., *Patriarcats*, in *D.T.C.* X, 2253–67.
Leclercq, H., *Justinien*, in *D.A.C.L.* (1928), VIII, 507–604.
Batiffol, P., *L'empereur Justinien et le siège apostolique* in *Recherches de sciences religieuses t.* XVI, (1926).
Bréhier, L., in F. & M. IV, 437–482.

Theological Aspect

Tixeront, Vol. III, ch. 5.
Denzinger, gives the text of John II's decision on the orthodoxy of "*One of the Trinity suffered*"; Justinian's canons of 543 against the Origenists; the Canons of the General Council of 553 condemning the Three Chapters.
Kirch gives extracts from Justinian's laws which illustrate his fusion of civil and ecclesiastical law; the oath of Palagius I at his consecration.

III. BYZANTINE CATHOLICISM

General Account

DUCHESNE, *op. cit.*, ch. 10–12.

PARGOIRE, *op. cit.*, ch. 2.

CHAPMAN, H. J., O.S.B., *The Condemnation of Pope Honorius* (pub. The Catholic Truth Society) is quite the best account in English of this affair and gives valuable extracts from the sources; cf. also the same writer's article *Honorius I* in CATH. ENCY.

BRÉHIER, L., in F. & M. IV, 483–93 and *ib.* V 55–210 for the events; in IV 535-58 and *ib.* V, 471–504 for the religious life and institutions.

CATH. ENCY., *Monothelites.*

AMANN, E., *Honorius I*, in *D.T.C.* VII (1922), 93–132.

   id.   *Martin I, ib.* X, (1928), 182–194.

Theological Aspect

TIXERONT, ch. 6.

DENZINGER gives the important passages of the letters of Honorius I to Sergius; the text of John IV's explanation of Honorius; the decrees of the Lateran Synod of 649; the defining passage of Agatho's letter to the general Council of 680; the definition of the General Council.

KIRCH gives practically the whole text of Honorius' first letter to Sergius, and all the fragments of the second; the important clauses of the *Ecthesis*; part of the text of John IV's explanation; the discussion between St. Maximus and the patriarch of Constantinople; the *Type* of Constans II; the Council of 681's judgment on Honorius; Leo II's confirmation of that condemnation and also his other references to Honorius; the canons of the Synod *in Trullo* of 692.

DE JOURNEL gives an extract from the synodal letter of St. Sophronius.

APPENDIX

POPES AND EMPERORS to 715

POPES	ACCESSION	DEATH	EMPERORS[1]
St. Peter[2]		65	Nero 54
Linus	67	79	Vespasian 69
Cletus	79	91	Titus 79
Clement I	91	100	Domitian 81
Evaristus	100	109	Nerva 96
Alexander	109	119	Trajan 98
Sixtus I	119	126	Hadrian 117
Telesphorus	125	136	
Hyginus	136	140	Antoninus Pius 138
Pius I	140	155	
Anicetus	155	166	Marcus Aurelius 161
Soter	166	174	
Eleutherius	174	189	Commodus 180
Victor I	189	20 Apr. 199	Septimius Severus 193
Zephyrinus	199	26 Aug. 217	Caracalla 211
Calixtus I	217	14 Oct. 222	Heliogabalus 218
Urban I	222	25 May 230	Alexander Severus 222
Pontian	230	28 Sept. 235	Maximin 235
Anterus	235	3 Jan. 236	
Fabian	236	20 Jan. 250	Decius 249[3]
Cornelius	Mar. 251	14 Sept. 253	Gallus 251
Lucius I	253	5 Mar. 254	Valerian 253
Stephen I	12 May 254	2 Aug. 257	
Sixtus II	Aug. 257	6 Aug. 258	
Denis	22 July 259	26 Dec. 268	Gallienus 260
Felix I	5 Jan. 269	30 Dec. 274	Claudius II 268
			Aurelian 270
Eutychian	5 Jan. 275	8 Dec. 283	Tacitus 275
			Probus 276
			Carus 282
Caius	17 Dec. 283	22 Apr. 296	*Eastern Emp. Western Emp.*
			Diocletian 284 Maximin 284
Marcellinus	30 June 296	25 Oct. 304	Galerius 305 Constantius I
			305
			Constantine I
			306
Marcellus I	307	15 Jan. 309	
Melchiades	2 July 310	11 Jan. 314	Licinius 311
Silvester I	31 Jan. 314	31 Dec. 335	Constantine I
			324

[1] The single date against an emperor's name is that of his accession.

[2] The dates of the popes down to, and including, Soter are not certain.

[3] Between Maximin and Decius insert the Gordians (238–244) and Philip the Arabian (244–249).

POPES	ACCESSION	DEATH	EMPERORS[1]	
			Eastern Emp.	*Western Emp.*
Mark	18 Jan. 336	7 Oct. 336		
Julius I	6 Feb. 337	12 Apr. 352	Constantius II 337	Constans I 337
				Constantius II 351
Liberius	17 May 352	24 Sept. 366	Julian 361	Julian 361
			Jovian 363	Jovian 363
			Valens 364	Valentinian I 364
Damasus I	1 Oct. 366	10 Dec. 384	Theodosius I 379	Gratian 375
				Valentinian II 382
Siricius	Dec. 384	26 Nov. 399		Theodosius I 392
			Arcadius 395	Honorius 395
Anastasius I	Dec. 399	401/2		
Innocent I	402	12 Mar. 417	Theodosius II 408	
Zosimas	18 Mar. 417	26 Dec. 418		
Boniface I	29 Dec. 418	4 Sept. 422		
Celestine I	10 Sept. 422	27 July 432		Valentinian III 425–455[2]
Sixtus III	31 July 432	19 Aug 440		
Leo I	Sept. 440	10 Nov. 461	Marcian 450–457	
			Leo I 457–474	
Hilary	12 Nov. 461	21 Feb. 468		
Simplicius	25 Feb. 468	10 Mar. 483	Zeno 474–491	
Felix III	483	25 Feb. 492	Anastasius 491-518	
Gelasius I	1 Mar. 492	19 Nov. 496		
Anastasius II	24 Nov. 496	19 Nov. 498		
Symmachus	22 Nov. 498	19 July 514		
Hormisdas	20 July 514	7 Aug. 523	Justin I 518–527	
John I	13 Aug. 523	18 May 526		
Felix IV	12 July 526	12 Oct. 530	Justinian I 527–565	
Boniface II	17 Sept. 530	17 Oct. 532		
John II	31 Dec. 532	27 May 535		
Agapitus I	3 June 535	22 Apr. 536		
Silverius	8 June 536	20 June 538[3]		
Vigilius	29 Mar. 537	7 June 555		
Pelagius I	7 June 555	3 Mar. 560		
John III	14 July 560	13 July 573	Justin II 565–578	
Benedict I	3 June 574	31 July 578	Tiberius II 578–582	
Pelagius II	27 Nov. 578	6 Feb. 590	Maurice 582–602	
Gregory I	3 Sept. 590	12 Mar. 604	Phocas 602–610	
Sabinian	13 Sept. 604	22 Feb. 606		
Boniface III	19 Feb. 607	12 Nov. 607		
Boniface IV	15 Sept. 608	25 May 615	Heraclius 610–641	
Deusdedit I	19 Oct. 615	8 Nov. 618		
Boniface V	23 Dec. 619	25 Oct. 625		
Honorius I	3 Nov. 625	12 Oct. 638		

[1] The single date against an emperor's name is that of his accession.
[2] The last effective emperor in the West. The actual last titular emperor was Romulus, nicknamed Augustulus, whom the Barbarian general Odoacer induced to abdicate in 476.
[3] Date of his death.

POPES	ACCESSION	DEATH	EMPERORS
Severinus	28 May 640	2 Aug. 640	
John IV	25 Dec. 640	12 Oct. 642	Constans II 641–668
Theodore I	24 Nov. 642	13 May 649	
Martin I	June 649	16 Sept. 655[1]	
Eugene I	10 Aug. 654	2 June 657	
Vitalian	30 July 657	27 Jan. 672	Constantine IV 668–685
Deusdedit II	11 Apr. 672	16 June 676	
Donus	2 Nov. 676	11 Apr. 678	
Agatho	June 678	10 Jan. 681	
Leo II	7 Aug. 682	3 July 683	
Benedict II	26 June 684	8 May 685	
John V	24 July 685	2 Aug. 686	
Conon	21 Oct. 686	21 Sept. 687	
Sergius I	15 Dec. 687	6 Sept. 701	Justinian II 685–695
John VI	30 Oct. 701	11 Jan. 705	and 705–711[2]
John VII	1 Mar. 705	18 Oct. 707	
Sisinnius	18 Jan. 708	7 Feb. 708	
Constantine	25 Mar. 708	9 Apr. 715	

[1] Date of his death.
[2] During the banishment of Justinian II, Leontius (695–698) and Tiberius III (698–705) were emperors.

INDEX

A

Abraham, 14

Acacius, 265; Schism of, 266–71.

Adoptionism, 100–1, 134.

Aeschylus, 11, 70.

Africa, beginnings of Christianity in, 152

Agapitus I, pope, 275.

Agatho, pope, 300–1.

Alexander the Great, importance of conquests, cultural, 4–6; religious, 6–7, 11, 20, 25–6, 128.

—— Severus, emperor, legalises Christianity, 163–4.

Alexandria, School of, 118–28; importance of see of, 153, 155, 156, 229.

Ambrose, St., Bishop of Milan, influence on early monasticism, 142; early theorist of relations between Church and Christian State, 187, 214, 217–20; career, 183, 216.

Ammonius Saccas, 118.

Anastasius, emperor, 268–70.

—— II, pope, 269.

Anomaeans, party of the, 210–13.

Anti-encyclion, 265.

Antioch, ecclesiastical importance of, 155–6.

Antony, St., of Egypt, 139–40.

Apocryphal writings, Christian, moral heresies in, 139.

Apollinarianism, 226–7, 240, 248, 250, 262.

Apollinaris of Laodicea, 226–7, 239, 243.

Apollonius of Tyana, 162, 169.

Apologists, the, 79–84.

Apostates, in the persecutions, 109, 112.

Aquileia, Council of (381), 220.

Arabia, beginnings of Christianity in, 153.

Arcadius, emperor, 231–4.

Aristotle, 5, 11, 100.

Arius, career and doctrine of, 188–91, 197.

Arles, Councils of (314), 150, 152; (353), 207.

Armenia, beginnings of Christianity in, 153.

Artemas, 101.

Ascension, origin of feast of, 148.

Asia Minor, Christian beginnings in, 153.

Athanasius, St., Bishop of Alexandria, 128, 141, 153, 194–210, 223, 224, 225, 226.

Atticus, patriarch of Constantinople, 235–6.

Augustine, St., Bishop of Hippo, and early monasticism, 142–3; also 96, 120, 124, 128.

Augustus, emperor, 3, 20.

Aurelian, emperor, intervention at Antioch against Paul of Samosata, 134.

B

Balkans, Christian beginnings in, 153.

Baptism, in the New Testament, 35, 36; liturgy of, in early Church, 84, 145, 146; controversy about repetition of, 114–17.

Bardasanes, 78.

Basil of Ancyra, 206–7; and the *homoiousion*, 211-12; and Liberius, 212.

—— St., Bishop of Ceserea, 128; and early monasticism, 140–1; and the Arian Emperor, 223–4; and the Meletian schism, 224–7; and Rome, 226–7.

Basilides the Gnostic, teaching of, 85–6, 125.

Boniface II, pope, 276.

C

Calixtus I, pope, St., career, 102–3; his reform of the penitential discipline, 103, 108; relations with St. Hippolytus, 103; with Tertullian, 103.

Carthage, Councils of (254), 114; (255), 115; (256), 115, 116.

Cassian, John, 144–5.

Catechumenate, 145–6.

Celestine I, pope, St., 152; and the heresy of Nestorius, 241-7.

Celibacy, consecration of, as a primitive ascetic practice, 137; of clergy, 151.

Celsus, 124.

Cerdon, 118.

Chalcedon, General Council of (451), 248–61.

Chapters, the Three, controversy, 279–85.

Charity, works of, in primitive Church, 138–9.

Christmas, origins of feast, 148.

Church, rôle in primitive Christian life, 34–7, 48–51, 53, 55, 89, 91, 122, 125–6, 145–7, 150–2.

Cicero, and the Paganism of his time, 13, 18, 19, 71.

Claudius, emperor, 3.